INSCRIPTIONS OF THE ŚARABHAPURĪYAS, PĀṆḌUVAṀŚINS AND SOMAVAṀŚINS

PART I
INTRODUCTION

INSCRIPTIONS OF THE ŚARABHAPURĪYAS, PĀṆḌUVAṀŚINS AND SOMAVAṀŚINS

PART I

INTRODUCTION

Ajay Mitra Shastri

INDIAN COUNCIL OF HISTORICAL RESEARCH
NEW DELHI
AND
MOTILAL BANARSIDASS
DELHI

First published: 1995

Published on behalf of

INDIAN COUNCIL OF HISTORICAL RESEARCH
35, Ferozeshah Road, New Delhi 110 001

by

MOTILAL BANARSIDASS
Bungalow Road, Jawahar Nagar, Delhi 110 007

Branches:
120 Royapettah High Road, Mylapore, Madras 600 004
16 St. Mark's Road, Bangalore 560 001
Ashok Rajpath, Patna 800 004
Chowk, Varanasi 221 001

Part I ISBN: 81-208-0635-2
Set ISBN: 81-208-0637-9

PRINTED IN INDIA

BY JAINENDRA PRAKASH JAIN
AT SHRI JAINENDRA PRESS, A-45 NARAINA, PHASE I,
NEW DELHI 110 028

To
my wife
Dr Yogeshwari Shastri
who stood solidly by me
in all my undertakings

INSCRIPTIONS OF INDIA PROGRAMME

The value of inscriptions as a source of early Indian history has been widely recognised. In fact, the epigraphic records scattered all over India, Pakistan and Bangladesh form a very important source for the reconstruction of the political and cultural history of the Indian subcontinent from the third century B.C. to about the fourteenth century A.D. But for these records composed in Sanskritic and Dravidian languages and incised on a variety of materials—primarily lithic objects and copper-plates—our knowledge of the early history of India would have remained perfunctory. The number of inscriptions noticed till date far exceeds one hundred thousand, and a large majority of them offer valuable historical information not available from any other source. The mass of scattered epigraphical wealth noticed or published in numerous Indian and foreign, mostly occidental, periodicals devoted to orientology and other occasional publications, many of them long defunct or out of print, spread over nearly last two centuries, is not easily accessible to the students of Indian history. Therefore, the necessity of bringing out properly edited and handy compilations of chronologically, dynastically, regionally or otherwise allied inscriptions had been felt for a long time. As early as 1877, a volume of Aśokan edicts was published by the Archaeological Survey of India as the inaugural volume of its prestigious *Corpus Inscriptionum Indicarum* series. It was followed by a couple of other volumes comprising post-Aśokan Kharoṣṭhī (or Kharoṣṭī) and Gupta and allied epigraphs. In the last six decades or more only four more volumes including the inscriptions of the Vākāṭakas, Śilāhāras, Paramāras and Candellas and those dated in the Kalacuri-Cedi era have been brought out. In view of the urgency of the matter for historical studies and with a view to supplementing the *Corpus* series, the Indian Council of Historical Research has undertaken an ambitious programme of the publication of epigraphs dating from *circa* sixth to fourteenth century A.D., the chronological limits being flexible according to dynastic or regional requirements. Fortunately, despite certain difficulties the programme has recorded a steady progress and as many as four volumes covering the inscriptions of the Maukharis, Later Guptas, Puṣpabhūtis, Yaśovarman of Kanauj, Pallavas, Western Gaṅgas and Gajapatis of Orissa have already been published and a few more are in the pipeline. The volumes released so far have evoked welcome response.

The present volume deals with the inscriptions of the Śarabhapurīyas, Pāṇḍuvaṁśins and Somavaṁśins who played a major role in shaping the destinies of the Chhattisgarh region of Madhya Pradesh and Orissa from about the sixth to the early twelfth century A.D.

'Prachi', 23 Vidya Vihar
Rana Pratap Nagar
Nagpur-440 022
October 1990

AJAY MITRA SHASTRI
Co-ordinator
Inscriptions of India Programme
Indian Council of Historical Research, New Delhi

PREFACE

The present work attempts to bring together the epigraphic records of certain dynasties that ruled over a large part of the present states of Madhya Pradesh and Orissa from about the sixth to early twelfth century A.D. The major dynasties covered in this work primarily ruled over the Chhattisgarh region of Madhya Pradesh and the adjoining areas of Orissa, known as Kosalā or Kosala (now popularly designated by historians as South Kosala in order to distinguish it from its northern namesake commonly called Uttara Kosala or simply Kosala), and later expanded eastwards so as to cover a major part of Orissa.

The work is divided into two parts. Part I provides necessary background to the second part and deals at length with the general features of the inscriptions and outlines the history of the dynasties concerned. Part II comprises four sections which are devoted to the inscriptions of the Śarabhapurīyas, Pāṇḍuvaṁśins of Mekalā, Pāṇḍuvaṁśins of Kosalā and Somavaṁśins of Kosalā and Orissa, each dynasty claiming a section. Originally, the work was proposed to be entitled "Inscriptions of the Śarabhapurīyas, Pāṇḍuvaṁśins and Śomavaṁśins of South Kosalā and Orissa", and there was no intention to include the records of the Pāṇḍavas of Mekalā who were till then not known to have been connected with the region. However, subsequent discovery of a record of the dynasty at Mallar in the Bilaspur district of Madhya Pradesh and the identification of the village donated thereby showed that at least for some time the region round Bilaspur, which formed a part of South Kosalā, was included in the territory under its last known member. It was, therefore, felt necessary to incorporate the inscriptions of this family also in the present work, and the title had accordingly to be suitably altered so as to drop any reference to territorial divisions.

Two of the inscriptions incorporated in the present work call for some remarks. It is now popularly held that Amarārya-kula known from the Mallar plates of Vyāghrarāja was the real name of what is commonly known among historians as the Śarabhapurīya dynasty. We do not subscribe to this notion, and the reasons have been discussed in detail at the proper place. Therefore, the only known record of this family, *viz.*, Mallar plates of Vyāghrarāja, has been included as an appendix to Section I comprising the inscriptions of the Śarabhapurīyas. The Malga plates of *Sāmanta* Indrarāja have been incorporated in an appendix to Section II devoted to the records of the Pāṇḍuvaṁśins of Mekalā, for there are cogent reasons to believe that he was closely connected with the Pāṇḍavas of Mekalā, though it is difficult to determine the exact nature of this relationship in the present state of our knowledge.

It would not be out of place to make a passing reference to certain important features of the present work. We have devoted a fairly large space to a detailed treatment of the inscriptions in Part I. We have dwelt not only upon the format, palaeography, language, orthography, contents, methods employed for dating and similar other points, but have also tried to trace the development of the draft of the inscriptions which will, wherever possible enable us to place even an incomplete charter in a historical perspective. This is, we feel, the first attempt of its kind. Dharmaśāstra injunctions regarding the preparation of deeds of land-grants and their actual epigraphic parallels have also been discussed in detail.

When the work was initially taken up, rather reluctantly, at the behest of Professor R.S. Sharma, the first Chairman of the Indian Council of Historical Research, it was felt that there was little scope for any original contribution regarding the history of the ruling families in question. However, as the work progressed, this notion proved wrong, and it was soon realized that the subject offered an almost virgin field with considerable scope for rethinking and reassessment of the extant evidence. First of all, the chronology was in a highly unsettled state refusing to yield itself to a dependable framework. A thorough reappraisal of the available material has enabled us to determine the chronology in a more convincing manner. To cite only a few important points, we have shown that the Śarabhapurīyas launched upon their political career towards the close of the fifth century and continued to rule up to the end of the sixth or early seventh century A.D. and that the Amarārya-kula chief Pravara-bhaṭṭāraka flourished about the same period as the termination of the Śarabhapurīya rule. As regards the Pāṇḍuvaṁśins of Mekalā, it has been shown convincingly that there is absolutely nothing to support the popular notion that they were feudatories of the Vākāṭakas. On the other hand, the extant evidence proves beyond doubt that the Pāṇḍava chief Bharatabala and his son and successor Śūrabala *alias* Udīrṇavaira (the latter brought to light for the first time by the discovery of his Mallar plates) flourished in the closing years of the sixth and early years of the following century A.D. when the Vākāṭakas had long disappeared from the political map of India. Likewise, after a critical assessment of all the extant evidence we have concluded that the Pāṇḍuvaṁśin chief Tīvaradeva came to power in the latter half of the seventh century A.D. and that the last known member of the dynasty, Śivagupta Bālārjuna, closed his reign about the end of the eighth century A.D. These views are not only backed by the available evidence but also present a more coherent historical picture of the area and period concerned, and it is a matter of gratification that they have already met with general acceptance by historians. A judicious analysis of the extra data has led us to date the commencement of the Somavaṁśin rule about the middle of the ninth century. Our chronology of the Pāṇḍuvaṁśins and the Somavaṁśins has resulted in reducing the gap between the close of the rule of the former and the commencement of that of the latter, thereby indicating a family relationship between the two lines, a conclusion which finds strong support from other pieces of evidence as well. We have been able to determine the order of succession of the Somavaṁśins, more particularly during the confused interval between Mahāśivagupta II Dharmaratha and Mahāśivagupta III Yayāti, more convincingly. To mention only a couple of other important points, the relationship between the Pāṇḍavas of Mekalā and *sāmanta* Indrarāja known from his Malga plates has been brought to light for the first time, and the evidence bearing on the question of the location of Trikaliṅga, which is very vital from the standpoint of the Somavaṁśins, has been examined dispassionately and, I think, in a convincing manner besides bringing some fresh literary and epigraphic evidence to bear upon the problem.

The references to inscriptions included in Part II of this work call for some explanation. They have been referred to by the serial order in which they appear in that Part. Thus, I:I means the first inscription of the first section (Śarabhapurīya Inscriptions) of Part II.

I expected to complete the present work long back. But due to serious eye trouble, which resulted in an inordinate disruption of my academic schedule, it has been delayed by over three years and could be submitted for publication only in 1983. Thereafter it has been with the press, so that it is now nearly seven years after its completion. However, care has been taken to incorporate the material that came to light as late as 1990, and the results of my research as a U.G.C. National Fellow have also been utilized to introduce fresh information.

I have received valuable help from various quarters in the preparation and publication of this work and it is with great pleasure that I express my gratitude to Professor R.S. Sharma, the first Chairman of the Indian Council of Historical Research, who was primarily responsible for initiating the Inscriptions Programme and at whose insistence the present work was undertaken. I am thankful to Professor K.M. Shrimali, Department of History, University of Delhi, for the arduous task of seeing the work through the press, while the credit for the job of preparing the index and errata goes to Shri Devendra Handa, Chairman, Department of Ancient Indian History, Culture and Archaeology, Panjab University, Chandigarh.

Before concluding, we crave the indulgence of the discerning readers for the misprints that have crept into the book despite careful proof-reading. The more serious ones have been listed in the errata.

AJAY MITRA SHASTRI

'Prachi', 23 Vidya Vihar
Rana Pratap Nagar
Nagpur-440 022
October, 1990

ABBREVIATIONS

ABORI	*Annals of the Bhandarkar Oriental Research Institute*
ARIE	*Annual Report on Indian Epigraphy*
ASI, AR	*Archaeological Survey of India, Annual Report*
BMC, AI	*Catalogue of Indian Coins in the British Museum*
	Catalogue of the Coins of Ancient India
BSS	Bombay Sanskrit Series
CASR	*Cunningham's Archaeological Survey Reports*
CII	*Corpus Inscriptionum Indicarum*
DMO	*Dynasties of Mediaeval Orissa* by Binayak Misra
DHNI	*Dynastic History of Northern India* by H.C. Ray
EI	*Epigraphia Indica*
HCIP	*History and Culture of the Indian People*
HDS	*History of Dharmaśāstra* by P.V. Kane
HO	*History of Orissa* by R.D. Banerji
IA	*Indian Antiquary*
IC	*Indian Culture*
ICPB	*Inscriptions in the Central Provinces and Berar* by Hira Lal
IE	*Indian Epigraphy* by D.C. Sircar
IEG	*Indian Epigraphical Glossary* by D.C. Sircar
IHQ	*Indian Historical Quarterly*
INC	*Indian Numismatic Chronicle*
IO	*Inscriptions of Orissa,* iv, by S.N. Rajaguru
JAHRS	*Journal of the Andhra Historical Research Society*
JAIH	*Journal of Ancient Indian History*
JAOS	*Journal of the American Oriental Society*
JAS	*Journal of the Asiatic Society,* Calcutta
JAS, Letters	*Journal of the Asiatic Society, Letters*
JASB	*Journal of the Asiatic Society of Bengal*
JBBRAS	*Journal of the Bombay Branch of the Royal Asiatic Society*
JBORS	*Journal of the Bihar and Orissa Research Society*
JESI	*Journal of the Epigraphical Society of India*
JIH	*Journal of Indian History*
JKHRS	*Journal of the Kalinga Historical Research Society*
JNSI	*Journal of the Numismatic Society of India*
JOI	*Journal of the Oriental Institute*
JPASB	*Journal and Proceedings of the Asiatic Society of Bengal*
JRAS	*Journal of the Royal Asiatic Society*

JRASB, Letters	*Journal of the Royal Asiatic Society of Bengal, Letters*
NHIP	*New History of the Indian People*
NS	New Series
NS	*Numismatic Supplement of the JASB*
NSP	Nirnay Sagar Press
OHRJ	*Orissa Historical Research Journal*
PAIOC	*Proceedings of the All-India Oriental Conference*
PIHC	*Proceedings of the Indian History Congress*
SBE	Sacred Books of the East
SBH	Sacred Books of the Hindus
SIE	*Studies in Indian Epigraphy*
SII	*South Indian Inscriptions*
VIJ	*Vishveshvaranand Indological Journal*

CONTENTS

PART I

INTRODUCTION

INSCRIPTIONS

The present work covers the epigraphic records of three dynasties, to wit, the Śarabhapurīyas, also called kings of Śarabhapura, the Pāṇḍuvaṁśins of Mekalā and Kosala and the Somavaṁśins. Practically all our knowledge of the history of these dynasties is based on the inscriptions left by them or by private individuals during the period of their rule.

These records are divisible into two broad groups on the grounds of the difference in the bases on which they are incised, *viz.*, (1) copper-plate charters and (2) lithic records. The former belong, without a single exception, to the members of these dynasties or their feudatories as the right of issuing copper-plate charters with the object of making or renewing land-grants was a royal prerogative. Most of the records of the second category, however, belong to private persons whose pious acts they purport to record. Some of these epigraphs, it is true, emanate from members of royal families; but they are not in the nature of royal charters from which they differ not only as regards the base but also in other respects like the style of composition and sometimes even scripts. It will, therefore, be in the fitness of things to deal with them separately within the dynastic framework.

I. ŚARABHAPURĪYA INSCRIPTIONS

What little we know of this dynasty is based almost entirely on the copper-plate grants issued by some of the members of this dynasty. Only one of the members, Prasanna or Prasannamātra, is known from another source, *i.e.*, coins. Not a single stone inscription belonging to any member of the family or to the period of its rule is known so far. Of the seventeen records of the dynasty reported to date, three belong to Narendra,[1] four to Jayarāja,[2] seven to Sudevarāja,[3] and two to Pravararāja.[4] Of the remaining grant only the middle or second plate has been found[5] and, as the name of the issuing chief is not recorded in the portion incised on the only available plate, its attribution is uncertain.[6] As many as sixteen records have

1. Nos. I:I-III.
2. Nos. I:IV-VII.
3. Nos. I: VIII—XIV.
4. Nos. I: XV-XVI.
5. No. 1:Appendix I. Another record, *viz.*, Mallar plates of Vyāghrarāja, is also generally attributed to the Śarabhapurīyas. But, as will be shown in the sequel, Vyāghrarāja and his two predecessors mentioned in the charter appear to have belonged to a different family.
6. It has been suggested that the plate belongs to Sudevarāja. But this surmise is based on some general considerations which cannot be depended upon for settling the issue.

been found at various places in the Chhattisgarh region of Madhya Pradesh whereas only one has been reported from the adjoining Kalahandi District of Orissa.[7]

All the grants of the family are written on a set of three plates of copper. Of these, the outer or first side of the first plate is invariably left blank as the writing on this side would have become illegible and worn out by constant handling and due to exposure to the inclemencies of weather. With the same object of the preservation of writing the outer side of the last or third plate was also intended to be left uninscribed. Actually, both the known complete charters of Narendra,[8] the first member of the family whose records have come down to us, and the Angura[9] and the first set of the Mallar plates[10] of Jayarāja have the outer side of the third plate blank. But later on it was found difficult to adjust and accommodate the draft on the inner sides of the first and the last plates and both sides of the middle plate and the remainder of the draft, which comprised a much smaller number of lines as compared to those on the other inscribed sides of the plates, came to be incised on the second side of the third plate. The Arang plates of Jayarāja, issued in the fifth year of his reign,[11] form the earliest record of the family on which the writing is continued on the second side of the last plate. Henceforth this feature is observed in all the records except the Dhamatari plates of Sudevarāja[12] and the Thakurdiya plates of Pravararāja,[13] the last known member of the dynasty, which retain the old fashion of leaving the second side of the third plate blank. It must be remembered, however, that in all the cases where both sides of the third plate bear writing, the outer side contains much fewer lines than the other inscribed sides of the plates, sometimes only a single line,[14] indicating thereby that the second side was actually expected to be left blank and that all cases of the continuation of writing on this side are due to the inability of the writer to accommodate the draft on the remaining sides of the plates. The practice of recording royal charters on a set of three copper-plates was continued by the Pāṇḍuvaṁśins and the Somavaṁśins who followed the Śarabhapurīyas in South Kosala.

7. No. I:IV.
8. Nos. I:I-II.
9. No. I: IV.
10. No. I: V.
11. No. 1: VI.
12. No. I: IX.
13. No. I: XV.
14. *E.g.*, Sirpur (No. I: X) and Kauvatal (No. I : XII) plates of Sudevarāja and Mallar plates of Pravararāja (No. I: XVI). The Mallar plates of the 9th year of Jayarāja (No. I: VII) have only a couple of lines on the second side of the last plate.

Plates

The **plates** are rectangular, their breadth being less than the length. According to the information available, the smallest plates are those employed for the Dhamatari grant of Sudevarāja which measure $3\frac{3}{8}$" x 3" and the largest those of the Kauvatal plates of the same king measuring 7.4" x 4.2". Other plates range between these sizes. All the three plates of a charter are generally of a uniform thickness, but there are a few exceptions.[15] Generally, the corners of the plates are angular, but in a few cases they are found somewhat rounded.[16] Some of the plates are broader at the ends than in the middle.[17] Ordinarily, new plates were used for engraving the records. However, the lower portion of the writing on the first side of the second plate and the whole writing on the second side of the same plate and the inner side of the third plate of the Mallar grant of Jayarāja's ninth regnal year is engraved on erasures. The practice of raising or rendering thicker the edges of the plates for the preservation of writing is observed only in one case, *viz.*, Mallar plates of Pravararāja.

The plates are held together by a copper ring which is passed through a hole made about the middle of the margin on the left. The hole is generally circular or nearly so, but in a few cases it is square or squarish.[18]

Seals

The ends of the ring are joined under a circular **seal** with a diameter of around 3".[19] Seals attached to all the grants have been found with the exception of the stray plate of Narendra,[20] the Mallar plates of the fifth year of Jayarāja, the incomplete Sarangarh plates of Sudevarāja[21] and the stray middle plate of the unattributable charter.[22] Strangely enough, the seal of Jayarāja is found attached to the Sirpur plates of the seventh year of the reign of Sudevarāja. Obviously, the seal of Jayarāja, several unused

15. The second plate of the Mallar grant of the 5th year of Jayarāja (No. I: V) and of the Thakurdiya charter of Pravararāja (No. I: XV) is thicker than the remaining plates.
16. The corners of both the Mallar grants of Jayarāja are, for instance, rounded.
17. *E.g.*, Mallar plates of Jayarāja's 5th regnal year (No. 1: V) and the Raipur plates of Sudevarāja (No. I: XIII).
18. Thus, the Mallar plates of the 9th year of Jayarāja's reign (No. I: VII), the Kauvatal plates (No. I: XII) and one of the sides of the Sarangarh plates (No. I: XIV) of Sudevarāja, the Mallar plates of Pravararāja (No. I: XVI) and the middle plate of the only unassignable grant have square holes.
19. Some seals are slightly less and others more in diameter. The Kurud plates of Narendra (No. I: II) and the Angura plates of Jayarāja (No. I: IV) have seals measuring 2·8" in diameter. The diameter of the seal of the Dhamatari plates of Sudevarāja is 3". Other seals measure $3\frac{1}{4}$" (Arang plates of Jayarāja, No. I: VI), $3\frac{5}{8}$" [Raipur (No. I:XIII) and Arang (No. I: XI) plates of Sudevarāja] and 3·2" (Thakurdiya plates of Pravararāja, No. I: XV).
20. No. I: III.
21. No. I: XIV.
22. No. I: Appendix I.

specimens whereof must have been lying in the records office, was attached by oversight to Sudevarāja's charter. Alternatively, it is not impossible that, for some reason not known to us, Sudevarāja's plates were detached from their original ring the ends of which were soldered under Sudevarāja's own seal and were erroneously joined to a seal originally attached to a grant of Jayarāja.[22a] The seals are invariably cast from moulds. As to their metal, Fleet states in connection with the Arang plates of Jayarāja and the Raipur plates of Sudevarāja that the seals attached to these charters have a strong yellow glint in them and give the impression of being of a kind of brass rather than of copper.[23] In reality, however, they seem to be of bronze. The somewhat countersunk, often concave surface, which is generally enclosed within a double-line border, is divided into two parts by a couple of horizontal lines, the lower half being of a slightly larger dimension. The upper portion bears in the centre in a low relief the figure of goddess Lakṣmī, nimbate, standing on a lotus and facing full front. Her right hand is bent and raised up and the left one held akimbo. In each of the two hands she seems to hold some indistinct object.[24] She is represented as being bathed by water poured from a vessel held in the uplifted and expanded trunk of an elephant standing on a water-lily on either side of the goddess. There are accessory devices on right and left corners. The object on the proper left is invariably a conch-shell or *śaṅkha*[25] while that on the proper right is either a water-lily[26] or wheel (*cakra*).[27] In a solitary case[28] the sun and moon represented by a pellet and a crescent respectively have been noticed in the uppermost portion. The upper portion of the lower half, almost in the centre of the seal, bears a two-line metrical legend composed in the *Anuṣṭubh* metre giving the name of the reigning monarch responsible for issuing the charter in question which is described as chastiser of the enemies[29] or as everlasting in the world.[30] The name of the king, who is

22a. Other instances of copper-plate charters to which the seals of the predecessors of the issuing chiefs must also be explained in a similar manner. For another view, see *ICPB*, 166-A, No. 177-b; *EI*, xxxi, 103 and note 4.

23. *CII*, iii, 191 and 196.

24. The object held by the goddess cannot be made out definitely. V.V. Mirashi thinks that the object held in her raised right hand on the seal of the Thakurdiya plates is lotus (*EI*, xxii, 17).

25. However, on the seals of the Thakurdiya and Mallar plates of Pravararāja (Nos. I: XV and XVI) we find water-lily on both sides.

26. On the seals of the Angura, Arang and Mallar (second set) plates of Jayarāja (Nos. I: IV, VI and VII) and the Nahna, Arang and Raipur plates of Sudevarāja (Nos. I: VIII, XI and XIII). As stated above, on the seals of the Thakurdiya and Mallar plates of Pravararāja we have water-lily on either side.

27. On the seals of Dhamatari and Kauvatal plates of Sudevarāja (Nos. I: IX and XI).

28. On the seal of the Kurud plates of Narendra (No. I: II).

29. In the legends on all the seals with the exception of those attached to the Nahna, Dhamatari, Kauvatal and Arang plates of Sudevarāja (Nos. I: VIII, IX, X and XI).

30. In the legends on the seals of the four charters of Sudevarāja specified in the previous note.

often described in conventional terms alluding to his military successes[31] or regular succession,[32] is preceded by the honorific *śrīmat*. Generally the name of the king's father[33] and sometimes that of his grandfather[34] are also given,[35] in a few cases in an ornate style. Below the legend is a device which is often described as 'floral'. However, from the seal attached to the Mallar plates of Pravararāja[36] it appears to consist of a jar or *pūrṇa-kumbha* flanked by water-lilies. These devices are significant inasmuch as they indicate the Vaiṣṇavite leanings of these chiefs, a conclusion vouched for by the internal evidence of the charters granted by them.

Palaeography

All the available inscriptions are written in what is popularly known as the **'box-headed' variety of the Central Indian alphabet** which itself is classed under the southern class of alphabets. The variety is so called because the tops of the letters give the appearance of small square boxes which are formed by sinking four short strokes in the form of a square which, as pointed out by Bühler, was an artificial development of the serif. The block of the metal inside the square is left out unscooped. In other words, the boxes are of the filled in type with the exception of only a few letters in the Sirpur plates of Sudevarāja[37] which present scooped out or hollow boxes. Southern characteristics are noticed in the curves at the lower ends of the letters *a*, *ā*, *k*, *ñ*, and *r*, *ḍ* with a rounded back and notch in the left limbs of *p* and *b* and occasionally in the upper horizontal line of *j* and the medial *au* which is bipartite in the earlier records. The influence of northern characteristics is also seen in a few cases. The rather strange appearance of this alphabet is mainly due to the contraction of the breadth and elongation of all the letters and the conversion of all the curves into angular strokes.[38] These characters bear a general resemblance to those of

31. Narendra's legend describes him as one who had conquered the earth by the edge of his sword while Jayarāja is said to have assailed (Nos. I: IV and V) or uprooted (No. I: VII) his enemies by prowess. Sudevarāja is also described in a similar manner ('uprooted', Nos. I: IX and XI; 'assailed', No. XIII). Pravararāja is stated to have acquired the earth by (the prowess of his own arms.
32. On the seals of Dhamatari and Kauvatal plates of Sudevarāja (Nos. I: IX and XII).
33. On the seals of the plates of Narendra (No. I: I-II), Jayarāja (Nos. I: IV-V and VII), Nahna and Arang plates of Sudevarāja (Nos.I: VIII and XI) and both the records of Pravararāja (Nos. I: XV-XVI). The legend on the seal of the Raipur plates of Sudevarāja (No. I: XIII) also probably mentioned his father's name.
34. On the seals attached to the Nahna, Arang and Raipur plates of Sudevarāja (Nos. I: VIII, XI, XIII).
35. The legends on the seals of the Dhamatari and Kauvatal plates (Nos. I: IX and XII) of Sudevarāja do not mention his father or grandfather.
36. No. I: XVI.
37. No. I: X.
38. *CII*, iii, 19; G. Bühler, *Indian Palaeography*, 83-84; G.H. Ojha, *Bhāratīya Prācīna Lipimālā*, 83.

the Vākāṭaka records which are, however, somewhat less stylised[39] and assignable to an earlier date, a fact vouched for by other historical considerations also. The characters of the earlier records such as the Pīparḍūlā, Kurud and Rawan plates of Narendra show less elongation and angularity as compared to those of the later records of the family, thereby indicating the direction of palaeographical development. Another direction in which the scriptual development took place was the extension of the top-stroke of the box-head into short horizontal lines on either side of which the beginnings are traceable in the records of Pravararāja and which is met with in a fully developed form in the copper-plate grants of the Pāṇḍuvaṁśins of South Kosala. One cannot be quite sure of the suggestion that the use of these characters in Kosala was due to the influence of the Vākāṭakas[40] as there is no definite evidence on this point.

We may now advert to a few points of detail. In the case of the *akṣara mā*, the medial *ā* is attached in two different ways, *viz*., (i) top-stroke as in the case of other *akṣaras*, and (ii) downward extension, sometimes showing a curve at the lower end, of the right vertical of the sign for *m*. Examples of both the types are met with in the Pīparḍūlā plates of Narendra while in the Kurud plates issued by the same king about twenty-one years later the medial is throughout indicated by the top-stroke. The other method is adopted in Narendra's Rawan plate[41] as well as in all the records of Jayarāja. In the Nahna, Sirpur, Arang and Raipur plates of Sudevarāja also we come across the same sign, but his remaining records revert back to the top-stroke which is employed throughout in both the extant records of the next king Pravararāja. Medial *ī* is also indicated in two different ways, *i.e*., (i) a dot in the centre of a circle, which denotes the short medial *i*, attached to the top of the letter and (ii) a short stroke, generally vertical, springing from the bottom of the circle. In the Pīparḍūlā and Rawan plates of Narendra we come across the second mode, but the upper end of the stroke inside the circle shows a leftward curve. In the records of Jayarāja both the signs are employed[42] whereas in the epigraphs of Sudevarāja it is generally indicated in the second way, though, it must be pointed out, the stroke is sometimes horizontal.[43] The records of Pravararāja

39. The characters of the Vākāṭaka copper-plate grants are less angular and elongated than those of their Śarabhapurīya counterparts.

40. *EI*, xxii, 17. The fact appears to be that this variety was widely prevalent throughout Central India.

41. In two of the three instances of *mā* met with in the record the medial *ā* is indicated by a hook attached to the lower end of the right limb whereas in the third case the stroke is attached to the upper portion of the right limb. The last case seems to be due to oversight.

42. In the Angura plates we find the second mode, though the stroke inside the circle is horizontal. In the second set of Mallar plates, on the other hand, it is vertical. The dot figures in the first set of the Mallar plates and the Arang plates.

43. In the Arang and Raipur plates. In the Dhamatari plates it assumes a peculiar, in some cases almost circular, form.

employ the first sign throughout. It seems that there is no fundamental difference between the two signs, the second sign or its variations being probably the result of an attempt to form the sign by a single stroke. For the medial *ū* we find three different signs employed—(i) one formed by the downward extension of the right limb of the letter which is again turned upward and the addition of a hook attached to the lower portion of the duplicated vertical line;[44] (ii) that formed by the elongation of the lower portion of the right limb of the letter and turning it slightly upward on left and additing a horizontal stroke, sometimes slightly curved, to the left of the elongation;[45] and (iii) a semi-circle open to right attached to the lower end of the slightly elongated right limb of the letter.[46] The medial *ṛ* differs from the subscribed *r* only in that the former shows a flourishing curve. The medial *o* sometimes originates as a single vertical stroke which is divided into two parts turning in opposite directions[47] while in other cases both the strokes emerge independently from the top-stroke of the letter.[48] As regards the medial *o* in *mo*, in most of the records one part is attached to the top of the letter and the other part to the lower end of its right limb[49] while in a few records of Sudevarāja[50] as well as in both the charters of Pravararāja both the strokes are attached to the top (box) of the letter independently. The medial *au* is bipartite in the earlier records and tripartite in the later ones.[51] In the records of Narendra both the parts of *j* are of equal breadth whereas in subsequent inscriptions the breadth of the upper half is considerably reduced as compared to the lower part which begins much further to left. The letters *ḍ* and *d* are clearly distinguished from each other. *T* is without a loop while *n* exhibits a loop invariably. The dot inside the circle of *th* sometimes takes the form of a horizontal stroke[52] and sometimes of an irregular circle joined to its

44. In most of the grants in letters like *bhū* and *sū*.
45. In the letters *cū* and *yū* in all the records up to the time of Sudevarāja.
46. In the letters *cū* and *yū* in the Thakurdiya and Mallar plates of Pravararāja.
47. In the Nahna and Arang plates of Sudevarāja.
48. In all the remaining records. Sometimes both the strokes show a sharp downward curve.
49. In both sets of Mallar plates of Jayarāja and the Nahna, Arang, Sirpur and Raipur plates of Sudevarāja.
50. In the Dhamatari, Kauvatal and Sarangarh plates of Sudevarāja. Also in the Kurud plates of Narendra, Angura and Arang plates of Jayarāja.
51. The Arang plates of Jayarāja, Dhamatari and Kauvatal plates of Sudevarāja and both the records of Paravararāja show the tripartite form while the Nahna, Arang, Sirpur and Raipur plates of Sudevarāja give instances of the use of bipartite form. Bipartite form is used in both the sets of the Mallar plates of Jayarāja also, but it is constructed in a different manner, *i.e.*, the right end of the upper part of the box of the letter goes up a little as a vertical line which culminates into a square box from the right top end of which flourish the two strokes.
52. In the Sirpur plates of Sudevarāja the line is straight while in the Dhamatari and Sarangarh plates of the same king it is curved at both the ends.

base.[53] *B* exhibits a notch in the left limb in the earlier records[54] while the breadth of its upper part is reduced on the left in all the later records.[55] The letter *m* shows a box attached to each of its upper ends barring only the subscribed one only in the Nahna plates of Sudevarāja. As for *l*, its right upper end is strongly curved as an arch over the letter and brought down as a vertical line on its left, in a few cases much below the base line of the letter.[56] The final *t* is smaller in size as compared to other letters and without a box-head and has one or two vertical lines above.[57] In the Dhamatari plates of Sudevarāja we come across the *halanta* mark also.[58] The use of the *jihvāmūliya* and the *upadhmānīya* is quite common, the former being exactly identical in shape with *m* and the medial *ā*, if required, being added to it exactly in the same manner as to *m*. The *visarga* is indicated either by a couple of dots or horizontal strokes placed one above the other.[59] We have **numerical symbols** for 2, 3, 4, 5, 7, 9, 10 and 20.

As for the use of **punctuation mark**, no fixed principle is observed. At places they are not used even though required while in many cases they are found employed even though their presence is not warranted. But generally speaking, they are employed at the end of sentences, halves of verses and of the verses themselves and to mark the conclusion of a record. A variety of marks is noticed employed for these purposes. They include one or a couple of vertical[60] or horizontal[61] lines, two dots placed one above the other,[62] sometimes separated by a horizontal line[63] and two vertical

53. In the Kurud and Rawan plates of Narendra and Nahna and Raipur plates of Sudevarāja.
54. In the records of Narendra.
55. In all the records of Jayarāja and his successors.
56. *E.g.*, in the Kauvatal plates of Sudevarāja and Thakurdiya and Mallar plates of Pravararāja.
57. In the Kurud plates of Narendra, the Angura, Mallar (both sets) plates of Jayarāja and the Nahna, Sirpur and Arang plates of Sudevarāja a single vertical line capped by a horizontal stroke is employed whereas we find two vertical lines with the crowning horizontal stroke in Pravararāja's inscriptions.
58. Text-lines 20 and 22.
59. : is used in the Pīparḍūlā and Kurud plates of Narendra, Angura plates of Jayarāja, Dhamatari and Kauvatal plates of Sudevarāja and Thakurdiya and Mallar plates of Pravararāja. The use of = is met with in the Mallar (second set) plates of Jayarāja and the Nahna, Sirpur, Raipur and Sarangarh plates of Sudevarāja. We come across both the forms in the Mallar (first set) and Arang plates of Jayarāja and Arang plates of Sudevarāja.
60. In the Kurud plates of Narendra. In a few places the joining of the two lines gives the mark a somewhat strange appearance.
61. A single horizontal line is noticed in the Angura, Mallar (second set) and Arang plates of Jayarāja and the Nahna and Sirpur plates of Sudevarāja. In Sudevarāja's Kauvatal plates it is curved slightly at both the ends. Two horizontal lines are seen in the Mallar (both sets) and Arang plates of Jayarāja and the Nahna, Sirpur, Arang, Raipur and Sarangarh plates of Sudevarāja.
62. In Jayarāja's Mallar (first set) plates and Sudevarāja's Nahna plates.
63. In Jayarāja's Mallar (first set) plates.

lines placed side by side, the left one with a hook at the top.[64] Two dots or horizontal lines, it must be pointed out, are also used for *visarga* and in several records they are employed both as *visarga* as well as to indicate a pause.[65] A device consisting of a group of six vertical lines, each following line being smaller than the preceding one, followed by a horizontal line, is used in the Mallar plates of Jayarāja's ninth regnal year to indicate the conclusion of the record.

Corrections

Reference may now be made to the **methods adopted for correcting** what had been erroneously engraved earlier. In cases where the error pertained to a small portion like a letter or a medial sign which was wrongly engraved, the correction was made by making necessary alterations. In all such cases traces of the originally incised letters or medial signs are quite clear.[66] In cases where correction by alteration was not found possible, the wrongly incised letter was cancelled by rubbing.[67] We also find instances of undesired portions being erased and desired words being engraved on the erasures.[68] When it was noticed that a few words were repeated by oversight, the duplicated portion was rubbed off.[69] It must be pointed out, however, that such attempts at correction are comparatively few and far between; numerous errors of a similar nature have been left out unrectified.

As regards **supplying omissions**, two different techniques are found to have been resorted to. We come across a few instances of an omitted letter written below the line without any indication as to where it is to be inserted, the place of insertion being determined only by the context.[70] In the Arang plates of Sudevarāja (text-line 7) we find the use of the *kākapada* mark (+) to denote the omission as well as before the portion to be supplied. The same mark has been employed for two different purposes in another grant of the same monarch.[71] At one place[72] we find it used before the word above the line in order to indicate that this is not its proper place. At another place[73] it is found used above the line with a view to indicate that

64. In Sudevarāja's Dhamatari and Pravararāja's Thakurdiya and Mallar plates.
65. *E.g.*, in the Mallar (both sets) and Arang plates of Jayarāja and the Nahna, Sirpur, Arang and Sarangarh plates of Sudevarāja.
66. *E.g.*, Mallar plates of Jayarāja, year 9 (text-line 5); Nahna (text-line 6) and Arang plates (text-line 3) of Sudevarāja and Thakurdiya plates of Pravararāja (text-line 1).
67. Raipur plates of Sudevarāja, text-line 11.
68. Kauvatal plates of Sudevarāja, text-lines 4, 9 and 10.
69. Mallar plates of Jayarāja, year 5, text-line 15.
70. Nahna (text-line 13) and Arang (text-lines 8 and 25) plates of Sudevarāja and Thakurdiya plates of Pravararāja, text-line 3.
71. Raipur plates.
72. Text-line 10.
73. Text-line 13.

something has to be inserted here. At yet another place[74] a couple of letters omitted by oversight have been engraved below the line with a *kākapada* mark and another *kākapada* is employed before, instead of after, the letter after which the omitted letters should have come. It would thus follow that no fixed principle is followed for supplying omissions.

Language and Orthography

All the records are composed in **Sanskrit** which seems to have served as the official language. **Prakritism** can, however, be noticed in some stray cases. In the Pipardula plates of Narendra (text-line 6), for instance, we come across the form Svāmippa used in place of Svāmyātman. Likewise, the word *haḍappagrāha* is found employed for *hṛtapragrāha* in the Mallar plates of the ninth year of Jayarāja (text-line 8). The same is true of the name Kansippasvāmin occurring in the Sirpur plates (text-line 10) of Sudevarāja and the form *akkaśālika* (for *akṣaśālika*) met with in the Dhamatari plates (text-line 28) of the same king. Prakritism is also noticed in the word *savvatsara* used in the Kurud plates of Narendra (text-line 20) and the Nahna (text-line 22) and Kauvatal (text-line 24) plates of Sudevarāja and in *sāvvatsara* figuring in the Amgura plates (text-line 28) of Jayarāja. The use of *tāmbra*[75] or *tāmvra*[76] for *tāmra* in a majority of inscriptions is indicative of the faulty pronunciation current in those days. The same applies to the word *ukirṇṇa* (for *utkīrṇa*) met with in the Kauvatal plates (text-line 25) of Sudevarāja and Thakurdiya plates (text-line 23) of Pravararāja and the employment of *gn* for *jñ* in the word *mukh-āgnayā* in the Arang plates of Sudevarāja (text-line 26), of *ṅgh* for *ṁh* in the names ending in *siṁha*[77] and that of *ṅ* in place of *anusvāra* before the palatal sibilant (*ś*) in words like *aṅśa*[78] (for *aṁśa*) and *viṅśa*[79] (for *viṁśa*). While the employment of the letter *ra* for *ṛ*[80] and of the latter for the *repha*[81] in a few cases emanates from faulty

74. Text-line 25. In text-line 17 of the same record we notice a *svastika*, but its purpose is not clear.
75. I: I, text-line 6; I: V, text-line 10; I: VI, text-line 11; I: VII, text-line 12; I: VIII, text-lines 10 and 23; I: IX, text-line 11; I: X, text-line 11; I: XI, text-line 13; I: XII, text-line 10; I: XIII, text-line 11; I: XIV, text-line 11; I: XVI, text-line 10; I: App. II, text-line 4.
76. I: XV, text-line 9.
77. I: IV, text-line 19; I: V, text-line 22; I: VI, text-line 24; I: VII, text-line 25; I: VIII, text-line 23 (here we have *sīṅgha* in place of the common *siṅgha*); I: IX, text-line 28; I: X, text-line 25; I: XII, text-line 25; I: XIII, text-line 28; I: XV, text-line 23; I: XVI, text-line 24. In the Arang plates of Sudevarāja, text-line 26, we find the use of *siṁgha* instead of *siṅgha*.
78. Arang plates of Sudevarāja, text-lines 10, 11 and 13.
79. Kurud plates of Narendra, text-line 20.
80. Mallar plates (first set) of Jayarāja, text-line 9; Dhamatari (text-line 6) and Raipur (text-line 9) plates of Sudevarāja.
81. Thakurdiya plates of Pravararāja, text-lines 12 (*darīśayatī* for *darśayati*) and 17 (*variśa* for *varṣa*).

pronunciation, the rather common use of *ri* instead of *ṛ*[82] and *vice versa*[83] are evidently due to the inability to distinguish between the pronunciations of the two letters. The transformation of the word *utkīrṇṇa* into *uktīrṇṇa*[84] or *uktirṇṇa*[85] in some cases illustrates metathesis while the frequent elision of the first consonant in the word *dvijāya* following *tasmād*[86] is an instance of haplology. The *sandhi* rules are often not observed.[87] The reduplication of the consonant following the *repha* is common whereas examples of the reduplication of the consonant preceding *r* are few and far between.[88] In one case we come across the use of *gh* for *h*.[89] There are numerous cases of the reduplication of *v* following an *anusvāra*.[90] The use of *anusvāra* for final *m* is very common.[91] Final *m* is often left out[92] while the same is the case with final *t* in a few places.[93] The replacement of final *m* by *anusvāra* is noticed in a number of cases.[94] We have numerous instances of unnecessary employment of double nasals[95] and the reduplication of the letter

82. I: I, text-line 19 (*tritiya* for *tṛtīya*); I: II, text-line 7 (*griha* for *gṛha*) and 8 (*prabhrity* for *prabhṛty*); I: V, text-line 3 (*pitri* for *pitṛ*); I: VI, text-line 10 (*vridhaye* for *vṛddhaye*); I: VII, text-line 10 (*bavrica* for *bahvṛca*); I: IX, text-line 12 (*sriṣṭaḥ* for *sṛṣṭaḥ*), etc.
83. *E.g.*, *tṛdaśa* in place of *tridaśa* in I: VII, text-line 5; I: VIII, text-line 6; I: X, text-line 6; I: XI, text-line 6; I: XII, text-line 5; I: XIII, text-line 6; I: XVI, text-line 6.
84. In the Mallar (first set, text-line 22) and Arang (text-line 23) plates of Jayarāja and the Sirpur (text-line 25), Arang (text-line 26) and Raipur (text-line 28) plates of Sudevarāja.
85. In the Angura plates of Jayarāja, text-line 18.
86. I: V, text-line 14; I: VI, text-line 15; I: VIII, text-lines 13-14; I: IX, text-line 15; I: X, text-line 15; I: XI, text-line 17; I:XII, text-line 14; I:XIII, text-lines 16-17; I: XIV, text-line 15; I: XV, text-line 13; I: XVI, text-line 14; I: App. I, text-line 8.
87. *E.g.*, Pīparḍūlā (text-lines 5,7 and 11) and Kurud (text-lines 2 and 4) plates of Narendra.
88. I: V, text-line 1; I: VI, text-line 1; I: VII, text-lines 1 and 8; I: VIII, text-line 1; I: X, text-line 1; I: XI, text-line 1; I: XIII, text-lines 1, 9, 10 and 12; I: XIV, text-line 1.
89. *Dāgha* (for *dāha*) in the Kurud plates of Narendra, text-line 7.
90. See, for instance, *saṁvvatsara* in the Mallar (first set, text-line 23) and Arang (text-line 24) plates of Jayarāja, Raipur plates (text-line 27) of Sudevarāja and Thakurdiya plates (text-line 22) of Pravararāja and *para-dattā*[*m**] *vvā* in text-line 20 of the last mentioned record.
91. *E.g.*, I: IV, text-lines 11 and 12; I: V, text-line 15; I: VI, text-lines 14 and 21; I: VII, text-lines 16 and 23; I: IX, text-lines 15 and 24; I: X, text-lines 15 and 22; I: XI, text-lines 17 and 24; I: XII, text-lines 14, 15 and 24; I: XIII, text-lines 16 and 23; I: XIV, text-lines 15 and 16; I: XV, text-lines 14 and 20; I: XVI, text-lines 14 and 21.
92. See, for instance, I: II, text-lines 14, 16 and 18; I: VI, text-line 16; I: VII, text-line 17; I: VIII, text-lines 13 and 14; I: IX, text-line 17; I: X, text-line 16; I: XI, text-line 18; I: XIII, text-line 17; I: XV, text-line 13; I: XVI, text-line 15.
93. I: VI, text-lines 19 and 20; I: VII, text-lines 20 and 21; I: XI, text-line 23.
94. I: IV, text-lines 11 and 12; I: V, text-line 15; I: VI, text-lines 14 and 21; I: VII, text-lines 16 and 23; I: IX, text-lines 15 and 24; I: X, text-lines 15 and 24; I: XI, text-lines 17 and 24; I: XII, text-lines 14, 15 and 21; I: XIII, text-lines 16 and 23; I: XIV, text-lines 15 and 16; I: XV, text-lines 14 and 20; I: XVI, text-lines 14 and 21.
95. This tendency is first noticed in the Mallar plates of Jayarāja (I: V, text-line 22; I: VII, text-lines 6, 15, 16 and 19) and is found to become more common in the records of Sudevarāja (I: IX, text-line 13; I: XI, text-lines 21 and 22; I: XII, text-lines 1, 2, 18 and 23) and Pravararāja (I: XV, text-line 18; I: XVI, text-lines 1, 2 and 16).

t following a nasal,[96] both noticed for the first time in the records of Jayarāja.[97] There are also a few examples of the substitution of *t* for a nasal followed by the letter *t*.[98] In some cases *visarga* and reduplicated sibilant are used side by side, which is grammatically erroneous.[99] The letter *t* preceding *s* is sometimes dropped as in *prativasyatha* (for *prativatsyatha*) occurring in the Mallar (first set, text-line 12) and Arang (text-line 12) plates of Jayarāja and the Nahna plates (text-line 13) of Sudevarāja. In a majority of the inscriptions of Jayarāja we come across a redundant *d* inserted between *Śarabhapurāt* and the following word *vikkrama*.[100] Attention must also be invited to the employment of the suffix *u* at the end of the words *saṁvat*[101] and *samvatsara*[102] in certain records which is due to the influence of Dravidian languages.[103]

Abbreviations

A few **abbreviations** are found employed. Thus, we come across *di* for *dina* or *divasa*[104] and *savva*[105] or *saṁvva*[106] for *saṁvatsara*, though the use of the words in their full forms is met with more often than of their abbreviated forms.

The inscriptions are composed in prose excluding only the customary imprecatory and benedictive verses at the end and the versified legend on the seal.

Grants

As stated above, all the available inscriptions of the dynasty are written on copper-plates and their object is to register land-grants in favour of a

96. I: IV, text-lines 9 and 16; I: V, text-lines 1, 2, 4, 11, 13, 16, 18 and 19-20; I: VI, text-lines 1, 12, 17 and 18; I: VII, text-lines 1, 2, 20 and 21; I: XVI, text-line 14.
97. As will be clear from the preceding and following examples, several orthographically strange features were introduced during the reign of Jayarāja.
98. I: V, text-line 2; I: VI, text-line 20; I: VII, text-lines 13-14. In a couple of cases (*ghorāddhakāraṁ*, I: V, text-line 7; I: VI, text-line 7) we notice that the nasal followed by *dh* is replaced by *d*.
99. *E.g.*, I: V, text-line 4. *Contra* the employment of a single sibilant where two sibilants are required (I: IX, text-line 9). Both these are due to defective pronunciation.
100. I: V, text-line 1; I: VI, text-line 1; I: VII, text-line 1. This was evidently due to the habitual pronunciation °*purād* = *vikram*° which owed itself to the observance of *sandhi* rules and the non-observance of *sandhi* in the examples in question.
101. I: XVI, text-line 23.
102. I: IX, text-line 27.
103. This characteristic is particularly noticed in Telugu. Owing to the impact of Telugu this feature is found employed in several mediaeval Marathi inscriptions.
104. I: II, text-line 20; I: VII, text-line 26; I: VIII text-line 22; I: X, text-line 24; I: XI, text-line 26; I: XII, text-line 24; I: XV, text-line 23. The word *diso* met with in the Mallar plates of the fifth year of Jayarāja (text-line 23) is perhaps not to be taken as an error and probably represents an error for *divasaḥ*.
105. I: X, text-line 24.
106. I: XI, text-line 26.

Brāhmaṇa[107] or a number of them[108] or a religious establishment.[109] The object of making the grant was invariably the augmentation of the religious merit of the donor's parents as well as the donor himself. The occasion of the gift is generally left unspecified,[110] The grants were generally made by the kings themselves. However, there are a few instances of grants which are stated to have been made by some other personages and later approved by the then ruling chief by issuing a copper-plate charter (*śāsana*). The grant recorded in the Pīparḍūlā plates of Narendra, for example, is said to have been made originally by one Rāhudeva and later endorsed by the monarch. Mallar plates of the ninth year of Jayarāja purport to register a grant stated to have been made by the *Hadappagrāha* Vatsa was later approved by the king. The Sirpur plates of Sudevarāja state that the grant recorded in them was made earlier by the honourable Nanna and later endorsed by Sudevarāja. A grant made by *Pratihāra* Bhogilla for the increase of his own as well as his parents' religious merit was endorsed by Sudevarāja by issuing his Arang charter. According to the same monarch's Raipur plates, he approved a grant made by Savitṛsvāmin in favour of his sons-in-law Nāgavatsasvāmin and Bandhuvatsasvāmin. Similarly the grant recorded in Sudevarāja's Sarangarh plates was reportedly made by the chief queen and some other members of the royal family and was later approved by the king. The unassignable stray plate also aimed at recording a similar grant, *viz.*, made by a certain Daṇḍacakra together with the young and elderly members of his family and later approved by the issuing chief. It will thus be seen that some of the personages responsible for making grants were royal officers, some other members of the royal family and the remaining ones probably landlords or *zagirdars*. It is obvious that they must have given away villages out of the land allotted to or held by them. They did not, however, enjoy the unrestricted right of alienation as, the land-grants being tax-free, it would have deprived the state of a considerable revenue by way of loss of land tax and therefore the permission of the king was deemed essential for all grants of land. The monarch's approval was also required specially as the grants were of a permanent nature while as regards government officers land was in all probability, allotted to them only for their own life-time.

107. In a majority of inscriptions the donee is a single Brāhmaṇa, groups of Brāhmaṇas and temples as grantees figuring only in a few cases specified in the following two notes.

108. Two Brāhmaṇas are referred to as donees in the Mallar plates of the ninth year of Jayarāja (No. I: VII) while the incomplete Sarangarh plates of Sudevarāja (No. I: XIV) record a grant in favour of as many as ten Brāhmaṇas. The Raipur plates of the same king (No. I: XIII) also refer to a couple of Brāhmaṇa donees.

109. The solitary Rawan plate of Narendra (No. I: III) is the only Śarabhapurīya charter recording a grant in favour of a religious institution, *i.e.*, a temple.

110. There are only three exceptions, *viz.*, Nos. I: II, I: V and I: XIII, which speak of donations made on the occasions of an ablution in the Gaṅgā, an *Uttarāyaṇa* and a lunar eclipse respectively.

Palm-leaf Charters

Reference must be made in this connection to the Kurud plates of Narendra which supply a very interesting piece of information regarding the materials employed for recording royal charters. It is averred that the grant rccorded therein was originally made by means of a charter written on plam leaves (*tāla-patra-śāsana*) by a personage spoken of as *parama-bhaṭṭāraka-pāda*, that the palm-leaf charter was burnt in a conflagration in the donee's house, and that after ascertaining that the grant was being enjoyed uninterruptedly by the donee it was endorsed by Narendra in favour of the original beneficiary's son by means of issuing a copper-plate charter. While we come across a few other allusions to the destruction of the original charters of a donatory nature and their renewal or confirmation by later rulers,[111] the record in question enjoys a unique position in the whole range of Indian epigraphy inasmuch as it affords us the only extant reference to the issuing of royal charters concerning land-grants recorded on palmyra leaves. Palm-leaf charters must have evidently been issued in a fairly good number but have not come down to us because of their perishable character.

Dates

All the complete epigraphic records that have been reported so far are dated. However, the **dates** are recorded only in years referred to as belonging to the increasingly victorious reign,[112] evidently of the ruling chiefs responsible for issuing the grants in question. All the dates follow a set pattern. They first mention the regnal year which is invariably followed by a reference to the month and the day thereof, the days being counted serially from 1 to 30 and there being no mention of the fortnight. The epigraphs themselves afford us absolutely no clue to ascertain as to whether the month mentioned was intended to be *pūrṇimānta* or *amānta.* But the Pāṇḍuvaṁśins of Kosala, who followed the Śarabhapurīyas, appear to have employed the *pūrṇimānta* system for dating their records as indicated by the Lodhia plates of Śivagupta Bālārjuna which first refer to the *tithi* as

111. Both the Nidhanpur and Dubi plates of Bhāskaravarman, the Bhauma-Nāraka king of Kāmarūpa, are clearly stated to have been issued in confirmation of grants made by earlier rulers of the dynasty. The original charters registering the grants are said to have been damaged, the former in a conflagration. See *EI*, xii, 66ff.; xix, 115ff. (Nidhanpur plates); xxx, 287ff. (Dubi plates).

112. A few variations deserve notice. The Pipardula plates of Narendra refer to the year only as increasing (*pravarddhamāna*) while the same monarch's Kurud plates speak of the year of the increasingly victorious reign (*pravarddhamāna-vijaya-rājya-savvatsara*). The same expression is met with in the Dhamatari plates of Sudevarāja with the only difference that the suffix *ū* is added at the end of the word *sambatsara.* In all the other records except two (Nos. I: VIII and I: XI) we find the expression *pravarddhamāna-vijaya* qualifying the year, the word *rājya* being left out. In the aforesaid two exceptions the year is mentioned without any descriptive eipthet.

Kārttika-paurṇamāsī which is then specified as *Kārttika-dina* 30.[113] It is, therefore, very likely, nay almost certain, that in the Śarabhapurīya charters also the *pūrṇimānta* scheme was intended even though it is not specifically stated even once. Reference may now be made to a few variations in the manner of specifying the dates noticed in the records under consideration. The Pīparḍūlā grant of Narendra, which is the record of the dynasty, mentions the date in words only whereas the Kurud plates of the same king and the Mallar grant issued in the fifth year of Jayarāja give it partly in words and partly in figures. Thus, in both these charters the year is mentioned both in words and figures whereas the day is specified only in figures. In all the other records, which are available in full, both the year and the day are indicated only in figures which are invariably specified in accordance with the old system of numerical notation. In one case there is a reference to the second or intercalary Bhādrapada.[114]

Draft and its Evolution.

Most of the records of the dynasty commence with the symbolic representation of the auspicious word *siddham*[114a] followed by the word *svasti.* The initial symbol was, on the authority of the eleventh century Arab writer Al-Biruni,[115] taken earlier to stand for *praṇava* or *om*. However, it is now generally admitted that he was misinformed or confused probably because the symbol was sometimes pronouned as *oṁ siddhiḥ* and that it really represents *siddham*, commonly translated as 'success' or 'hail'.[116] After these auspicious words, which constitute the *maṅgala,* we invariably find the mention of the place of issue which is generally Śarabhapura in the earlier records and Śrīpura in a few later charters.[117] The Kurud plates of Narendra provide the only example of a charter issued from a military camp.[118] Next are noticed the description of the issuing monarch and his order about the land-grant. This is followed by an exhortation to the future kings to uphold the grant, which is sought to be strengthened by a few imprecatory and benedictory stanzas, and the date. The concluding item is the mention of the scribe. In some cases the date and the reference to the engraver change their position and the latter is accorded precedence over the former.[119] This general framework is found followed in all the epigraphs without a single exception.

113. See *infra*, No. III: VIII. 114. No. I : X.

114a. The symbol is not found in the Mallar (both sets) and Arang plates of Jayarāja and the Nahna plates of Sudevarāja. The device is formed by a more or less cursively drawn semi-circle open to right or left. Many variations, some of which are due to the desire for ornamentation, are noticed as will be obvious from a glance at the plates.

115. E. Sachau, *Al-Beruni's India*, i, 173.

116. *EI*, xvii, 352; *Proceedings of Indian History Congress*, 1939, 471ff.; D.C. Sircar, *Indian Epigraphy*, 92-93, 95.

117. Only Dhamatari and Kauvatal plates of Sudevarāja and both the available grants of Pravararāja were issued from Śrīpura.

118. The plates were given from the *vijaya-skandhāvāra* located at Tilakeśvara.

119. In the Mallar (both sets) and Arang plates of Jayarāja.

It will be instructive to trace the **evolution of the draft** of the copper plate charters of the kings of Śarabhapura. The first four records, it will be clear from a perusal, have a very simple draft which gets elaborated during the reign of Jayarāja. This point can be best brought home by a somewhat detailed analysis of the contents of these records. The draft of the first known record of the family, viz., Pīparḍūlā plates of Narendra, is extremely simple and in the nature of matter of fact statement without any unnecessary elaboration. After the auspicious words *siddham*, represented symbolically, and *svasti* and the allusion to Śarabhapura, whence the charter was issued, the inscription refers to the illustrious *Mahārāja* Narendra about whom no information is supplied. Next follows the grant portion. It simply records the donation of a village by an individual for his own merit in favour of a Brāhmaṇa by means of a copper-plate charter and its ratification by the king. The address in respect of the grant is extremely simple and the addressees are the agriculturist householders inhabiting the village led by the Brāhmaṇas. As for the grantee, his Veda and *gotra* are specified. The only privilege conferred on the donee through this charter was the exemption from the entry of the *cāṭas* and *bhaṭas* (regular and irregular soldiers) and the villagers were asked to make over to the donee all the revenues in kind and cash. Next comes the request to the future district officers (*bhoga-patis*) to maintain the gift village and a couple of imprecatory and benedictive stanzas, attributed to Vyāsa, are cited in support of this entreaty. The record concludes with the specification of the date and the mention of the engraver.

The second stage in the development of the draft is noticed in the same monarch's Kurud plates which were issued twenty-one years later than the above-mentioned grant. The development is seen in the following matters. The king is now described, for the first time, in the preamble as a devout worshipper of *Bhagavat* (*i.e.*, Viṣṇu) and as meditating upon the feet of his parents. The addressees of the charter are now 'commanded' *samājñāpayati*) instead of being 'informed' (*bodhayati*) as in the previous grant. The villagers are, for the first time, asked to be obedient to the donee and the list of offerings to be made to him is considerably elaborated. It now includes *bhoga* or periodical offerings, *bhāga* or royal share of the agricultural produce, grains and cash. The exhortation is now addressed to the future kings and not to the district officers as in the preceding charter. The number of imprecatory and benedictive verses quoted in the name of Vyāsa is now increased to three. Whereas in the earlier grant the regnal year is qualified only by the word *pravarddhamāna*, 'increasing' or 'prosperous', in the charter under review it is found elaborated to *pravarddhamāna-vijaya-rājya*, 'increasingly victorious reign' or 'prosperous and victorious reign'. The date, which was formerly given in words only, is now specified in a mixture of words and figures, the year being expressed both in words and figures and the day only in figures. It will be seen that most of these features, some of them in a more elaborated form, are noticed in all the later records of the family.[120]

Chronologically speaking, the next record of the family is the Amgura grant of Jayarāja which marks a further stage in the evolution of the draft. The new features noticed in it are as under. The grant is, for the first time, said to have been made for the increase of the religious merit of the donor's parents as well as of the grantor himself. The reference to the making of the grant with the pouring of water (*udaka-pūrvaṁ*), which we come across in a few later records, is met with here for the first time. The catalogue of offerings to be brought by the villagers to the donee is now standardised and includes only *bhoga* and *bhāga*. The number of benedictive and imprecatory stanzas quoted in the name of Vyāsa is now raised to four. The date is expressed only in figures, a feature met with in practically all the later inscriptions of the family.[121]

The draft of the next record, *viz.*, the Mallar plates given by Jayarāja in the fifth year of his reign is much more developed and has almost attained the standardised form. The new features noticed in this epigraph may be outlined as follows. The description of the king is found fully developed. It is said that his feet were washed by the waters that were flowing forth from the radiance of the crest-jewels of the feudatories subdued by his prowess, that he was the cause of the tearing out of the parted hair of the women of his enemies and that he was the giver of cattle, earth and wealth (*vikkram-opanata-sāmanta-cūḍāmaṇi-prabhā-prasek-āmbubhir = dhauta-pāda-yugalo-ripu-vilāsinī-sīmant-oddhararaṇa-hetur = vasu vasudhā-go-pradaḥ*). The two adjectives describing the king's religious affiliation and devotion to parents, which have heen noticed in connection with the last two grants, also continue. The gift village is, for the first time, described as leading to happiness and fame in the abode of the lord of gods, *i.e.*, heaven (*tridaśa-pati-sadana-sukha-pratiṣṭhā-kara*) and the grant is said to have been intended to endure as long as the universe with its darkness removed by the rays of the sun, the moon and the stars lasts (*yāvad = ravi-śaśi-tārā-kiraṇa-pratihata-ghor-āndhakāram jagad = avatiṣṭhate tāvad = upabhogyaḥ*). Again, the grant is, for the first time, reported to have carried with it right to the major and minor deposits (*sa-nidhi, s-opanidhi*) and to have been exempted from all the taxes (*sarvva-kara-visarjjita*). This is in addition to the exemption from the entry of regular and irregular soldiers which is specified in the Pīparḍūlā plates of Narendra but omitted in the preceding

120. The Rawan grant of Narendra is incomplete and, therefore, nothing can be said about the draft of the second and third plates. The same is true of Sudevarāja's Sarangarh plates. However, the draft of the only available plate of the Rawan grant closely resembles the Kurud plates in regard to formal matters and as such has to be placed close to it and definitely later than the Pīparḍūlā grant.

121. The Mallar plates of the fifth year of Jayarāja constitute the only exception.

two grants. As for the imprecatory and benedictive stanzas, we have now also four. But of these, the first verse, which is met with here for the first time, is anonymous and is separated from the remaining three stanzas, which are ascribed to Vyāsa, by a small prose passage asking the addressees to protect the grant. These three verses are found in the previous grant also, but their order is slightly changed. And this order is adhered to in all the subsequent epigraphs of the family. Strangely enough, verse 1 of the Pīparḍūlā plates and verse 2 of the Kurud and Amgura plates, which is found in all the later records, is dropped in this inscription.

The draft thus developed with five (instead of the four of the previous record) imprecatory and benedictive stanzas is repeated without any alteration in Jayarāja's Arang plates dated in the fifth year of his reign. The finally developed draft is met with in the next epigraph, *viz.*, Mallar plates of the same ruler's ninth regnal year. The only noteworthy difference between this and the preceding record is that the former inserts the word *makuṭa*, 'crown', between', *sāmanta* and *cūḍāmaṇi* in the description of the issuing chief. This draft is repeated without any substantial change in all the subsequent charters of the family.

II. RECORDS OF THE PĀṆḌAVAVAṀŚINS OF MEKALĀ

The Pāṇḍavavaṁśins of Mekalā found a place on the historical map of India several decades later than the Śarabhapurīyas.[122] Nothing was known about this dynasty up to as late as October 1940 when the Bamhani plates[123] were discovered. Even though nearly four decades have elapsed since the discovery of the first record of the dynasty, only two more records, one of them incomplete, have come to light so far. And these two epigraphs also have been brought to light within the last five years.[124] All the three records known to date are copper-plate grants which form the sole source of information regarding the history of the family.

One of these charters (Bamhani plates) was found in the erstwhile Rewa State in the Baghelkhand region of Madhya Pradesh while the remaining two records have been discovered at Burhikhar, a part of the present township of Mallar in the Bilaspur District of Madhya Pradesh. The Bamhani and one of the records found at Mallar are complete[125] while the remaining inscription from the latter place remains incomplete.[126]

122. The first Śarabhapurīya epigraph was noticed by Cunningham in 1863 though it was discovered some time prior to the middle of the last century.
123. No. II: I.
124. The Mallar plates of Śūrabala were published in the *Studies in Indian Epigraphy* (Journal of the Epigraphical Society of India), iii, for the year 1976 while the incomplete Mallar plate was first brought to scholarly notice at the time of the third annual conference of the Epigraphical Society of India held at Udipi in March 1977.
125. Nos. II: I-II.
126. For an account of this plate, see *ABORI*, lviii-lix, 435-36.

Both the complete epigraphs belong to Śūrabala who was also known as Udīrṇavaira. It was earlier believed that the Bamhani plates emanated from Bharatabala; but the discovery of the Mallar plates of Śūrabala leaves no doubt that the former also belong to Śūrabala and, as will be shown in the sequel, their earlier erroneous ascription to Bharatabala was due to the carelessness of the scribe or the officer responsible for the preparation of the draft who left out some important portions.[127] The remaining epigraph is known only from a stray plate containing only a portion of the record and does not admit of attribution unless the remaining plates are found.

Plates

Both the complete records are incised on a **set of three copper-plates.** The outer side of the first plate of both the sets is left uninscribed. In the case of the Bamhani plates the second side of the last plate is also left blank while both the sides of the Mallar grant are inscribed. However, the fact that only three lines are incised on the outer side of this plate as against eleven lines on the first plate and the first side of the second plate, thirteen on the second side of the second plate and fourteen lines on the inner side of the third plate leaves no doubt that originally the second side of the third plate of this record also was intended to be left uninscribed for the sake of the preservation of writing, but the writing had to be continued on this side owing to the failure of the scribe to accommodate the matter on the remaining sides of the plates intended to be used for this purpose.

The **plates** are rectangular, their length being invariably larger than the breadth. Broadly speaking, they are somewhat larger in the middle than at the corners.[128] The Bamhani plates are the largest and measure about 19.5 cms. long and 11.25 cms. broad while the Mallar plates, which come next in chronological order, are 18.5 cms. in length and 10.6 cms. in breadth The solitary extant plate of the remaining unassignable charter measures 17.5 cms. long and 10.25 cms. broad. The extant material, thus, seems to indicate that with the passage of time there was a slight diminution in the size of the plates during the same reign though it is not possible to arrive at a definite conclusion on this point until the remaining plates of the Burhikhar charter and other grants of the family or of the same reign come to light. The ends of the inscribed sides of the plates are neither raised into rims nor rendered thicker for the protection of the writing, a feature noticed in the case of numerous copper-plate records.

The **hole for the passage of the copper-ring**, which kept the plates together, is invariably circular[129] and is cut in the centre at the top unlike

127. See editorial notes on No. II: I.
128. The stray plate of the only unattributable charter is somewhat irregular in shape.
129. The diameter of the hole ranges from 0·6 cm. to 1·875 cms (stray plate and Bamhani plates respectively), that of the Mallar plates being 0.8 cm.

all the remaining copper-plate records included in this volume which have the hole in the left margin.[130] It must be pointed out in this connection that this feature is noticed in the case of the copper-plate charters of the Parivrājaka *Mahārājas* Hastin[131] and Saṅkṣobha[132] as well as of the *Mahārājas* of Uccakalpa, *viz.*, Jayanātha[133] and Śarvanātha[134] hailing from the Baghelkand region and must be regarded as a regional characteristic though a few similar stray cases from other areas are also not unknown.[135] The ends of the ring are soldered under a roughly circular **seal** with a diameter of a little over 2 cms.[136] The surface of the **seal** of the Mallar plates is divided into two almost equal parts by a horizontal line with a short slanting downward projection at the left end. The upper half accommodates a rather roughly carved figure of a bull (Nandin) couchant to left while in the lower portion we have a single-line legend in prose consisting of a single word, in nominative singular, which may have been one of the titles of the issuing monarch. The seal attached to the Bamhani plates bears neither emblem nor legend. It may be reasonably supposed that this seal also must have borne the same device and inscription as met with on the seal of the Mallar plates and that they are totally worn out without leaving any trace whatever. Alternatively it is not impossible that for some reason the device and the legend could not be impressed and consequently the seal was left blank.

Palaeography

The **characters** of the inscriptions belong to the southern class of alphabets prevalent in Central India or, as Fleet would term it,[137] 'a variety, with southern characteristics, of the Central India alphabet'. In this variety tops of most of the letters are formed by small triangles with their apex downwards which characteristic has given it its popular meaningful name 'nail-headed'. The variety is similar to the box-headed one with the difference that the tops of letters are triangular instead of square and there is no perceptible effort to turn all curves into angles. Some other instances of the use of the nail-headed characters are known from Central India and elsewhere, but most of them show northern characteristics.[138] While the triangle or nail-head forms a distinguishing feature of this variety, the initial vowels *i*, *e* and *au* and the consonants *kh*, *j*, *ṇ*, *b* and *l* do not show

130. The only exceptions are Nos. II: Appendix (Malga plates of Indrarāja) and IV: Appendix II which have ring-holes on the top and right margin respectively.
131. J.F. Fleet, *Inscriptions of the Early Gupta Kings and their Successors*, *CII*, iii, nos. 21-24.
132. *Ibid.*, no. 25. 133. *Ibid.*, nos. 26-27.
134. *Ibid.*, nos. 28-31. 135. *E.g.*, Poona plates of Prabhāvatīguptā.
136. The seal of the Bamhani plates has a diameter of 3/4" while the diameter of the seal to which the ends of the ring of the Mallar plates are soldered is 2·2 cms.
137. *CII*, iii, 18. 138. For some examples, see *EI*, xxvii, 132, fn. 4.

triangular tops. The letter *m* has invariably a box-head instead of a triangle while in a few cases (*g*, *ṭ*, *th*, *dh*, *v* and *ś*) the triangle has turned almost into an oblong. The initial *i* is indicated by a couple of dots placed horizontally with an indented curve above them. The top horizontal line of *j* shows a slight notch in the middle. The medial *i* is expressed by a circle whereas the length of the medial is indicated by a dot inside the circle. The numerical symbol for 2, which is met with in the Bamhani plates, bears a close resemblance to its modern Nāgarī form. We notice the *halanta* mark in final *t* in the Bamhani (text line 45) as well as Mallar plates (text-line 46) while the *jihvāmūlīya* and *upadhmāniya* are conspicuous by absence. The sign for *visarga* is exactly like its present form consisting of a couple of dots placed vertically.

A few instances of **punctuation marks** are met with in the Bamhani plates. At one place (text-line 1) it consists of two dots placed one above the other as in the case of *visarga* whereas elsewhere in the same record we have one [139] or two[140] curved horizontal strokes used as marks of punctuation. However, no regularity is observed in this matter. Sometimes we find one such stroke employed correctly after a half verse (text-lines 19 and 22), but elsewhere two strokes are used for the same purpose (text-line 29). Similarly, at the end of a stanza we come across sometimes one (text-lines 6, 13, 21 and 46) and sometimes two such strokes (text-lines 8 and 28). At the end of the record a couple of strokes is employed to mark the conclusion. There are several instances of the omission of the mark where it is required and of its occurrence where it is not called for.

Language and Orthography

The **language** is Sanskrit and all the three extant records are composed in a mixture of prose and verse. The *praśasti* (eulogy) portion is drafted in a variety of metres and the verses describing the attainments of different monarchs are interspersed with short prose passages introducing individual rulers. As usual, the grant portion is in prose.

As for **orthographical peculiarities**, mention must be made of the use of *anusvāra* for final *n* as in *śrīmāṁ* for *śrīmān*,[141] *dayāvāṁ* for *dayāvān*,[142] *snehavāṁ* for *snehavān*[143], *digantāṁ* for *digantān*,[144] *śīkarārdrāṁ* for *śīkarārdrān*,[145] *akulāntāṁ* for *akulāntān*[146] and *loke=smiṁ* for *loke=smin*[147]; of *ṅ* in place of *anusvāra*, as for example, in *vaṅśa* for *vaṁśa*;[148] of *gh* for *h*, *e.g.*, in *rāja-siṁ*(or *ṅ*) *ghaiḥ* for *rāja-siṁhaiḥ*;[149] of *ṛ* for *ri* as in *śṛtāṃ*

139. Text-lines 6, 13, 19, 21, 22, 26, 29, 35, 46, 47.
140. Text-lines 8, 28, 29, 49.
141. No. II: I, text-lines 10, 33; No. II: II, text-lines 7, 14, 20, 27, 36.
142. No. II: I, text-lines 4-5.
143. No. II: I, text-line 18,
144. No. II:I, text-line 12.
145. No. II: I, text-line 13.
146. *Ibid.*, text-line 12.
147. *Ibid.*, text-line 3; No. II: II, text-line 8.
148. No. II: I, text-line 41 (*vaṅśe*); No. II: II, text-lines 11 (*vaṅśa*), 34 (*vaṅśaḥ*).
149. *Ibid.*, text-line 32 (*rāja-siṅghaiḥ*); No. II: I, text-line [*rāja-sighai* (*ṅghai*) *ḥ*]. .

for *śritāṃ*[150] and *tṛdaśā* for *tridaśa*;[151] of *ra*[152] or *ri*[153] for *ṛ* and *v* instead of *b*[154] and *vice versa*;[155] of the *anusvāra* and *ñ* or *n*[156] simultaneously where only one of them is required and that of a redundant *visarga* after *anusvāra*;[156a] and the reduplication of the consonants preceding[157] and following[158] the *repha*. All the features but for the last one are evidently due to faulty pronunciation prevalent in those days though, it may be pointed out, correct forms are also met with.

Object

The **object** of the stray plate remains unknown while the remaining two charters aim at recording grants of villages. Whereas the Bamhani plates purport to register the king's grant in favour of a Brāhmaṇa, the donee of the Mallar plates was a temple of god Jayeśvara-bhaṭṭāraka and the grant was made in favour of this temple by a private individual, *viz.*, Narasiṁha, son of Bota and grandson of the trader (*vaṇik*) Manoratha, who had received the granted village from the king with whose permission he made the grant. Whether the king gave the village after receving some money from the grantor, by way of compensation for the loss of land revenue cannot be ascertained.[159] The purpose of the grant, though not specified in the record, was evidently the maintenance of the temple including the provision of worship and repairs. As the inscription aims at recording a grant in favour of the temple in question, it is described as the charter (*śāsana*) of the illustrious Jayeśvara-bhaṭṭāraka.

Dates

Both the complete records are dated, the date of the remaining incomplete record, if recorded originally, being unknown as it must have been

150. *Ibid.*, text-line 25.
151. No. II: II, text-lines 3. Also *tṛśūla* for *triśūla* in text-line 1.
152. No. II: I, text-line 5 (*graha* for *gṛha*).
153. *Ibid.*, text-line 22 (*vyākriṣya* instead of *vyākṛṣya*).
154. See °*r—vvabhūva* in place of °*r—bbabhūva* in *ibid.*, text-line 8.
155. *Ibid.*, text-line 46.
156. *Ibid.*, text-lines 48 (*likhitaṁñ* = *c* = ; here *anusvāra* is redundant), 16 (*samaṁnvitāyā* [*ḥ**] where *anusvāra* is superfluous), 7 (*praśaṁnsī* where *n* is unnecessary)

156*a*. See *śāsanaṁḥ* and *Mekalāyāṁḥ* in No. II: II, text-lines 4 and 6 respectively.

157. *E.g.*, *puttra* (No. II: I, text-lines 8, 13, 16-17), *dharittrī* (ibid., text-line 11), °*kkrānta* and *śattru* (No. II: II, text-line 9).
158. *E.g.*, *kīrtti* (No. II: I, text-line 2), *mūrtti* (*rttī*)*ḥ* (*ibid.*, text-line 4), °*r—yyaśobhiḥ* (*ibid.*, text-line 3), °*r—vvabhūva* (*ibid.*, text-line 8), *audāryya* and *cāturyya* (*ibid.*, text-line 16).
159. In a few records we notice a clear reference to such considerations while a majority of copper-plate grants maintain reticence on this point though in all probability in most cases compensation in some or other form was involved. For a full discussion on this point, see D.C. Sircar, *Indian Epigraphy*, 114-19.

recorded on the missing last plate. But the dates are given not in an era but only with reference to the issuer's reign and specify not only the year, which is spoken of as that of the increasingly (or prosperous and) victorious reign, but the month, the fortnight, the *tithi* and the *nakṣatra* also. The Mallar plates mention, in addition to all these details, the weekday (*Budha-dina*) also. It would be noticed that the dates of these records are much more elaborate than those of the Śarabhapurīya grants.

Draft

The extant complete charters open with the auspicious formula *siddham*, (expressed by a symbol) *svasti* (no. II:I) or *om svasti* (no. II:II).[160] This is followed by the eulogy, composed in a mixture of prose and verse, chronicling the history of the dynasty up to the time of the donor. In the Mallar plates the *praśasti* portion is preceded by the statement that this charter of the illustrious Jayeśvara-bhaṭṭāraka, who is described a bit elaborately, is written with the permission of Udīrṇṇavaira. The first two members of the dynasty are described only in verses while the subsequent chiefs are introduced by short prose passages interspersed in the versified *praśasti*. This is followed by the notification containing the king's order in respect of the grant including such details as the specification of the gift village, the donee and the privileges bestowed on the grantee. Next follows the exhortation to future members of the dynasty to uphold the grant which is sought to be supported by some imprecatory stanzas.[161] The epigraphs end with the mention of the date, the writer and the engraver.[162]

The draft of both the charters is almost identical with only a few minor differences. Some of the stanzas met with in the *praśasti* portion of the Bamhani plates are repeated in the Mallar grant which was issued six years later.[163] But most of the verses found in the former are omitted in the latter[163a] which, again, contains a few stanzas which are introduced in it for the first time.[164] There seems to be a deliberate attempt to reduce the number of verses in the Mallar plates. Thus, while there are as many as

160. The form of the opening symbol of this grant, differs considerably from that of the Bamhani plates and bears some resemblance to that of the *praṇava*. If this is also taken to stand for *siddham*, we shall have to regard it as another form of the symbol.

161. The verses, which are not attributed to any authority, are preceded by the curse that one revoking the grant, will incur five great sins.

162. While the Mallar plates simply name the writer and the engraver, the Bamhani grant, which is earlier, mentions the names of their fathers together with their occupations also. The name of the engraver is spelt differently in the two records (Mihiraka in the Bamhani plates and Mahiraka in the Mallar plates).

163. Verses 1, 5, 10 and 11 of the Bamhani plates are found reproduced in the Mallar plates as verses 1, 4, 6 and 7 respectively without any change.

163*a*. As many as seven verses (2-4 and 6-9) of the Bamhani plates are dropped in the Mallar plates.

164. Only three stanzas (2, 3 and 5) are new.

eleven eulogistic stanzas in the Bamhani plates, we have only seven in the Mallar plates. The same tendency towards brevity is noticed in the grant portion and imprecatory verses. The Bamhani grant names five officers and contains three imprecatory stanzas as against only two officers and two imprecatory verses met with in the Mallar plates. Even as regards the concluding item, *i.e.*, mention of the writer and the engraver, the Bamhani charter refers to their parentage which is omitted in the Mallar plates.

Malga Plates of Sāmanta Indrarāja

Reference may now be made to the **Malga plates of Indraraja**[165] which we have tried for the first time to place in a historical perspective. This charter bears a close similarity to the known records of the Pāṇḍavavaṁśins of Mekalā. Thus, all these plates have ring-hole in the middle at the top and the legend on the seals attached to them consists of a single word giving the name of the ruling chief in the nominative singular preceded by the honorific *śrī*. The initial portion of all these records consists of a versified eulogy. The officers mentioned in connection with the royal command about the grant in the Bamhani and the Malga plates are also identical. The same is true of the privileges accompanying the grant. The exhortation for the protection of the grant is addressed in all these records to the future members of the grantor's family and the violators of the grant are threatened with the five great sins. Droṇāka, the engraver of the Malga plates, is described, like Mihiraka who incised the Bamhani and Mallar grants, as son of the goldsmith Īśvara. All the three records mention *nakṣatra* in connection with the date. It may, therefore, be reasonably concluded that the *Sāmanta* Indrarāja, the donor of the Malga plates, was connected with the Pāṇḍavavaṁśins of Mekalā though, at the moment, it is difficult to determine the nature of this relationship.[166]

III. RECORDS OF THE PĀṆḌAVAVAṀŚINS OF SOUTH KOSALA

While the Śarabhapurīyas and the Pāṇḍavavaṁśins of Mekalā are known to us only from their copper-plate grants, for the Pāṇḍavavaṁśins of South Kosala we have both copper-plate charters and lithic records. As the two categories differ from each other fundamentally, they may be dealt with separately.

A. *Copper Plate Charters*

We have in all ten copper-plate charters of one of which only a solitary plate, the last one, is available. Of the remaining grants, three belong to

165. No. II: Appendix II.
166. For a full discussion of this question, see introduction to No. II: Appendix II.

Tīvaradeva,[167] one to his son Nannarāja (II)[168] and five to Śivagupta Bālārjuna.[169] The stray plate,[170] though not containing the issuing chief's name, can be attributed, with a fair degree of certitude, to Śivagupta Bālārjuna on account of its general features and date.[171] The only available grant of Tīvaradeva's son, Nannarāja, was, for some unascertainable reason, left incomplete and it is doubtful if the grant recorded in it was ever made.[172] All these records have been found in the Chhattisgarh region of the present Madhya Pradesh, Mallar in the Bilaspur District yielding the largest number, viz., three, followed by Bonda in the Raigarh District which has given us two records. All other localities have yielded one grant each.

Plates

All the complete extant charters comprise a **set of three copper-plates**. The second or middle plate bears writing on both sides, while the outer or first side of the first plate is, as a rule, deliberately left uninscribed. In all but a couple of cases the outer or second side of the third or last plate is also left plain. Even as regards the two exceptions, *i.e.*, the Baloda plates of Tīvaradeva[173] and the Bonda plates of Śivagupta Bālārjuna,[174] the outer side bears only a single line. That in these two cases also the second side was originally desired to be left uninscribed will be plain from a comparison of the inscribed sides of the plates. In the first case, the outer side of the last plate bears only one line, while all the other inscribed sides of the three plates bear ten lines each. As for the second exception, we have seven lines of writing on each of the other inscribed sides, while the second side of the third plate has only a single line comprising a couple of letters and a numerical figure. It is apparent that the writing was intended to be completed on the inner side of the last plate but had to be continued on its outer side due to slight error of judgment on the part of the writer or the engraver. It may be pointed out in this connection that the executors of writing on the copper-plates of the Pāṇḍuvaṁśins of South Kosala were much more successful than those of the Śarabhapurīya charters most of which show the continuation of writing on the outer side o.' the third plate. The outer sides of the first and last plates were left or intended to be left uninscribed as the writing on these sides would have been worn out and become illegible due to repeated handling and vagaries of weather.

167. Nos. III: II-IV.
168. No. III: V.
169. Nos. III: VI-X.
170. No. III: Appendix II. Also *vide VIJ*, xv, 117-20.
171. For a detailed discussion of these points, see *ibid.*, xv, 117-19.
172. For a full consideration of this point, see *JOI*, xxv, 67-69.
173. No. III: IV.
174. No. III: VII.

The **plates** are, as usual, rectangular and their length is invariably larger than the width. The smallest plates are those of the incomplete Aḍhabhāra grant of Nannarāja. They measure 20 cms. in length and 12.375 cms. in breadth. The plates used for the Baloda grant, which are the largest, measure 23.75 cms. long and 13.43 cms. broad. Their height is, however, less than that of some other plates including the Bonda (8.55 cms,)[175] and Rajim (9.68 cms.)[176] plates of Tīvaradeva and the Bardula plates of Śivagupta Bālārjuna[177] which have the maximum breadth, *viz.* 9cms. The sizes of the remaining plates range between these two limits. The plates are generally of a uniform size throughout, there being only a few exceptions. Thus, the plates of the Bonda and Baloda grants of Tīvaradeva are slightly more in length and height in the middle than at the ends and the corners of the former are somewhat rounded. The second plate of one of the Mallar charters of Śivagupta[178] is slightly thicker than the remaining two plates. The edges of the plates are neither raised nor rendered thicker; but the writing in most cases is in a fairly good state of preservation. The plates invariably have a **hole** about the middle of the margin on proper right for the passage of the copper ring which held them together. The ring-hole is circular with the solitary exception of that on the plates of the Baloda grant of Tīvaradeva which is square. The ends of the ring are joined together under a circular seal with a diameter ranging between approximately 7.70 and 9.2 cms[179].

The **seals** of all the copper-plate charters except those of the incomplete Aḍhabhāra grant of Nannarāja and the stray plate attributable to Śivagupta have come down to us. They fall into two groups, *viz.*, those of Tīvaradeva, the first member of the dynasty whose copper-plate grants are extant, and of Śivagupta, which differ considerably from each other. First as regards the seals of the former. They have a raised circular border, and the rather deep countersunk surface within the frame-of this border is divided into two unequal parts by a couple of horizontal lines. The upper part, which is nearly ½ of the lower portion, bears, in relief, a seated figure of Garuḍa, facing full front, shown with human head and a bird's body with spread out wings and grasping a serpent with raised hood in each of his two hands. On its left there is a *cakra* or wheel and on right a *śaṅkha* or conch-shell, both being well-known attributes of god Viṣṇu. The upper half of the lower portion, about the centre of the seal, is occupied by a metrical legend in

175. No. III: II.
176. No. III: III.
177. No. III: VI.
178. No. III: X.
179. The seals of the Bonda and Rajim plates of Tīvaradeva and the Bardula plates of Śivagupta have a diameter of 7.70 cms, while the diameter of the Baloda plates of Tīvaradeva and the Bonda, Lodhia (as well as the first Mallar plates) and Mallar (second set) of Śivagupta is 8.125, 8.95, 8.75 and 9.2 cms respectively.

the *Anuṣṭubh* metre given in two lines. The verse speaks of the issuer of the grant, Tīvaradeva, whose name is preceded by the honorific *śrīmat*, as the lord of Kosala (*Kosal-ādhipati*) and refers to the charter (*śāsana*) in question as aiming at the increase of religious merit and intended to be as durable as the moon and the stars. Below the legend there is a floral device, probably a full-blown lotus. It will be noticed that the devices on the seal are in conformity with the religious leanings of Tīvaradeva who styled himself a 'devout worshipper of Viṣṇu' (*parama-Vaiṣṇava*), for while the mythical bird Garuḍa is well known as Viṣṇu's mount (*vāhana*), the wheel and the conch-shell, as well as the lotus, are his equally famous cognisances. We have no information about the seals of the chiefs flourishing between Tīvaradeva and Śivagupta, for while the only extant record of Tīvaradeva's son Nannarāja remained incomplete and without a seal, records of other intervening rulers are yet to be discovered. However, as Nannarāja retained his father's sectarian title (*parama-Vaiṣṇava*), it may be presumed with a fair amount of probability that he allowed all the features of his father's seal to remain unchanged except only the legend which he must have suitably altered to insert his own name. After Nannarāja there occurred a revolutionary change in the religious persuasions of the dynasty and Vaiṣṇavism was replaced by Śaivism. This change is reflected in the devices on the seals which, however, retained the general framework initiated by Tīvaradeva. Thus, Śivagupta's seals, like those of Tīvaradeva, are circular and have a raised border. Their countersunk surface is also divided into two portions by two straight horizontal lines, the lower portion being nearly twice in size as compared to the upper portion. Again, the upper portion bears religious devices, while we have legend and another device in the lower portion. But the devices in the upper part are, however, quite different from those we meet with on the seals of Tīvaradeva. Garuḍa is replaced by the representation of a slim, couchant, humped bull (Nandin), the mount of god Śiva, flanked by a trident (*triśūla*), an attribute of the god, in front and a *pūrna-ghaṭa* (a jar with overflowing foliage) behind. The legend, separated from the aforesaid devices by a couple of horizontal lines, refers to Śivagupta, who is mentioned, without any honorific, as son of the illustrious Harṣagupta and as possessing good qualities and speaks of his charter being as lasting as the universe. The allusion to parentage, it will be observed, is a feature that was introduced for the first time. Beneath the legend we have a full-blown lotus flanked by a long-stalked leaf on either side.

It is pertinent to note in this connection that the general framework of the Pāṇḍavavaṁśin seals including the shape, raised frame and the division of the surface into two parts by a couple of horizontal lines was inherited from the seals of the Śarabhapurīyas. The legends on the seals of both the dynasties are in two lines and in the *Anuṣṭubh* metre and their general pattern is also similar. In particular, the seals of Tīvaradeva bear a much closer resemblance to the Śarabhapurīya seals. And this is quite natural as both the Śarabhapurīyas and Tīvaradeva were devotees of Viṣṇu, a fact that accounts for the representation, in common, of the wheel and the conch-shell on the seals of both, though the central devices, Abhiṣeka-Lakṣmī and Garuḍa on their respective seals, are different. Even though the sectarian devices in the upper part underwent a revolutionary change before or during Śivagupta's reign, the general framework of the seals remained unaltered.

Palaeography

Like the Śarabhapurīya records, all the extant copper-plate charters of the Pāṇḍavavaṁśins of South Kosala are written in the **box-headed variety of the Central Indian alphabet**, with southern peculiarities. The box-heads are square and of the filled in or unscooped variety. All the letters show box-heads except only *i*, *e*, *ṅ*, *j*, *ñ*, *ṇ*, *b*, *l* and the final consonants where they are conspicuous by absence. The box-head forms the sole distinguishing mark between *e* and *c* which have otherwise an identical shape. As compared to the Śarabhapurīya records which also employ the same variety, the characters of these inscriptions evince the tendency towards elongation[180] and angularism in a considerably more accentuated manner. The equalisation of all the verticals, turning of all the curves into sharp angles and the contraction of the breadth impart a peculiar appearance to this alphabet. The projection of the top-line of the crowning box on both sides adds to the strangeness of this alphabet. These tendencies are to be noticed in a more or less pronounced form in practically all the Pāṇḍuvaṁśin records, more particularly in the inscriptions of Śivagupta Bālārjuna. Special mention must be made in this context of the last mentioned monarch's Mallar plates (second set)[181] where the top-line is so much projected on either side that in most cases the upper parts of all the vertical lines of a letter are joined together and look like emanating from the same horizontal line. Peculiarities of the southern alphabet are to be seen in a stereotyped manner in the leftward curves (now turned into angles) at the bottom of the initials *a* and *ā* and the consonants *k*, *ñ* and *r*, the notch in the left limb of the letters *gh*, *p*, *ph*, *b*, *l* and *h*, the round-backed *ḍ*, which is clearly distinguished from *d*, and the turning of the right vertical of *l* to the left of the letter. Turning our attention to some of the peculiarities, it may be pointed out that in the Bonda plates of Śivagupta[182] the letters *a*, *ā* and *kh* show a superfluous curve appended to the vertical on the right.[183] In the case of

180. P.B. Desai, however, is of the opinion that the tendency for elongation is not a general sign of development in the script, but only an individual trait of the scribe. See *EI*, xxvii, 288.
181. No. III: X.
182. No. III: VII.
183. *E.g.*, *api* (text-line 19), *agne* (text-line 21), *ācchettā* (text-line 24) and *sukhaṁ* (text-

the initial *a* this feature is noticed in the same king's Mallar plates (second set) also.[184] This redundant curve is not found in any other record of Śivagupta or, for that matter, any other member of the dynasty. We come across a solitary instance of the omission of the two dots constituting the lower portion of the initial *i*,[185] evidently by oversight. In one case the medial *ṛ* turns to right as in modern Nāgarī[186] while everywhere else it turns to left. The medial *au* is invariably tripartite. The *anusvāra* is generally indicated by a point above the concerned letter as in modern Nāgarī. In a few exceptional cases, however, it is denoted by a circle[187] or a horizontal stroke[188] at the same place. In the case of *j*, the lower limb is placed to the proper right as compared to the upper part, though the form with both parts commencing from the same level is also met with. There is not a single case of notch in the upper horizontal line. The dot inside the elongated circle (or oval) of *th* is often found turned into a circle joined a little to the lower portion of the letter. The subscribed *r* often resembles the medial *ṛ*[189] and in a few cases it has actually been read as *ṛ*.[190] The *visarga*, generally indicated by two dots placed vertically, is similar to its modern Nāgarī counterpart; but sometimes it takes the form of a couple of circles one below the other.[191] The *jihvāmūlīya*, which has a form exactly like that of *m* and is placed above the letter before which it is to be pronounced, is met with, though rarely,[192] while the *upadhmānīya* does not occur even once. There is only one instance of the use of *avagraha*.[192a]. We come across final *t* and *m*[193]. The final consonants, which are invariably without a box and smaller in size in comparison to other letters, are generally indicated by adding a slanting stroke to the bottom. A peculiar form is met with in

---

line 15). As against it, the necessary curve of *ñ* in *prajñā* (text-line 3) is dropped, possibly due to inadvertence.

184. See No. III. X, text-lines 19 (*api*) and 21 (*agne°*). But no such curve is noticed in the case of *ā* and *kh*.

185. No. III: II, text-line 7 (*iv-ākṛta*). But subsequently in the same line we find these dots.

186. No. III: III, text-line 4.

187. No. III: IV, text-line 23. But elsewhere in the same record a dot is employed for the same purpose.

188. No. III: X, text-lines, 6, 9, 12, 16 and 22.

189. See No. III: V, text-lines 1, 7 and 9. The same is true of No. III: IV. In no. III: VIII, text-lines 4,5,11, 13 and 14 the curve is so much pronounced that it has actually been read as *ṛ*.

190. In no. III: VIII, text-lines 4, 5, 11, 13 and 14.

191. No. III: IV, text-lines 3, 4, 6, 10, 21, 22, 24, 27, 33, 37 and 38. But elsewhere in this very record the *visarga* is formed by two dots. Essentially the two forms are identical and the difference is due to the scribe.

192. III: II, text-line 42; III: IV, text-line 41.

192a. III: Appendix II, text-line 7.

193. For final *t*, see III: II, text-lines 8, 38, 39 and 42; III:III, text-line 33; III:IV, text-line 8; III: VII, text-lines 23 and 28. For final *m*, *vide* III:II, text-line 2; III: IV, text-line 2; III:V, text-line 24.

the Bonda plates of Śivagupta where it is encircled by a curve.[194] We find the *numerals* 1,[195] 2,[196] 5,[197] 6,[198] 7,[199] 8,[200] 9,[201] 10,[201a] 20,[202] 30,[203] and 50.[204] The form of 1 resembles, to some extent, its modern counterpart inasmuch as it is indicated by a vertical stroke with a slight leftward curve on its top. The numeral 2 does not occur independently but only as forming part of the numbers 12[205] and 22.[206] In both cases it bears a close resemblance to its modern form. The figure 3, forming the first component of 30, too, is similar to its modern Nāgarī counterpart. There is not a single example of its occurrence by itself. The figure for 5 also bears a close resemblance to its modern Nāgarī form. We get two different forms of the symbol for 7, one forming the second component of 57 met with in the Lodhia plates of Śivagupta and the last plate of another grant assignable to the same chief[207] and the other figuring independently.[208] Like the former the latter, too, is a numerical symbol. However, it appears to represent 'rather an intermediate form between the numerical symbol and the decimal figure'.[209] The sign for 8 is a fully developed decimal figure of the southern type as indicated by the vertical line which shows a slight bend to the left.[210] Specially noteworthy in the present context is, however, the representation of 30 involving the employment of zero in a couple of records of Śivagupta.[211] It shows that the decimal notation had become well-known in South Kosala in the later phase of the Pāṇḍuvaṁśin rule. However, the use of numerical symbols for 50 and 7 for expressing 57 in the same epigraphs is a pointer to a transitional phase when both the old and the new systems of numeral notation were used simultaneously. All the other compound numbers

194. No. III: VII, text-line 28 (final *t*).
195. No. III: II, text-line 42.
196. No. III: VI, text-line 30; No. III: VII, text-line 28.
197. No. III: II, text-line 42.
198. No. III: VII, text-line 29.
199. No. III: III, text-line 36 (Fleet doubted whether it represents 7 or 9, but he thought that on the whole it is intended for 7); III:IV, text-line 40; III:VIII, text-line 32; III: Appendix II, text-line 7.
200. No. III: III, text-line 36.
201. No. III:IV, text-line 40; No. III: VI, text-line 30.
201a. No. III: VI, text-line 30.
202. No. III: IV, text-line 40; No. III-VII, text-line 28.
203. No. III: VIII, text-line 32; III: Appendix II, text-line 7.
204. No. III:VIII, text-line 32; III:Appendix II, text-line 7.
205. No. III: VI, text-line 30.
206. No. III:VII, text-line 28.
207. No. III: VIII, text-line 32; III:Appendix II, text-line 7.
208. No. III: III, text-line 36; no. III: IV, text-line 40.
209. J.F. Fleet, *Inscriptions of the Early Gupta Kings and their Successors*, *CII*, iii, 292, fn. 1.
210. *Ibid.*, fn. 2.
211. No. III:VIII, text-line 32; III: Appendix II, text-line 7.

occurring in earlier records of the dynasty are represented according to the old system.[212]

Punctuation Marks

We do not observe any regularity in the employment of **punctuation marks.** They are often found used where they are not required and are conspicuously absent where they are required by the context. Similarly, a single mark of punctuation is used where double punctuation is called for and *vice versa.* Examples of such irregularities are too numerous to be cited in detail. A single mark of punctuation is formed by a curved vertical line,[213] sometimes with a hook to left at its upper end,[214] or a straight vertical line.[215] A double punctuation is indicated by a couple of curved vertical lines the first of which shows a hook on top left.[216] In a few cases a mark of punctuation is found used at the end of a record, evidently as a mark of conclusion. In four out of six intances of this kind we find the use of two curved vertical strokes, that on the left with a hook on top.[217] There is only a single example of the employment of a curved vertical stroke as a closing mark.[218] In a solitary case we come across a couple of vertically placed dots used for the same purpose.[219] It is noteworthy in this context that these dots, which constitute *visarga,* are never used as a mark of punctuation in any other Pāṇḍuvaṁśin copper-plate inscription, whereas we have numerous instances of their use to mark a punctuation in the Śarabhapurīya records and a single case in a record of the Pāṇḍavavaṁśins of Mekalā.

Corrections

There is also some indication of the methods adopted for **rectifying errors.** There are several cases of cancellation by striking off redundant medial signs originally incised by oversight.[220] We have a few examples of correcting by modifying the erroneously engraved letters also. Thus, in one case *va* is found altered into *ṭa* (III: III, text-line 21) while elsewhere the engraver

212. These numbers are 12, 22 and 27.
213. No. III: II, text-line 25; no. III: V, text-line 24; No. III:VII, text-line 29; no. III: IX, text-line 21.
214. No. III: II, text-line 27; no. III:VI, text-lines 12ff.; no. III:IX, text-lines 19 and 24.
215. No. III: VIII, text-lines 6 and 8.
216. Most of the instances of a double mark of punctuation are of this type. Sometimes a couple of curved lines serve the same purpose (No. III: IV, text-line 8).
217. III: II, text-line 42; III: IX, text-line 28; III: X, text-line 28; III: Appendix II, text-line 7.
218. III: VII, text-line 29.
219. III: IV, text-line 41.
220. See III: II, text-lines 4, 6, 8, 27, 29 and 35; III: III, text-lines 18, 22, 24 and 26; III: VI, text-line 14; III: IX, text-line 2.

first began to incise *pitro°* which he later corrected to *mātā* (III: III, text-line 22). In one instance we find the correct form incised on an erasure (III: IV, text-line 40). Reference may now be made to the Baloda plates of Tīvaradeva which afford information about a very interesting device used for introducing corrections. At one place on the first plate of this charter in a syllable a square hole was cut into the plate and a fresh piece of copper inserted into the hole. This was probably intended for correcting the syllable which might have been spoiled accidentally into the original engraving.[221]

We have also a couple of instances to illustrate the **mode of supplying letters which were dropped by oversight** by the engraver. In both these cases the missing letter is engraved below the line exactly at the place where it should have been incised without any other indication of its proper position.

Language and Orthography

The **language** of all the records is Sanskrit which affords, however, a few instances of Prakritism or impact of local dialects. Leaving out the cases of erroneous spellings and defective pronunciation to which attention will be invited in due course, this element is limited to a few words only. The word *phaliha* forming part of the name of one of the donees of the Bonda plates of Tīvaradeva[222] is a Prakrit form of the Sanskrit word *sphaṭika*. The word *sāppū* in the name of another grantee of the same record[223] probably represents a local dialectal form of which the meaning cannot be ascertained. The suffix *u* employed to mark nominative singular of *a*-stem in a few words in a couple of the charters of Tīvaradeva[224] is perhaps traceable to Dravidian linguistic impact. As stated above, this element is noticed in a few Śarabhapurīya grants also.

Attention may now be drawn to **orthographical peculiarities**. The use of the medial sign for *i* in place of that for *ī* and *vice versa* is noticed very commonly[225] and serves to illustrate the inability of the semieducated people to distinguish between them as is the case even now. The same is true of the employment of the initial *ṛ* for *ri*[226] which shows that the common people did not make any distinction between the pronunciations of these letters. This is best illustrated by the simultaneous use of the medial signs for *ṛ* and *ī* while writing *śṛī*[227] which is indicative of the confused

221. III: IV, text-line 10. Also see *EI*, vii, 103.
222. *Rā(A) vattri (nti) phalihasvāmin*, III:II, text-line 26.
223. Sāppūpakṣasvāmin, *ibid.*, text-line 27.
224. III: III, text-line 36 (*saṁvatsaru*, *divasu* and *aṣṭha(ṭa)mu*); III:IV, text-line 40 (*samvatsaru*).
225. The instances of the use of *i* for *ī* are much more numerous than *vice versa*. See III: III-IV and VII-X. In some records both types of instances are met with, the former being commoner than the latter.
226. *E.g.*, *nistṛṅśa* (III:III, text-line 4) and *tṛvikrama* (III:VII, text-line 12).
227. III: VIII, text-lines 4, 5, 11, 13 and 14.

state of the scribe's mind. The *anusvāra* preceding *ś*[228] and *s*[229] is often substituted by the guttural nasal (*ṅ*). We have only a single instance of the replacement of the final *n* by *ṅ* in *puruṣāṅsamājñāpayati* for *puruṣān samājñāpayati* in the Mallar plates (second set) of Śivagupta (text-line 8). These errors are also due to faulty pronunciation. There is only a solitary case of the employment of the dental nasal (*n*) for the guttural one in *du(di) nmukha* for *diṅmukha* in the Rajim plates of Tīvaradeva (text-line 3), which is apparently due to oversight; for in other records of the same chief the word is spelt correctly. Twice *anusvāra* is also found replaced by the dental nasal.[230] Examples of the use of *anusvāra* for final *m* are too numerous to be cited in detail. The *anusvāra* followed by *b*[231] or *v*[232] is sometimes substituted by *m*. In a few words like *Brāhmaṇāṁ* for *Brāhmaṇān*,[233] *sa-pradhānāṁ* for *sa-pradhānān*[234] and *puruṣāṁ* for *puruṣān*,[235] the *anusvāra* is found employed in place of the final *n*. In a few cases, final *n*[236] and *m*[236] are dropped altogether. The use of *tāmbra*[228] and *tāmvra*[239] in lieu of *tāmra* illustrates faulty pronunciation obtaining in those days. The verbal forms *lalaṁnti* and *pataṁnti*[240] provide instances of the use of two nasals side by side, the first one being, of course, redundant. The occasional use of the dental nasal for the cerebral one in the word *punya* for *puṇya*[241] is illustrative of defective pronunciation still current in common parlance. The reduplication of the consonants preceding[242] and following[243] *r* was quite common, the latter feature

228. See, for instance, *vaṅśa* (III: III, text-line 16; III:IV, text-lines 18-19; III:V, text-line 5; III:VI, text-line 4; III-VII, text-line 5); *nistriṅśa* (III: II, text-line 4; III:III, text-line 4; III: IV, text-line 5); *nṛśaṅśa* (III: III, text-line 27; III:IV, text-line 32); *triṅśataḥ* (III:VI, III: IV, text-line 27); *viṅśati* (III: II, text-line 30); *anyāṅś-ca* (III: VI, text-line 8; III:VII, text-line 8); *dvāviṅśa* (III:VII, text-line 28); *Taraḍaṅśaka* (III: IX, text-lines 5-6 and 11).

229. See *nṛśaṅsa*: III: VI, text-line 21; III:VII, text-lines 17-18; III-IX, text-line 19; III: X, text-line 18; °*haṅsopādhyāya*: III: VI, text-lines 12 and 13.

230. III: V, text-line 22 (*nṛśaṅsā*); III:VI, text-line 12 (°*haṅsopādhyāya*).

231. *Sambatsare*: III, VII, text-line 28; III: VIII, text-line 31.

232. See *dattām = vā* and *samvat*: III: II, text-lines 40 and 42 respectively.

233. III: III, text-line 19; III: V text-lines 10-11; III: VI text-line 6; III: VII text-line 7.

234. III: VI, text-line 6.

235. III: VI, text-line 8.

236. III: VIII, text-lines 6 and 8; III: IX text-lines 6 and 9: III:X, text-line 6.

237. III: VIII, text-line 20; III: X, text-line 19.

238. III: VI, text-line 16; III:VII, text-line 13; III: VIII, text-line 16.

239. III: IX, text-line 13; III: X, text-line 14.

240. III: V, text-lines 21-22. *Saṁmbhavaḥ* (III: VII, text-line 5) provides a similar example.

241. III: III, text-line 16; III: V, text-line 15.

242. *E.g.*, *kalattra*; III:II, text-line 8; III-IV, text-line 9; *puttra*: III: III, text-line 23; *sāputtrika*: III: II, text-line 22; *śattru*: III:II, text-line 8; III:IV, text-line 9.

243. See, for example, *darppaṇa*: III:I, text-line 3; III-I, text-line 3; III:IV, text-line 3; *karṣṣaṇa*: III: II, text-line 4; III-IV, text-line 4 *durllalita*: III-II, text-line 4; III: IV, text-line 4; *addhvaryyu*: III:II, text-line 23; *śauryya*: III:VII, text-line 3; ***Yajurvveda*, III: II, text-line 23**; *sarvva*: III-II, text-line 22, etc.

being commoner. We have, of course, several examples where such consonants are not reduplicated. The examples of the reduplication of the consonants followed by the medial *ṛ* are extremely rare.[244] The letter *dh* followed by *y* (as in °*nuddhyāta*[245] and *upāddhyāya*[246]) and *v* (*e.g.*, *addhvaryvu*[247]) is also sometimes reduplicated. As against this, we have an instance of the omission of *d* in *budhvā* used in lieu of *buddhvā* in the Lodhia plates of Śivagupta (III: VIII, text-line 30). This as well as *kṛtivāsaso* for *kṛttivāsaso*[248] and *Kārtikeya* for *Kārttikeya*[249] where one *t* is found dropped afford examples of haplology. The same is true of the more frequent dropping of a *d* in *udiśya* in place of *uddiśya.*[250] Much more numerous are the instances of the elision of the terminal *t* and *d* when they are followed by words commencing with the same letters, *e.g.*, *asmadattiḥ* for *asmad* = *dattiḥ*[251] *etadvayaṁ* for *etad* = *dvayaṁ*[252] and *jagatraya* in place of *jagat* = *traya.*[253] The word *uktīrṇa* for *utkīrṇa*[254] and *ākṣetpā* for *ākṣeptā*[255] provide instances of the change in the position of letters or metathesis. The use of *v* for *b*[256] and *vice versa,*[257] the latter being more common, serve to illustrate the indiscriminate use of these letters commonly noticed in certain areas even in our own times. The occasional use of the dental sibilant for the palatal one[258] and *vice versa,*[259] the

244. *Sannidhāttṛ*: III: VII, text-line 8.
245. III: II, text-line 18; III: IV, text-line 21.
246. III: II, text-line 23.
247. III:II, text-line 23.
248. III: IX, text-line 3.
249. III: VI, text-line 3; III:IX, text-line 3.
250. III: IV, text-line 30; III: V, text-line 21; III: VIII, text-lines 17-18; III: IX, text-line 17; III:X, text-lines 16-17. The remaining inscriptions contain the correct form.
251. III: VIII, text-line 28.
252. III:III, text-line 28; III: IV, text-line 32; III: V, text-line 23; III-VI, text-line 21; III:VII, text-line 18; III-VIII, text-line 19, etc.
253. III: II-IV, text-line 1.
254. III: II, text-line 42; III: IV, text-line 41. Similar examples are found in the Śarabhapurīya records also.
255. III: VI, text-line 26.
256. See, for instance, *vahala* for *bahala* (III:II-IV text-line 5;), *Indravala* for *Indrabala* (III: IV, text-line 18) and *vahubhir*° for *bahubhir*° (III: VI, text-line 27).
257. See *abhibṛddhaye* for *abhivṛddhaye*: III:III, text-line 22; III: IV, text-line 29; III:VI, text-line 16; III: VII, text-line 13; III-VIII, text-line 15; *prativastabyam* for *prativastavyam*: III: III, text-lines 25-26; III: V, text-line 20; III: VI, text-line 19; III: VII, text-line 16; III:X, text-line 16; *bapuṣi* for *vapuṣi*: III:III, text-lines 9-10; III: IV, text-line 11; *byavasthā* for *vyavasthā*: III:III, text-line 8; *Byāsa* for *Vyāsa*: III:III, text-line 30; III:VII, text-line 20; III:VIII, text-line 21: *bā* for *vā*: III:III, text-line 34; III:V, text-line 26; III:VII, text-line 26; *saṁbat* for *saṁvat*: III: VII, text-line 28; *sambatsare* for *saṁvatsare*: III:VII, text-line 28; III: VIII, text-line 31; *pūrbva* for *pūrvva*: III:VIII, text-line 16; *sarbva* for *sarvva*: III: VIII, text-lines 8 and 9; °*bvasudhā* for °*vvasudhā*: III: VIII, text-line 25.
258. *E.g.*, *akṣasālika* for *akṣaśālika*: III:II, text-line 42; *prasamita* and *sūra* in lieu of *praśamita* and *śūra* respectively: III:III, text-line 17.
259. *Nṛśaṅśa* for *nṛśaṁsa*: III:III, text-line 27; III:IV, text-line 32.

latter being rather rare, also illustrate the lack of distinction in the pronunciation of these letters among the common people. The use of *ucchrijya* for *utṣrjya* met with in a few records of Śivagupta,[260] is also due to faulty pronunciation. The rather frequent non-observance of *sandhi* sometimes proves useful, specially when proper names are involved, as it enables us to know the correct forms of names.[261] The grants of Tīvaradeva are drafted in a **mixture of prose and verse** the *praśasti* portion containing a verse and a long prose passage composed in a highly ornate style and eulogising the issuer and the rest of the portion barring only imprecatory stanzas and the metrical legend on the seal being in prose. The records of his successors, on the other hand, are composed entirely in prose with the usual exception of the imprecatory verses and the inscription on the seal.

Abbreviation

Di for *dina* is the only abbreviation noticed in the date portion of a few of our records.[262] *Saṁvatsara* is found abbreviated as *saṁ* in a solitary grant.[263]

Contents

All the charters purport to record grants of land for a single Brāhmaṇa[264] or a group thereof with each one of them mentioned specifically (the maximum number being twenty-five)[265] or a religious institution[266] with the object of augmenting his own as well as his parents' religious merit. As many as six out of nine complete grants specify the occasions when the gifts were made. They are a sacred *tithi*[267] or a *saṅkrānti*[268] or an eclipse.[269] All the grants were made by the king himself. But four of them are reported to have been made at the request of some other individuals. Two grants were made at the request of his near relatives, *viz.*, son-in-law Nannarāja (III: IV) and maternal uncle Bhāskaravarman (III: IX), by Tīvaradeva and Śivagupta Bālārjuna respectively. Of the remaining two grants, both of Śivagupta, one is said to have been made at the behest of a Śaiva teacher

260. III: VI, text-line 23; III: VII, text-line 20; III: IX, text-line 21.
261. See III:II, text-line 19, where it is possible to determine the correct form of the name of the village Avaḍika due to non-observance of *sandhi* (*Bondaka-Avaḍika-sahita*). Had *sandhi* been observed, it would have become impossible to ascertain whether the name was Avaḍika or Āvaḍika.
262. III:II, text-line 42; III:IV, text-line 40; III: VI, text-line 30.
263. III: Appendix II, text-line 7.
264. All the grants barring the cases noted in the following two notes were made in favour of a single Brāhmaṇa.
265. III:II (25 Brāhmaṇas); III: III (2); III: VI (13).
266. III: IV (a *sattra*); III: VIII and X (Śaiva temples); III: IX (a Buddhist monastery).
267. III:III (Jyeṣṭha dvādaśī); III:VI (Kārttika śukla dvādaśī); III:VIII (Kārttika paurṇāmāsī).
268. III: V (Bhādrapada kṛṣṇa dvādaśī saṅkrānti) and VII (Pauṣa-saṅkrānti).
269. III: IX (solar eclipse on Āṣāḍha Amāvāsyā).

(III:VIII) and the other at the request of a certain Śivanandin (III: X) about whom no other information is given. The religious establishments referred to as grantees included a free feeding house or *sattra* (III: IV), two Śaiva temples (III: VIII and X) and the order of Buddhist monks living at a small monastery or *vihārikā* (III: IX). We have no instance of a land-grant originally made by another person and later approved by the king, a feature well known from the Śarabhapurīya records.

Dates

All but two records contain **dates** all of which are given in terms of regnal years of the donors concerned.[270] The years are invariably referred to as falling within the increasingly victorious reign.[271] Thereafter we find reference to the month and the day. The mode of indicating the date in the grants of Tīvaradeva is almost exactly identical with that followed by the Śarabhapurīyas inasmuch as both refer to the regnal year, the name of the month and the day within the month counted serially without any allusion to the fortnight. In the reign of Nannarāja II, however, the practice of referring to the fortnight was initiated,[272] though it was not always followed in the subsequent records of the dynasty. Of the five complete records of Śivagupta, only three are dated and of them also the date portions of only two grants mention the fortnight, one referring to the first fortnight (III: VII) and the other to the bright (*śukla*) fortnight (III: VI). It is not stated clearly as to which of the fortnights, dark or bright, was treated as the first fortnight of a month. But the Lodhia plates, which first mention *Karttika paurṇamasī* and then describe it as the 30th day of Kārttika, leave no doubt that the months referred to in the records of the Pāṇḍuvaṁśins of South Kosala are to be taken as *pūrṇimānta*.[272a]

The dates are specified in three different ways. The Bonda (III: II) and Baloda (III: IV) plates of Tīvaradeva and the Bardula plates of Śivagupta (III: VI) specify the dates only in figures, whereas in the Rajim plates of Tīvaradeva (III: III) and the stray plate of Śivagupta (III: App. II) we find them indicated partly in words and partly in figures. The Rajim plates give

270. The two exceptions are provided by the two sets of Mallar plates of Śivagupta (III: IX and X). One of these records (III: IX) mentions the *tithi* on which the grant was made, but the regnal year remains unknown.

271. Or 'prosperous and victorious reign' (*pravardhamāna-vijaya-rājya-saṁvatsara*). Sometimes we have *rajye* and *saṁvatsaru* or *saṁvatsare* in lieu of *rājya* and *saṁvatsara* respectively.

272. The grant recorded in the Aḍhabhāra plates of Nannarāja II is said to have been made on Bhādrapada kṛṣṇa dvādaśī. But as the record remained incomplete, the date, if intended to be given at the end, is missing.

272a. It has been suggested by V. V. Mirashi and Lochan Prasad Pandeya (*EI*, xxxv, 62-63) that both *pūrṇimānta* and *amānta* systems were current in South Kosala during the period of the Pāṇḍuvaṁśin rule and that the month of Pauṣa mentioned in Śivagupta's Bonda plates has to be taken as *amānta*.

the year only in figures while the day is specified both in words and figures. In the plate of Śivagupta, on the other hand, the year is mentioned both in words and figures and the day only in figures. As against this, the Bonda and Lodhia plates of Śivagupta (III: VII and VIII) specify the dates in word as well as in figures. But no chronological inference can be drawn in this regard as the stray plate of Śivagupta, issued a couple of months after the Lodhia plates, is dated partly in words and partly in figures.

In a few epigraphs the date is found specified twice, once in connection with the occasion of the grant and for the second time at the end.[272b] The former refers to the moment of making the grant, while the latter has reference to the date when the royal order concerning the grant was formally recorded on plates. A comparison of these dates reveals that three of the grants in question were made and recorded on the same dates[273] But the grant mentioned in the Rajim plates of Tīvaradeva was made on the 12th day of the month of Jyeṣṭha, while it was formally recorded on plates on the eighth day of Kārttika, *i.e.*, a little less than five months later.

Draft

The charters of Tīvaradeva commence with the symbol for *siddham* which is followed by a stanza composed in the *Āryā* metre praising the king in general terms. Next we find a reference to the place of issue (Śrīpura) preceded by the word *svasti.* Thereafter comes a long prose passage eulogising the chief. This eulogy not only alludes to the numerous qualities of physique, head and heart reportedly possessed by him but names his father and grandfather and the family to which he belonged besides mentioning his overlordship over the whole of Kosala and his religious leanings as well as his devotion to his parents. Next follows the king's order in respect of the land-grant which is invariably addressed to the inhabitants of the village/villages to be granted. In one case the king is said to have honoured the Brāhmaṇas before issuing the order (III:III). This portion names the gift village/villages and the administrative division[274] in which it/they was/were situated, the privileges transferred with the grant, the donee/donees, the purpose of the grant and the obligations of the villagers. The privileges transferred to the grantee by the Baloda

272b. III: III, VI, VII and VIII. The Aḍhabhāra plates of Nannarāja II mention the occasion of the grant, but whether the *tithi* was to be recorded at the end cannot be determined. The Mallar plates (first set) of Śivagupta also speak of the *tithi* of making the grant but not specify any date at the end.

273. The Bardula, Lodhia, and possibly, Bonda plates of Śivagupta.

273a. We have several other instances of grants formally registered long after they were made.

274. *Bhukti* (III: II-III) or *mārga* (III:IV). In subsequent records we find mention of *viṣaya* (III: V-VII) and *bhoga* (III: VIII-X), the latter being evidently the same as *bhukti*.

plates (III:IV) inciuded hidden treasures and deposits (*nidhi* and *upanidhi*), collection of all the taxes and exemption from the entry of irregular and regular soldiers. These are common to the remaining two grants also. But the Bonda plates add the right to collect the fines for the ten offences (*daś-āparādha*) and the property of a person dying without a heir (*aputrika-veṇī*). The Rajim grant, which does not refer to any of these two privileges, speaks of another privilege af uncertain nature called *dāradraṇaka*. The grant is invariably said to have been made with the object of augmenting the donor's as well as his parents' religious merit[275] and it was intended to endure as long as the rays of the sun, the moon and the stars continue to remove the darkness of this world.[276] The villagers were ordered to give the donee the royal share of agricultural produce (*bhāga*) and periodical offerings (*bhoga*) as due. This section is followed by an exhortation to the future kings to protect the grant, and six imprecatory stanzas are quoted four of which are ascribed to Vyāsa. Last comes the date of the formal registration of the grant and, in two cases, the reference to the engraver whose father is also named.

This pattern is generally followed with some rather minor alterations in the subsequent records of the family. The Aḍhabhāra plates of Nannarāja II, which constitute, chronologically speaking, the next record of the dynasty, follow the above-mentioned features in a general manner; but the eulogistic verse following the *siddham* symbol is dropped. An interesting feature of this grant is a long prose passage describing the donor's father in hyperbolic language while the grantor himself is described very briefly. While Tīvaradeva's records name two earlier generations, Nannarāja II's only known grant names only his father. It contains a reference to the worship of the Brāhmaṇa residents of the donated village, and to the list of privileges referred to in the Baloda plates of Tīvaradeva is added exemption from all the oppressions. For the first time we find the statement that the grant was made by means of a charter (*śāsana*). As the grant is incomplete, it is difficult to ascertain if its concluding portion was also similar to that of Tivaradeva's.

The draft of Śivagupta's grants bears a general resemblance to that of Nannarāja II's. But it omits reference to the place of issue. The eulogy mentions only the grantor's father. The notification invariably contains reference to honouring the Brāhmaṇas, but the list of the addressees of the royal order about the grant is enlarged. It now includes not only the inhabitants of the donated village but also its headman (*Pradhāna*) and all the royal officers including the *Samāhartṛ*, *Sannidhātṛ* and others along with

275. The object is stated sometimes before and sometimes after the mention of the donee/donees (for the former, see III: III; and for the latter, III: II and IV).

276. The Sanskrit expression for this was borrowed verbatim from the Sarabhapurīya grants and was later modified slightly.

their subordinates (*Karaṇa*) posted from time to time.[277] *Daś-aparādha* is added to the donee's privileges listed in the Aḍhabhāra plates. The charter by means of which the grant was made is now said to have been written on copper-plates (*tāmra-śāsana*). The expression *yāvad-ravi-śaśi-tārā-kiraṇa-pratihata-ghor-āndhakāraṁ jagad-avatiṣṭhate tāvad-upabhogyaḥ*, which is met with in the Śarabhapurīya records and was borrowed therefrom in the grants of Tīvaradeva and Nannarāja II, is now replaced by *ā-candr-ārka-sama-kāl-opabhog-ārtham* which, again, occupies a different position. The same six imprecatory verses as are found in Tīvaradeva's grants are quoted in Śivagupta's charters also. The Lodhia plates, however, contain two more stanzas not met with in any other record of the dynasty.[278] Most of his copper-plate grants end with the date which is, however, dropped in both the sets of the Mallar plates. The stray plate ascribable to Śivagupta is his only record containing a reference to the scribe. Why this item is dropped in all the other grants cannot be ascertained.

The foregoing analysis will reveal that the copper-plate grants of the Pāṇḍuvaṁśins of Kosala have a great affinity, palaeographical and otherwise, with the Śarabhapurīya charters, and it is quite natural as the Pāṇḍuvaṁśins were political successors of the kings of Śarabhapura. The grants of both the dynasties are written in box-headed characters and composed in Sanskrit. Their drafts are also very similar and some of the expressions are common to them. The differences between the two sets of grants are of a minor nature inasmuch as the general framework of both is almost identical, whereas a few items of the Śarabhapurīya epigraphs are found a bit enlarged and developed in the charters of the Pāṇḍuvaṁśa.

B. *Lithic Records*

Leaving aside extremely fragmentary inscriptions which could not be adequately studied and published owing to the bad state of their preservation, we have, in all, seven stone inscriptions of the time of the Pāṇḍuvaṁśins. They are generally engraved on slabs of stone which were originally fixed into the wall or some other part of the religious structures whose construction or some pious act connected therewith they purport to record. The slabs are square or rectangular in shape and of varying sizes depending upon the volume of the text to be incised. They were more or less rubbed

277. All the records of Śivagupta do not refer to the royal officers in the same manner. Thus, the Bardula and the first set of Mallar plates (III: VI and IX) mention all the officers as enumerated above. But the Bonda (III:VII) and Mallar (second) plates (III:X) drop reference to the subordinates, while the Lodhia plates (III:VIII) omit both village headman and subordinates.

278. Verses 7 and 8. Verse 8 of the Lodhia plates is repeated in the solitary plate of another record attributable to the same king but issued about couple of months later.

smooth before engraving. Portions of stones bearing three of these inscriptions are borken as a result of which considerable portions of these records are lost. The remaining parts of these epigraphs as well as other inscriptions have become indistinct at places as a result of being exposed to the inclemencies of weather for well over a millennium.

All but two of these epigraphs are from Sirpur, ancient Śrīpura, in the Raipur District of Madhya Pradesh. Of the remaining two epigraphs, one comes from the village Senkapat, some two miles to the south of Sirpur (III: XV). As regards the other inscriptions (III: I) there is considerable difference of opinion about its findspot. Various localities including Bhandak in the Chanda District of Maharahtra, Ratanpur in the Bilaspur District of Madhya Pradesh and Arang in the Raipur District have been named as its possible findspots, there being no definite evidence on this point. But Vinayakrao Aurangabadkar's account, which summarises its contents, appears to favour Arang.[279] Thus, the findspots of all the lithic records of the dynasty lie in the Raipur Bilaspur region of Madhya Pradesh.

Palaeography

All these records are engraved in **characters** belonging to early Nāgarī or what has often been described as northern class of alphabets[280] and represent the so-called Kuṭila variety that was prevalent throughout northern India and Nepal from the sixth to the ninth century A.D.[281] Many of the letters bear a close resemblance to their modern Nāgarī counterparts, though, strangely enough antiquated forms of a few letters like *i*, *j*, *ṇ*, *th*, *dh* and *bh* are also met with. The initial *a* is similar to its form in use in Nāgarī in western India at present. The medial *ā* is sometimes indicated by a top-stroke and sometimes by a vertical stroke to the proper left of the letter emanating from the top horizontal line. The medial sign for *e* is either formed by a top-stroke or *śiro-mātrā* or by a stroke on proper right or *pṛṣṭha-mātrā* which is, however, not yet fully developed. Interestingly enough, both the forms are often met with side by side in the same record. The forms of medial *i*, *ī*, and *ṛ* resemble their modern Nāgarī counterparts. Medial *u* and *ū* are also generally similar to their modern Nāgarī descendants except in the case of *pū*, *bhū* and *rū*. Medial *ū*, in *pū* and *bhū* takes the form of a curved horizontal stroke to the left springing from the bottom

279. For a full discussion on this point, see notes on the inscription and the historical account of the dynasty in the introduction.

280. This name is applied rather loosely to the characters used over a very wide area of the Indian sub-continent. Another name of this alphabet which appears to have been popular in ancient times, in Siddhamātṛikā.

281. The letters of the Kuṭila variety have small wedges or just short horizontal strokes on top. The script is sometimes designated as acute-angled alphabet also. The name Kuṭila is probably given on account of the flourishing *mātrās* and the leftward slant of the verticals of the letters.

of the letter. Both *u* and *ū* are attached to the middle of *r*, the latter being brought a little further downwards. In a few cases, however, medial *ū* in *rū* is turned upwards.[282] For medial *ai*, we find either two *śiro-mātrās* or one *pṛṣṭha-mātrā* and one *śiro-mātrā*. Likewise, in medial *au* we have a *pṛṣṭha-mātrā* and a *śiro-mātrā*. All these features indicate that the characters of these inscriptions as those of other contemporary records from northern India represent a transitional phase between late Brāhmī and modern Nāgarī.

As we have seen above, copper-plate grants of the Pāṇḍuvaṁśins are incised in box-headed characters. It is rather strange that two different alphabets should have been used during the same period in the same region and by the same dynasty for different types of records, one exclusively for copper-plate inscriptions and the other for lithic records. It seems that the rulers got their official charters incised in box-headed characters as a matter of convention, while stone inscriptions, which were not official documents, were written in the characters in common use during the period. This is indeed a unique example of conventionalism carried to an extreme.

Punctuation Marks

Punctuation is indicated by a single or double *daṇḍa* (vertical stroke). It is sometimes just a straight line and sometimes curved; but in a majority of cases we find a short horizontal or slanting stroke on the left emanating from the middle or bottom of the single *daṇḍa* or the first of the double *daṇḍa* mark. Generally a single *daṇḍa* is found at the end of the first half and a double *daṇḍa* at the end of the second half of a verse as well as after an invocation. But instances of indiscriminate employment of the marks of punctuation are also too numerous to be enumerated exhaustively. Two of these inscriptions afford us marks of conclusion at the end. That at the end of one of the Sirpur inscriptions (III: XII) consists of a couple of vertical lines followed by a circle. At the close of the Senkapat inscription (III: XV) we find a couple of double *daṇḍas* with a device resembling the letter *tha* between them. The first of the double *daṇḍa* mark on left shows the horizontal projection to left, and the two vertical lines are so formed as to appear joined on the top. The verticals of the double *daṇḍa* mark on the right are, on the contrary, almost straight. The conclusion of the *praśasti* portion of the Nagpur Museum inscription of the time of Nannarāja is marked by a device consisting of a circle surrounded by a cresent or semi-circle on each of the four sides between two double *daṇḍa* marks.[283] This device is met with on a number of early Indian coins including punch-marked, uninscri-

282. III: XI, text-lines 7 (*gurūpacaraṇe*) and 12 (*rūpaiḥ*). In text-line 1, medial *u* of *ru* in the word *puruṣottamāya* is also bent upwards, evidently due to oversight.

283. III: I, text-line 17, at the end of verse 38 with which the *praśasti* comes to an end. Subsequent verses do not form part of the eulogy.

bed cast copper and local series, though it is difficult to determine its exact significance.

Language and Orthography

The **language** is Sanskrit and all the records, with the exception of the occasional auspicious formula at the beginning[284] and mention of the scribe at the end,[285] are couched in verses composed in a variety of metres. Some of the noteworthy **orthographical features** are (i) the change of *anusvāra* followed by the palatal sibilant into *ṅ*[286] or *n*[287] the latter being rarer, and of that followed by *gh* (for *h*) into *ṅ*;[287a] (ii) the employment of the sign of *v* for *b*,[288] (iii) of *anusvāra* for final *m*,[289] and (iv) of the *repha* in place of *ṛ*.[290] The last feature as well as the use of the dental for the palatal sibilant[291] and of the dental nasal in lieu of the cerebral one[292] is met with rather rarely. Most of these afford illustrations of erroneous pronunciation prevalent during the period in question. There are a few instances of the use of *upadhmānīya*,[293] while we have none of *jihvāmūlīya*. At one place *setikā* is used for *śvetikā*.[294] However, in spite of the few errors noticed in these respects, the text of stone inscriptions is definitely much more correct than that of copper-plate records. The reason of this striking difference between the two sets of records lies in the fact that, while persons responsible for drafting copper-plate inscriptions were ordinary people with little pretension to scholarship, the composers of stone inscriptions were, to judge from their compositions, accomplished and well-read poets of high merit.

284. We find such formulae at the commencement of III:I, XI, XIII and XV. Of these, the first contains only a salutation without naming the deity, though Buddha appears to be intended. III: XI begins with a salutation to Puruṣottama and the last two with an obeisance to Śiva.

285. III: XII is the only record naming the engraver in a prose sentence at the end.

286. *E.g.*, *vaṅśa* (III:I, text-line 7; III:XV, text-line 3); *tayor = aṅśe* (III: XI, text-line 20); °*daś-āṅśā* (III: XI, text-line 21); *vyañjan-āṅśena* and *vyañjan-āṅśa* (III: XII, text-lines 8 and 9 respectively); *sudhāṅśo*° (III: XII, text-line 1); *śīt-āṅśu* (III: XV, text-line 3).

287. *Mīmānsā* (III: I, text-line 19); *dhvanse* (III: XI, text-line 7).

287*a*. *E.g.*, *nṛsiṅhaḥ* (III: XI, text-line 3).

288. For some of the instances, see III: I, text-line 2 (*lavdha*), 3 (*paricumvita*), 6 (*kuṭumvinī*, *pravala*, *vāliśa*, *vudha* and *vāliśaṃ*), 8 (*valaṃ* and *suvahuśaḥ*), 11 (*prāravdha*), 16 (*vrahmacārī*, *namovuddho* and *vodhisatva*; III: XI, text-line 8 (*vandha*); III: XII, line 7 (*vibhrad*), etc. Even the name Bālārjuna is often wrongly spelt beginning with *v* instead of *b*.

289. *E.g.*, see III: XI, text-lines 15, 23, 24, 25; III: XIII, text-line 2.

290. *Vrahac = chalena* in place of *bṛhac* = chalena (III: XI, text-line 14).

291. *Sālā* for *śālā* (III: I, text-line 16).

292. *Raghunā* for *Raghuṇā* (III: I, text-line 14).

293. III: I, text-lines 11, 12 and 13.

294. III: XII, text-line 8

Nature and Contents

While copper-plate grants are official charters purporting to register royal orders concerning land-grants, stone inscriptions are private records. It is no doubt true that some of the records refer to pious acts of the members of the royal family, but still they can by no stretch of imagination be described as official records. They aim at recording pious acts of private benefactors such as construction of temples and gifts of land in their favour for defraying the expenses on their maintenance and repairs, rituals and other activities connected therewith,[295] arrangements for the perpetual provision of flowers or flower-garlands for the worship at the temples,[296] and provision of food for the Buddhist monks living at a monastery built by the donor.[297] It is not improbable that the grants of villages and plots of land mentioned in these inscriptions were actually made through copper-plate charters and are recorded in the epigraphs in question only because they appertained the structures on which they were fixed.[298]

All these epigraphs open with the *siddham* symbol which is, in a majority of cases, followed by a short religious formula in prose paying obeisance to the central divinity or personage of the religious sect with which the record is concerned.[299] Next come one or more stanzas invoking favours from the concerned deity or personage.[300] The *siddham* symbol, the prose formula and the versified invocation together constitute what is commonly called *maṅgalācaraṇa* and is ordinarily met with in numerous ancient and medieval Sanskrit compositions. It was believed to ensure completion of and long life for the work. The invocation precedes the *praśasti* often giving an account of the history of the dynasty to which the contemporary ruler of the area in question belonged, the attainments of the then monarch being specially highlighted. In one case (III: I) we find mention of a ruler who did not belong to the contemporary ruling dynasty but who was

295. Thus, III: I records the construction of a Buddhist temple and its renovation at a later date, while the object of III: XI is to describe the building of a temple of Hari and provisions for its maintenance and repairs.

296. III: XIII and XIV.

297. III: XII.

298. Such a possibility has been pointed out in connection with some of the cave inscriptions of the Sātavāhanas and the Kṣaharāta chief Nahapāna. See D.C. Sircar, *Indian Epigraphy*, 108-09.

299. III: I, XI, XIII and XV contain such a formula. But in III: I the deity so saluted is not named, though Buddha is obviously implied.

300. The Arang inscription of the time of Nannarājādhirāja (III:I) has four verses in praise of Buddha, while we have three stanzas praising Viṣṇu and his man-lion incarnation in the Sirpur Lakshmaṇa temple inscription of the time of Śivagupta (III: XI). The Senkapat inscription (III: XV) of the time of the last named king contains two verses, one each in praise of Bhava and Pārvatī, whereas the remaining three inscriptions of the reign of the same chief and found at Sirpur (III:XII-XIV) contain a single invocatory stanza, the first in praise of Sugata and the rest invoking Śiva.

responsible for the original construction of the structures whose renovation is purported to be recorded. Next follows a detailed description of the pious act the recording of which is the main purpose of the inscription. In a few cases we come across a fulsome account of the terms and conditions governing the donation.[301] The mention of the composer and the engraver, about whom only a few details are given, forms the concluding item. None of the records supplies date.

Some of the inscriptions fall into two parts and appear to have been clearly treated as such originally also. The first part of the inaugural inscription of this section (III: I), for instance, ends with verse 38 which mentions the poet responsible for composing the *praśasti* and is followed by a device which appears to mark the conclusion. The subsequent portion including an imprecatory stanza and reference to the contemporary ruler forms the second part. Similarly, the Sirpur Lakshmaṇa Temple Inscription of the time of Śivagupta also consists of two parts: the first part recording the *praśasti* and the principal pious act, *viz*., construction of the temple, comes to an end with verse 23, while the following portion outlining the regulations governing the grant forms something like an appendix.

These epigraphs are of great importance for the reconstruction of the history of the Pāṇḍuvaṁśins. It is instructive to note in this connection that the earliest extant records of the duration of their rule are inscriptions engraved on stone which supply us valuable historical information not available from any other source. Names of and details about many of the early and later members of the dynasty including Udayana, Bhavadeva Raṇakesarin and Chandragupta as well as Raṇakesarin, brother of the last known chief of the family, would have remained in oblivion but for these records. It will not be an exaggeration if we state that most of our information about the various aspects of the history of the dynasty is derived from stone inscriptions set up during its sovereignty.

Stone inscriptions are important not only for historical studies, but also as a source of the history of Sanskrit literature. While most of the copperplate inscriptions are in the nature of matter of fact statement in a simple language,[302] lithic records constitute beautiful examples of Sanskrit poetry of no mean order. There is no doubt that their composers were accomplished poets who had mastered poetics and had great command over the language. Bhāskarabhaṭṭa,[303] Cintātura Īśāna,[304] Kṛṣṇanandin, son of

301. Such conditions are found outlined in detail in the Sirpur Lakshmaṇa temple inscription and briefly in the Senkapat inscription.

302. Except for a long eulogistic prose passage in Tīvaradeva's grants and a short one in Nannarāja II's and Śivagupta's grants. But these passages bestow only conventional praise on the ruler and contain little historical information.

303. He composed Nannarājādhirāja's Arang inscription.

304. The Sirpur Lakshmaṇa temple inscription was composed by him.

Devanandin,[305] and Sumaṅgala, son of Tāradatta,[306] who composed these *praśastis*, deserve a high place in the annals of classical Sanskrit literature. Their names would have remained unknown but for these inscriptions as no other works composed by them have come to light.

IV. RECORDS OF THE SOMAVAṀŚINS

As in the case of the Pāṇḍava of South Kosala, for the Somavaṁśins or Somakulins also we have copper-plate grants as well as stone inscriptions, though the number of the latter is much smaller than that of the former.[307] In view of the difference of nature between the two categories of records, it will be in the fitness of things to dwell upon them independently, copper-plate charters naturally claiming a precedence.

The members of the Somavaṁśa are known to have issued copper-plate grants on a much larger scale than those belonging to any of the preceding dynasties.[308] In fact, the number of the copper-plate charters of this family is almost equal to that of the same category of records of all the three dynasties taken together whose records have been dealt with so far. The credit of issuing the largest number of grants easily goes to the second member of the dynasty, *viz.*, Mahābhavagupta I Janamejaya, the first ruling chief of the family for whose reign we have epigraphic records. As many as thirteen grants of his reign have been reported so far.[309] For the next reign, that of Mahāśivagupta I Yayāti, we have six grants,[310] whereas Mahābhavagupta II Bhīmaratha is represented by a couple of charters one of which belongs to the king himself[311] while the other was issued by a feudal chief during his reign.[312] For Mahāśivagupta II Dharmaratha[313] and Mahāśivagupta III Yayāti[314] we have only one record each. The position is better with regard to Mahābhavagupta IV Uddyotakesarin who is known from four copper-plate grants[315] besides as many lithic records.[316] Of the reign

305. He was responsible for the composition of III: XIII.
306. He authored III: XII, XV and III: Appendix I.
307. Including the fragmentary Sūrya image inscription of Karṇa's reign form Gandhibeda (IV: Appendix III), we have only four stone inscriptions, while the reamining thirty-three records of the family are copper-plate charters.
308. Seventeen plates of the Śarabhapurīyas, three of the Pāṇḍavavaṁśins of Mekalā and ten of the Pāṇḍavavaṁśins of South Kosala are known, while for Somavaṁśins alone we have as many as thirty-three grants.
309. Nos. IV: I-XI and Supplementary Inscriptions I-II.
310. Nos. IV: XII-XVII.
311. No. IV: XVIII.
312. No. IV: XIX.
313. No. IV: XX.
314. No. IV: XXI.
315. No.s IV: XXII and XXIV; Appendix II: Supplementary Inscription III.
316. Nos. IV: XXIII, XXV and XXVI.

of Mahāśivagupta V Karṇarāja, only a single grant has been found so for.[317] The same is true of Indraratha whose only known record, *viz.*, the Banpur plates, has not been edited adequately.[318] We also have a grant of a Somavaṁśin chief named Someśvara[319] whose exact relationship with the Somavaṁśins of Trikaliṅga cannot be determined at present and a stray plate of a charter.[320]

All the records with known findspots have been reported from the modern state of Orissa, their provenances being situated in an area stretching from the Sambalpur-Balangir tract adjoining the Chhattisgarh region of Madhya Pradesh to the coastal district of Puri. A glance at the list of findspots will reveal a general concentration in the area extending from Sambalpur-Balangir to Cuttack.[321] Actually, first seven grants of Mahābhavagupta I Janamejaya issued up to the seventh year of his reign have been found in the Sambalpur-Balangir region and the three Chaudwar grants of the thirty-first year of the same king's reign[322] are the earliest records of the dynasty to be reported from the Cuttack region. From this period onward the find of the epigraphic records of the Somavaṁśins in this area becomes a routine affair.[323] The first record of the dynasty to be reported from the Puri region is the Mahulpara copperplate grant of Mahāśivagupta II Dharmaratha[324] after which we find a fairly good number of inscriptions, both copper-plate and lithic, of the family in this area.[325] It is interesting to note that even though the Sambalpur-Balangir area, where a majority of earlier records has been found, does not altogether cease to yield records of the subsequent period, their incidence is less as compared to those found in the other region.[326] But the area continued its association with the dynasty up to the last and an inscription of the time of Karṇa has been reported recently from the Balangir District.[327] These facts are important inasmuch as they corroborate and supplement

317. No. IV: XXVII.
318. IV: Appendix I.
319. IV: XXVIII.
320. IV: Appendix IV.
321. As many as twenty-three (IV: I-IV, VI-XI, XIII-XIX, XXI-XXII, XXVIII, Appendix II and IV and Supplementary Inscriptions I-V are definitely known to have been found in this area and three more records are likely to have been discovered in the same region. (IV:V, XII and XXIV).
322. Nos. IV: VIII-X.
323. Nos. IV: XIV, XVIII, XXII and XXVIII have been reported from this region.
324. No. IV: XX.
325. Nos. IV: XXIII, XXV and XXVI and Appendices I and III are said to have been found in the coastal area and illustrate the expansion of the Somavaṁśin power in that direction.
326. Only seven records of this period (Nos. IV: XXI and XXVIII, App. II and Supplementary Inscriptions I-II and V are reported from the Sambalpur-Balangir area, while all the remaining records with definitely known provenance have been found in the Cuttack-Puri region.
327. Supplementary Inscription V.

the inferences drawn from the internal evidence of the records themselves regarding the fluctuating fortunes of the Somavaṁśin power and the shifting of its centre from the west to the east.

Plates

Like the grants of the Śarabhapurīyas and the Pāṇḍuvaṁśins, the charters of the Somavaṁśins are also incised as a rule on a **set of three copper-plates** and are accordingly described in one of them as *tri-phalī-tāmra-śāsana* (*i.e.*, a charter consisting of three plates of copper).[328] The first side of the first plate is invariably left uninscribed and the record commences on its inner or second side. The exterior of the last or third plate also appears to have been intended to be left blank and is actually found so left in a vast majority of cases. In other words, the inscription generally comes to an end on the interior of this plate. It is, of course, true that in a few cases the writing is found continued on the reverse of the third plate also;[329] but these form exceptions which may be easily explained as due either to the inability of the scribes to accommodate the mater on the sides of the plates intended to be inscribed or to some other reason which is not difficult of ascertainment. The earliest extant example of this kind is afforded by the Sonpur grant of Mahābhavagupta I Janamejaya the last two lines whereof are incised on the outer side of the third plates.[330] However, a glance at the text will show that the record was actually originally completed on the inner side of the third plate. But the last two lines (48-49) had to be scored out as some serious errors had crept in and had to be re-engraved on the outer side as no space was available on the inner side. The Cuttack plates of the ninth year of the reign of Mahāśivagupta I Yayāti[331] provide the next instance of this type. In this case as many as seven lines (60-66) are incised on the reverse of the third plate. This can be satisfactorily explained away on the ground that, this being the first record consisting of as many as sixty-six lines, the scribe found it difficult to complete it on the interior of the third plate and had no option but to continue the remainder of the draft on its external side. The same may be said regarding the Patna plates of the same monarch's twenty-eighth regnal year which consist of as many as seventy-five lines, the last six of which had to be incised perforce on the second side of the last plate,[332] and the Balijhari plates of Mahābhavagupta IV Uddyotakesarin comprising seventy-eight lines, the last eight of which are found engraved on the exterior of the third plate.[333] The continuation of writing on the second side of the third plate in the case of the

328. Nos. IV: VIII-X, text-line 46.
329. Nos. IV: VI, XIV, XVII, XXII, XXIV and XXVIII.
330. No. IV: VI.
331. No. IV: XIV.
332. No. IV: XVII.
333. No. IV: XXII.

last-named chief's Mahakosala Historical Society's grant[334] and the Kelga grant of Someśvara[335] is obviously due to the employment of plates of a smaller size for incising these records. The problem of confining the writing to the inner side of the last plate even if the record was extra-ordinarily large or the plates employed for receiving the record were of a smaller size could have been easily solved by using an additional plate. But that the writers of these grants did not do so illustrates amply a strict adherence on their part to the convention of using only a set of three plates which was popularised by the Śarabhapurīyas and the Pāṇḍavas.

The **plates** used for these grants are, as a rule, rectangular, their breadth being invariably smaller than the length. The same uniformity is, however, not observed with regard to the actual size of the plates which varies widely from charter to charter. The smallest plate is that employed for the incomplete Mahada grant of Mahābhavagupta IV Uddyotakesarin and measures 7.8 cms. in width and 16.5 cms. in length.[336] Next come the Kudopali plates issued by a feudal chief during the reign of Mahābhavagupta II Bhīmaratha and are 10 cms. broad and 19 cms. long.[337] The plates of the Jatesinga-Dungari grant of Mahāśivagupta III Yayāti, which are the next smallest, measure 10 cms. broad and 20 cms. in length.[338] The Ratnagiri grant of Mahāśivagupta V Karṇa[339] is incised on the largest plates measuring 21.75 to 22.25 cms. in width and 35 cms. in length. The above-mentioned Mahada plate illustrates the smallest width (7.8 cms) followed by that of the aforesaid Kudopali and Jatesinga-Dungari plates measuring 10 cms. The smallest length is again exemplified by the stray Mahada plate (16.5), the next lowest in length being the Kelga plates of Someśvara (17.5 cms.)[340] and the Mahulpada plates of Mahāśivagupta II Dharmaratha (18.4 cms).

While normally plates of a uniform size are employed for incising a record, we come across a few instances of the use of plates of different sizes for the same charter. The first plate of the Ratnagiri grant of Karṇa, for instance, measures 38.75 x 22.25 cms, the second plate, 35 x 22.25 cms. and the third plate, 35 x 21.75 cms. Likewise, the first two plates of the Kelga grant of Someśvara are 10 cms broad and 20 cms long, while the breadth and length of the last plate are a little more, *viz.*, 10.625 and 20.625 cms. respectively.

334. No. IV: XXIV. Four lines are incised on the outer side of the last plate.
335. No. IV: XXVIII. Only a single line is engraved on the exterior of the third plate which is a clear evidence of the scribe's inability to accommodate the matter on the sides of the plates really meant for receiving the writing.
336. No. IV: XIX.
337. No. IV: XIX.
338. No. IV: XXI.
339. No. IV: XXVII. As will be seen in the sequel, the plates used for this grant are of different sizes.
340. No. IV: XXVIII.

Generally speaking, the width and the length of a plate are not the same at every point. It is noticed in most cases that the plates are longer in the middle than at the ends and broader at the ends than in the middle. The width of the plates used for the first record of the dynasty included in this volume, *i.e.*, Vakratentali grant of Mahābhāvagupta I Janamejaya, for example, varies from 10.625 cms. to 11.875 cms. while the length ranges from 22.2 cms. to 22.5 cms. The same is true of many other records.[341] In such cases we cannot speak of an absolute width or length which varies from point to point and mention has often to be made of the maximum and minimum width and length. The corners of the plates are mostly angular, there being only a few instances of rounded corners.[342] The surface of most of the plates of these grants as that of the plates of the grants of the other dynasties dealt with in the present volume is even. But here are a few exceptions which may be noted. Thus, the edges of the plates of the three Chaudwar grants of Mahābhavagupta I Janamejaya are fashioned slightly thicker than the inscribed portion so as to serve as rims for the protection of the writing from friction. The plates of the second Kalibhana grant of Mahābhavagupta I Janamejaya[343] and those of the Orissa Museum grant of the fourth year[344] and the Patna grant of the eighth year of the reign of Mahāśivagupta I Yayāti[345] also have raised edges. There are also instances of copper-plate charters the edges of only one or two plates of which are raised. The ends of only two of the three plates of the Patna grant of the sixth year of the reign of Mahābhavagupta I Janamejaya[346] are raised, while in the case of the Ratnagiri grant of Mahāśivagupta V Karṇa only the last plate has a raised rim. The question as to why the edges of all the plates of these grants were not fashioned thicker or raised into rims cannot be answered satisfactorily. It may, however, be added that even though the edges of a vast majority of plates are not raised into rims, the writing is, on the whole, in a fairly good state of preservation.

The plates are held together in their proper order by means of a **copper-ring** which is passed through a hole bored in the margin. In all but one cases the hole is made at the centre of the margin on the left. The solitary exception is provided by the stray Mahada plate of Uddyotakesarin[346a] which has the ring-hole on the right. This unusual position of the hole does not admit

341. The width of the Satallama plates of Mahābhavagupta I Janamejaya, for instance, varies from 13·25 cms. to 13·425cms. Further, they are longer in the middle than at the top or at the bottom.
342. The corners of the Nibinna plates of Mahāśivagupta I Yayāti (IV: XV) and the Kudopali plates of Mahābhavagupta II Bhīmaratha (IV: XIX) are, for example, rounded.
343. No. IV: XI.
344. No. IV: XII.
345. No. IV: XIII.
346. No. IV: III.
346*a*. No. IV: Appendix II.

of a satisfactory explanation. The hole is generally circular or nearly so; but that of the Patna plates of Mahābhavagupta I Janamejaya's sixth regnal year is square.[347] Broadly speaking, the joints of the ring are soldered under the seal which had to be attached as a mark of authentication.

Seals

Seals affixed to a majority of complete copper-plate charters have been found. Only those attached to the first Kalibhana and Gaintala grants of Mahābhavagupta I Janamejaya, the Orissa Museum and Cuttack plates of Mahāśivagupta I Yayāti and the Ratnagiri plates of Mahāśivagupta V Karṇa are missing. From a technical point of view the extant seals may be divided into two distinct groups. Most of them were cast in moulds and affixed to the two ends of the copper-ring holding the plates in position. They are generally of bronze and occasionally of brass.[348] In a few cases, however, the ends of the ring are said to have been secured in the lower portion of a lump of copper 'which bulges out on either side along the ring' to form a circular or oval seal (actually space on which the seal is impressed).[349] In one case the seal is said to have been impressed on the upper surface of this lump of copper,[350] while in another instance the devices noticed on this lump are reported to have been 'cut in relief'.[351] A pin or nail was sometimes driven with a view to make the fixture of the seal to the ends of the ring durable.[352] The diameter of the upper surface of the seal measures between 2.850 cms and 9 cms the minimum and maximum diameters being those of the seals attached to the Satallamā plates of Mahābhavagupta I Janamejaya[353] and the Patna plates of the eighth year of the reign of Mahāśivagupta I Yayāti[354] respectively. The seals bear on a somewhat contersunk surface in relief either a device only or both a device and a legend. The common device is the abhiṣeka-Lakṣmī or gaja-Lakṣmī motif which is seen on a vast majority of those seals on which the devices and legends are still legible. Generally, the goddess is represented as seated in the *padmāsana* attitude on a full-blown lotus and being bathed by an elephant on either side of the goddess. The elephants are also shown as standing on fully expanded lotuses with their trunks raised in the attitude of bathing the goddess. In some cases, the lotuses, on which the elephants stand, rise as high as the shoulders of the goddess. On the seal of

347. No. IV: III. The shape of the ring-hole is not always quite regular.
348. The seal of the second set of the Kalibhana plates of Mahābhavagupta I Janamejaya is said to be of brass.
349. See Nos. IV: I, XV, XVII and XXI.
350. No. IV: I. See *EI*, xi, 93.
351. No. IV: XV. *Vide EI*, xi, 95.
352. Nos. IV: I and V.
353. No. IV: V.
354. No. IV: XIII.

the Satallamā plates of Mahābhavagupta I Janamejaya the goddess is further flanked by a lamp-stand on either side. On two of the Chaudwar plates of the same monarch, the goddess is said to be represented as seated on throne instead of lotus.[355] On the seal of one of the Patna plates of the sixth year of the same chief, Pratapachandra Ghosha conjecturally identified the seated figure as that of Rāmacandra seated on lotus and surrounded by lotus leaves and flowers and discerned conjecturally the figure of Hanumān in the lower portion.[356] However, though the representations on the seal are rather indistinct, the central figure is evidently that of the goddess Lakṣmī, while the lower part, as pointed out by Fleet, seems to contain only a floral device.[357] While in many instances we have only the usual device of abhiṣeka-Lakṣmī, in a few cases the legend is also noticed. The legend is in simple prose and gives only the king's name preceded by the honorific *śrī*.[358] The seal of Mahābhavagupta IV Uddyotakesarin's Mahakosala Historical Society's plates is quite distinct from any other seal of the dynasty. In the centre we have a humped and horned bull standing to right, above it a crescent and below it a two-line legend giving the monarch's name in the usual manner.[359] It is interesting to note in this connection that the seals attached to other complete charters of the same king bear the usual device of gaja-Lakṣmi. The change was probably deliberate, introduced with a view to bring it in tune with the religious leanings of the family as well as himself. The seal attached to the Kelga plates of Someśvara,[360] a later member of a collateral branch of the dynasty, is interesting inasmuch as it is fashioned like a lotus flower. Its

355. Nos. IV: VIII and X.
356. *JASB*, xlvi, 174.
357. *EI*, iii, 341.
358. The legend is preserved only on a couple of Somavaṁśin seals, *viz.*, Chaudwar plates of Mahābhavagupta I Janamejaya (No. IV: X) and Mahakosala Historical Society's plates of Mahābhavagupta IV Uddyotakesarin (No. IV: XXIV). On the latter, it ends in genitive singular, and the same must have been the case with that on the former, though Fleet describes it as ending with the word *deva* without any case ending. B.C. Mazumdar read tentatively the much-defaced legend on the Vakratentali plates of Mahābhavagupta I Janamejaya as *Śrī-Janmejayadeva* [*rājasya* ?]. See *EI*, xi, 93. But we feel that in view of the legends on the other two seals which give the name Mahābhavagupta, the legend on this seal also most probably must have been *Śrī- Mahābhavaguptarājadevasya*. A few other seals also must have borne the legend, which is, however, completely worn out and consequently illegible.
359. The legend is *Śrī-Mahābhavaguptarājadevasya*. Lochan Prasad Pandeya, who originally published this record, described the animal as 'facing the proper right' (*EI*, xxii, 235). However, if the photograph accompanying his paper is to be relied upon (*ibid.*, plate facing p. 137), the bull faces proper left, not proper right. Further, the legend is not quite clear in the plate.
360. B.C. Mazumdar, who first published these plates, erroneously took the elephants flanking the figure of the goddess as creepers and observed that the posture of the goddess indicating peaceful meditation is hardly consistent with the figure of any goddess (*EI*, xii, 237).

inner side is hollow, whereas its lower external and middle rings consist of fifteen and fourteen petals respectively. On its surface, however, we have the usual gaja-Lakṣmī motif.[361]

Reference may now be made to the seals affixed to the grants of the feudatory chiefs acknowledging the suzerainty of the members of the Somavaṁśa. The seal of the Sambalpur University Museum plates of the Rāṣṭrakula chief Devapya, a feudatory of Mahābhavagupta I Janamejaya,[362] bears only a short prose legend giving the name of the chief in genitive singular preceded by the honorific *śrī*. On the seal attached to the Degaon charter of the Rāṣṭrakūṭa chief Mugdhagondala, who also acknowledged the suzerainty of Mahābhavagupta I Janamejaya, we have the figure of Garuḍa with outstretched wings and beak-like nose in a low relief in a running posture with its left hand extended to front as if to catch the snake which is shown below.[362a] The seal attached to the Kudopali plates of *Rāṇaka* Puñja,[362b] who was a feudal chief under Mahābhavagupta II Bhīmaratha, bears in the centre in a high relief the figure of a sitting swan facing proper left, above it but considerably separated from it, a crescent, and below it, the legend *Rāṇaka-śrī-Puṁja*. The device, which is quite different from that seen on any other seal of the Somavaṁśins, should not surprise us as the *Rāṇaka* was only a feudatory of a Somavaṁśin ruler and had otherwise no association with the family.

We have some information about the manner of preservation of only one of these copper-plate charters. The Sonpur plates of Mahābhavagupta I Janamejaya are reported to have been found preserved in a massive oblong lithic coffer measuring about 42 cms. in length, 30 cms. in breadth and 32½ cms. in height, covered with a slipping lid. The coffer was obviously specially designed for the safe deposit of the charter.[363]

Palaeography

The **characters** belong to the Nāgarī alphabet of the northern class, commonly designated as the 'northern class of alphabets', a nomenclature employed by us also following the common practice while introducing the texts of the Somavaṁśin inscriptions. To be somewhat more specific, they belong to the Gauḍī alphabet which sprang from the earlier Siddhamātṛkā alphabet and was prevalent in eastern India including Bihar, Bengal, Assam Orissa as well as in Nepal from the tenth to the fourteenth century A.D. This name, which was actually in vogue in those days as vouched for by

361. No. IV: XXVIII.
362. Suppl. Inscr. I.
362a. Suppl. Inscr. II.
362b. No. IV: XIX.
363. xxiii*EI*, 248.

Al-Biruni,[363a] has to be preferred to the alternative nomenclature, Proto-Bengali, popularised in modern times by G. Bühler[364] and used by modern epigraphists.[365] It was from this script that the modern regional alphabets used in Bengal, Bihar, Orissa, Assam and Nepal finally originated. But the alphabet of the Somavaṁśin inscriptions cannot be described as pure Gauḍī, but as an admixture of Gauḍī and Devanāgarī characters, with the former element predominating in some records and the latter element in others.[366]

We may now pass on to some interesting **palaeographical features** of our records. By and large, the characters bear a close resemblance to their modern Nāgarī counterparts. The only exceptions are the forms of *i*, which retains its earlier form,[367] *e*, *o*, which bears a close resemblance to *u*,[368] and *dh* and *bh* which have yet to reach their modern forms. There is little difference between the signs for *dh* and *v* except that there is no top-line on *dh*. The final letters[369] are distinguished from the ordinary ones either by the absence of the top-line or by the use of the *halanta* mark. In some cases we come across altogether peculiar forms of the final letters.[370] As for the medial signs, the most interesting feature is the common use of the *pṛṣṭha-mātrā* or a vertical line attached to the left of the letter to indicate the medial *e*. This is, however, not universal and in many cases we notice simultaneous employment of the *pṛṣṭha-mātrā* and a flourishing top-stroke for the same purpose side by side.[371] In one case, *viz.*, Mahakosala Historical Society's plates of Mahābhavagupta IV Uddyota-kesarin,[372] we do not find the use the *pṛṣṭha-mātrā* at all, the medial vowel being indicated either by a top-stroke or by a short horizontal stroke showing a slight downward curve on left. In earlier inscriptions, the medial *u* is indicated by a curve open in its upper portion attached to the bottom of the letter on left as in modern Nāgarī while *ū* is indicated either

363*a*. See E. Sachau, *Al-Biruni's India*, i, 173. Mentioned along with other regional alphabets, it is also called Gaurī and is said to have been used in Pūrvadeśa or the Eastern country. Also see D.C. Sircar in *Journal of Ancient Indian History*, iv (1970-71), 117 and 120.

364. *Indian Palaeography*, 77.

365. *E.g.*, *IHQ*, xx, 238.

366. The Gauḍī element, for instance, is more predominant in the second Kalibhana grant of Mahābhavagupta I Janamejaya than in the first.

367. We have both the forms consisting of a couple of horizontally placed circles with a horizontal line above (Nos. IV: I, text-line 16; XXII, text-line 16: the horizontal line in this case shows curves at both ends) or below (No. IV: VI, text-line 21).

368. The only major difference is that the sign for *o* has no head-line.

369. Of these, *t*, *n* and *m* are met with very often.

370. *E.g.*, see the forms of *n* (No. IV: VIII, text-lines 5, 7, 9 and 21) and *m* (*ibid.*, text-lines 8, 27 and 30).

371. The instances are too common to be enumerated exhaustively.

372. No. IV: XXIV.

by a sign resembling subscribed *v* or by a semi-circle open at the bottom attached to the bottom of the letter on left.[373] While in later times this form of the medial *u* continues, a sign resembling subscribed *v* is often employed for this purpose,[374] while a curve or semi-circle open to right is added to the bottom of the letter in order to indicate the medial *ū*. The signs used for indicating the medial *ā*, *i*, *ī* and *ṛ* are identical with those in vogue in Nāgarī at present.

As for **numbers**, the decimal notation, which had come into existence a few centuries earlier, had come into popular use, and all the figures in tens,[375] except a solitary instance,[376] are expressed according to the new system. The lone exception met with in the cuttack grant of Mahāśivagupta I Yayāti, however, indicates that the old system had not yet gone out of vogue completely.[377] In our inscriptions we come across the numerals 1, 2, 3, 4, 5, 6, 7, 8, 9, 10, 11, 12, 13, 15, 17, 18, 24, 28, 31 and 34. Some of these figures have forms quite similar to their modern Nāgarī counterparts[378] while others present a somewhat different appearance[379].

The earliest extant record of the family, to wit, Vakratentali plates of Mahābhavagupta I Janamejaya, shows fully developed and beautifully drawn top-lines covering the entire upper portion of the letters barring

373. The resemblance to subscribed *v* in a few cases is probably due to a strong curve in the left limb of the semi-circle. In *pu* and *vu*, the medial *u* resembles subscribed *r* (see Nos. IV: I, text-lines 26 and 34, and II, text-line 20). In *ru* and *rū*, the medial sign for *ū* and *ū* is always attached in the middle.

374. For numerous clear examples of both, see the Brahmeśvara temple inscription of Uddyotakesarin and the Ratnagiri plates of Karṇa (Nos. IV: XXVI and XXVII).

375. Of these we have 11, 12, 13, 15, 17, 18, 24, 28, 31 and 34. For the figure of 10, see next note.

376. In the Cuttack plates of Mahāśivagupta I Yayāti (No. IV: XIV), text-line 65, the number 13 is expressed by the symbols for 10 and 3.

377. This system, called *akṣarapallī* as distinguished from the new system styled *aṅkapallī*, is known to have remained in use side by side with the decimal system till quite late times as seen from the Buddhist manuscripts from Nepal and Jain manuscripts from Gujarat and Rajasthan dating as late as sixteenth century A.D. See Bühler, *Indian Palaeography*, 97ff.; G.H. Ojha, *Bhāratīya Prācīna Lipimālā*, 108-109.

378. The figures for 2, 3 and 8 are quite close to their modern Nāgarī forms, though they were yet to assume the final form. The figure for 8 is almost similar to its modern form. The figure for 3 is almost identical with its modern counterpart; but it is often placed horizontally or obliquely.

379. The figure for 1 consists only of a curved vertical stroke and has yet to develop the loop in the upper portion. Its upper part is often found bent on left, but in a solitary case (No. IV: XXV, text-line 1) the bend is on right. The figure for 5 looks like a cursive form of the English figure for the same number. Forms of 4 and 6 are quite different from their present Nāgarī counterparts. The sign for 9 (No. IV: XIV, text-line 65) bears a slight resemblance to its modern Nāgarī form prevalent in western India. The figure for 7 (No. IV: VI, text-line 44) looks like modern Nāgarī 1. But at another place (No. IV: XIV, text line 20) we have a hook instead of the loop.

only a few cases which may be regarded as exceptions.[380] The practice of putting top-lines is continued without a single exception in all the inscriptions of this chief issued up to the seventeenth year of his reign. In the Chaudwar grants of the thirty-first year of the reign of the same king[381] we come across, for the first time, imperfectly formed scooped out triangles or nail-heads on tops of some of the letters. The next record of his reign, *viz.*, Kalibhana grant of the thirty-fourth regnal year[382] presents numerous instances of solid triangular tops. This change from top-lines to triangular tops is found carried to its logical conclusion in the records of Mahāśivagupta I Yayāti, all of which have solid or scooped out nail-heads on tops of letters.[383] This is again followed by a strange development in the reverse direction the beginnings of which may be traced in the extension of the ends of nail-heads to such an extent as to serve the purpose of top-lines. This feature is noticed in some of the records of Mahāśivagupta I Yayāti himself[384] and becomes more and more pronounced with the passage of time.[385] Next we come across an admixture of nail-heads and top-lines,[386] the latter becoming more predominant with the passage of time.[387]

380. No. IV: I. The letters *ṭ* and *dh* and final consonants as well as initial *i* are without top-lines. Top-lines could not be added to a few other letters like *g*, *ś* and sometimes *ṇ* which do not have vertical lines in the upper portion.

381. Nos. IV: VIII-X.

382. No. IV: XI.

383. The Orissa State Museum (No. IV: XII), Nibinna (No. IV: XV) and the two Patna plates (Nos. IV: XVI and XVII) have solid nail-heads, while scooped out tops are met with in the first Patna (No. IV: XIII) and Cuttack (No. IV: XIV) plates. But in the third Patna plates (No. IV: XVII), we notice an admixture of solid and scooped out heads. The same is true of the Cuttack plates of Mahābhavagupta II Bhīmaratha (No. IV: XVIII) also, though solid tops are comparatively fewer.

384. See, for instance, the Nibinna plates (No. IV: XV). Mahāśivagupta I Yayāti's Cuttack plates afford some rare instances of the use of top-line also.

385. *Vide* Mahābhavagupta II Bhīmaratha's Cuttack plates (No. IV: XVIII) and the Kudopali plates of his feudatory Puñja (No. IV: XIX).

386. See Mahāśivagupta II Dharmaratha's Mahulpada plates (No. IV: XX).

387. In the Jatesinga-Dungari charter of Mahāśivagupta III Yayāti and Balijhari plates of Mahābhavagupta IV Uddyotakesarin (Nos. IV: XXI and XXII) we generally find the use of top-lines, examples of nail-heads being few and far between. The Lalatendukesari and Navamuni cave inscriptions (Nos. IV: XXIII and XXV) and the Mahakosala Historical Society's plates and the Brahmeśvara temple inscription (No. IV: XXVI) of Mahābhavagupta IV Uddyotakesarin have top-lines which tend to be continuous in his incomplete Mahada grant (No. IV: Appendix II) which contains, however, some rare solid nail-heads also. Strange though it might appear, the last known copper-plate grant of the family, *viz.*, Ratnagiri plates of Karṇa (No. IV: XXVII), reverts back to solid nail-heads which are found in most cases, top-lines being noticed in other cases. But the upper horizontal line of the nail-head is extended to right to function as a top-line.

Punctuation Marks

No regularity is observed regarding the employment of **marks of punctuations** which are often found used at places where they are not required and are not employed where they are actually called for. Generally speaking, one or two vertical lines, the latter generally at the end of a stanza, are used for this purpose. Where two vertical lines are used, a short horizontal stroke is attached to the middle of the first line on left. In a few cases, this stroke is attached even to a single vertical line. Sometimes the attachment to the left of the first line assumes a strange form.[388] The lines are generally curved at the lower end almost exactly like the lower ends of the vertical lines of the letters.

Mention may now be made of a few interesting devices employed to mark the conclusion of the record. Two circles placed one below the other are found used as a mark of conclusion in the concluding line of the Vakratentali plates of Mahābhavagupta I Janamejaya. There is also a second mark consisting of a couple of vertical lines, the first with a peculiar hook on top, in the same line which also appears to have been used for the same purpose.[389] Another strange conclusion mark originating from two vertical lines is noticed at the end of the first Patna plates of the same monarch.[390] His Satallamā grant[391] has a couple of vertically placed circles used as a closing mark, while in the first Kalibhana plates we have a mark which consists of these circles together with a couple of vertical lines and a strange horizontally placed mark on right employed for the same purpose.[392] The second Kalibhana plates contain the same closing mark except only the last mentioned device.[393] The Sonpur grant has for this purpose two sets of a couple of vertical lines with a curved horizontal stroke intervening between them.[394] In the Patna plates of Mahāśivagupta I Yayāti we find the same device; but two sets of a single instead of two vertical lines are employed.[395] Two sets of two vertical lines separated by a circle are noticed in the Jatesinga-Dungari charter of Mahāśivagupta III Yayāti,[396] whereas we come across two vertical lines followed by a device consisting of a semi-circle facing but separated from a short vertical stroke in Mahāśivagupta IV Uddyotakes-

388. See, for examples, No. IV: II, text-line 33; III, text-line 23; V, text-line 44; XII, text-line 4; XXIV, text-lines 4, 17, 19 and 27.
389. No. IV: I, text-line 39.
390. No. IV: II, text-line 45.
391. No. IV: V, text-line 44.
392. No. IV: IV, text-line 48.
393. No. IV: XI, text-line 52.
394. No. IV: VI, text-line 57.
395. No. IV: XIII, text-line 50.
396. No. IV: XXI, text-line 46. The same device with a little elaboration of vertical lines and a semi-circle inside the circle is met with in No. IV: XXIV, text-line 36 also where the grant actually concludes.

arin's Mahakosala Historical Society's plates.[397] The most elaborate device is met with in his Navamuni cave inscription. It consists of two circles placed one above the other, a couple of joined vertical lines, a floral device, two connected vertical lines and a *siddham*-like mark, in a row from left to right.[398] It will thus be seen that the conclusion of a record was not unoften indicated by a distinctive device.

A floral design flanked by a single vertical line on left and two such lines on right is also noticed in the Mahakosala Historical Society's plates after the imprecatory stanzas and before the date.[398a]

Corrections

We may now pass on to the devices adopted for **correcting errors** and supplying omissions. Superflous letters engraved by oversight, when detected were cancelled by erasing.[399] In case an unwanted letter or a group thereof was found incised due to slip, it was erased and correct letters or letters were engraved in its place.[400] It may be pointed out, however, that we do have instances of errors being left undetected and consequently uncorrected.[401]

We have numerous examples of **letters or words originally left out but supplied later**. Some interesting cases may be illustrated here. The word *Kosalāyāṁ* left out unincised in text-line 13 of the Sonpur plates of Mahā-bhavagupta I Janamejaya[402] was later engraved in smaller letters in the space above the ring-hole opposite line 17, its proper place being indicated by a *kākapada* (+) at both the places. The expression *gām = ekaṁ* omitted by oversight in line 42 of the Orissa State Museum plates of Mahāśivagupta I Yayāti[403] is found supplied in smaller characters below the line between the *akṣaras sva* and *da* with a *kākapada* at the end, indicating that this word is to be supplied elsewhere and does not belong to the line in the midst of which it is actually incised. But strangely enough, there is absolutely no indication of the place where it is actually to be supplied as in the preceding case. These are the only examples of the use of the *kākapada* mark in the inscriptions under reference. In most other cases, letters originally omitted by inadvertence are found engraved below the line where they

397. No. IV: XXIV, text-line 38.
398. No. IV: XXV, text-line 3.
398a. No. IV: XXIV, text-line 33. Its exact significance is not clear.
399. See, for examples, Nos. IV: XV, text-line 41; XIX, text-lines 14 and 18; XXI, text-line 4.
400. Nos. IV: V, text-line 11; XIX, text-lines 1 and 3. A portion of line 7 and the whole of the following line of the Kudopali plates of Puñja (No. IV: XIX), are engraved on an erasure.
401. Cf. No. IV: V, text-line 44, where *vi* in *Kaivilāsa* (correct Kailāsa) incised by oversight has been left uncancelled.
402. No. IV: VI.
403. No. IV: XII.

ought to have been written without any indication of their proper place.[404] We have a solitary example of an originally left out letter being inserted in its proper place in the concerned line itself.[405]

Numbering of Verses

While there are several Somavaṁśin records composed in a mixture of prose and verse, the **verses have been generally left unnumbered.** The lone exception is the Cuttack grant of Mahāśivagupta I Yayāti where an attempt has been made to number the stanzas serially. But here also only the first seven verses have been numbered and these too incorrectly.[406]

Language and Orthography

All the grants are couched in **Sanskrit**, though the impact of local dialect and popular but incorrect pronunciation is noticeable at many a place. Prakritism or local dialectal elements may be illustrated by numerous words and names like *saṭa* for *ṣaṣṭha*,[407] *aṭṭhāvīsa* for *aṣṭāviṁśa*,[408] *vaccha* for *vatsa*[409], *Kauccha* for *Kautsa*,[410] Ucchavaṇāga for Utsavanāga,[411] *samvacchare* for *saṁvatsare*,[412] *maccha* for *matsya*,[413] *kṛccha*[414] or *kṛcchna*,[415] for *kṛtsna*, *kumvara*[416] or *kuvmāra*[417] in place of *kumāra*, Sāvatha for *Śrāvasti*[418] *vināṇi*[419] or *vināṇī*[420] in place of *vijñāni*, *khiti* for *kṣiti*,[421] *sotā* for *srotas*,[422]

404. For examples, see Nos. IV: VI text-lines 20 and 41; IV, text-lines 8 and 43; XIX, text-line 16; XX, text-lines 8 and 15.
405. No. IV: V, text-line 20.
406. Thus, number 1 is wrongly placed after verse 2 and number 2 is similarly erroneously given after the second quarter of verse 3. The numbered verses belong to the ***praśasti*** portion.
407. No. IV: XXVII, text-line 66.
408. *Ibid.*, text-line 33.
409. Nos. IV: I, text-line 13; VII, text-lines 15 and 52.
410. No. IV: II, text-line 10.
411. No. IV: XV, text-line 50.
412. Nos. IV: II, text-line 40; III text-line 41; IV, text-line 44; V, text-line 40, etc.
413. No. IV: Appendix II, text-line 4; Appendix IV, text-line 3.
414. Nos. IV: II, text-line 45.
415. No. IV: IV, text-line 9; V, text-line 5.
416. No. IV: XXVIII, text-line 7. This is very close to the modern colloquial pronounciation of the word, *viz.*, *kuṁvara*.
417. *Ibid.*, text-line 25. This is obviously an error for *kumvara*, the precursor of the modern *kuṁvara*, met with in line 7 of the same inscription.
418. No. IV: Appendix IV, text-line 9.
419. No. IV: XVI, text-line 64.
420. No. IV: XVII, text-line 75.
421. No. IV: XIX, text-line 17.
422. No. IV: XX, text-line 20. This word (*sotā*) in the sense of a fountain is in common use in some of the modern Indian vernaculars also.

ukṛta,[423] *utkarita,*[424] *utkarnita,*[425] *utakirṇṇa*[426] and *uktīrṇṇa*[427] in place of *utkīrṇṇa* or *utkīrṇa, tāmvra*[428] and *s-āmvra*[429] in place of *tāmra* and *s-āmra* respectively and *pla* for *pala.*[430] The employment of *j* in place of *y*, which is quite common in Oriya and other vernaculars in eastern India, is met with rather rarely in Jayāti[431] and *jo*[432] instead of Yayāti and *yo* respectively. The list of privileges conferred on the donees noticed in some of the later grants of the dynasty also contains a few words of linguistic interest which were obviously borrowed from the local dialect. Of these mention may be made of *andhāruvā* or *arthāruvā, praty-andhāruva* or *praty-arthāruvā, aturāvaḍḍi, antakāvaḍḍi* or *rintakāvaḍḍi, ciṭola, ciṭṭola* or *ciṅgola, viṣayāli tantalika* and *vasāvakī* which do not find a place in any standard lexicon.[433] Some of the personal names also seem to have a tinge of local or non-Sanskritic elements. These include Vaccha, Koighoṣa, Rayaṇa(ṇā) Ojjhā, Evuli, Nārāpagaṇḍa, Koṇḍa or Koṇḍadeva, Appa, Dāddi, Vāpūka, Sānthakara, Avala, Āllava, Vṛllā, Tiku, Ullā, Māhūka, Devu, Iyoka, Yapa, Kāko, Chicchaṭeśvara, Panāka or Pannāka, Ucchavaṇāga, Uhlāsa,[434] Rāccho, Kumbhaṇḍipāla, Vāheru, Maṅgāka, Māhūṇadevī, Chittalladeva, Śaṅkhuka, Ābhābhakara and Herūka.[435] Some of these names, it is interesting to note, were borne by persons hailing from higher sections of society including Brāhmaṇa donees and government officers holding responsible positions.

As regards **orthographical peculiarities**, re-duplication of consonants following *r* is quite common, though not invariably carried out. The cases of the employment of the vowel *ṛ* in place of *ri* are numerous,[436] while

423. No. IV: I, text-line 39.
424. No. IV: XVIII, text-line 73. This is actually a grammatically incorrect verbal form.
425. No. IV: VIII, text-line 49.
426. No. IV: XI, text-line 52.
427. No. IV: XXII, text-line 77. This is actually an illustration of haplology.
428. Nos. IV: V, text-line 19; VI, text-lines 21 and 50; VII, text-lines 20, 51 and 52; VIII, text-lines 14 and 46; XI, text-line 16; XIV, text-line 38; XV, text-line 19; XVI, text-line 28; XIX, text-lines 18 and 35; XXI, text-line 45; XXII, text-lines 47 and 74; Appendix II, text-line 11; XXVIII, text-line 20; IV: Appendix IV, text-line 13. In IV: XXIV, text-line 14, we have *tāvra.*
429. Nos. IV: V, text-line 14; VI, text-line 17; VII, text-lines 14-15; Appendix II, text-line 3.
430. No. IV: III, text-lines 45 and 46.
431. No. IV: XIV, text-line 64. Earlier in the same record (text-line 20, verse 7) we have the correct form of the name.
432. No. IV: XVII, text-line 60. As the common practice appears to have been to employ *j* instead of *y*, it must have required great caution to use *y* which is found commonly.
433. For these terms, see nos. IV: XX-XXII and XXVIII; Appendix II and IV.
434. An error for Ullāsa which is common even now.
435. See index for these names.
436. See, for nstance, Tṛkaliṅgādhipati (nos. IV: I, text-line 4; II, text-line 3; III, text-line 3; IV; text-line 12; V, text-lines 8 and 31; VI, text-line 9; XI, text-line 48), *tṛjagtai* (nos. IV: VI, text-line 47; VII, text-line 47, *tṛdaśa-pati* (nos. IV: II, text-line 45;

those of the use of *ri* for *ṛ* are extremely rare.[437] No distinction is made between *b* and *v* and the sign for *v* alone is employed. This is evidently due to the lack of differentiation in the pronunciation of the two letters in eastern India. *Anusvāra* is frequently used instead of final *m* and its instances are too numerous to be enumerated exhaustively. The cerebral nasal (*ṇ*) is often substituted by the dental one (*n*) as in *pratigṛhnāti* for *pratigṛhṇāti*,[438] *punya* for *puṇya*.[439] *hiranya* instead of *hiraṇya*,[440] *nṛpānāṁ* instead of *nṛpāṇāṁ*,[441] *kalyāna* in place of *kalyāṇa*,[442] *śān-opalo* for *śāṇ-opalo*,[443] Vaiṣnavī for Vaiṣṇavī,[444] *grahena* instead of *graheṇa*[445] and *utkirnita* for *utkīrṇa*[446] as against the extremely rare substitution of *ṇ* for *n* as in *ṇāga* for *nāga*[447] and *vināṇi* (or *-ṇī*) for *vijñāni*.[448] This reflects the common practice of pronouncing only the dental nasal among the ordinary people in some regions including eastern India which obviously obtained in those days as now. An analogous situation appears to be reflected in the rather indiscriminate employment of the sibilants. In common parlance no distinction appears to have been made between the different sibilants, the dental one being much more common than the other two. This is illustrated by the rather common use of *s* for *ś* and *ṣ* as in *nisiddha*,[449] Sivagupta,[450] *kusalī*,[451] *pisuna*,[452] *sāsana*,[453] Kesava,[454] *sāstra*,[455] *saṅkā*,[456]

IV, text-line 9), *kṛyate* (no. IV: XVIII, text-line 11), *Vetṛka* (nos. IV: VI, text-line 14; XVI, text-line 28; XXI, text-line 22).

437. See *Samāhatri*, *Sannidhatri* (no. IV: V, text-line-line 11) and *pitribhiḥ* (no. IV: XIX, text-line 32).
438. See nos. IV: I, text-line 26; VI, text-line 31; XI, text-line 26; XIII, text-line 24; XIX, text-line 24 (*pratigṛhnanti*); XX, text-line 47; XXI, text-line 35; XXIV, text-line 23.
439. See nos. IV: V, text-lines 19 and 30; XIX, text-lines 18, 25 and 27; XXII, text-lines 47 and 59; XXIV, text-lines 13 and 24; Appendix II, text-line 6.
440. *Vide* no. IV: V, text-line 20.
441. See no. IV: XII, text-line 46.
442. *Vide* no. IV: XIX, text-line 6.
443. See no. IV: XXII, text-line 3.
444. *Vide* no. IV: XXII, text-line 56.
445. See no. IV: Appendix II, text-line 7.
446. See no. IV: VIII, text-line 49...
447. Nos. IV: XIII, text-line 40; XV, text-line 50.
448. See nos. IV: XVI, text-line 64; XVII, text-line 75.
449. For *niṣiddha*: See no. IV: V, text-line 14.
450. For Śivagupta. See nos. IV; VI, text-line 10; XIII, text-line 4; XIV, text-line 25.
451. In place of *kuśalī*; nos. IV: VI, text-line 12; XII, text-line 17; XIII, text-line 4. Also see *kusalinaḥ* in no. IV: XXVIII, text-line 8.
452. Instead of *Piśuna* nos. IV: VI, text-line 14; XII, text-line 19; XV, text-line 7; XVIII, text-line 33.
453. The correct form is *śāsana*. *Vide* nos. IV: VI, text-lines 21, 25 and 50; XI, text-lines 16 and 50; XII, text-line 53; XXII, text-line 74; XXVIII, text-lines 20-21.
454. Keśava is the correct form. See no. IV: VI, text-line 24.
455. For *śāstra*. See nos. IV: VI, text-lines 26 and 45; XIII, text-line 16; XIV, text-line 42; XXVIII, text-line 33.
456. No. IV: XXI, text-line 46.
456. For *śaṅkā* nos. IV: XII, text-line 32; XIII, text-lines 17-18; XIV, text-line 44; XXVIII, text-line 37. In no. IV: VI, text-line 28, we have *saṁkā*.

satāni,[457] *hutāsana*,[458] *dasame*,[459] *sīkṣa*,[460] Kosala-*dese*,[461] Kāsyapa,[462] *ātmanas=ca*,[463] *yaso*,[464] *pāsa*,[465] *satru*,[466] *syāma*,[467] *Māhesvara*,[468] *Dāṇḍapāsika*,[469] *das-āparādha*,[470] *pravesa*,[471] Paramesvara,[472] Chicchaṭesvara,[473] *sudhyati*,[474] Sūlapāṇi,[475] °*sarmman*,[476] *viseṣa*,[477] *sudi*,[478] *visada*,[479] *sṛṅga*,[480] *sasvad*,[481] *rasmi*,[482] Gurjjaresvara,[483] Vaisākha,[484] *sālin*,[485] *śīt-ānsu*,[486] *nistrinsa*,[487] *sān-opala*,[488] *uddisya*,[489] *yas=ca*,[490] *sa-gartt-osara*,[491] *saṣṭhi*,[492]

457. Instead of *śatāni* which is the correct form. See no. IV: VI, text-lines 32-33. Also see *S(Ś)atena* in nos. IV: XII, text-line 40; XIII, text-line 25; XIV, text-line 48.
458. Correct form is *hutāśana*, *Vide* nos. IV: VI, text-line 37; XIV, text-line 54; XVIII, text-line 62.
459. For *daśame*. See no. IV: VI, text-line 43.
460. *Śīkṣā* is the correct form *Vide* no. IV: VI, text-line 45.
461. In place of *-deśe*: nos. IV: XI, text-lines 4-5; XIII, text-line 5; XV, text-line 5 (*desa*).
462. For Kāśyapa. See no. XI. text-line 12.
463. Correct form is *ātmanaś=ca*: no. IV: XI, text-lines 15-16.
464. For *yaśo*. See nos. IV: XI, text-line 16; XIII, text-line 12; XXII, text-line 47.
465. *Pāśa* is the correct form: nos. IV: XI, text-line 29; XII, text-line 41; XIV, text-line 50.
466. Instead of *śatru*: no. IV: XII, text-line 2.
467. Correct form is *śyāma*: no. IV: XII, text-line 2.
468. Instead of *Māheśvara*: nos. IV: XII, text-lines 13 and 49; XIII, text-line 3; XXVIII, text-line 23(Mahesvara for Maheśvara).
469. *For Dāṇḍapāśika*: nos. IV: XII, text-line 19; XV, text-line 7; XVII, text-line 31; XVIII, text-line 33; XX, text-line 29; XXI, text-line 21.
470. *Daś-āparādha* is correct: nos. IV: XII, text-line 21; XV, text-line 10.
471. For *praveśa*: no. IV: XII, text-line 23.
472. For *Parameśvara*: nos. IV: XII, text-line 50; XIII, text-lines 3 and 36.
473. Instead of Chicchaṭeśvara: no. IV: XII, text-line 54.
474. For *śudhyati*: no. IV: XIV, text-line 49.
475. For *Śūlapāṇi*: no. IV: XIV, text-line 54.
476. In °*sarmmaṇe* for *śarmmaṇe*: nos. XV, text-line 16; XXII, text-lines 45 and 49.
477. Instead of the correct form *viśeṣa*: nos. IV: XVII, text-line 4; XXVIII, text-line 29.
478. For *śudi* which itself stands for *śuddha dina*: nos. IV: XVII, text-line 75; XXI, text-line 45.
479. In place of *viśada*: no. IV: XX, text-line 7.
480. *Śṛṅga* is the correct form: no. IV: XX, text-line 8.
481. Instead of *śaśvad*: no. IV: XX, text-line 13. Also see *saśvat* in no. IV: XXII, text-line 69.
482. For *raśmi* which is the correct form: no. IV: XX, text-line 14.
483. The correct form is Gurjjareśvara: no. IV: text-line 13.
484. For Vaiśākha: no. IV: XXI, text-lines 44 and 45.
485. Correct form is °*śālin*. See no. IV: XXII, text-line 1.
486. For *śīt-āṁśu*: no. IV: XXII, text-line 10.
487. Instead of *nistriṁśa*: no. IV: XXII, text-line 17. In text-line 70 we have *nīstriṁsa*.
488. *Śāṇ-opala* is the correct form: no. IV: XXVII, text-line 2.
489. For *uddiśya*: no. IV: XXVIII, text-line 23.
490. In place of *yaś=ca*. See no. IV: XXVIII, text-line 34.
491. For *sa-gartt-oṣara*. See no. IV: XV, text-line 12.
492. In place of the correct form *ṣaṣṭi*. *Vide* no. IV: XV, text-line 26.

pīyūsa,[493] *bhavisyati,*[494] *abhisikta,*[495] etc. We also notice a number of examples of the rather indiscriminate employment of the palatal[496] and cerebral[497] sibilants instead of the dental one. Instances of the interchange between the palatal and cerebral sibilants are comparatively few and far between.[498] There is a solitary case of the use of *ī* instead of *yī* in *Kāṇva-śākh-ādhyāī,*[499] and of the substitution of *ī* for *i* in *ity-uvagatya.*[500] In a few cases final *n* is found replaced by *anusvāra,*[501] while the dental nasal is sometimes substituted for *anusvāra.*[502] Examples illustrating the replacement of *anusvāra* preceding a sibilant by *ṅ* are many, *viz.*, *vaṅśa,*[503] *vaṅśi,*[504] *vaṅśe,*[505] *triṅśattame,*[506] *dvātriṅśa,*[507] *viṅśati,*[508] *nistriṅśa,*[509] *ratnāṅśu,*[510] *śīt-āṅśu*[511] and *dhvaṅsana.*[512] We have also a few instances of the letter *h*

493. For *pīyūṣa. Vide* no. IV: XXII, text-line 2.
494. Correct form is *bhaviṣyati*: no. IV: XXII, text-line 58.
495. For *abhiṣikta*: no. IV: XXVIII, text-line 4.
496. See, for example, *ś(s)alila, puraśś(s)ara, ś(s)ama,* (no. IV:V, text-line 18), *vaś(s)eta (t)* (no. IV: V, text-line 26), Koś(s)ala (no. IV: XV, text-line 4), Koś(s)al-endra (no. IV: VIII, text-line 48), *samāvāś(s)ita* (no. IV: XII, text-line 1), *ś(s)ita* (no) IV: XIV, text-line 65), *āś(s)akti* (no. IV: XVIII, text-line 12), *śāś(s)ana* (no. IV: XVII, text-line 70), *sāś(s)anena (ibid.*, text-line 42), *jal-āvaś(s) ecana* (no. IV: XVIII, text-line 6), *ś(s)arvvān* (no. IV: XVIII, text-line 63), *kumbhīnaś(s)āḥ* (nos. IV: XXII, text-line 20; XXVII, text-line 16), *ś(s)rotaḥ* (no. IV: XXII, text-line 38), *ś(s)īmani* (no. XXVII, text-line 10), Madhuś(s)ūdana (no. IV: XXVII, text-line 18), etc.
497. See *ṣ(s)a-nidhiḥ* (no. IV: VIII, text-line 8), *ṣū(su)tena* (no. IV: VIII, text-line 49), Koṣ(s)ala (nos. IV: XI, text-line 4; XXI, text-line 18; XXII, text-lines 24 and 72; XXVII, text-line 19), *ṣ(s)ama* (no. IV:XVIII, text-line 43) and Toṣ(s) alīya (no. IV: XXVII, text-line 33).
498. For the replacement of *ṣ* for *ś* see *kuṣ(ś)alī* (no. IV: III, text-line 4), *kūṣ* (*kuś*)*alī* (no. (IV: II, text-line 4), *vaṁṣ(ś)-odbhava* (no. IV: XIX, text-line 8), etc. The substitution of *ś* for *ṣ* is illustrated by *varś(ṣ)a* (no. IV: XIX, text-line 23), *bhaviś(ṣ)yati* (no. IV: XIX, text-line 27), Riśi (Hṛṣī)keśa (no. IV: II, text-line 15), etc.
499. No. IV: II, text-line 17.
500. *Ibid.*, text-line 21.
501. See *pārthiv-endrāṁ*(n): no. IV: II, text-line 37; *V(B)rāhmaṇāṁ(n)*: no. IV: III, text-line 5; *preyāṁ(n)*: IV: XVII, text-line 68; *bhagavāṁ*(n): no. IV: XIX, text-line 26.
502. See, for instance, *dhvansana* for *dhvaṁsana* (nos. IV: XVI, text-line 9; XVII, text-line 8; XX, text-line 7), *dhvansaika* for *dhvaṁsaika* (no. IV: XX, text-line 23); *śīt-ānsu* for *śīt-āṁśu* (no. IV: XVII, text-line 10) *nistrinsa* in place of *nistriṁśa* (no. IV: XXII, text-line 17), *ratn-ānsu* for *ratn-āṁṣu* (no. IV: XXII, text-line 22), *vinsati* for for *viṁśati* (no. IV: XXIII, text-line 3), etc.
503. For *vaṁsa*: no. IV. II, text-line 45; IV, text-line 9; V, text-line 6; XXI, text-line 15; XXII, text-line 10.
504. Instead of the correct form *vaṁśī*: no. IV: II, text-line 45.
505. In place of *vaṁśe* which is the correct form: no. IV: IV, text-line 10.
506. The correct form is *triṁśattame*. See no. IV: XI, text-line 49. In no. IV: VIII, text-line 44 we have *triṅśattime.*
507. For *dvātriṁśa. Vide* no. IV: XX, text-lines 16-17.
508. *Viṁśati* is the correct form. See no. IV: XVI, text-line 61.
509. For *nistriṁśa*: no. IV: XXII, text-line 10.
510. Instead of the correct form *ratn-āṁśu*: no. IV: XX, text-line 14.
511. The correct form is *śīt-āṁśu. Vide* no. IV: XXI, text-line 15.
512. For *dhvaṁsana*: no. IV: XIV, text-line 8.

following an *anusvāra* being replaced by *g* or *gh*, while the *anusvāra* itself gives place to the lingual nasal. Thus, we come across the name Siṁhadatta turned into Siṅgadata[513] or Siṅghadatta.[514] Errors in respect of the medial signs for *i* and *u* are very common and signs of long medials are often found employed where those of short ones are expected and *vice versa.*[515] Examples of the substitution of *t* for *n* followed by *t* are rare,[516] while there are several instances of the deletion of one of the two identical consonants not intervened by any other letter.[517] We have several instances of the use of the *avagraha* sign.[518]

Abbreviations

As regards **abbreviations**, we find only a few of them used in our records. These include *śudi* or *sudi*[519] for *śuddha dina*, *i.e.*, a day of a bright fortnight, and *vadi*[520] for *bahula dina*, *i.e.*, a day of a dark fortnight, which are not met with in the earlier inscriptions incorporated in the present volume but had obviously become well established and were in popular use during the period represented by the records under consideration. We have a single instance of the employment of the abbreviated form Phālgu for Phālguna[521] and three examples of the use of Mārga for Mārgaśīrṣa.[522] In a few records *sa* or *saṁ*[523] is found used for *saṁbaddha* while referring to

---

513. No. IV: XVIII, text-lines 68-69.
514. No. IV: XVII, text-line 69. Also see nos. IV:XX, text-line 7; XXIV, text-line 12.
515. Examples of such indiscriminate use of medial signs are too numerous to be enumerated exhaustively.
516. *E.g.*, *valgayatt(nt)i*: no. IV: XX, text-line 46; *att(nt)ar*: *ibid*, text-line 60.
517. See, for example, *jagatraya* (*jaga* = *traya*): no. IV: XVII, text-line 17; Udyotakesarī for Uddyotakesarī: no IV: XXII, text-line 27. Also see for the same spelling nos. IV: XXIII and XXV, text-line 1. Elsewhere the name is spelt correctly. Another similar instance is *udyotita* for *uddyotita*: no. IV: XXIII, text-line 3.
518. See nos. IV: VI, text-line 45; XVI, text-line 19; XVII, text-lines 23 and 73; XVIII, text-line 35; XX, text-lines 31, 36 and 53; XXI, text-line 23; XXII, text-line 7; XXVII, text-lines 5 and 18; XXVIII, text-line 29.
519. *Śudi:* nos. IV: I, text-line 37; II, text-line 41; IV, text-line 45; V, text-line 41; VI, text-line 44; VII, text-line 45; VIII, text-line 46; XII, text-line 53; XVI, text-line 62; XVII, text-line 75; XVIII, text-line 73; XXVII, text-lines 67 and 68. *Sudi*: nos. IV: XV, text-line 48; XXI, text-line 45. In no. IV: III, text-line 42 we have *śrudi.*
520. *E.g.*, nos. IV: XI, text-lines 49 and 50; XX, text-line 62; XXII, text-line 76. Interestingly enough, while *vadi* itself was used as an abbreviation of *bahula dina*, we come across an example of the use of the expression *vadi dina* (no. IV: XXIV, text-line 34), showing thereby that sometimes *vadi* was erroneously taken in the sense of the dark fortnight and not as denoting a day of the dark fortnight.
521. No. IV: IV, text-line 45.
522. Nos. IV: XV, text-line 48; XVIII, text-line 73; XXII, text-lines 76 and 77. In no. IV: XV, text-line 47, we have the corrupt form Margasi.
523. *Sa* is met with in no. IV: XXII, text-line 33, and *saṁ* in nos. XXVII, text-line 33 and XXVIII, text-line 8. Of these, the first stands for the form *sambaddha* and the second for *saṁbaddha*, both of which are grammatically correct. It is interesting to note

an administrative division as attached to a district. At one place[524] we find the expression *rūpyaka-pala* abbreviated as *rupla*.

Draft

The earliest extant record of the dynasty, Vakratentali plates of Mahābhavagupta I Janamejaya, is in prose barring only the customary benedictory and imprecatory stanzas. The next grant, *viz.*, the same king's Patna plates, is also drafted in a similar manner, but a verse in praise of the monarch is added at the end. The same laudatory stanza is repeated in the first Kalibhana and Satallamā grants, but instead of being given at the end it is now inserted after a long prose passage describing the place of issue.[525] The Sonepur charter also contains a eulogistic verse which is inserted after the specification of the date and prior to that of the writer, but this stanza is different from the one met with in earlier grants. This verse is found repeated along with that found in earlier records in the Gaintala plates at the same place as in the preceding grant. With a slight change,[526] this verse is retained as the second of the two laudatory stanzas, the first being found for the first time, in the three Chaudwar grants and the second Kalibhana charter. In all these records both these stanzas are given before the mention of the date. It will be seen that the number of laudatory stanzas in the records of Mahābhavagupta I Janamejaya was very small, never exceeding two, and their place was not fixed. From the time of the next king, Mahāśivagupta I Yayāti, however, versified *praśasti* comprising a fairly large number of stanzas at the beginning became an almost regular feature of copper-plate charters, grants without such verses being very few.[527] The number of such *praśasti* stanzas went on increasing with the passage of time.[528] These stanzas may be classified into two

that these abbreviations are, for the first time, employed during the reign of Uddyotakesarin.

524. No. IV: III, text-line 46. While the first *akṣara* is undoubtedly an abbreviation of *rūpyaka*, the second one, *pla*, is obviously a corrupt, may be colloquial, form of the word *pala*. The same form is met with in the preceding line where there is no question of abbreviating it. The correct form is found used in no. IV: II, text-line 19.

525. No. IV: III does not contain any eulogistic stanza. It is rather surprising as the *Mahāsandhivigrahin* and the writer of this record were the same as those mentioned in the preceding and following records, *viz.*, first Patna and Kalibhana plates.

526. Dharmmakandarppadeva, probably a *biruda* of the king, is substituted in these grants for Janamejayaśrīḥ met with in earlier grants.

526a. In no. IV: XIII three *praśasti* stanzas are given at the end.

527. Such grants are nos. IV: XV, XXI and XXIV. No. IV: XIX, which, too, does not contain any laudatory verse, belongs to a feudatory chief and not to the dynasty itself.

528. Thus, the first known grant of Mahāśivagupta I Yayāti, Orissa State Museum plates (no. IV: XII) contains only four laudatory stanzas, while the Cuttack (no. IV: XIV) and the two Patna grants (nos. IV: XVI and XVII) have seven, seven and eight stanzas respectively. In the Cuttack plates of Mahābhavagupta II Bhīmaratha (no. IV: XVIII), Mahulpada plates of Mahāśivagupta II Dharmaratha (no. IV: XX),

groups, *viz.*, (i) those in praise of the place from which the charter in question was issued and (ii) those eulogising the issuing monarch. While the verses extolling the king are met with in the very first known grant of this king, those in praise of the place of issue are for the first time met with in the Cuttack plates of the ninth year of his reign.[528a] And what is even more interesting in this connection, more verses (4) are devoted in this grant to the eulogy of the place of issue than to that of the king himself (3). But while the eulogy of the issuing monarch, often with a brief account of earlier reigns, became an almost regular feature, the versified *praśasti* of the place of issue did not find that much favour and, judging from the extant evidence, was discontinued after the reign of Mahāśivagupta II Dharmaratha.[529] Another interesting feature is the occurrence of one or more stanzas in praise of the person occupying the office of the *Mahāsāndhivigrahika* and sometimes of the occupant of the office of the *Mahākṣapaṭalin* also in a few records in connection with the reference to the writer at the end. The insertion of a verse or verses indirectly praising an officer, apparently having no connection with the grant, is noticed in the Somavaṁśin records as early as the seventeenth year of the reign of Mahābhavagupta I Janamejaya and is found continued right up to the close of his reign.[530] But the practice of introducing a stanza or stanzas devoted exclusively to the exaltation of one or both of the aforesaid officers was first initiated by Mahāśivagupta I Yayāti and is noticed for the first time in the Cuttack plates of the ninth year of his reign. Thereafter it became an almost regular feature.[531]

Balijhari plates of Mahābhavagupta IV Uddyotakesarin (no. IV: XXII) and Ratnagiri plates of Karṇa, we have nine, ten, eleven and seventeen stanzas respectively. The Banpur grant of Indraratha (No. IV: Appendix I) has fourteen verses.

528a. It may be pointed out in this context that a long prose passage describing the place of issue in conventional terms is met with in a few records of Mahābhavagupta I Janamejaya. It is first noticed in his first Kalibhana plates and is found repeated in the Satallamā, Sonepur and Gaintala plates and appears to have been discontinued thereafter as it is not found in any subsequent grant.

529. It is not found in the grants of Mahāśivagupta III Yayāti, Mahābhavagupta IV Uddyotakesarin and Karṇa as well as in the grant of Someśvara. But the Banpur plates of Indraratha contain five stanzas in praise of the place of issue.

530. We find one such stanza in the Sonepur and Gaintala plates of the seventeenth year and two each in the Chaudwar and second Kalibhana plates of the thirty-first and thirty-fourth years respectively. But these verses are apparently in praise of the king, though they actually extol the minister.

531. The Cuttack and the second Patna plates of Mahāśivagupta I Yayāti and the Cuttack plates of Mahābhavagupta II Bhīmaratha contain a single stanza in praise of the *Sandhivigrahin* at the time. The last-mentioned record also has a verse referring to the *Kāyastha* responsible for writing it. No other record contains such a stanza. In the Mahulpada plates of Mahāśivagupta II Dharmaratha we have a couple of stanzas, one praising the *Sandhivigrahin* and the other the *Mahākṣapaṭalādhyakṣa*. The same is the case with the Balijhari charter of Mahābhavagupta IV Uddyotakesarin. Two

All but seven[532] copper-plate charters were issued by sovereign monarchs belonging to the dynasty. Of the seven exceptions, four were issued by feudatory chiefs,[533] one by a chief who was a collateral member of the dynasty and assumed sovereign titles but described himself as *Kumārādhirāja* and *Paśçima-Laṅkādhipati* and not as *Mahārājādhirāja* and *Trikaliṅgādhipati* as other imperial members of the dynasty did,[534] and another by a member of the family who styled himself *Paramabhaṭṭāraka, Paścimalaṅkādhipati, Mahākumārādhirāja, Parameśvara* and *Yuvarāja.*[534a] The seventh remaining record being incomplete,[535] it is not possible to decide as to whom it belonged though it is not unlikely that it, too, was issued by the same chief to whom we owe the fifth of these charters. Since the issuers of the first four of these charters were feudal chiefs, they had, as clearly averred in the records, to seek the permission of their overlords before issuing the grants.

Object and Occasions

The **object** of all the charters is to register grants of one or more villages[536] in favour of certain individuals or religious establishments with the object of the increase of the religious merit and fame of the donor himself as well as his parents. Individual grantees are generally Brāhmaṇas, the solitary exception being the Ratnagiri plates of Karṇa which aim at recording the grant of a village in favour of a lady named Karppūraśrī. Most of the grants were made in favour of a single individual, examples of grants made in favour of a number of Brāhmaṇas being few.[537] We have in all three **institutional grants**, *viz.*, Sonepur plates of Mahābhavagupta I Janamejaya, Kelga plates of Someśvara and Banpur plates

verses are devoted to the description of the *Sandhivigrahin* and one to that of the *Mahākṣapaṭalādhyakṣa*. Nos. IV: XV, XVI, XXI, and XXIV do not contain such stanzas.

532. These records are nos. IV: XIX, XXVIII; Appendix IV, Supplementary Inscriptions I, II, IV and V.

533. Kudopali plates of Puñja: no. IV: XIX.

534. Kelga plates of Someśvara who claimed his descent from a sovereign monarch belonging to the Soma-kula.

534a. Supplementary Inscription IV (Nuapatna plates of Dharmaratha).

535. No. IV: Appendix. II.

536. The Cuttack plates of Mahābhavagupta II Bhīmaratha (no. IV: XVIII) and the Jatesinga-Dungari plates of Mahāśivagupta III Yayāti (no. IV: XXI) record the donation of two villages each to a single Brāhmaṇa donee while the Balijhari plates of Mahābhavagupta IV Uddyotakesarin aim at granting two villages in favour of two Brāhmaṇa brothers (no. IV: XXII). We have no charter referring to the grant or more than two villages.

537. The maximum number of Brāhmaṇa donees is four which is mentioned in the first Patna plates of Mahābhavagupta I Janamejaya (no. IV: II). The same chief's second Patna plates (no. IV: III) and Mahābhavagupta IV Uddyotakesarin's Balijhari charter (no. IV: XXII) record grants in favour of two grantees each.

of Indraratha.[538] The first of these records a grant in favour of a traders' organisation of Kamalavana which hailed from Khadirapadra and was stationed at Suvarṇapura at the time of the grant. This traders' organisation on its part gave away the village for the provision of worship (lit., *bali*, *caru* and *naivedya*) at and repairs of the temples of Keśava and Āditya. Though the Kelga plates apparently record a grant to a Brāhmaṇa, it is said to have been made in favour of god Maheśvara-bhaṭṭāraka, indicating thereby that the Brāhmaṇa donee was probably the priest of the temple and the donation was meant to enable him to provide for worship and other necessities of the temple. The Banpur plates clearly aver that the grant was made for the provision of *bali*, *caru* and *naivedya* to the goddess Khadiravarṇī-bhaṭṭārikā.

The **occasions** on which the grants in question were made are generally left unspecified, there being only five records mentioning such occasions. The earliest grant of the family, *i.e.*, Vakratentali charter, was given away by Mahābhavagupta I Janamejaya on the occasion of the Viṣuvat *saṅkrānti*,[539] and his grandson Mahābhavagupta II Bhīmaratha made his only known grant on the occasion of a solar eclipse (no. IV: VIII). A Rāṣṭrakūṭa feudatory of Janamejaya I also made a grant on the same occasion.[539a] The only extant charter of Mahāśivagupta III Yayāti, *viz.*, Jatesinga-Dungri plates, is reported to have been made over to the donee on the 'auspicious *tithi*' Amāvāsyā. The gift recorded in Mahābhavagupta IV Uddyotakesarin's Mahakosala Historical Society's plates is stated to have been given away on the occasion of a Siṁha *saṅkrānti*. A lunar eclipse formed the occasion of the same monarch's grant registered in his incomplete Mahada charter. The Kelga grant of Someśvara was made on 'an auspicious *tithi*' of the month of Māgha, but the *tithi* itself has been left unnamed. But in all probability it was Māghī Pūrṇimā which is regarded as highly sacred.

Dates

All the complete charters are dated, the **dates** being invariably indicated in the years of the reigns of the issuing chiefs. The only apparent exceptions are the Kudopali grant of *Raṇaka* Puñja[540] and the charters of some other

538. See nos. IV: VI, XXVIII and Appendix. I.

539. The Nuapatna grant of Dharmaratha (Supplementary Inscription IV) was also made on the occasion of a Viṣuvat *saṅkrānti*. There are two Viṣuvat *saṅkrāntis*, *viz.*, Meṣa and Tulā *saṅkrāntis* when the length of the day and night is equal. See P. V. Kane, HDS, v, 213.

539a. Supplementary Inscription I.

540. No. IV: XIX. The mode of dating in this record is different from that noticed in other records. It mentions only the thirteenth year of Mahābhavagupta II Bhīmaratha's reign without specifying the *tithi* at the beginning and not at the end as in most other records.

vassals[540a] which specify the dates not in terms of the years of their own chieftainship but in those of their suzerains. This is quite in keeping with the practice seen commonly followed in numerous other records. The years are spoken of as belonging to the 'victorious' (*vijaya-rājya*) or increasingly victorious' or 'prosperous and victorious' reign (*pravarddhamāna-vijaya-rājya*) of the king.[541] The mention of the year is followed by the specification of the month, fortnight and *tithi*. In most cases the fortnight is described as bright or dark[542] and in a few records as first or second.[543] A vast majority of inscriptions records the date including the year, fornight and *tithi* first in words which are followed by the specification of the first and the third items in figures, the second item being indicated in an abbreviated form. These two modes of expressing the date, *i.e.*, in words and figures, are more often than not clearly distinguished from each other by the use of the word *aṅka* between them.[544] There is only a solitary case, *viz.*, the Cuttack grant of Mahāśivagupta I Yayāti, where the specification af the date in words and figures is combined, *i.e.*, first the year is mentioned in words and figures and then the *tithi* is indicated in a similar manner, unlike other records which first specify both the year and the *tithi* together in words and then both are indicated together in figures. The Mahulpada plates of Mahāśivagupta II Dharmaratha are the only record where the date is indicated only in figures. The Mahakosala Historical Society's plates of Mahābhavagupta IV Uddyotakesarin give the date partly in

540*a*. See Supplementary Inscriptions I-II and IV-V.

541. No regularity or development is noticed in this regard. In the first six records of Mahābhavagupta I Janamejaya we get the expression *vijaya-rājye*, the word *pravarddhamāna* being prefixed to it for the first time in this Gaintala plates, and the combined expression *pravarddhamāna-vijaya-rājye* or *pravarddhamāne vijaya-rājye* is found in all the subsequent records of this king. The word *pravarddhamāna*, strange though it may appear, is again omitted in the first two charters of the next king, Mahāśivagupta I Yayāti (nos. IV: XII and XIII). Finally, it re-appears in the Cuttack plates of the ninth year of his reign and is met with in all the subsequent records of the family with the solitary exception of the Mahulpada plates of Mahāśivagupta II Dharmaratha where we do not get any allusion to the reigning king in connection with the date.

542. It is interesting to note that while in several cases the white fortnight is referred to as *sita-* or *śukla-pakṣa*, in other records the contraction *śu di or su di*, which actually connotes a 'day of the bright fortnight', is used in the sense of 'bright fortnight' and the word *tithi* is often suffixed to it, though redundantly. See, for instance, nos. IV: VIII-X. The contraction *va di*, actually standing for *bahula dina* or a 'day of the dark fortnight' is employed in a similar manner much more frequently. *Vide* nos. IV: XI, XXII and XXIV.

543. While the *dvitīya-pakṣa* or second fortnight is clearly mentioned in the first Kalibhana and Satallamā plates of Mahābhavagupta I Janamejaya, the use of the expression *prathama-pakṣa* or first fortnight, though not actually met with, can be easily inferred.

544. We have the expressions *yatr-āṅkataḥ*, *yatr-āṅkato*, *yatr-āṅkato-pi*, *yatr-āṅken-āpi*, *aṅke*, *aṅkataḥ* and *yatr-āṅke*. Nos. IV: XI, XIV and XV do not contain any such expression.

words and partly in figures *i.e.*, the year is given only in words and the *tithi* only in figures.

The first Kalibhana and Satallamā grants of Mahābhavagupta I Janamejaya first describe the *tithis* as the *pratipad* of the second fortnight (*dvitīya-pakṣa*) of the month of Phālguna and as *dvādaśī* of the second fortnight of the month of Kārttika which are later specified in figures as the first day of the bright half of Phālguna and as the twelfth day of the bright half of Kārttika respectively. This leaves no room for doubt that the dark fortnight was regarded as the first half of a month and that the months referred to in our records have to be taken as *pūrṇimānta*. Records of other dynasties also clearly indicate the popularity enjoyed by the *pūrṇimānta* system in medieval Orissa and adjoining area of present Madhya Pradesh.

We have no definite evidence to ascertain if the copper-plate charters were issued on the same days on which the land-grants recorded therein were actually made. As has been shown earlier, there are instances to show that sometimes there was a long gap between the date on which the grant was made and that when it was formalised by issuing a royal charter. The same may have been the case with some of the Somavaṁśin grants also though the extant records do not enable us to arrive at a definite conclusion on this point.[545]

Kara-śāsanas

Generally speaking copper-plate charters aimed at turning granted village/s into permanent rent-free holdings, and this fact is stated in unambiguous terms in all the records without a single exception.[546] There are, however, two records which register land-grants on the explicit condition of the annual payment of a stipulated amount by way of tax by the donees. Both these charters belong to the sixth year of the regin of Mahābhavagupta I Janamejaya and were issued from the same place (nos. IV: II and III). One of these records registers the grant of a village in favour of four Brāhmaṇas on the stipulation of the payment of tax amounting to eight *palas* of silver every year by the grantees.[547] The other charter records the grant of a village to two Brāhmaṇa brothers on the condition of the payment of five *palas* of silver as tax, obviously annual.[548] Both these grants evidently belong to the category of *kara-śāsana* or 'a charter recording a land-grant on the condition of the payment of tax' a number of which have been found

545. For some instances of this kind see the treatment of the Śarabhapurīya and Pāṇḍavavaṁśin records.

546. The expression used for this purpose is *tāmra-śāsanen-ā-karīkṛtya pratipāditaḥ*.

547. *Prati-varṣa-dātavya-rūpyak-āṣṭa-pala-kara-dānaṁ viniścitya* (no. IV: II, text-lines 19-20).

548. *Kara-pañca-rūpya-plāni-niṣṭaṅkya kara-śāsanam= idaṁ dattaṁ yatra ru pla* 5 (no. IV: III, text-lines 45-46). For another example of a *Kara-śāsana* of the time of Mahābhavagupta I Janamejaya, see Supplementary Inscription II.

in Orissa and form an interesting feature of medieval Orissan epigraphy.[549] The second of these grants is explicitly called a *kara-śāsana*. But what is strange is that even though these grants were made on the condition of the payment of a stipulated annual tax, the expression *tāmra-śāsanen-ā-karīkṛtya pratipāditaḥ, i.e.* 'given after making (the village) rent-free by means of a copper-plate charter', which is actually applicable only to revenue-free grants, is repeated with reference to these revenue-paying grants also. Not only that, the customary benedictory and imprecatory stanzas befitting a charter conveying a revenue-free grant are also cited as if the grants conveyed through these charters were revenue-free.[550] As pointed out by D. C. Sircar, this was probably due to the fact that ancient Indians did not look at the sale or conditional grant of landed property favourably and therefore represented even sale or revenue-paying grant of land as an outright revenue-free gift. This is explicitly stated by Vijñāneśvara in his Mitākṣarā commentary on the *Yājñavalkya-smṛti.* It is stated that the sale of landed property[551] being forbidden and its gift being extolled, even when it is to be sold it should be sold in the garb of a gift after giving water and gold.[552] Reference may in this connection be made to the expression *tṛṇ-odaka* which is referred to as one of the taxes listed in the Kelga plates of Someśvara.[553] Literally meaning 'grass and water', it is found used in some medieval Orissan records in the technical sense of a fixed cess payable to the king in the case of *kara-śāsana* grants.[554]

Some of the records leave the impression that even though the grants recorded therein are said to have been made by the issuing chiefs, the grants may have actually been made by others. Thus, the Sonepur grant of Mahābhavagupta I Janamejaya purports to record the gift of a village by the king in favour of a traders' body (*vaṇik-sthāna*) of Kamalapura which in turn made it over to a couple of temples of Keśava and Āditya. Now, if the gift was actually made as stated in the record, one would have to believe that the traders' organisation played the role only of an intermediary and no merit could accrue to it from the gift. Secondly, it would be difficult to explain as to why the monarch did not give the village direct to the temples in question himself instead of routing the grant through the traders' body.

549. For these records, see D.C. Sircar, 'Some Kara-Śāsanas of Ancient Orissa', *JRAS*, 1952, 4-10; *IE*, 111-13.

550. Apparently there is no difference between the *kara-śāsanas* and other charters recording revenue-free grants.

551. The word used in this connection is *sthāvara*, 'stationary'; but in the present context it refers to landed property alone.

552. *Sthāvarasya-vikraya-pratiṣedhāt....dāna-praśaṁsāc=ca vikraye='pi kartavye sahiraṇyam=udakaṁ dattvā dāna-rūpeṇa sthāvara-vikrayaṁ kuryāt.*
Mitākṣarā on *Yājñavalkya-smṛti*, ii. 114.

553. No. IV: XXVIII, text-line 17.

554. For instances of the use of the word in this technical sense, see *JRAS*, 1952, 6-7, nos. II and III, *IE*, 111-12.

It therefore appears very likely that the king actually sold or gave away the village to the traders' body in return for some consideration. The role of the traders' body cannot be explained in any other way.

Reference may also be made here to the Kelga plates of Someśvara which record the grant of a village in favour of a Brāhmaṇa at the request of a couple of high officers. Although there is no clear indication, in all likelihood the granted village was situated in the *jāgīr* or fief of the officers concerned who must have compensated the loss of revenue to the state, at least partially. Alternatively, it is possible that they actually paid some money to the king in return for which the latter turned it into a rent-free holding.[555]

Mahābhavagupta I Janamejaya's Sonepur plates record a grant which is said to have been made by means of a couple of characters. First, the village in question was given to the *vaṇik-sthāna* of Kamala-vana by means of a copper-plate charter. Thereafter the *vaṇik-sthāna* gave it away in favour of two temples after entering it into a charter (*śāsanīkṛtya*). It seems that first the king issued a copper-plate charter recording the transfer of the village to the *vaṇik-sthāna* which got another charter issued in favour of the temples in question. What we have probably represents either the second charter or a gist of both the charters. This is the only instance of its kind in the entire range of Somavaṁśin epigraphy.

Contents

All the grants begin with an auspicious formula or *maṅgala* which is very simple. In most cases it consists of the symbol for *siddham* which is followed by the word *svasti*.[556] In four inscriptions we find the *siddham* symbol and the word *svasti* separated from each other by the symbol for *om*[557] and in a single case, Mahakosala Historical Society's plates of Mahābhavagupta IV, by the well-known Śaivite formula *Oṁ namaḥ Śivāya*. In keeping with the ancient practice, the word *svasti* always precedes the reference to the place

555. For some other similar instances, see D.C. Sircar, *IE*, 114-15. A few grants which were probably made by persons whose names are not recorded in connection with the grant are also known. See *ibid.*, 115-18.

556. See nos. IV: I-III, VII, XII, XIV-XIX, XXI and XXVIII. In nos. IV: VIII-X, in addition to *siddham svasti* we have the word *svasty-astu, i.e.*, let there be success, after the mention of the place of issue.

The *siddham* symbol in all our records is basically the same though the exact form differs from record to record, the differences being due to the writers' predilections and, in some cases, a perceptible attempt at ornamentation. The symbol is always open to right.

557. These records are IV: IV,XI, XIII and XX. It is interesting to note that the *om* symbol, which is quite close to its modern form, looks like initial *o* with an *anusvāra*. See no. IV: IV, text-line 1. But in many other cases the *anusvāra*-like mark is absent (nos. IV: XI, XIII, XX and XXIV).

of issue[558] and in a few records, where the mention of the place of issue is separated from the *siddham* symbol by *praśasti* stanzas, the word *svasti* finds place just before the place of issue,[559] and not immediately after siddham or *siddham om* or siddham *oṁ namaḥ Śivāya* as in other cases. Some of the records, it is interesting to note, have an auspicious formula at the end also. Thus, at the end of the Vakratentali plates of Mahābhavagupta I Janamejaya we have the well-known formula *maṅgalaṁ mahāśrīḥ*.[560] The Cuttack plates of Mahāśivagupta I Yayāti have a double *praṇava* or *oṁ* at the end,[561] while the Cuttack grant of Mahābhavagupta II Bhīmaratha contain the auspicious word *śivaṁ* after the specification of the date and before the mention of the engraver.[562] This is quite in conformity with the belief obtaining in those days that works containing *maṅgala* at the beginning, in the middle and at the end get fame.[563]

The *maṅgala* is generally followed by the mention of the place wherefrom the charter in question was issued. The only exceptions to this general rule are the Balijhari and Sankhameri grants of Mahābhavagupta IV Uddyotakesarin[563a] and the Ratnagiri plates of Karṇa which contain a versified account of the dynasty as well as the issuing monarch between the *siddham* symbol and the reference to the issuing place.[564] This place is invariably specified in ablative singular. Some of the issuing places are mentioned by themselves without any other descriptive expression following them.[565] In the absence of any other word indicating a military camp or temporary residence attached to them, these have to be taken as capital cities. This conjecture finds support from the fact that in a number of other cases, expressions connoting such camps or residences are found suffixed to the names of the issuing places. Thus, the first three grants of Mahābhavagupta I Janamejaya are said to have been issued from the victorious camp, in the first case stationed at Suvarṇṇapura[566] and in the other cases at Mūrasīman.[567] The second Kalibhana charter of the same king was also reportedly given from the victorious military camp pitched at Suvarṇṇa-

558. The practice of using the word *svasti* prior to the mention of the place of issue was followed even while writing letters. See my *India as seen in the Kuṭṭanī-mata of Dāmodaragupta*, 163-64. Also see *Lekha-paddhati* (Gaekwad Oriental Series, No. 19), 58-59.
559. In nos. IV: XXII and XXVII eleven and seventeen eulogistic verses respectively intervene between *siddham* and *svasti*.
560. No. IV: I, text-line 39. This formula is noticed in a number of medieval records.
561. No. IV: XIV, text-line 66.
562. No. IV: XVII, text-line 75.
563. *Maṅgal-ādīnī maṅgala-madhyāni maṅgal-āntāni ca śāstrāṇi prathante.*
563*a*. These two items are separated by eleven stanzas. See No. XXII and Supplementary Inscription III.
564. Seventeen verses intervene between these two items. See IV: XXVII.
565. See nos. IV: V, VI, XVI, XVII, XVIII, XX, XXII, XXVII and XXVIII. In no. IV: IV Mūrasīman, the issuing locality, is styled a *pattana-vara*, *i.e.*, 'the best of towns'.
566. It is called a *vijaya-skandhāvāra*. In most cases the word *śrī* or *śrīmat* is prefixed to the expression referring to the 'victorious camp'.
567. In these records we have the expression *vijaya-kaṭaka*. See nos. IV: II and III.

pura,[568] whereas his Gaintala and Chaudwar plates are stated to have been granted from a similar camp situated at Ārāma.[569] Two of the charters of the next monarch, Mahāśivagupta I Yayāti,[570] the only known grant of Mahāśivagupta III Yayāti[571] and the Mahakosala Historical Society's plates of Mahābhavagupta IV Uddyotakesarin[572] are reported to have been given away from the victorious military camps stationed at Vinītapura, *pattana* Suvarṇṇapura and Kisarakellā respectively. Only the Kudopali charter of *Rāṇaka* Puñja is said to have been given from his residence at Vāmaṇḍāpāṭī.[573] With the passage of time this item was elaborated and the beginnings of this elaboration can be traced back to the first Kalibhana grant of the sixth year of the reign of Mahābhavagupta I Janamejaya where we get for the first time a long prose passage eulogising the issuing place in a conventional manner. Similar prose *praśasti* of the issuing place is met with in a few other records of his reign while it is conspiciuous by its absence in others.[574] What is interesting is that the same description is applied to different issuing places which is a clear indication of its conventional character.[575] The only other grant containing a prose passage in praise of the issuing locality is the Jatesinga-Dungari charter of Mahāśivagupta III Yayāti.[575a] Versified description of the place of issue is for the first time met with in the Cuttack plates of Mahāśivagupta I Yayāti. The versified eulogy is found continued not only in some of his other grants[575b] but in the charters of Mahābhavagupta II Bhīmaratha and Mahāśivagupta II Dharmaratha[576] also. The employment of the same stanzas for the description

568. No. IV: XI.
569. Nos. IV: VII and VIII-X.
570. Nos. IV: XII and XIII. In the latter grant there is no expression like *samāvāsita* between the name of the locality and the expression connoting the camp which is simply mentioned as a *kaṭaka.* Vinītapura, where the camp was situated, is erroneously mentioned in ablative singular.
571. No. IV: XXI.
572. No. IV: XXIV. This is the only record which speaks of the camp as *mahāvijaya-kaṭaka, i.e.*, 'great victorious camp'. Again, no honorific like *śrī* or *śrīmat* is used for the locality or the camp.
573. No. IV: XIX. It must have been Puñja's headquarters.
574. It occurs in nos. IV: V, VI and VII while nos. IV : VIII-X and XI do not contain such description.
575. The description of Mūrasīman in nos. IV: IV and V and of Ārāma in no. IV: VI as well as of the military camp at the latter place in no. IV: VII is almost identical.
575a. No. IV: XXI. The eulogy of the camp pitched at Suvarṇṇapura met with in text-lines 1-11 is the longest prose *praśasti* of the issuing place found in the Somavaṁśin records.
575b. Four verses describe Vinītapura in Mahāśivagupta I Yatāti's Cuttack plates. The same four stanzas are repeated in both of his Patna grants in connection with the description of Yayātinagara.
576. Nos. IV: XVIII and XX. Both these records contain four stanzas each eulogising Yayātinagara. These verses are the same as those met with in nos. IV: XIV, XVI and XVII.

of Vinītapura and Yayātinagara makes the conventional character of the eulogy evident.[577] But the eulogy of the issuing locality, whether in prose or in verses, was altogether discontinued after Mahāśivagupta III Yayāti and is conspicuously absent in the records of the members of the dynasty.[578]

The next item is the mention of the donor who is generally referred to as meditating upon the feet of his father both of whom are spoken of with the usual titles which are *Parama-Māheśvara*, *Paramabhaṭṭāraka-Mahārājādhirāja-Parameśvara*, *Soma-kula-tilaka* and *Trikaliṅgādhipati*.[579] In the earlier records this item is quite simple but gets elaborated in subsequent charters and some more space is now devoted to a rather hyperbolic description of the issuer. The first trace of elaboration is noticed in the first Kalibhana plates of Mahābhavagupta I Janamejaya where a *praśasti* stanza eulogising him is added immediately after the prose passage describing Mūrasīman wherefrom the grant was issued.[580] This verse is found repeated at the same place in the Satallamā plates also. A regular full-fledged eulogy in verses is first met in the Orissa State Museum plates of Mahāśiva-

577. The four stanzas of the Cuttack grant of Mahāśivagupta I Yayāti describing Vinītapura are repeated in subsequent records for the description of Yayātinagara.

578. No such *praśasti* is found in the records of Mahābhavagupta IV Uddyotakesarin (nos. IV: XXII, XXIV and Supplementary Inscription III) and Karṇa (no. IV: XXVII).

579. All the rulers are mentioned with the word *mahat* prefixed to their names. The only exception is Mahābhavagupta I Janamejaya's father, who is called simply Śivagupta in all the records except only the Satallamā plates of his son where the word *mahat* is added to his name also (no. IV: V, text lines 6-7). Again, in the first Kalibhana grant of his son, Śivagupta is styled simply *Mahārāja* (no. IV: IV, text-line 10). He as well as all of his descendants are referred to with the imperial title *Paramabhaṭṭāraka-Mahārājādhirāja-Parameśvara* in all the other records. Śivagupta is styled *Parama-Māheśvara* only in the Sonepur and second Kalibhana grants of his son. The styles *Soma-kula-tilaka* and *Trikaliṅgādhipati* are never applied to him. All other rulers are given full titles, both political and sectarian, and generally the father and the son are endowed with the same titles. There are, however, a few exceptions. In the first Patna and Nibinna plates (nos. IV: XIII and XV) of Mahāśivagupta I Yayāti his father is denied the titles *Soma-kula-tilaka* and *Trikaliṅgādhipati*. The denial may, however, be purely accidental. The draft of the Jatesinga-Dungari grant of Mahāśivagupta III Yayāti (no. IV: XXI) is quite different from that of the other records and the usual manner of mentioning the reigning monarch and his predecessor is not followed. The Mahakosala Historical Society's plates of Mahābhavagupta IV Uddyotakesarin (no. IV: XXIV) style the donor *mātā-pitṛ-pād-ānudhyāta* but omit any specific reference to his father or predecessor. The formal portion of the Ratnagiri plates of Karṇa (no. IV: XXVII) also omits reference to the benefactor's father.

580. No. IV: IV, text-lines 7-10. This stanza is, however, found earlier in the first Patna plates of this king, but there it occurs at the end of the record and not at the place where *praśasti* normally appears. The Gaintala plates contain a long prose passage extolling the donor after imprecatory stanzas and before the date. Similar laudatory prose passages are met with in the three Chaudwar and the second Kalibhana charters (nos. IV: VIII, text-lines 34-37; XI, text-lines 37-40). The Gaintala, Chaudwar and the second Kalibhana grants also contain two stanzas each in praise of the benefactor the first after the date and the rest before it.

gupta I Yayâti which contains four stanzas in praise of the issuer and his father. Thereafter versified *praśasti* is found in a number of grants of the last named monarch as well as his descendants and the number of such stanzas naturally grows with the passage of time with a view to accommodate the increasing number of preceding generations.[581] The largest number of eulogistic stanzas, seventeen, is found in the Ratnagiri plates of Karṇa. Mention must in this connection be made of the Jatesinga-Dungari charter of Mahāśivagupta III Yayāti which is the only copper-plate grant to contain a long prose *praśasti* of the issuer. It is noteworthy that the traditional prose formula mentioning the donor and his father together with the titles borne by them is found repeated even in those records where they have already been referred to in the versified *praśasti* even at the risk of redundance immediately after the *praśasti.* This is indeed an instance of the faithful observance of conservativism in regard to a set epigraphical formula. The eulogistic verses as well as prose passages sometimes supply valuable useful information.

Next follows the royal order about the grant. The monarch is invariably described as *kuśalin*, *i.e.*, 'in good health', thereby signifying that he made the grant in question in a sound mental and physical state with a full sense of responsibility and that the deed recording the gift must be regarded as valid.[582] Then there is mention of the gift village or villages and the administrative division wherein it/they was/were situated. Next the king is often stated to have honoured the Brāhmaṇas,[583] before issuing the order concerning the grant. This is followed by a list of personages to whom the royal order was addressed. This list included the agriculturist house-

581. The versified *praśasti* is absent only in the first Patna and Nibinna grants of Mahāśivagupta I Yayāti (nos. IV: XIII and XV), the Kudopali plates of *Rāṇaka* Puñja (no. IV: XIX), the Jatesinga-Dungari plates of Mahāśivagupta III Yayāti (no. IV: XXI) and the Mahakosala Historical Society's Charter of Mahābhavagupta IV Uddyotakesarin (no. IV: XXIV). The Cuttack and the second and third Patna grants of Mahāśivagupta I Yayāti contain three, three and four *praśasti* stanzas respectively (nos. IV: XIV, XVI and XVII) whereas we have five, six and eleven such verses in the Cuttack plates of Mahābhavagupta II Bhīmaratha, Mahulpada plates of Mahāśivagupta II Dharmartha and the Balijhari and Sankhameri charters of Mahābhavagupta IV Uddyotakesarin (nos. IV: XVIII, XX and XXII and Supplementary Inscription III) respectively.

582. This expression is met with in a large majority of copper-plate grants hailing from different parts of the Indian sub-continent and was a legal pre-requisite of making a grant.

583. In most records we have simply an allusion to honoring the Brāhmaṇas, but in some grants beginning with Mahāśivagupta I Yayāti's Orissa State Museum plates (no. IV: XII) we find the adjective *tad* = *viṣayīya* prefixed to the Brāhmaṇas. Actually, this was an error, for it was physically impossible to honour all the Brāhmaṇas of a district while making a land-grant and the adjective was really meant to qualify the officers mentioned in connection with the grant as it really does in a few of the grants (see nos. IV: I-XI, XIII, XV-XVI and XXI).

holders inhabiting the donated village/s[584] and a host of royal officers and other dignitaries including, in many cases, members of the royal family such as the queens and princes and nobles and royal favourites.[585] In the earlier records the number of the addressees of the royal command is quite small including only such officers as were actually connected with the administration of the village and were thus directly concerned with the grant. With the passage of time, however, this list, like other items, also underwent considerable elaboration and more and more personages found place in it. To illustrate the point, while the Vakratentali charter of Mahābhavagupta I Janamejaya mentions only nine addressees, the Sonepur and Gaintala plates of the same chief name eleven addressees, the Chaudwar plates thirteen and the Cuttack and Nibinna plates of Mahāśivagupta I Yayāti fourteen each. The verbal form used to express the royal act of ordering is invariably *samājñāpayati*, 'commands'. In the Ratnagiri plates of Karṇa alone we find the expressions *anunayati*, 'requests', and *bodhayati*, 'informs', in addition to the usual *samājñāpayati*. What has been stated about the addressees is true of the privileges and exemptions transferred to the donee/donees along with the land grant also. Their number is as meagre as seven in the two Patna grants and eight in the Vakratentali and first Kalibhana plates of Mahābhavagupta I Janamejaya but grows to ten in the two Patna plates of Mahāśivagupta I Yayāti, fifteen in the Mahulpada plates of Mahāśivagupta II Dharmaratha, twenty in the Balijhari charter of Mahābhavagupta IV Uddyotakesarin and as high as twenty-five in the Ratnagiri grant of Karṇa. The Kelga charter of Someśvara approaches the last mentioned record very close inasmuch as it specifies twenty-four such privileges. The gradual increase in the number of these privileges is an index of the growth of the obligations of the cultivators towards the state. This item is of great importance for the study of the revenue system in medieval Orissa under the Somavaṁśins.

The mention of the beneficiary/beneficiaries of the grant, which constitutes the next item, remained a rather simple affair from beginning to end and escaped the process of elaboration to which most other items were subjected. The change that it underwent was of a minor nature. The grantee is generally mentioned together with his *gotra*, *pravara*, the place from which he hailed originally (*vinirgata*) and the place of his residence at the time when the grant was made (*vāstavya*). In a few cases the *anupravaras*

584. They are referred to only in nos. IV: I-V, XXI and XXIV. In other records they are omitted, probably inadvertently.

585. *Avarodha-janas*, 'inmates of the royal harem' are mentioned in all the records. But a few grants refer to '*rājñī*', 'queens', in addition to the 'inmates of the royal harem' (see nos. IV: XV, XVI, XVIII, XX and XXVII). The difference, if any intended, between them is not clear. There are noticed some minor variations in the list of the addressees which may be due to the inadvertence on the part of the officers responsible for drafting official charters and not much significance need be attached to them.

and the *śākhā* of the Veda, to which the donee belonged, are also found specified.[586] In the earlier records only the father of the donee is named but in later charters his grand-father is also often mentioned. The second generation preceding the grantee is first mentioned in the second Kalibhana grant which is the last record of the reign of Mahābhavagupta I Janamejaya and thereafter it became a common practice.[587]

The grant is invariably reported to have been made with the pouring of water, which signified the transfer of the gift village, to be enjoyed as long as the moon, stars, sun and the earth endure for the augmentation of the religious merit and the fame of the grantor's parents as well as of the donor himself and it was solemnised by issuing a deed engraved on copper-plates (*tāmra-śāsana*) which transformed the granted village into a revenue-free holding. The inhabitants of the donated village are exhorted to offer the donee all the dues which they had been offering to the donor so far. Next we come across exhortation to the future rulers to maintain the grant as if it were their own grant and in support of this entreaty imprecatory and benedictory stanzas lauding the making and upholding the land-grant and condemning its violation are cited as from Dharmaśāstra. The number of these verses ranges between seven and fourteen, the former number being met with in the Kelga plates of Someśvara and the latter in the Gaintala plates of Mahābhavagupta I Janamejaya and the third Patna grant of Mahāśivagupta I Yayāti.[588] These stanzas are of a customary nature and many of them are found to be common to all the records. Several of these verses are met with in the copper-plate charters of other dynasties also.

The imprecation is generally followed by the specification of the date of the record which is of great value for ascertaining the length of the reigns of individual rulers. As stated above, the dates are given invariably with reference to the reigns of the monarchs in question. In this connection the king is again mentioned with sovereign titles which are used for him earlier while referring to the donor. It is interesting to note in this connection that whereas earlier the king is generally mentioned by the name beginning with *mahat* and ending in *gupta*, the date portion refers to him by his other name like Janamejaya, Yayāti, Bhīmaratha, Uddyotakesarin and Karṇa. The only exceptions are the Chaudwar plates where the king is named as Mahābhavagupta and the Jatesinga-Dungari grant which mentions the donor by both the names together as śrī-Mahāśivagupta-śrī-

586. For the specification of the *anupravaras* see nos. IV: II and VII and for that of the Vedic *śākhā* see nos. IV: I-V, VII-XI, XIII, XIV, XVI, XVII, XVIII, XXI, XXII and XXIV.

587. Only in nos. IV: XIX and XXIV the donee's grandfather is not named. In the latter record the donee's name has been left out by inadvertence.

588. Thus, we find eight verses in no. IV: XXIV, eleven in nos. IV: II, V, XIV, XXI and XXII, and twelve in nos. IV: I, VI, XVIII and XXVII, and thirteen in nos. IV: III, IV, VIII-X, XI, XII, XIII, XV, XVI and XX.

Yayāti. The Mahulpada plates of Mahāśivagupta II Dharmaratha and the Mahakosala Historical Society's plates of Mahābhavagupta IV Uddyotakesarin do not name the king in connection with the date. Some of the records give a full compliment of titles to the monarch whereas others omit the twin titles *Soma-kula-tilaka* and *Trikaliṅgādhipati* while specifying the date.[589] But these differences, minor as they are, do not appear to be of much significance and are apparently due to inadvertence on the part of the writers.[590]

Next we come across reference to the writer who was in a majority of cases the *Kāyastha* or clerk attached to the office of the *Mahāsandhivigrahin* (or *-hika*) or *Sandhivigrahin* both of whom are clearly named. Barring the solitary exception of the Sonepur grant of the seventeenth year of the reign of Mahābhavagupta I Janamejaya all the charters of his reign name only these two officers in connection with the writing of the official records.[591] The *Mahākṣapaṭalin*[591a] figures as the writer for the first time in the aforesaid Sonepur grant and is found mentioned in this capacity in several records of Mahāśivagupta I Yayāti and his successors.[592] The Orissa State Museum plates of his reign, which constitute his first record, are reported to have been written with his permission,[592a] but all other records mentioning him are stated to have been written by him. It is interesting to note that whether a charter was written by the *Kāyastha* or the *Mahākṣapaṭalika* (or *-laka*), the *Mahāsandhivigrahin* or *Sandhivigrahin* is invariably referred to and it was evidently under his instructions and supervison that copper-plate charters were written. In a couple of charters the *Sandhivigrahin* himself figures as a writer.[593] The only record wherein this item is omitted is the Cuttack grant of Mahāśivagupta I Yayāti. Strangely enough, it mentions the *Sandhivigrahin* by name, but it stops at that and does not

589. These two epithets are first mentioned in connection with the date in Mahābhavagupta I Janamejaya's Sonepur grant of the seventeenth year of his reign and are thereafter met with in nos. IV: VIII-XVIII while they are conspicuously absent in others.

590. For other details about the dates see *supra*, pp. 69-71.

591. The second Kalibhana plates are said to have been written with the permission of the *Mahāsāndhivigrahika*, though the writer has been left unnamed. But it may be presumed that he was also a *Kāyastha*.

591a. Other forms of the designation met with in our records are *Mahākṣapaṭalaka* (no. IV: XV), *Mahākṣapaṭalika* (no. IV: XII) and *Mahākṣapaṭalādhyakṣa* (nos. IV: XX and XXII). For the occurrence of the form *Mahākṣapaṭalin*, see nos. IV: VI and XXVII

592. See nos. IV: XII, XV, XX, XXII and XXVII.

592a. This charter may have been written by a subordinate of the *Mahākṣapaṭalika*. Alternatively, it is possible that the *Mahākṣapaṭalika* himself wrote the record and that the wording alone is defective.

593. These records are the Jatesinga-Dungari plates of Mahāśivagupta III Yayāti and the Mahakosala Historical Society's plates of Mahābhavagupta IV Uddyotakesarin (nos. IV: XXI and XXIV). The act of writing is not mentioned in the Cuttack plates of Mahāśivagupta I Yayāti.

refer to the act of writing, may be due to inadvertence. It is not impossible that the record was also actually written by the *Sandhivigrahin* himself though a clear statement to that effect is missing. Further, we often find one or more verses in praise of the *Mahāsāndhivigrahika* and the *Mahākṣa-paṭalika.*

The concluding item concerns the specification of the engraver who is named in a majority of records.[594] In some of the records the scribe's father is also named,[595] but in most cases he is mentioned alone. He is sometimes referred to as an artisan (*vijñānin*) or goldsmith (*suvarṇakāra*).[596] Two of the grants, one belonging to Mahābavagupta IV Uddyotakesarin's reign and the other to that of Karṇa are said to have been inscribed by the artisan belonging to the goldsmiths's lane [*suva*(or *sva*) *rṇa-vīthi*].[597] In a solitary record the scribe's father is said to have been a trader (*vaṇik*) and it is not improbable that his son also adopted the same occupation.[598]

The order in which the contents of copper-plate charters have been adumbrated in the foregoing paragraphs is generally adhered to in a vast majority of cases. But we notice some slight alterations in this order in a few records. As stated above, the specification of the writer normally follows the date. But this order is found reversed in a few cases.[599] Secondly, while most of the records generally conclude with the mention of the scribe, some have an auspicious formula or *maṅgala* at the end.[600] Then, the Kudopali plates of *Rāṇaka* Puñja, the drafting of which is somewhat different from that of the remaining records, close with the statement that whatever has been written on this copper-plate charter (*tāmra*) is authentic (*pramāṇa*). Such a statement, which is rather uncalled for, is not found in any other record included in this volume. The same is true of the concluding stanza of the Mahakosala Historical Society's plates of Mahābhava-gupta IV entreating the learned to adopt an attitude of forgiveness towards whatever faults might have crept in the charter. Such statements are sometimes met with in manuscripts but are rather rare in epigraphic records.

B. *Stone Inscriptions*

We have in all four lithic records incised during the rule of the Soma-vaṁśins. As many as three of them belong to the reign of Mahābhavagupta IV Uddyotakesarin and only one to that of Karṇa. Of the three epigraphs

594. This item is conspicuously absent only in nos. IV: II-III, XXI and XXIV.
595. See, for instance, nos. IV: I, IV-XI and XIII.
596. For the mention of *vijñānin* see nos. IV: XIII, XVI-XX, XXII, XXVII, and Supplementary Inscription III and for that of *suvarṇakāra* see no. IV: IV.
597. Nos. IV: XXII and XXVII.
598. See no. IV: VII. The same must evidently be true of no. IV: VI which was inscribed by the same person whose father is, however, named without the epithet *vaṇik.*
599. *Vide* nos. IV: XVII, XVIII and XX.
600. Nos. IV: I and XIV. For the treatment of the *maṅgala* at the end see *supra.*

of the time of Uddyotakesarin, two are found engraved in the Lalāṭendukesarī and Navamuni caves on the Khandagiri hill near Bhubaneswar.[601] The third inscription is incised on a slab originally attached to the Brahmeśvara temple at Bhubaneswar.[602] The epigraph of the reign of Karṇa is engraved on the back of a stone image of Sūrya reported to have been found at the village of Gandhibedha in the Balasore District and presently deposited in the Orissa State Museum, Bhubaneswar.[603]

Palaeographically these records bear a close resemblance to the copper-plate charters of the dynasty and call for no special remarks. The only note-worthy point is that directly emanating from a member of the royal family and belonging to the *praśasti* category, the Brahmeśvara temple inscription is engraved with much greater care than the other three records. The language of all the four records is Sanskrit, but that of the Lalāṭendukesarin cave inscription is highly corrupt. This record was evidently drafted by a semi-educated person. Because of indifferent drafting this short inscription comprising just five lines offers some **orthographical features** which throw welcome light on popular pronunciations as against the grammatically correct forms met with in carefully drafted records. Interesting from this point of view are the rather common use of *j* instead of *y* in Jasanandika (text-line 4) and of *kha* for *kṣa* as in *karma-khayaḥ* (text-line 5). The elision of one of the two identical consonants not separated from each other by a vowel as in Udyotakesari (text-line 1) and udyotita (text-line 3) is also interesting and, as shown above, is noticed in copper-plate grants also *Tasmīna* for *tasmin* and *thāne* for *sthāne* (text-line 2) and the form Pārasyanātha instead of Pārśvanātha (text-line 5) are obviously drawn from popular pronunciation. If R.D. Benerji is right in taking *isaṇa* (text-line 3) in the sense of 'temple', the usage is of some interest lexicographically.

The Lalāṭendukesarin and Navamuni cave inscriptions of the reign of Uddyotakesarin and the Gandhibeḍha image inscription of Karṇa's time are in prose, while the Brahmeśvara temple inscription of the former's reign is composed in verses in a variety of metres except only the auspicious formula (*siddham om*) at the beginning and a prose passage at the end specifying the date and the scribe. The last-mentioned record is a beautiful composition, is styled a *praśasti* (eulogy) and was composed by *Bhaṭṭa* Puruṣottama who proudly calls himself *kavi-vara*, 'an excellent poet'.

All the four inscriptions are private records and aim at recording pious deeds of private persons. The first two inscriptions are connected with Jainism and record pious acts like the renovation of some edifices and install-

601. Nos. IV: XXIII and XXV.

602. No. IV: XXVI. The present whereabouts of this record are not known.

603. No. IV: Appendix III. The inscription is fragmentary and only the initial portion mentioning Karṇa is now extant.

ation of the Tīrthaṅkara images. The Gandhibeḍha inscription of Karṇa's reign refers to the installation of the Sūrya image on the back of which it is incised. The Brahmeśvara temple inscription is also a private record though the person whose pious acts it purports to record happens to be an important member of the royal family, *viz.*, Kolāvatī, the mother of the reigning king. It speaks of the construction of the Brahmeśvara temple and dedication of a few dancing girls (*dārikā*) to it by the royal mother.

These records fall into two classes: (i) ordinary and (ii) *praśasti*. The Brahmeśvara temple inscription belongs to the latter category and the rest to the former. All the three records of the first category open with the auspicious symbol for *siddham* which is followed by the specification of the date which is invariably with reference to the then king's reign. But while the Lalāṭendukesarin and Navamuni cave inscriptions of Uddyotakesarin's time refer to the king without any regal title, the Gandhibeḍha inscription of Karṇa's reign mentions the monarch with full imperial titles as in the copper-plate charters. The first two epigraphs specify only the regnal year, other details like the month, fortnight and *tithi* being omitted. The same may have been the case with the Gandhibeḍha inscription though its present damaged condition has deprived us of its exact date and other details. Next we find mention of the pious deed with which the records conclude.

The Brahmeśvara temple, inscription which alone represents the *praśasti* type of records, commences with the auspicious formula *siddham om*. It is followed by a long versified eulogy tracing the history of the ruling family from the very beginning to the time of the reigning monarch. Next we get a brief description of the donatrix and a rather ornate account of the pious act performed by her. Then follows an exaggerated though brief reference to the poet responsible for composing the *praśasti* and a prayer for the long life of the *praśasti*. The specification of the date, which follows, is exactly like the one we are accustomed to in copper-plate inscriptions. The closing item relates to the mention of the engraver.

Had we had a larger number of stone inscriptions of the time of the family in question, we would, it may be reasonably assumed, have had a greater variety as in the case of the Pāṇḍuvaṁśins of South Kosala. We may perhaps hope to get some more lithic records in the years to come. But looking to the comparative figures of the discoveries of copper-plates charters and stone inscriptions during the last over sixty-five years, it is evident that the number of stone inscriptions of the Somavaṁśins is not likely to be impressive unless some miraculous discovery upsets this calculation.

V. SOME OBSERVATIONS ON COPPER-PLATE CHARTERS

A glance at the copper-plate grants included in this volume will reveal similarities in some important matters. Thus, all the records, without a single exception, are incised on a set of three rectangular plates of which the outer side of the first is invariably blank while the second side of the last plate is also either left uninscribed or was intended to be so left though because of the scribe's inability to accommodate the matter on the sides of the plates originally desired to be inscribed the writing had often to be continued on this side. The plates of all the records are held in position by a copperring passing through a hole bored about the middle of the margin on the left; only in a few exceptional cases the hole is cut on the right. There is considerable similarity in respect of seals as well inasmuch as all of them bear a device and legend, versified in the case of the Śarabhapura kings and the Pāṇḍuvaṁśins of Kosala and in prose in other cases, and the name of the ruling chief found on the seal is somewhat different from that in the body of the record itself. All these inscriptions are composed in Sanskrit with some local dialectal or Prakritic elements. We notice a general similarity in drafting and a number of expressions are common to the records of the three dynasties of Kosala and the adjoining area of Orissa. The dates are invariably indicated with reference to the regnal years of the issuing monarch without the use of any known reckoning and the months mentioned are always *pūrṇimānta*. Even the wording of the date portion bears great similarity. Many of the imprecatory and benedictory stanzas are also common. Inscriptions of the two earlier dynasties of Kosala, Śarabhapurīyas and Pāṇḍuvaṁśins, are in an identical script, *viz.*, box-head variety of the Central Indian alphabet, which becoming unintelligible and going out of vogue with the passage of time, had to be abandoned by the Somavaṁśins in favour of the northern class of alphabets which were in common use. These important similarities bind the copper-plate charters of the three dynasties of Kosala into a coherent unit and provide the justification for their inclusion in a single volume. There is noticed considerable elaboration in regard to many items with the passage of time, but the fundamental unity remains undisturbed.

The same cannot be said about the three grants of the Mekalā Pāṇḍuvaṁśins which form a distinct unity and differ from the other records in many respects but are included in this volume as they have an important bearing on the history of the period and the area in question.

Interesting light on the nature of copper-plate charters is thrown by a few Dharmaśāstra texts which give detailed instructions about the execution of royal charters recording land-grants. Yājñavalkya, for instance, advises the king as follows: 'having made a land-grant or bestowed a *nibandha*,[604] the

604. The word *nibandha* is taken by later scholiasts in the sense of a fixed or stipulated contribution to the Brāhmaṇas or religious establishments. As its illustrations are cited 'so many *rūpakas* (silver coins) on a load of commodities', 'so many leaves on a bundle of leaves' (Vijñāneśvara), 'owners of fields in this village should give so much per field per *mensem* or *per annum*' (Aparārka), etc.

king should cause a document (*lekhya*) to be prepared for the information of the good future kings. He should next issue a permanent charter (*śāsana*) written on (a piece of) cloth or on copper-plate, marked at the top (*i.e.*, outside)[605] with his own seal, mentioning his ancestors as well as himself, the amount or extent of the gift and boundaries of the gift land[606] and date[607] and bearing his own signature.'[608] Viṣṇu gives similar instructions.[609] Vasiṣṭha as cited in the *Vyavahāra-prakāśa* gives a little more detailed account. Important points of this description are that after giving land to the Brāhmaṇas the king should execute a charter which must specify the year, month, fortnight and day, the monarch's name, the grantee together with his ancestors, *gotra* and the Veda studied by him, the extent of the gift land and the king's signature. These details should be written by the donor himself. The officer in charge of peace and war (*sandhi-vigraha-kārin*) should write the royal charter when ordered by the king himself and mention his own name. And lastly, the charter should be marked with the royal seal.[610] Bṛhaspati defines *dāna-patra* as a charter on plates (*patra*)

605. *Upari*, in the original, has been taken in this sense in Vijñāneśvara's Mitākṣarā commentary. But it may also be taken to mean 'on top' as in the case of many charters the seal is really found fixed in the upper portion of the first plate or the only plate in case of single-plate charters.

606. Viśvarūpa, the earliest known commentator of the *Yājñavalkya-smṛti*, understands *dāna-cched-opavarṇanam*, the expression in the original, as referring to the result of making and violating a gift and illustrates it by quoting a well-known imprecatory stanza, *i.e.*, *ṣaṣṭiṁ varṣa-sahasrāṇi*, etc. Aparārka does likewise. But according to Vijñāneśvara, *dāna-ccheda* denotes the boundaries and extent of the gift-land (*dīyate iti dānaṁ kṣetr-ādi tasya chedaḥ chidyate anen-eti chedaḥ nady-āvāṭau nivartanaṁ tat—parimāṇaṁ ca*).

607. Vijñāneśvara rightly points out that the date may be indicated in two ways, *i.e.*, the number of years elapsed since the time of the Śaka king or the benefactor's regnal years: *kālena ca dvi-vidhena—Śaka-nṛp-ātītarūpeṇa saṁvatsara-rūpeṇa ca kālena.* The specification of the Śaka era is only illustrative, the intention being to refer to well-known reckonings. The Śaka era is spoken of because it was very popular in the Deccan where the commentator flourished.

608. *Yājñavalkya- smṛti*, I, 318-20:

दत्त्वा भूमिं निबन्धं वा कृत्वा लेख्यं तु कारयेत् ।
आगामि भद्रनृपतिपरिज्ञानाय पार्थिवः ॥
पटे वा ताम्रपट्टे वा स्वमुद्रोपरिचिह्नितम् ।
अभिलेख्यात्मनो वंश्यानात्मानं च महीपतिः ॥
प्रतिग्रहपरीमाणं दानच्छेदोपवर्णनम् ।
स्वहस्तकालसंपन्नं शासनं कारयेत्स्थिरम् ॥

609. Lakshmanasastri Joshi (Ed.), *Dharmakośa*, Vyavahārakāṇḍa, I, Part I, 349.

610. *Dharmakośa*, Vyavahārakāṇḍa, I, Part I:

दत्त्वा भोगान् द्विजातिभ्यो रत्नानि विविधानि च ।
राजा भूमिं च कुर्वीत तेषां तस्याश्च शासनम् ॥

recording a permanent irrevocable and inviolable land-grant.[611] He further states that after granting land, etc., the king should have a charter written on copper-plates or cloth. It should specify the place of issue, lineage (of the donor and the beneficiary), etc. It should state that the grant is made in favour of such and such a person for the merit of the parents as well as his own self, it is inviolable, irrevocable, free from all taxes, intended to last as long as the moon and the sun endure and to be inherited in the family through sons and grandsons, the grantor and the maintainer get heaven while one who violates it goes to hell for sixty thousand years.[612] It must bear the seal, mention date (lit., year, month, etc.), bear signatures of the benefactor (*dhan-ādhyakṣ-ākṣara*) and be written by the *Sandhivigrahin* and the writer.[613] A few stanzas quoted in the name of Vyāsa in the *Kṛtya-kalpataru*

क्रियाकारकसंबन्धं समासार्थक्रियान्वितम् ।
समामासतदर्धाहर्नृपनामोपलक्षितम् ॥
प्रतिग्रहीतृजात्यादिसगोत्रब्रह्मचारिकम् ।
संनिवेशप्रमाणं च स्वहस्तं तु लिखेत्स्वयम् ॥
संधिविग्रहकारी च भवेद्यस्तत्र लेखकः ।
स्वयं राजा समादिष्टः स लिखेद्राजशासनम् ॥
स्वनाम विलिखेत् पश्चान्मुद्रितं राजमुद्रया ।
ग्रामक्षेत्रगृहादीनामीदृक्स्याद्राजशासनम् ॥

611. भूमिं दत्त्वा तु यत्पत्रं कुर्याच्चन्द्रार्ककालिकम् ।
अनाच्छेद्यमनाहार्यं दानलेख्यं तु तद्विदुः ॥

Cited in *Dharmakośa*, I, Part I, 364.

612. This is actually the gist of a commonly quoted imprecatory stanza given in note 606 above. Hereafter Bṛhaspati cites another imprecatory verse, *i.e.*, *Sva-dattāṁ para-dattāṁ vā*, etc., by way of illustration.

613. दत्त्वा भूम्यादिकं राजा ताम्रपत्रे पटेऽथवा ।
शासनं कारयेत् धर्म्यं स्थानवंशादिसंयुतम् ।
मातापित्रोरात्मनश्च पुण्यायाऽमुकसूनवे ।
दत्तं मयाऽमुकायाद्य दानं सब्रह्मचारिणे ॥
अनाछेद्यमनाहार्यं सर्वभागविवर्जितम् ।
चन्द्रार्कसमकालीनं पुत्रपौत्रान्वयानुगम् ॥
दातुः पालयितुः स्वर्ग्यं हर्तुर्नरकमेव च ।
षष्टिवर्षसहस्राणि दानच्छेदफलं लिखेत् ॥
स्वदत्तां परदत्तां वा हरेद्यस्तु वसुंधराम् ।
षष्टिवर्षसहस्राणि विष्टायां जायते कृमिः ॥
समुद्रं वर्षमासादिधनाध्यक्षाक्षरान्वितम् ।
ज्ञातं मयेति लिखितं संधिविग्रहलेखकैः ।
एवंविधं राजकृतं शासनं समुदाहृतम् ॥

Quoted in *Dharmakośa*, I, Part I, 364-65.

enjoin that commanded by the king himself, the writer (*i.e.*, clerk) attached to the *Sandhivigrahin* should write the royal charter on a plate of copper or cloth. It (the charter) should mention the place (*of issue*), genealogy, the country (*i.e.*, administrative division concerned), the village (*to be donated*), assembled Brāhmaṇas and other respectable officers and should be addressed to the agriculturist householders and others down to the Chāṇḍālas. It should state that it is given for the merit of the donor's parents as well as the donor himself, refer to the beneficiary as well as his father together with the former's Veda and state that the grant is as durable as the moon and the sun and to pass in the donee's family through his sons and grandsons, that it is inviolable and irrevocable and exempted from all dues, that the heaven is in store for the grantor and the upholder of the grant and hell for its violator. It should be written in clear hand, should specify the year, month and its half (fortnight) and day and should be endowed with the royal seal.[614]

It will follow from the foregoing extracts that the normal contents of copper-plate charters were expected to include a reference to the place wherefrom it was given, the donor and his family, the administrative division and the village/villages concerned, royal order concerning the grant and its purpose, the extent and boundaries of the gift land, the donee together with his *gotra* and Veda, exemptions conferred on the donee, expression of the desire for the permanence of the grant, exhortation to the

614. राज्ञा तु स्वयमादिष्टः संधिविग्रहलेखकः ।
ताम्रपट्टे पटे वाऽपि विलिखेद्राजशासनम् ॥
क्रियाकारकसंबन्धं समासार्थक्रियान्वितम् ।
संनिवेशं प्रमाणं च स्वहस्तं च लिखेत्स्वयम् ।
मतं मेऽमुकपुत्रस्य अमुकस्य महीपतेः ॥
समासासतदर्धाहर्नृपनामोपलक्षितम् ।
प्रतिग्रहीतृजात्यादिसगोत्रब्रह्मचारिकम् ॥
स्थानं वंशानुपूर्व्वं च देशं ग्राममुपागतम् ।
ब्राह्मणांस्तु तथा चान्यान्मान्यानधिकृतान् लिखेत् ॥
कुटुम्बिनोऽथ कायस्थदूतवैद्यमहत्तरान् ।
म्लेच्छचण्डालपर्यन्तान् सर्वान् संबोधयन्निति ।
मातापित्रोरात्मनश्च पुण्यायामुकसूनवे ।
तत्तं मयाऽमुकायाथ दानं सब्रह्मचारिणे ॥
षष्टिवर्षसहस्राणि दानच्छेदफलं तथा ।
आगामिनृपसामन्तबोधनार्थं नृपोलिखेत् ॥
सामान्योऽयं धर्मसेतुर्नृपाणां काले काले पालनीयो भवद्भिः ।
सर्वानेतान् भाविनः पार्थिवेन्द्रान भूयो भूयो याचते रामभद्रः ॥

Quoted in *Dharmakośa*, I, Part I, 375-76.

future monarchs to maintain the grant, imprecatory and benedictory stanzas and the date. It was to be written by an official writer, preferably the *Sandhivigrahin* or the writer attached to him, and marked by the royal seal. The object of the preparation of the charter was to inform the future rulers who were expected to maintain the grant and copper-plate charters were accepted as legal documents in courts of judicature.

A glance at the copper-plate inscriptions incorporated in the present volume would show that the instructions given in the Dharmaśāstra texts about the preparation of royal charters concerning land-grants are generally followed in them. Earlier records like those of the Śarabhapurīyas and Pāṇḍuvaṁśins are in consonance with the simpler instructions found in the works of earlier authorities like Yājñavalkya and Viṣṇu while the more elaborate instructions given by Vasiṣṭha, Bṛhaspati and Vyāsa, whose works belong to a comparatively much later date,[615] are found reverberated in the Somavaṁśin grants. As we have shown above, practically all the items of the contents of copper-plate charters went through the process of elaboration with the passage of time and this elaboration is reflected in the later Dharmaśāstra texts. It is not unlikely that the Dharmaśastra writers really drew upon actual specimens of copper-plate charters of their own times rather than *vice versa*.[616] In fact, a comparative study of copper-plate inscriptions and relevant portions of the Dharmaśāstra works is likely to prove of great value for determining the time and locale of the composition of the latter.

II

POLITICAL HISTORY

Having dwelt upon the inscriptions included in the present volume, we may now advert, briefly of course, to the history of the dynasties represented by them. We know very little about the history of South Kosala prior to the rise of the Śarabhapurīyas about the close of the fifth century A.D. The available evidence seems to indicate that it formed part of the Maurya and Sātavāhana empires.[617] For over a century after the fall of the Sātavāhanas we know practically nothing about the history of this area. When the curtain rises about the middle of the fourth century A.D. we find that the area was under a certain Mahendra who, according to the famous Allahabad pillar inscription,[617a] was first defeated and then re-instated in

615. For the dates of these works, see P.V. Kane, *HDS*, i, 168ff.
616. The instructions of Vyāsa, for instance, appear to be based on the early medieval copper-plate inscriptions of eastern India, more specially of Bengal. A study of Dharmaśāstra texts on these lines is bound to be very interesting and instructive.
617. Whether the Śuṅgas and the Kāṇvāyanas had anything to do with this region cannot be ascertained in the present state of insufficient information.
617*a*. Fleet, CII, iii, 7, text-line 19.

the rule of Kosala by the Gupta emperor Samudragupta. Unfortunately nothing is known about the family to which Mahendra belonged and what happened to his territorial possessions after him. The conjectures that he hailed from the Śarabhapurīya[618] or Nala[619] dynasty cannot be taken seriously in the absence of the evidence to bear them out. We are again in total oblivion till about the end of the fifth century A.D. Even though the kingdom of Kosala is reported to have been returned to its ruler Mahendra by Samudragupta, it is not impossible that after the termination of his rule, it was annexed and brought under their direct rule by the Imperial Guptas. In any case, we have enough evidence of the growing Gupta influence which is symbolised by the use of the Gupta era[620] and the coins of Mahendrāditya and Kramāditya.[620a] During this period the area also appears to have been raided by the Vākāṭaka king Narendrasena whose commands, it is boastfully claimed, were obeyed by the lords of Kosalā, Mekalā and Malava.[621] But we tread surer grounds with the rise of the Śarabhapurīyas about the close of the fifth or early in the sixth century A.D.

1. ŚARABHAPURĪYAS

The members of this dynasty are styled 'Kings of Śarabhapura' or 'Śarabhapurīyas' as a vast majority of the records of this family was issued from the town known as Śarabhapura.[622] And this nomenclature has got currency in the absence of any information on this point in their numerous records which describe the issuing monarch without naming the family to which he belonged. It has recently been suggested on the basis of the Malhar plates of Vyâghrarāja[623] that the dynasty was known as Amarārya-kula[624] which is the same as the Amaraja-kula from which Lokaprakāśā,

618. K.D. Bajpai and S.K. Pandey (*Malhar* 1975-77, 7 and 31) regard him as the younger brother of the Śarabhapurīya chief Narendra known from the Kurud (no. I:II) and Rawan (no. I:III) plates for which there is absolutely no evidence. The *Kausalaka* Mahendra referred to in the Allahabad pillar inscription of Samudragupta may be reasonably identified with the *Māhārāja* Mahendra whose baked clay seal bearing an inscription (*Mahārāja-Mahendrasya*) in early Gupta Brāhmī characters has been found from the Gupta level in the excavations at Mallar (*ibid.*, 7, 31 and 35).
619. P.L. Mishra, 'A New Light on the Nalas of Chattisgarh', *IHQ*, xxxvi, 247-59.
620. See the Arang plates of *Mahārāja* Bhīmasena II, dated G. 282 (*EI*, ix, 342ff.; Hira Lal, *ICPB*, 94-96, no. 170. There is controversy about the date of this record, but Hira Lal's reading of the year, *viz.*, 282 appears to be correct.
620a. *JNSI*, xxii, 184-87.
621. *CII*, v, 81, text-lines 27-28; *Vidarbha Saṁśodhana Maṇḍala Vārṣika*, 1971, 75, text-lines 22-23; 1977, 171-72, text-lines 17-18.
622. Of the sixteen records referring to the place of issue as many as eleven were issued from Śarabhapura. See nos. I: I, III-VIII, X-XI and XIII-XIV.
623. No. I: Appendix II.
624. *EI*, xxxiv, 48. Also see B.C. Jain, *Mahanta Ghāsīdāsa Smāraka Saṅgrahālaya Purā-*

queen of Bharatabala, the Pāṇḍavavaṁśin ruler of Mekalā, is said to have hailed.[625] But this surmise cannot be accepted, for, as will be shown in the sequel, Vyāghrarāja, the issuer of this charter, and other members of the family named in this grant had nothing to do with the Śarabhapurīyas. We are, therefore, left with no alternative but to retain this nomenclature, inadequate though it may look, derived from the place of issue of the early charters of the rulers in question.

Śarabhapura

As stated above, most of the charters of the Śarabhapurīyas were issued from Śarabhapura. The first known grant of this family, *viz.*, the Pīparḍūlā plates of Narendra, was given away from this locality. And as the issuer of this charter, Narendra, who is the earliest known monarch of the family, is said to have been a son of Śarabha, we shall not be far from the truth if we assume that the township was founded by or christened after Śarabha. As regards its identification, however, there is total uncertainty and numerous conjectures have been hazarded. Alexander Cunningham first surmised that by the elision of the initial *ś* it may, through the forms 'Arabhpura' or 'Arbhi', be represented by the modern Arvi, the chief town of the tahsil of that name, in the Wardha District of the Maharashtra State. Alternatively he thought that it might be identical with the modern Sambalpur or Sambhalpur, the chief town of the Sambalpur District of Orissa.[626] But, as pointed out by Fleet[627] and Sten Konow,[628] neither of these propositions can be upheld. The former himself observed that if Śarabhapura is represented by any modern town, one must look in the maps for some such name as Sarbhor or Sābhor. He did not suggest any specific identification. Hira Lal, who believed that the Śarabhapurīyas were responsible for ousting the Pāṇḍuvaṁśins from the Chhattisgarh region,[629] was of the opinion that 'it may perhaps have been a new name imposed on the conquered city of Śrīpura by the victor from the fabulous animal of that name (*śarabha*), who is believed to be a match for a lion, with reference to the claim of the Sirpur dynasty to be *Kesarīs* (lions)'.[630] This suggestion cannot, however, be taken seriously as it is now accepted

---

tattva Upavibhāga meṁ Saṅgṛhīta Vastuoṁ kā Sūcī-patra, Part VI; *Utkīrṇṇa Lekha*, *Introduction*, 7-8.

625. Nos. II: I, text-line 29, verse 10; II, text-lines 29-30, verse 6.
626. *Archaeological Survey Reports*, xvii, 57f.
627. *CII*, iii, 193.
628. *EI*, xiii, 106.
629. *Ibid.*, xi, 186; *ICPB*, 101.
630. *EI*, xi, 186, fn. In his *ICPB*, 105, however, he states that Śarabhapura has not yet (1932) been identified. In support of his proposed identification Hira Lal states that the inscriptions of the Śarabhapurīyas have been found in the country round about and in close proximity of Sirpur, *i.e.*, at Arang, Raipur, Khariar and Sarangarh which enclose Sirpur from all directions, north, south, east and west.

by common consensus that the kings of Śarabhapura preceded the Pāṇḍuvaṁśins in the rule over Śrīpura. Secondly, the idea of the new name being imposed on Śrīpura in allusion to the mythical animal *śarabha* which is a match for a lion is based on the faulty notion that the Pāṇḍuvaṁśins assumed the title of *Kesarin*. It is no doubt true that a couple of the members of this dynasty are known to have borne names or titles terminating with the word *kesarin*. There is, however, nothing to indicate that the family was known as Kesarin. Extant epigraphical evidence proves beyond doubt that Śarabhapura was different from Śrīpura. It is instructive to note that Sudevarāja, the penultimate member of the dynasty, issued the Nahna plates of the second year, Sirpur and Arang plates of the seventh year, the Raipur plates of the tenth year and the undated[631] Sarangarh plates from Śarabhapura whereas the Dhamatari plates of the third year and the Kauvatal plates of the seventh year were given away from Śrīpura.[632] Pravararāja, who was probably a younger brother of and succeeded Sudevarāja, issued both of his known charters from Śrīpura. It is evident that Sudevarāja continued to have his capital at Śarabhapura till at least the tenth year of his reign but made Śrīpura his second capital sometime in or prior to his third regnal year[633] and that his successor Pravararāja finally shifted his capital to Śrīpura. When the Pāṇḍuvaṁśins dispossessed the Śarabhapurīyas of their dominions, they continued to have their capital at Śrīpura. The distinction between the two cities is also indicated by the fact that Sudevarāja's charters issued from Śarabhapura were inscribed by Droṇasiṁha while those given away from Śrīpura were engraved by Golasiṁha. Both the extant charters of Pravararāja, which were issued from Śrīpura, were also incised by Golasiṁha. While commenting on the Śarabhavaram plates issued by a district officer from Cīkūrapura, Sten Konow proposed to identify Śarabhapura with the findspot of the record, Śarabhavaram, situated at a distance of some twenty miles to the north-west of Rajahmandry (Rajamahendri) and ten miles from the bank of the river Godavari in Andhra Pradesh.[634] This conjecture was based on the consideration that the Śarabhavaram charter is written in an alphabet which is almost identical with that employed in the charters of the Śarabhapurīyas, it is dated exactly in the same manner as the grants of the kings of Śarabhapura and that the seal attached to it shows the representation of a conch which is noticed on the seals of the Śarabhapura charters also. Konow also pointed out that similar village names includ-

631. Only the first plate of this grant has been found, the remaining two plates remaining untraced. In keeping with the usual practice, the date must have been given on the third plate.

32. Nos. I: VIII, X-XI and XIII-XIV were issued from Śarabhapura and nos. I: IX
6 and XII from Śrīpura.

633. This is the date of his Dhamatari plates (no. I: IX).

634. *EI*, xiii, 108.

ing Śarabhapura occur in other places also in the neighbourhood of Śarabhavaram. He was fully aware of the fact that this suggestion was merely a 'loose guess': but still he felt that Śarabhapura should be looked for not in Raipur or its immediate neighbourhood, but farther to the south. However, notwithstanding the close similarity between the names Śarabhapura and Śarabhavaram and the occurrence of the very name Śarabhapura in the neighbourhood of the latter the fact remains that absolutely no evidence connecting the Śarabhapura kings with any part of Andhra Pradesh has come to light to date and as such Konow's surmise fares no better than Hira Lal's.

Lochan Prasad Pandeya, who was very familiar with the topography of the Chhattisgarh and adjoining area, suggested to identify Śarabhapura with a few localities bearing phonetically similar names in the Sambalpur District of Orissa and in the Bilaspur District of Madhya Pradesh. At first he proposed to equate it with Sarabhgarh, the chief town of a big zamindari of the same name in the Gangapur feudatory state (now in Sambalpur District) in Orissa.[635] V. V. Mirashi regarded this suggestion as plausible.[636] Alternatively, Pandeya thought that its identification with a locality called Saravā near Sheori-Narayan and the river Mahanadi or with another place known as Sarbhar near Nandaur in the Bilaspur District is not impossible.[637] In view of the close phonetic resemblance between the names concerned and the fact that many of the epigraphic records and coins of the Śarabhapura kings have been reported from this area, the identifications proposed by Pandeya, particularly the first one, are not improbable, although in the absence of any definite evidence on the point the question cannot be answered finally in the present state of our knowledge. Two points, however, deserve special attention in this connection. Similarity between place-names alone is not enough for the purpose of identification. Antiquity of the locality with which Śarabhapura is proposed to be identified must also be ascertained before any identification is accepted. Secondly, it must be remembered that at the time Pandeya proposed his identifications, most of the Śarabhapurīya inscriptions discovered till then were known to have been found in the Sambalpur region of Orissa and the Raigarh-Bilaspur region of Madhya Pradesh. But as we know now, all the three known records of Narendra, the first ruler of the dynasty known from his own inscriptions, as well as several other epigraphs of the other members of the family have been found in the Raipur District. It is therefore not impossible that Śarabhapura, which served as the capital of the dynasty from the very start, was actually situated in the Raipur region.

635. *Proceedings of All-India Oriental Conference*, Vth Session, i, 461. Also see *EI*, xxiii, 17; xxvi, 229, fn. 2.

636. *Ibid.*, xxii, 17.

637. *IHQ*, xix, 144.

D. C. Sircar, perhaps taking cue from Hira Lal, is inclined to opine that Śarabhapura was situated quite close to Śrīpura (modern Sirpur) in the Raipur District of Madhya Pradesh and that Pravararāja founded the new capital very near the old city of Śarabhapura which had served as the capital of his forefathers. He is led to this conclusion by the fact that the inscriptions issued from this city have all been found about the Raipur District.[638] This contention is supported by Moreshwar G. Dikshit on the ground of the discovery of Narendra's copper-plate charter at Kurud which is situated in the Raipur District as well as of a coin of Prasannamātra in the lowest stratum at Sirpur which was superimposed by buildings attributed to the Pāṇḍava kings, which shows the early association of the Śarabhapura kings with Sirpur.[639] But, as already pointed out while examining Hira Lal's view, there is enough evidence to show that the two cities were not situated in close proximity to each other. The fact that two different scribes had to be engaged for inscribing the charters issued by the same monarch (Sudevarāja) from Śarabhapura and Śrīpura clearly indicates that they were separated by a long distance.[640] Śrīpura is, for the first time, mentioned in the records of Sudevarāja who was separated from Prasannamātra, whose coin is reported to have been recovered at the lowest stratum in the excavations at Sirpur (ancient Śrīpura), by at least two reigns, viz., those of Jayarāja and Mānamātra-Durgarāja. The discovery of a single coin of Prasannamātra does not necessarily indicate his (and for that matter early Śarabhapurīyas) association with Śrīpura. It is common knowledge that in ancient India coins once issued continued to circulate for a long time, sometimes even after the issuing king or dynasty to which he belonged was supplanted by another.[641] Secondly, it is noteworthy that Prasannamātra is the only Śarabhapurīya king whose coins have been reported so far. As his successors are not known to have issued their own coins, it is very likely, nay almost certain, that they continued to use his specie as legal tender. As such, the stratum yielding Prasannamātra's coin need not of necessity be associated with him. It is instructive to note in this connection

638. *IHQ*, xix, 144; *EI*, xxxiii, 155.

639. *Ibid.*, xxxi, 264. For a brief account of the Sirpur excavations see Moreshwar G. Dikshit in *Raviśaṅkara Śukla Abhinandana Grantha* (Hindi), Nagpur, 1955, Itihāsa Khaṇḍa, 184-91.

640. *Cf. EI*, xxxiv, 29. Both the charters of Sudevarāja given from Śrīpura (nos. I: IX and XII) were inscribed by Golasiṁha while the rest of grants, all issued from Śarabhapura, were engraved by Droṇasiṁha.

641. *E.g.*, punch-marked coins continued to circulate for a few centuries after their manufacture. Then there is sufficient epigraphic evidence to prove that the silver coins of the early Kalacuri king Kṛṣṇarāja, called *Kṛṣṇarāja-rūpaka*, remained in circulation for at least one and a half centuries after the termination of the reign of the issuer. *Vide* Anjaneri plates of Bhogaśakti, dated (Kalacuri) 461 (=710-11 A.D.), which refer to taxes levied in *Kṛṣṇarāja-rūpakas* (V.V. Mirashi, *Inscriptions of the Kalachuri-Chedi Era, CII*, iv, 151, text-lines 38-39).

that barring this solitary coin no evidence of the Śarabhapurīya association has been found in the excavation and all the other structural remains and antiquities unearthed at Śrīpura belong to the post-Śarabhapurīya period.[642] In view of these facts it is obvious that the city of Śrīpura was probably founded by Sudevarāja during whose reign it appears to have been given the status of the second capital while the capital was finally shifted to this city either by Sudevarāja himself sometime after the tenth year of his reign or by his successor Pravararāja.

The latest theory on this question is that of K. D. Bajpai and S. K. Pandey who, after a lengthy examination of the earlier views on the subject, feel inclined to identify Śarabhapura with the village of Mallar (or Malhar) in the Bilaspur District of Madhya Pradesh. In support of their contention they point out the fact that several records of the rulers in question issued from Śarabhapura have been found at and around Mallar and that a large number of towns and villages referred to in these charters can be shown to be situated in the districts of Bilaspur and Raipur and part of the Raigarh District not far away from Mallar, actually within a radius of about fifty kilometres from it. The high antiquity and prosperity of Mallar that have come to light as a result of their excavations at the site also appear to have induced Bajpai and Pandey to favour this identification.[643] However, we find it difficult to accept this view as it is not supported by any strong evidence. It is no doubt true that the situation of Mallar answers well the requirements of an ideal capital of a kingdom comprising South Kosala and its antiquity and cultural wealth are also beyond doubt. A good number of the inscriptions of the family have also been found at the site. But these facts by themselves do not indicate that it represents Śarabhapura. As pointed out above, Śarabhapura was probably founded by Śarabha, the first known member of the family. There is some difference of opinion about his period. While most scholars assign him to the close of the fifth century A.D., Bajpai and Pandey are inclined to place him in the beginning of the fourth century A.D.[644] Be that as it may, for the present purpose it will suffice to state that the excavated evidence takes back the antiquity of Mallar to *circa* 1000 B.C. And as such this city could not have been founded by Śarabha during whose reign it was in a flourishing condition as revealed by the remains exhumed in course of excavations. Secondly, excavations have not yielded any evidence to indicate that it was anciently known as Śarabhapura, whereas we learn from the Ratanpur stone inscription, dated Kalacuri 915, and the Mallar stone inscription, dated Kalacuri 919, of the

642. These include a few Buddhist structures and inscriptions assignable to the time of Mahāśivagupta Bālārjuna, the last known Pāṇḍuvaṁśin king. For these remains, see *Śrī-Raviśaṅkara Śukla Abhinandana Grantha*, Itihāsa Khaṇḍa, 184-91, and for inscriptions, see no III : XII of this volume.

643. *Malhar 1975-77* 25-29.

644. *Ibid.*, 32.

time of the Kalacuri kings Pṛthvīdeva II[645] and Jājalladeva II[646] respectively that during the early medieval period it was called Mallāla or Mallāla-pattana. The supposition of Bajpai and Pandey that its name was changed from Śarabhapura to Mallāla-pattana during the Kalacuri period in allusion to the god Malhārī Śiva[647] fails to carry conviction in the absence of any supporting evidence.

It will follow from the foregoing discussion that the question of the location of Śarabhapura cannot be answered definitely in the present state of insufficient information and we have no alternative but to await future discoveries which may throw light on this vexed issue. However, as the earliest records of the dynasty have been reported from the Raipur District, the possibility of its ultimately being located in the Raipur area, but at a considerable distance from Sirpur, cannot be ruled out.

Genealogy

Generally speaking, the Śarabhapurīyā records are not of much historical interest inasmuch as they are singularly bereft of any genealogical account[648] which could help us reconstruct their history on a secure basis. It is only the metrical legends on the seals attached to them that often give us not only the name of the reigning monarch but also that of his father and sometimes also of the grandfather. And as such these short epigraphs have been of great help in reconstructing the history of the dynasty with some degree of certainty. There are, however, still a few points about which considerable uncertainty and consequent divergence of opinion prevail. We may refer to them in brief here.

As the earliest known member of the family, Narendra, describes himself as the son of Śarabha after whom the dynastic capital was christened, Śarabha may justifiably be taken to be the founder of the dynasty. His son Narendra was probably the next member of the family, there being at present no evidence to indicate that their reigns were intervened by that of any other ruler. The next member of the family whose copper-plate charters have been found is Jayarāja. But the inscription on the seals of Jayarāja's grants refers to him as the son of Prasanna[649] who has been rightly identified with Prasannamātra known from the legend of some

645. V.V. Mirashi, *Inscriptions of the Kalachuri-Chedi Era, CII*, iv, 506, verse 23.

646. *Ibid.*, 515, verse 21.

647. K.D. Bajpai and S.K. Pandey, *Malhar 1975-77*, 29.

648. The only exceptions are furnished by the Dhamatari and Kauvatal plates which name the father of the issuing chief, Sudevararāja.

649. The expression used is *Prasanna-tanaya, i.e.*, son of Prasanna. According to Fleet and some other scholars, the reading of the relevant expression on some of the seals is *Prasanna-hṛdaya, i.e.*, the heart of Prasanna. But as suggested by D.C. Sircar, in these cases also the correct reading is *tanaya* and not *hṛdaya*.

repousse coins.[650] However, in the absence of necessary evidence it is not possible at present to ascertain his relationship with Narendra. It has been conjectured that he was probably Narendra's successor and may have been his son as well.[651] But this cannot be regarded as certain and it is not impossible that the reigns of Narendra and Prasannamātra were separated from each other by one or more reigns.[652] In any case, this is still one of the uncertain points in the history of the Śarabhapurīyas. Lochan Prasad Pandey once surmised that Prasannamātra flourished prior to Narendra and that the latter conquered Śarabhapura from the former but was soon driven away by Jayarāja or Sudevarāja.[653] But being opposed to known historical facts, this conjecture need not be taken seriously. While there is, thus, some uncertainty about the immediate predecessor of Prasannamātra, there seems to be no doubt about the fact that he was himself succeeded by Jayarāja who clearly describes himself as Prasanna's son. From some of the seal-inscriptions of Sudevarāja we learn that Prasanna had another son named Mānamātra who was himself Sudevarāja's father.[654] No record of Mānamātra himself has been reported so far. However, the text of the Dhamatari and Kauvatal plates of Sudevarāja shows that Mānamātra was also known as Durgarāja. As the prefix *mahat* and the termination *rāja* are attached to his name, there can be no doubt about the fact that he followed Jayarāja on the throne. Mānamātra-Durgarāja was succeeded by Sudevarāja who is described figuratively in some of his seal-inscriptions as born from the moon in the form of Mānamātra who had himself emerged from the ocean that was Prasanna and in the text of his Dhamatari and Kauvatal charters as the son of Mahā-Durgarāja. Mānamātra-Durgarāja had another son named Pravararāja as we learn from the seal-inscriptions of the latter. As we have seen above, Sudevarāja made Śrīpura his second capital whereas Pravararāja appears to have finally shifted his headquarters to that town as indicated by the fact that both of his known charters were issued from there. On the basis of the evidence outlined above, the genealogy of the Śarabhapura kings was till recently reconstructed as follows:—

650. The prevalence of *mātra*- ending names among the Śarabhapura kings is noteworthy in this connection.

651. V.V. Mirashi, *Studies in Indology*, i, 249; *The Classical Age* (ed. R.C. Majumdar), 219.

652. This point can be settled only by future discoveries.

653. *IHQ*, xix, 143, fn. 9.

654. See the seal-inscriptions of the Nahna and Arang plates (nos. I: VIII and X) of Sudevarāja and the Thakurdiya and Malhar plates of Pravararāja (nos. I: XV and and XVI).

Śarabha

Narendra

Prasanna or Prasannamātra

Jayarāja — Mānamātra-Durgarāja

Sudevarāja — Pravararāja

The recent discovery of the Mallar plates of Vyāghrarāja[655] has, however, added new dimensions to the problem. Issued from Prasannapura, this inscription aims at recording the grant by Vyāghrarāja of the village Kunturapadra situated in the Pūrva-rāṣṭra in favour of the Brāhmaṇa *Dīkṣita* Agnicandrasvāmin, son of *Dīkṣita* Durgasvāmin. The grant was issued on the twenty-seventh day of the month of Pauṣa in the regnal year which has been variously deciphered as 4[656] or 41.[657] The donor, Vyāghrarāja, is represented as the younger brother of the illustrious king Pravara-bhaṭṭāraka who is compared to the traditional kings Pṛthu and Manu. Pravara-bhaṭṭāraka himself is stated to have been the son of Jaya-bhaṭṭāraka. Pravara-bhaṭṭāraka is further described as the very moon on the horizon that is the Amarārya-kula. Prasannapura, the place of issue, may have been so called after Prasannamātra of the Śarabhapura dynasty even as Śarabhapura was named after Śarabha. The names Jaya and Pravara are met with during the period represented by this inscription only among the Śarabhapurīyas. Pūrva-rāṣṭra, wherein the donated village was situated, is also mentioned in a couple of Śarabhapurīya epigraphs.[658] In view of these considerations it has been suggested that this record also belongs to the Śarabhapurīyas. Accordingly, Jaya-bhaṭṭāraka of this charter has been identified with the Śarabhapurīya chief Jayarāja and his son Pravara-bhaṭṭāraka has been designated as Pravara or Pravararāja I in order to distinguish him from the homonymous son of Mānamātra-Durgarāja who is consequently re-designated as Pravararāja II. It is not clear from the inscription if Vyāghrarāja also ruled as an independent monarch, for he is merely referred to as Pravara-bhaṭṭāraka's younger brother. According to this view, Jayarāja was succeeded by his son Pravararāja I (Pravara-bhaṭṭāraka of the inscription) who was followed by

655. See no. I: Appendix II. Also see *EI*, xxxiv, 45-50.

656. V.V. Mirashi, *Studies in Indology*, i. 260, fn. 4; Bal Chandra Jain, *Catalogue of the Archaeological Section of the M.G.M. Museum, Raipur*, vi: Inscriptions (Hindi), 175. This possibility is conceded by D.C. Sircar and G. Bhattacharya also.

657. *EI.*, xxxiv, 50, text-line 23.

658. Nos. I: VI, text-line 4; I: XII, text-line 4.

his uncle Mānamātra-Durgarāja. The genealogy reconstructed on these lines may be given as follows:—

1. Śarabha
2. Narendra
3. Prasanna or Prasannamātra
4. Jayarāja
5. Pravararāja I
Vyāghrarāja
6. Durgarāja-Mānamātra
7. Sudevarāja
8. Pravararāja II[659]

As against the above reconstruction of the genealogy and the order of succession proposed by D.C. Sircar and G. Bhattacharya, Bal Chandra Jain, who is also inclined to attribute this inscription to the Śarabhapurīyas, proposes to interpret its evidence in an altogether different manner. According to him, Pravara-bhaṭṭāraka of this record is none else than Pravararāja known from the Thakurdiya and Mallar plates. In order to reconcile the evidence of this record with the other Śarabhapurīya epigraphs, he conjectures that Pravararāja's (or, for that matter, Pravara-bhaṭṭāraka's) father had as many as three different names, to wit Jayarāja (or Jaya-bhaṭṭāraka), Mānamātra and Durgarāja. According to this interpretation, Vyāghrarāja was yet another son of Jayarāja-Mānamātra-Durgarāja.[660] If we were to follow this view, the order of succession would be as follows:—

1. Śarabha
2. Narendra
3. Prasanna or Prasannamātra
4. Jayarāja-Mānamātra-Durgarāja
5. Sudevarāja
6. Pravararāja
Vyāghrarāja

However, if one examines the inscription closely the difficulties involved in attributing it to the Śarabhapurīyas will become obvious. There are greater dissimilarities than correspondences between the Śarabhapurīya records on the one hand and the Mallar plates of Vyāghrarāja on the other.

659. *EI*, xxxiv, 47. This interpretation is admitted by V.V. Mirashi also. See his *Studies in Indology*, i, 249.

660. B.C. Jain, *op.cit.*, introduction, 7-8. This possibility was hinted at by Sircar and Bhattacharya also. See *EI*, xxxiv, 47, fn. 2.

The former, as shown earlier, are written in the box-headed characters of the Central Indian alphabet whereas the latter are engraved in the nail-headed alphabet with hollow or linear triangular marks forming tops of letters. The style of the latter is highly ornate as compared to that of the former which are composed in a very simple and, generally speaking, matter-of-fact style. And lastly, the seals of the two sets of records are quite different from each other. As pointed out above, the seals attached to the Śarabhapura charters bear the Abhiṣeka-Lakṣmī or Gaja-Lakṣmī device accompanied by some auxiliary devices in the upper portion while the lower half invariably contains a two-line legend in the *Anuṣṭubh* metre and sometimes another device below it. The seal affixed to Vyāghrarāja's charter on the other hand, bears a group of three devices in a row from left to right, *viz.*, the side-view of a wheel, the head of an animal or bird (perhaps Garuḍa)[661] and a conch-shell, in the upper part and a single-line prose legend giving the name of the issuer prefixed by the honorific *śri* in the nominative singular (*śri-Vyāghrarājaḥ*). The draft is also quite dissimilar to that of the other set of records which got finally standardised during the reign of Jayarāja and is met with in a practically unaltered form in all the records of the family thereafter. To illustrate the point, both the sets of records commence with the mention of the place whence the charter was issued. But in the Śarabhapura inscriptions this item is quite simple inasmuch as the locality is mentioned without any description whatsoever whereas in Vyāghrarāja's charter it is described in some detail. The former do not give any account of the issuing monarch's ancestry[662] and the name of the family while the latter refers to the benefactor's elder brother and father besides specifying the name of the family. The type of short conventional description of the king in the records of the Śarabhapura chiefs is conspicuous by its absence in the other epigraph which describes the grantor's elder brother, who was evidently the reigning king at that time, in a manner quite unlike that of the Śarabhapura charters. The notification regarding the grant also presents certain new features unfamiliar from the Śarabhapurīya grants. Thus, the records of the Śarabhapurīyas first refer to the district and the granted village and then the royal command concerning the grant is addressed to the villagers in general without specifying any particular section of the population. As against this, in the record of Vyāghrarāja we find reference to the worshipping of the Brāhmaṇas, both present and future, while the addressees are the king's servants, and it is after this that we find mention of the district and the village. The privileges accompanying the grant and the dues which the residents of the donated villages are

661. D.C. Sircar and G. Bhattacharya think that it may be a lion to front. See *EI*, xxxiv, 45.
662. The only exceptions are the Dhamatari and Kauvatal plates of Sudevarāja who is described therein as the son of Mahā-Durgarāja. See nos. I: IX, text-line 4 and XII, text-line 3.

ordered to pay to the donee according to the Śarabhapura charters are not met with in Vyāghrarāja's Mallar plates. We notice a considerable difference in regard to the benedictive and imprecatory stanzas also. Only two of such verses are fully and one partly common to both the sets of inscriptions while the rest are not. The manner of referring to the scribe is also quite dissimilar.

Attention must also be invited to another important point. While we have a large number of Śarabhapurīya copper-plate inscriptions, not even in a single record do we come across the expression *bhāṭṭāraka*, which is found used with the names of the elder brother and father of Vyāghrarāja, suffixed to the monarch's name. Conversely, the word *mahat*, which is found prefixed to the names of all the Śarabhapurīya chiefs from Jayarāja onwards in the initial portion of the text of the copper-plate charters issued by them,[663] is not attached to the kings' names in Vyāghrarāja's record. In view of these and other considerations we find it difficult to attribute this inscription to the Śarabhapurīyas. The three personages of the Amarārya-kula mentioned in this inscription had therefore nothing to do with the Śarabhapurīyas. The fact that they ruled from Prasannapura also proves nothing, for we know that the disappearance or change of dynasties did not of necessity result in the abandonment or shifting of the capital.[664] We feel that the Amarārya-kula kings Jaya-bhaṭṭāraka and Pravara-bhaṭṭāraka were probably ruling contemporaneously with the later members of the Śarabhapura family in a part of South Kosala not included in the dominions of the Śarabhapurīyas and taking advantage of the decline of the Śarabhapurīya power occupied the Mallar region sometime about the close of the sixth or the commencement of the seventh century A.D.[665] This explains why the Amarāryakula[666] is spoken of in the records of the Pāṇḍavavaṁśins of Mekalā as ruling in Kosala.[667] It need hardly be stressed that in view of what has been said in these pages the commonly accepted notion that the Amarārya-kula was the same as what is popularly called Śarabhapurīya dynasty has to be given up.

Chronology

The chronology of the Śarabhapura rulers constitutes an equally vexed

663. In the seal-inscriptions these monarchs are mentioned without the prefix *mahat*. This word is not prefixed to the name of Narendra and apparently this practice became popular from the time of Jayarāja when *rāja*--ending names came into fashion.

664. Note, for instance, the case of the Pāṇḍuvaṁśins who supplanted the Śarabhapurīyas but continued to have their capital at Śrīpura which was raised to the status of the capital of Kosala during the reigns of Sudevarāja and Pravararāja.

665. For a detailed discussion on the Mallar plates of Vyāghrarāja and the problems concerning them see I: Appendix II.

666. Under the name Amaraja-kula.

667. See nos. II: I, text-line 29, verse 10; II, text-lines 29-30, verse 6.

problem, and in the absence of definite evidence most of the theories ventured on the subject are more or less in the nature of guesswork.

It is universally admitted that the Śarabhapurīyas and the Pāṇḍuvaṁśins were chronologically close to each other. Hira Lal thought that the former supplanted the latter whom they ousted from Śrīpura.[668] However, this view has naturally not found favour with historians. As shown earlier, Śrīpura was accorded the status of a capital during the closing years of the Śarabhapurīya rule and it continued to enjoy the same position under the Pāṇḍuvaṁśins. This fact should leave no doubt that the Śarabhapurīyas were predecessors, not successors, of the Pāṇḍuvaṁśins.[669] This conclusion also finds support from the facts that the records of two of the early members of the latter dynasty seem to have borrowed certain phrases from those of the former[670] and show a comparatively more developed form.[671] The characters employed in the epigraphs of the Pāṇḍuvaṁśa monarchs are also admittedly much more developed than those met with in the inscriptions of the Śarabhapura chiefs.[672] And lastly, if the *Mahāsāmanta* Indrabalarāja, who is stated to have held the office of the *Sarv-ādhikār-ādhikṛta* or Chief Minister and is mentioned as the *dūtaka* in the Dhamatari and Kauvatal plates of Sudevarāja, has been correctly identified with Indrabala, son of the first known Pāṇḍuvaṁśin monarch Udayana and grandfather of Mahāśiva Tīvara (or Tīvaradeva as he is popularly known),[673] no further evidence is required to establish the priority of the Śarabhapura chiefs to the Pāṇḍuvaṁśins.

668. *EI*, xi, 186; *ICPB*, 101.

669. Otherwise we shall have to assume that the Śarabhapurīyas, whom Hira Lal took to be the successors of the Pāṇḍuvaṁśins, shifted the Kosala capital from Śrīpura to Śarabhapura and that the latter enjoyed this position for some generations till Sudevarāja and Pravararāja again revived the earlier glory of Śrīpura and made it their capital. Even if we were to believe with Hira Lal that Śarabhapura and Śrīpura were the same, it will have to be assumed that the early members of the Śarabhapura family changed the name of Śrīpura to Śarabhapura and retained the latter name for a few generations whereafter it again reverted back to the older discarded name which is simply riduculous.

670. The passage *yath-āsmābhir = ayaṁ grāmaḥ...yāvad = ravi-śaśi-tārā-kiraṇa-pratihata-ghor-āndhakāraṁ jagad = avatiṣṭhate tāvad = upabhogyaḥ*, which is met with in all the records of the kings of Śarabhapura from the fifth year of the reign of Jayarāja (it is first noticed in his Mallar plates of this year, see no. I:V) onwards, is found borrowed *ad verbatim* in the Bonda, Rajim and Baloda plates of Mahāśiva Tīvaradeva and the Adhabhara plates of his son and successor Nannarāja II (nos. III: II-V) but was given up later as indicated by the grants of Śivagupta Bālārjuna.

671. *Cf.* The description of the king in the records of Tīvaradeva and Nannarāja II (nos. III: II-V) which is much more elaborate than that found in any Śarabhapurīya grant and is full of long eulogistic compounds.

672. They are more elongated and angular and their box-heads often show small horizontal strokes attached to their tops.

673. *IHQ*, xx, 275; xxii, 63. However, this identification cannot be regarded as certain.

Some earlier historians were inclined to place the Śarabhapura chiefs in the eighth or ninth century A.D. Hira Lal, who, as stated above, believed in the anteriority of the Pāṇḍuvaṁśins to the Śarabhapurīyas and dated the Sirpur Lakshmaṇa temple inscription of Śivagupta Bālārjuna in the eighth or ninth century A.D. on palaeographical grounds,[674] naturally assigned the then known Śarabhapurīya records to the same period.[675] Even those who did not subscribe to Hira Lal's chronology, dated the Śarabhapurīya rule only a little prior to 800 A.D.[676] The main ground for this late dating was provided by the employment in their grants of the box-headed characters similar to those found in the Vākāṭaka records which, too, were relegated to the eighth century A.D. on the basis of the identification, proposed by Fleet,[677] of the Later Gupta king Devagupta, son of Ādityasena, mentioned in the Deo-Barnark inscription,[678] with the homonymous ruler whose daughter Prabhāvatīguptā was married to the Vākāṭaka king Rudrasena II.[679] But the discovery of the Poona plates of Prabhāvatīguptā,[680] who is described therein as the daughter of Candragupta[681], showed the erroneousness of this identification and proved once for all that the Vākāṭakas were contemporaries of the Imperial Guptas and the date of the Śarabhapurīyas had also to be pushed back to an earlier period[682] and the Śarabhapura kings are no longer placed in such a late age as the eighth and ninth centuries A.D.

674. *EI*, xi, 184 and 185; *ICPB*, 100.

675. Hira Lal gave the date of the Arang plates of Jayarāja and the Raipur plates of Sudevarāja as eighth or ninth century (*ICPB*, nos. 175 and 176) and of the Khariar (the same as our Nahna) and Sarangarh plates of Sudevarāja as eighth century A.D. (*ibid.*, no. 177; *EI*, ix, 283).

676. Sten Konow observed that the Sirpur Lakshmaṇa temple inscription of Śivagupta seemed to belong to *circa* 800 A.D. which, he thought, was not much later than the grants of the Śarabhapura kings (*ibid.*, xiii, 108). With reference to Sudevarāja's Nahna plates, however, the same scholar stated that its date could not be settled (*ibid.*, ix, 172). Fleet was uncertain about the Śarabhapurīya records and wavered between the periods not much distant from that of Goparāja (510 A.D.) known from the Eran inscription and a date about a couple of centuries later than Goparāja (*CII*, iii, introduction, 14). The latter alternative was apparently due to the shifting of the period of the Vākāṭakas also by about two centuries later than believed earlier (*ibid.*, introduction, 15-16).

677. *Ibid.*

678. *Ibid.*, 213-18, no. 46.

679. *CII*, v, 19, text-line 11; 24, text-line 15; 30, text-line 15; 40, text-line 7; 45, text-lines 11-12; 50, text-lines 11-12, etc.

680. *IA*, xli, 214-15; *EI*, xv, 39-44; *CII*, v, 5-9. These plates showed for the first time that Prabhāvatīguptā's father Devagupta was none else than the Gupta emperor Candragupta II Vikramāditya who had Devagupta as his 'dear name'. The Riddhapura plates also give Candragupta as Prabhāvatīguptā's father's name. See *ibid.*, 33-37. All other records mention him by his other name Devagupta.

681. *Ibid.*, 7, text-line 7. Also see *ibid.*, 36, text-line 7.

682. This was first pointed out effectively by V.V. Mirashi while editing the Thakurdiya plates of Pravararāja. See *EI*, xxii, 8ff.

According to a recent theory,[683] Mahendra of Kosala (*i.e.*, South Kosala), one of the rulers of Dakṣiṇāpatha first defeated and then reinstated by the Gupta emperor Samudragupta,[684] was a member of the Śarabhapurīya dynasty. It has been suggested that he was in all probability a younger brother of *Mahārāja* Narendra, son of Śarabha, known from his Pīparḍūlā, Kurud and Rawan plates. It is accordingly held that the Śarabhapurīyas launched upon their political career about the beginning of the fourth century A.D.[685] However, but for the name-ending (*i.e.*, Indra) of Mahendra and Narendra and the fact that the former, like the Śarabhapura kings ruled over South Kosala, there is, in the present state of insufficient information, nothing to connect Mahendra with the Śarabhapurīyas.[686] Moreover, such an early date for the commencement of the Śarabhapurīya power does not go well with the well-developed box-headed characters used in the grants of Narendra and his successors and need not be taken seriously in any historical discussion at least for the present.

An effort has been made to fix the date of the Śarabhapurīyas with reference to that of the Pāṇḍuvaṁśa king Tīvaradeva who was the first member of the dynasty whose copper-plate grants issued from the erstwhile Śarabhapurīya capital Śrīpura have come down to us.[687] The *raison d'etre* for adopting this approach lay in the belief that the date of Tīvaradeva could be fixed definitely on the basis of the evidence furnished by the Viṣṇukuṇḍin and Maukhari records and as the Śarabhapurīya rule in South Kosala was believed to have been supplanted by Tīvaradeva himself it was felt that if the date of the Pāṇḍava chief could be ascertained that of the Śarabhapurīyas could also be easily found out. But as will be shown in the sequel while discussing the chronology of the Pāṇḍuvaṁśins, recent epigraphic discoveries have knocked out of bottom the supposed independent epigraphic evidence for the date of Tīvaradeva which itself has to be determined with reference to the Śarabhapura chiefs. Let us, therefore, see as to what other evidence we have for the determination of the age of the Śarabhapurīyas.

As we have seen above, the Śarabhapurīyas commenced their political career with Śarabha after whom their early capital was called Śarabhapura.

683. K.D. Bajpai and S.K. Pandey, *Malhar 1975-77*, 32.

684. *CII*, iii, 7, text-line 19.

685. K.D. Bajpai and S.K. Pandey, *op.cit.*, 30-32. A clay sealing bearing the inscription *Mahārāja-Mahendrasya* in early Gupta Brāhmī characters found in the excavations at Mallar has been cited in support of this contention. The fact that the inscription on the sealing is not in box-headed characters employed in all the extant Śarabhapurīya records, however, goes against the supposed connection of Mahendra with the Śarabhapurīya dynasty.

686. Moreover, in the event of accepting this connection an unnecessary break of over a century between Mahendra and Narendra on the one hand and the later members of the Śarabhapurīya family on the other will have to be postulated as has actually been done by Bajpai and Pandey.

687. See, for instance, *EI*, xxii, 18-22.

It is now generally admitted that this Śarabha is probably identical with Śarabharāja, the maternal grandfather of Goparāja who, according to an Eran inscription of G. 191 or 510 A.D.,[688] accompanied his friend Bhānugupta in a battle and died after a fierce fight.[689] If this identification is accepted, Śarabha or Śarabharāja may be placed roughly in the last quarter of the fifth century A.D.[690] The last known date of Śarabha's son Narendra is the twenty-fourth year of his reign.[691] It may thus be assumed that he ruled for about twenty-five years and his reign may be dated from *c.* 500 to *c.* 525 A.D. It is not known as to who succeeded Narendra. The next known ruler of the family is, however, Prasanna or Prasannamātra who is known from some coins and seal-inscriptions of his son Jayarāja and grandson Sudevarāja. His relationship with Narendra and the length of his reign still remain unknown and no light on these questions is likely to be thrown unless his own epigraphic records are available. However, assuming that his reign as well as that of his immediate predecessor, if any at all, covered a period of about twenty-five years, we may date the conclusion of Parasannamātra's reign about 550 A.D. The latest known date of his son and successor, Jayarāja, being his ninth regnal year,[692] his rule may be taken to have lasted for at least a decade, *i.e., c.* 550-*c.* 560 A.D. Jayarāja was followed by his brother Mānamātra *alias* Durgarāja about whom we know nothing except the name which is known from the Dhamatari and Kauvatal plates of his son Sudevarāja as well as from the inscriptions attached to the same monarch's Nahna and Arang plates and Pravararāja's Thakurdiya and Mallar plates. As no record of his own reign has come to light so far, we do not know as to how long he ruled. We may tentatively assign him a short period of about ten years and date the termination of his reign about 570 A.D. Mānamātra-Durgarāja's son and successor, Sudevarāja, ruled for at

688. *CII*, iii, 91-93.
689. This identification was first hinted at by Fleet who was, however, not inclined to accept it. He observed that there is 'much less to identify either of the *Rājas* (Jayarāja and Sudevarāja) mentioned in them (Arang plates of Jayarāja and Raipur plates of Sudevarāja respectively) with Goparāja's maternal grandfather' (*ibid.*, iii, introduction 14). The case for the identity was first clearly put up by V.V. Mirashi. See *EI*, xxii, 17.
690. Mirashi, however, proposed to place Śarabharāja in c. 460-80 A.D. *Vide* his *Studies in Indology*, i, 250. Earlier he dated him roughly in the second half of the fifth century A.D. See *EI*, xxii, 17. D.C. Sircar, who also took the identification of Śarabha with Śarabharāja of the Eran inscription for granted, originally placed Śarabha in the period *c.* 465-80 A.D. (*IHQ*, xix, 144. Also *cf. A History and Culture of the Indian People* III: *The Classical Age*, 219, where Śarabha and his son Narendra are roughly assigned to the 'closing decades of the fifth century A.D.'). But subsequently after the discovery of the Kurud plates of Narendra's twenty-fourth regnal year he rightly proposed to bring down the date of Śarabha to the end of the fifth century A.D. (*EI*, xxxiii, 156).
691. Kurud grant of Narendra (no. I: II) was issued in this year.
692. This is the date of Jayarāja's second Mallar charter (no. I: VII).

least a decade as can be inferred from his latest known grant which was issued in the tenth year of his reign.[693] Even supposing that he did not rule any further, his rule could not have come to an end prior to *c.* 580 A.D. Pravararāja, who was younger brother of and succeeded Sudevarāja, is known from a couple of his copper-plate grants both of which were given in the third year of his reign. If he, too, is given a reign of about ten years, the termination of his reign may be dated around 590 A.D. Nothing is known about the Śarabhapurīyas after Pravararāja. Even if we assume that the rule of the dynasty came to a close with the end of Pravararāja's reign, the termination of the family must be dated within a few years of this date.

A passing reference may be made here to the Mallar plates of Vyāghrarāja which, according to the prevailing view, have some bearing on the problem under consideration. As shown earlier, we do not think that this record has anything to do with the Śarabhapurīyas. But in case the current theory that assigns kings Jaya-bhaṭṭāraka and his son Pravara-bhaṭṭāraka and the latter's younger brother Vyāghrarāja to the Śarabhapurīya dynasty is conceded, provision will have to be made for their reigns also. In that case the termination of the Śarabhapurīya rule will have to be dated still later.

It would be seen that this chronology is primarily based on the assumption that Śarabha, the founder of the Śarabhapurīya dynasty, is the same as Śarabharāja, the maternal grandfather of Goparāja, known from the Eran inscription dated 510 A.D. But it has been argued recently, though without sufficient reason, that this identification cannot be taken for granted as it is based merely on the sameness of names which ought not to be taken seriously, especially as we know of other instances of more than one chief of the same name ruling in different parts of the country in almost the same period.[694] It has also been stated in support of this contention that Eran, the find-spot of Goparāja's inscription in the proximity whereof Śarabharāja appears to have been ruling and the Chhattisgarh area where the Śarabhapurīyas are known to have ruled are situated hundreds of miles apart. In short, the very basis of the above chronology has been challenged.[695] We do not propose to examine this argument in extenso here as the same has been done elsewhere.[696] It would suffice to point out here that this identification is not based merely on the identity of names but also on

693. This date is furnished by his Raipur plates (no. I: XII).

694. By way of an example reference may be made to the fact that several chiefs named Vyāghra are known to have been ruling in different parts of North and South India during the Gupta period.

695. V.V. Mirashi, 'The Date of Tīvaradeva', *JESI*, vi, 1-4. It is interesting to note in this connection that this identification was first clearly advocated by Mirashi himself. He now feels it necessary to challenge it only to strengthen his theory of an early date for Tīvaradeva which is not warranted by the extant evidence.

696. Ajay Mitra Shastri, 'A Note on the Date of Tīvaradeva', *ibid.*, 5-11.

other considerations which lead to the conclusion that the period of Śarabharāja and that of the commencement of the Śarabhapurīya rule were not separated by a long gap.[697] Secondly, the Eran inscription under reference need not be taken to indicate that either Śarabharāja or his daughter's son Goparāja were ruling in the Eran region. The epigraph states about Goparāja that he had accompanied his friend Bhānugupta to Eran where he fought a great battle and fell fighting.[698] Thus, if the statement of the inscription were to be taken in a proper perspective, we shall have to conclude that like Bhānugupta, Goparāja also came to Eran from somewhere else. And even if it is conceded for argument's sake that Goparāja ruled over the Eran region, it does not necessarily follow that his maternal grandfather also ruled in the same area; for it is well known that even in those days when swift means of communication were not available, matrimonial relations were often contracted between families settled in areas situated hundreds of miles away from each other, specially in royal families. It is not impossible, therefore, that Śarabharāja was actually ruling in the Chhattisgarh region, though one cannot be quite sure on this point.[699]

Be that as it may. Fortunately, apart from the identification of the two Śarabhas we have some other evidence in favour of dating the commencement of the Śarabhapurīya rule about the close of the fifth century A.D. Fleet at first thought that the characters of the Śarabhapurīya grants 'indicate that they may perhaps be attributed to a period not far distant from that of Goparāja.'[699a] This statement was made with reference only to the Arang plates of Jayarāja and the Raipur plates of Sudevarāja which alone were incorporated by Fleet in his *Inscriptions of the Early Gupta Kings and their Successors*.[700] It was suggested by V.V. Mirashi that the box-headed characters were in use in Kosala owing to the influence of the Vākāṭakas and he referred in this connection to the assertion in the Balaghat plates of Pṛthivīṣeṇa II that the king of Kosala was a feudatory of his father Narendrasena.[701] He thought that this king of Kosala was 'probably one of "the Kings of Śarabhapura" '. He did not, however, name the Śarabha-

697. As pointed out by Fleet (*CII*, iii, introduction, 14), palaeographically the records of Jayarāja and Sudevarāja cannot perhaps be placed far distant from the Eran inscription of Goparāja.

698. *Śrī-Bhānugupta jagati pravīro rājā mahān pārtha-samo = ti-śūraḥ |*
ten = ātha sārddhan = tv = iha Goparājo mittr = ānugatyen kil = ānuyātaḥ |
D.C. Sircar, *Select Inscriptions*, i, 346.

699. Mirashi thinks that the early Śarabhapura chiefs ruled in the Gangapur area of Orissa. But the earliest records of the family have been found in the Raipur District which was obviously the home province of the dynasty.

699a. *CII*, iii, introduction, 14.

700. *Ibid.*, 191-200, nos. 40 and 41.

701. *EI*, xxii, 17. For Balaghat plates see *CII*, v, 79ff. The inscription actually states that the commands of Narendrasena were honoured by the lords of Kosala, Mekala and Mālava (see text-lines 27-28). The same statement is found in the Mahurjhari and Mandhal plates of Pṛthivīṣeṇa II.

purīya chief. But from the fact that he placed the first known Śarabhapura king Śarabha in *circa* 460-80 A.D.[702] it is obvious that this was the chief he had in his mind. In any case we have no evidence of the Vākāṭaka influence in South Kosala prior to the time of Narendrasena. A study of the extant Śarabhapurīya records reveals that all the kings of Śarabhapura beginning with Śarabha's son Narendra were for all practical purposes, sovereign rulers and there is absolutely no trace in their charters of their acknowledging the hegemony of the Vākāṭakas.[703] Now, Narendrasena's son and successor Pṛthivīṣeṇa II was one of the most powerful members of the main line of the Vākāṭakas and his rule lasted till about the close of the fifth century A.D. In all likelihood he maintained his hold over Kosala and no independent sovereign power could have conceivably come into existence during his reign. It follows that the Śarabhapurīyas could have launched upon a sovereign political career only around 500 A.D. This conclusion is also vouched for by the palaeographical evidence as it is generally admitted that the characters of the Śarabhapurīya charters are more advanced as compared to those of the Vākāṭaka records.

Very important light is thrown on this question by the evidence afforded by the Kurud plates issued by Śarabha's son Narendra in the twenty-fourth year of his reign. This epigraph records that the grant mentioned in it was originally made by the *Parama-bhaṭṭāraka-pāda* in favour of a Brāhmaṇa after taking bath in the Gaṅgā and conveyed by means of a charter written on palmyra leaves (*tāla-patra-śāsana*) and that when the charter was burnt in a household conflagration it was ascertained by official investigation that the donated village was in continuous enjoyment of the donee and renewed by *Mahārāja* Narendra by issuing a copper-plate charter to the original grantee's son for the increase of the merit of the *Parama-bhaṭṭāraka-pāda* himself. Moreshwar G. Dikshit, who edited the grant, took the expression *Parama-bhaṭṭāraka-pāda* to refer to the father of Narendra.[704] But as pointed out by D.C. Sircar,[705] the absence of the word for 'father' renders this suggestion untenable. On the other hand, it must be remembered that *Parama-bhaṭṭāraka* in association with *Mahārājādhirāja* was used as an imperial title by the Gupta emperors[706] and the statement that the grant

702. *Studies in Indology*, i, 250.
703. As will be shown later, Narendra continued to acknowledge nominal authority of the Guptas down to the end of his reign. We do not know much about Prasannamātra. But the expression *vikram = opanata-sāmanta-cūḍāmaṇi-prabhā-prasek = āmbubhir = dhauta-pāda-yugalaḥ* first noticed in the Mallar grant of the fifth regnal year of Jayarāja, leaves no doubt that he had formally assumed independent power by that time. This expression is regularly met with in all the subsequent records of the family.
704. *EI*, xxxi, 263.
705. *Ibid.*, 267-68.
706. The Imperial Guptas generally used the title *Mahārājādhirāja* which is invariably found in all their official records beginning with the Allahabad pillar inscription of

was originally made after bathing in the Gaṅgā can be easily explained with reference to the Imperial Guptas as they had their capital at Pāṭaliputra on the bank of the river Gaṅgā. It would thus follow that the title in question is intended to refer to the Gupta emperor who originally made the grant as well as the one whose suzerainty was acknowledged by Narendra. The facts that the Gupta overlord is left unnamed and that Narendra is not described as meditating upon the feet of the *Parama-bhaṭṭāraka*, however, show that the suzerainty was only nominal and outlying areas like Chhattisgarh had already started drifting away from the Gupta empire. Such a situation points to early sixth century A.D. when several erstwhile Gupta feudatories like the Later Guptas and the Maukharis[707] are known to have been struggling for power while at the same time continuing to acknowledge the authority, howsoever nominal it might have been, of the Imperial Guptas. We can therefore reasonably conclude that Śarabha started his career as a feudatory of the Guptas in the closing year of the fifth century A.D. and that his son Narendra, who flourished in the beginning of the sixth century, continued to acknowledge the Gupta authority, though only nominally, down to the close of his reign.

It will be noticed that our view about the date of the termination of the Śarabhapurīya rule is at variance with those of some other scholars. V.V. Mirashi was at first inclined to date this event in *c.* 535 A.D.,[708] though of late he has tried to push it back by a few years.[709] D.C. Sircar favoured the middle or the third quarter of the sixth century A.D. for the reign of the last known Śarabhapurīya king Pravararāja.[710] The latter position is obviously close to our position on this question. When Mirashi proposed the first date, records of Narendra who ruled for nearly a quarter of a century were totally unknown. Moreover, he laboured under the impression that the early Śarabhapura chiefs ruled in the eastern part of the Chhattisgarh region and that when Pravararāja made an attempt to expand his dominions

---

Samudragupta. The word *bhaṭṭāraka* is added to it for the first time in the Mathura pillar inscription of the fifth regnal year of Candragupta II (D.C. Sircar, *Select Inscriptions*, i, 277). From the time of Kumāragupta I, we start getting a more showy title, *Parama-bhaṭṭāraka*, which is, however, not used in all cases and *Mahārājādhirāja* continues to hold the field. These titles were not assumed by any other power during this period.

707. Iśānavarman, the fourth Maukhari king, it is interesting to note, was the first member of the dynasty to assume soverign titles. Among the Later Guptas also Kumāragupta, the fourth member of the dynasty, was probably the first to assume independent power. Both these chiefs flourished about the middle of the sixth century.

708. *EI*, xxii, 22.

709. *JESI*, iv, 1-5.

710. *A History and Culture of the Indian People*, III: *The Classical Age* (ed. R.C. Majumdar), 220. Had the Kurud plates been known when D.C. Sircar wrote, he would have certainly dated the termination of the Śarabhapurīya rule very close to the priod to which we assign this event.

westward he came into conflict with the Pāṇḍava chiefs who were contemporaneously ruling over the Bhandak region and were trying to conquer Kosala. Moreover, at that time only six of the seventeen Śarabhapurīya records were known. Much new evidence including many more records of the family has since come to light which renders a review of this position necessary. Similarly, when Sircar wrote on Śarabhapurīyas the Kurud plates which prove that Narendra had a long reign lasting about twenty-five years were unknown. The above discussion of the chronology of the Śarabhapurīyas takes note of all the extant evidence including that which came to light after Mirashi and Sircar wrote and this fact will account for the difference of opinion, major or minor, which is quite natural.

Historical Outline

We may now proceed to give a brief outline of the political history of the dynasty.

Śarabha

The first member of the dynasty known to us so far is Śarabha. No record of the reign of Śarabha himself has been reported to date, and all that we know about him is derived from the legends on the seals attached to the Pīparḍūlā and Kurud plates of his son and successor Narendra as well as from another contemporary record. Śarabhapura, the capital of the dynasty, was obvioulsy founded by and named after him.[711] The city has not been identified so far, but, as has been stated above, it was probably situated in the Raipur region of Madhya Pradesh. It can, therefore, be reasonably concluded that the principality over which he ruled was situated somewhere in South Kosala and in all likelihood comprised the Raipur area where the records of his son Narendra have been found. As pointed out earlier, he is generally identified with Śarabharāja, the maternal grandfather of Bhānugupta's contemporary Goparāja who died in a battle at Eran in 510 A.D.[712] His rule may accordingly be placed in the last quarter of the fifth century A.D.[713] It follows from the Kurud plates of Narendra that like his daughter's son Goparāja he, too, acknowledged the authority of the Guptas and ruled over his principality as their feudatory. As shown above, the *Parama-bhaṭṭāraka-pāda*, who made the original grant recorded in them

711. That the town was founded by Śarabha himself is clearly proved by the Pīparḍūlā plates which were given by his son Narendra in the third year of his reign.

712. This identification has been recently challenged by V.V. Mirashi, though without justification. It is all the more surprising as the identification was first clearly postulated by Mirashi himself. See *JESI*, vi, 1-4. For his earlier view see *EI*, xxii, 17; *Studies in Indology*, i, 249-50.

713. K.D. Bajpai and S.K. Pandey place Śarabha about the beginning of the fourth century A.D. and differentiate him from Goparāja's homonymous maternal grandfather (*Malhar 1975-77*, 32). Mirashi dated Śarabha's rule in *c.* 460-80 A.D.

after bathing in the Gaṅgā[714] and for the augmentation of whose religious merit the grant was renewed by Narendra, could only be the contemporary Gupta emperor who alone could have enjoyed the title of *parama-bhaṭṭāraka* during the period in question. The influence of the Imperial Guptas in South Kosala is vouched for by discovery of the coins of Mahendrāditya[715] and Kramāditya[716] and the employment of the Gupta era in epigraphic records.[717] The coins of Prasannamātra, which are modelled on those of Mahendrāditya and Kramāditya, also point in the same direction. The Gupta emperor Budhagupta, who was on the throne in the last quarter of the fifth century, was obviously Śarabha's overlord.

Narendra

Śarabha was succeeded by his son Narendra who assumed the title of *Mahārāja*. Three of his records, all copper-plate inscriptions, have been reported so far. All the three have been found in the Raipur District of Madhya Pradesh. The first *i.e.*, (Pīparḍūlā) grant is dated in the third and the second (*i.e.*, Kurud) in the twenty-fourth year of his reign, while the third (*viz.*, Rawan) is incomplete. He therefore appears to have ruled for about a quarter of a century, and his reign may be dated tentatively in *c.* 500-525 A.D. The Pīparḍūlā plates and the incomplete Rawan were issued from Śarabhapura, which was evidently his capital, and the Kurud plates from the king's victorious (military) camp (*vijaya-skandhāvāra*) stationed at Tilakeśvara. The latter record probably indicates that at the time of making this grant he was engaged in a military campaign. The villages mentioned in these records, in so far as they are identifiable, have been located with some degree of certainty in the Raigarh, Bilaspur and Raipur districts, indicating that a major part of this area was incorporated in Narendra's dominions. It is quite likely that Narendra added considerably to the territory inherited by him from his father Śarabha. We find some support for this suggestion in his real-inscriptions which aver that he had conquered the earth by the edge of his sword. (*khaḍga-dhārā-jitabhuvaḥ*). In his inscriptions we find no other information about him execpt that he was a devout worshipper of *Bhagavat* or god Viṣṇu.[718] In keeping with his sectarian affiliation, he introduced on his seal the figure of Abhiṣeka-Lakṣmī which was continued by all his descendants.

714. Moreshwar G. Dikshit, who took *Parama-bhaṭṭāraka-pāda* to mean the donor's father, thought that the river Gaṅgā mentioned here could only be the Mahanadi which is one of the most important rivers of this region. See *EI* xxxi, 263-64.

715. *JASB, NS*, xliv, no. 309; *JNSI*, x, 137; xvi, 216-17; *OHRJ*, i, 137.

716. *JNSI*, xxii, 184-187.

717. *EI*, ix, 342ff.; *ICPB*, 94-96. There is difference of opinion about the reading of the date, some taking it to be G. 282 and others G. 182. The former reading appears more probable.

718. Narendra and all the members of the dynasty are styled *Parama-Bhāgavata*.

His Kurud plates show that like his father he continued to acknowledge the supremacy of the Imperial Guptas till at least the twenty-fourth year of his reign. It is interesting to note that these plates refer to his overlord in a respectful manner as *parama-bhaṭṭāraka-pāda* while he himself is given the comparatively simpler title *Mahārāja* and the grant was renewed by him not for the increase of his own merit but that of his overlord. During this period the Gupta empire was disintegrating advantage of the prevailing political uncertainty, Narendra started ruling almost as an independent monarch. This is indicated by the non-mention of the name of the *Parama-bhaṭṭāraka-pāda*, the absence of an expression like *parama-bhaṭṭārakapād-ānudhyāta*, which is often found employed by feudatory chiefs, for Narendra himself, and the non-employment of the Gupta era as well as the use of his own regnal years for the purpose of dating.

Prasanna or Prasannamātra

It is not known definitely as to who succeeded Narendra. We know, however, that the next ruler was Prasanna who is known only from the seal-inscriptions of his son Jayarāja and grandson Sudevarāja. His full name was Prasanna-mātra which is found on his coins.[719] These coins, which are of base gold,[720] are manufactured by the repoussé technique like those of Mahendrāditya and Kramāditya as well as of the Nalas. The surface of the obverse of these coins is divided into two halves by a horizontal line. The upper part, which is shorter than the lower one, bears the standing figure of Garuḍa with spread out wings in the centre flanked by a crescent moon and a wheel on proper right and the sun and a conch-shell left. The lower portion bears the legend *śrī-Prasannamātra* in the box-headed characters.[721] The coins of Prasannamātra have been reported from an extensive area including the Kalahandi District of Orissa and the Chanda District of Maharashtra besides the Chhattisgarh region of Madhya Pradesh which was his home province.[722] The findspots of his coins may indicate that he ruled over an extensive

719. In the seal-inscriptions of his successors he is referred to simply as Prasanna.

720. Lochan Prasad Pandeya described these coins as of silver with a faint polish of gold all over. But actually they appear to be of base gold.

721. B.C. Jain has distinguished two varieties of Prasannamātra's coins in the Bhandara (Chanda District, Maharashtra) hoard, to wit, variety 'A' bears a cluster of six dots below the letter *sa* of the legend while variety 'B' has a pitcher with or without a cover in place of the cluster of six dots (JNSI, xvi, 217). As pointed out by him, the six coins in the Central Museum, Nagpur, published by V.P. Rode (*ibid.*, xii, 8-10), belong to the second variety. Richard Burn regards these pieces as seals or medals (*Annual Bibliography of Indian Archaeology*, vii, 12). For other references, see *Proceedings of All-India Oriental Conference*, Vth Session, i, 46ff.; *IHQ*, ix, 595; xv, 475-76; R.C. Majumdar and A.S. Altekar (ed.) *A New History of the Indian People*, vi: *The Vākā-ṭaka-Gupta Age*, 87, fn. 3; *ASI, AR*, 1926-27, 230.

722. Recently a few coins of Prasannamātra have been found at Khariar in the Kalahandi District of Orissa. I owe this information to my friend Professor N.K. Sahu.

region though, it must be remembered, it is not always safe to infer the extent of a king's dominion solely from the provenance of his specie.[723] The issue of coins by him seems to indicate that he was a powerful ruler and had probably thrown off the yoke of the Guptas and started ruling as a sovereign monarch for all intents and purposes. It must, however, be remembered that in ancient India minting was not regarded as a royal prerogative and coins issued by semi-independent provincial governors are known.[724] It is possible, therefore, that like Narendra, Prasannamātra also continued to concede the authority, though only nominal, of the Gupta overlord practically for the entire duration of his reign. As will be shown below, this conclusion is supported by the evidence of Jayarāja's grants. He appears to have founded a town named Prasannapura which is mentioned as situated on the river Niḍilā in the Mallar plates of Vyāghrarāja.[725] Later it became the capital of the Amarārya-kula. In the absence of any record of Prasannamātra himself it is difficult to ascertain his regnal period. We may, however, assign him and his possible predecessor, if any, a period of some twenty-five years, *viz circa* 525-550 A.D.

Jayarāja

Prasannamātra was followed on the throne by his son Jayarāja who is represented by four copper-plate charters dated from the third to the ninth year of his reign. Assuming that he ruled only for a short period of about ten years, we may date his reign from *c.* 550 to *c.* 560 A.D. He was the first member of the dynasty to prefix the word *mahat* to his name and this practice became so popular that it was adhered to not only by all his successors but also by the Pāṇḍuvaṁśins, and the Somavaṁśins *i.e.*, this practice was prevalent in the Chhattisgarh region of Madhya Pradesh and the adjoining area of Orissa for over six centuries. To him, again, is due the credit of giving the standard form to the draft of the copper-plate grants which was adhered to by all his descendants. His records, all of which were issued from Śarabhapura, have been found in the Kalahandi District of Orissa and the Bilaspur and Raipur districts of Madhya Pradesh, indicating that he maintained intact the dominions bequeathed to him by his royal predecessor. The same conclusion can be drawn from the localities mentioned in his records which have been satisfactorily identified in the same area. The allusion to his assailing the enemies by his

723. Being portable and useful to meet necessities of life, coins often travel to localities far away from the area for which they were originally meant.

724. See the *Senāpati, Mahāsenāpati, Talavara, Mahātalavara, Mahāgrāmika*, etc. coins. *Vide* D.C. Sircar, *Studies in Indian Coins*, 139-44.

725. It is also not impossible that the town was actually founded by his son who christened it after his father.

valour in the seal-inscriptions[726] and the statement that his feet were washed by the waters in the form of the flowing forth of the radiance of the jewels in the locks of hair on the tops of the heads of the feudatory chiefs who had been subjugated by his prowess in the initial portion of his records[727] probably indicate that he made fresh conquests. The reference to the feudal chiefs bowing down at his feet, it is interesting to note, is conspicuous by its absence in the Amgura plates of his third regnal year and is first met with in the grants issued in the fifth year of his reign.[728] It may perhaps indicate that he formally renounced the Gupta suzerainty and declared his independence sometime between his third and fifth regnal years. V.V. Mirashi is of the opinion that Jayarāja defeated Bhīmasena II of the so-called Rājarṣi-tulya-kula known from his Arang plate and occupied the Arang region.[729] But we find it difficult to acquiesce in this suggestion as the Arang plate of Bhīmasena is actually dated in the Gupta year 282 (=601 A.D.),[730] and not in G. 182 as Mirashi believes,[731] and consequently Bhīmasena II flourished considerably later than Jayarāja.[732] The identification of Jayarāja with Jaya-bhaṭṭāraka mentioned in the Mallar plates of Vyāghrarāja as suggested by D.C. Sircar and G. Bhattacharya also, as we have shown above, is not feasible. B.C. Jain's view that Jayarāja was also known as Mānamātra and Durgarāja besides Jayabhaṭṭāraka is also improbable.

Mānamātra-Durgarāja

Jayarāja probably died without an issue to succeed him and was, therefore, succeeded by his brother Mānamātra who is described as Prasanna's son in some of the seal-inscriptions of his son and successor Sudevarāja. In two of his copper-plate charters (Dhamatari and Kauvatal plates) the same Sudevarāja is said to have been the son of Mahā-Durgarāja. It is, thus, apparent that Mānamātra was also known as Durgarāja (or Mahā-Durgarāja). The word *mahat* prefixed to his name reveals that he did assume regal power. In the absence of his own records it is not possible to determine the

726. The initial portion of his copper-plate charters from fifth year onward also describes him as the cause of the tearing of the parted hair of the ladies of the enemies. This expression is found repeated in all the subsequent records of the dynasty.
727. This statement is, for the first time, met with in Jayarāja's records and consequently appears to be based on some historical facts. The phrase is, however, repeated by all his descendants. No historical significance need be attached to this borrowing.
728. It is first noticed in the Mallar (first set) and Arang plates of this year (see nos. I: V and VI).
729. *Studies in Indology*, i. 253.
730. *EI*, ix, 342ff.; *ICPB*, 94-96, no. 170; *IHQ*, xxii, 62-63.
731. *EI*, xxvi, 227-30; *Studies in Indology*, i, 252-57.
732. Even if we were to accept Mirashi's view for the sake of argument, Bhīmasena II and Jayarāja would not be contemporaries.

duration of his reign. But we shall not be far removed from the factual position if we place his reign in *c.* 560- *c.* 570 A.D.

Sten Konow proposed to identify Mānamātra with the early Rāṣṭrakūṭa king Mānāṅka and the former's son Sudevarāja with the latter's son Devarāja chiefly on the ground of similarity between these names. In support of his contention he drew attention to lexicographical works which regard *aṅka* and *mātra* as synonymous.[733] This conjecture was later endorsed by J. Dubreuil.[734] While editing the Pāṇḍaraṅgapallī plates of Avidheya, M.H. Krishna identified Avidheya as the third son of Devarāja (or Sudevarāja) and postulated the theory of an extensive Rāṣṭrakūṭa empire comprising large parts of Madhya Pradesh, Maharashtra and Karnataka.[735] This problem has been thoroughly examined by A.S. Altekar[736] and V.V. Mirashi[737] who have demonstrated the untenability of these suggestions which need not detain us here.

Likewise, the conjecture of Lochan Prasad Pandeya that Durg, the chief town of the district of the same name in Madhya Pradesh, was established by and named after Durgarāja[738] has been shown to be untenable by Hira Lal[739] who invites attention to a couple of stone inscriptions found at Durg one of which refers to king Śivadeva and the other to Śivadurga and Śivapura associated together, indicating that the fort and the town were separated in the time of Śivadeva who lent his name to both of them. He rightly concluded that the present name Durg or Drug is a contraction of Śivadurga.

Sudevarāja

Mānamātra-Durgarāja appears to have been succeeded by his son Sudevarāja who gives the name of his father as Mahā-Durgarāja in his Dhamatari and Kauvatal plates and as Mānamātra in some of his seal-inscriptions. As many as seven copper-plate inscriptions of his reign have been discovered so far. Their find-spots are situated in the present Raipur, Bilaspur and Raigarh districts of Madhya Pradesh and the Kalahandi District of Orissa and their dates range from the second to the tenth year of his reign. The Dhamatari and Kauvatal plates of the third and seventh years respectively were given from Śrīpura and the rest from the hereditary capital Śarabha-

733. *EI*, ix, 172. It must be pointed out, however, that this identification was postulated by Konow very doubtfully. He himself pointed out that the difference in the characters of the Śarabhapura records and the Uṇḍikavāṭikā grant of Abhimanyu and the seals of the two sets of records makes this identification doubtful.
734. *Ancient History of the Deccan*, 77.
735. *Mysore Archaeological Survey Report*, 1929, 197ff.
736. *ABORI*, xxiv, 148ff.
737. *ABORI*, xxv, 25ff.; *Studies in Indology*, i, 195ff.
738. *IHQ*, xxi 295.
739. *ICPB*, 136, no. 232.

pura. It seems, therefore, that he founded the town of Śrīpura and made it something like his second capital sometime in or prior to the third year of his reign. Śarabhapura, of course, continued to be the main capital. This is clearly shown by the fact that his latest known grant, to wit, the Raipur plates of the tenth year of his reign, was issued from Śarabhapura. As his latest record is dated in his tenth regnal year, there is no doubt that he ruled for at least ten years, if not more. Accordingly, his reign may be tentatively dated from *c.* 571 to *c.* 580 A.D.

In some of his seal-inscriptions he is stated to have extirpated his enemies by his valour and, according to some scholars, this expression indicates that Sudevarāja had some new conquests to his credit. But as such statements are met with in connection with other rulers also,[740] they need not be taken seriously. Of course, this is not to deny the possibility of such conquests by Sudevarāja.

The Dhamatari and Kauvatal plates inform us that Indrabalarāja, who acted as their *dūtaka* or executor, occupied the office of the *Sarvādhikārādhikṛta* under Sudevarāja at least from the third to the seventh year of his reign. This Indrabalarāja is commonly identified with the homonymous son of the Pāṇḍuvaṁśin king Udayana and grandfather of Tīvaradeva. But one cannot be quite sure about this identification which is based solely on the identity of names.

Pravararāja

That Pravararāja was a brother of Sudevarāja is known from his seal-legends which speak of him as a son of Mānamātra. As pointed out earlier, another son of Durgarāja-Mānamātra, Sudevarāja, made Śrīpura his second capital, though Śarabhapura continued to enjoy the status of the chief capital. As both the known charters of Pravararāja were issued from Śrīpura, it may be reasonably concluded that during his reign the capital was finally shifted to Śrīpura. It would thus follow that Sudevarāja was succeeded by Pravararāja who was probably his younger brother. Only a couple of records of Pravararāja have been found so far and both of them are dated in the third year of his reign. He may have ruled for a few years more and the termination of his reign may be dated around 590 A.D.

In the inscription on the seals attached to his charters he claims to have acquired the earth by the prowess of his own arms. This claim is different from the vague claims made by his predecessors and seems to be based on facts. We may, therefore, reasonably conclude that he had to his credit some important conquests which probably resulted in the annexation of some new territory. But in the absence of necessary evidence it is not possible to be more precise on this point.[741] The allusion to fresh territorial

740. *E.g.*, Narendra and Jayarāja.
741. Mirashi thinks that Pravararāja tried to extend his kingdom westwards in consequence of which he came into conflict with Tīvaradeva. See *EI*, xxii, 17.

acquisitions in the seal-epigraphs has led B.C. Jain to the conclusion that the kingdom of Śrīpura was established by Pravararāja who, being more ambitious, left Śarabhapura and entrenched himself at Śrīpura and that after his death this newly founded kingdom of Śrīpura was also added to Sudevarāja's ancestral principality of Śarabhapura.[742] However, in the present state of our knowledge this suggestion cannot be regarded as anything better than a gratuitous assumption without any evidence to support it.

Pravararāja is the last known Śarabhapura chief and nothing is known about the dynasty after him. Making a little allowance for the rule of his possible successor, if any, and for the extension of the earlier reigns beyond the latest recorded years we may tentatively date the end of the Śarabhapurīya rule about the close of the sixth century A.D.

The termination of the Śarabhapurīya rule appears to have been brought about by the rise of some other powers as evidenced by the epigraphic records found in South Kosala. As we have seen above, one of these was the Amarārya-kula whose members Jaya-bhaṭṭāraka, Pravara-bhaṭṭāraka and Vyāghrarāja appear to have flourished about the end of the sixth or the beginning of the following century A.D.[743] Bhīmasena II of the so-called Rājarṣi-tulya-kula, who issued his Arang plates in G. 282 (=601 A.D.), also appears to have contributed to the decline of the Śarabhapura family.[744] Śūrabala Udīrṇavaira, the last known member of the Pāṇḍava dynasty of Mekalā, also probably extended his rule to the Chhattisgarh region as can be reasonably inferred from his recently discovered Mallar charter given in the eighth year of his reign.[745] All these incursions must have been at the

742. B.C. Jain, *op. cit.*, Introduction, 8.

743. Although the localities mentioned in the Mallar plates of Vyāghrarāja, which are our only source of information about the Amarārya dynasty, have not yet been identified, their discovery at Mallar and the mention of Prasannapura, evidently named after the Śarabhapurīya chief Prasannamātra, should leave no doubt that the dynasty ruled at least for a while in South Kosala. Our dating of the plates around 600 A.D. finds support from the records of the Pāṇḍavas of Mekalā who, as will be shown in the sequel, also flourished about the same time and had matrimonial relations with the Amarāya-kula.

744. *EI*, ix, 342-45. Recently it has been suggested that the correct reading of the figure for hundred is 100 and not 200 so that the date of the record is actually 181. This suggestion is primarily based on the absence of a horizontal stroke attached to the right of the figure for 100. See V.V. Mirashi, *Studies in Indology*, i, 252ff.; *EI*, xxvi, 228. Also see *JOI*, xxiii, 335ff. It may, however, be added without questioning this statement that there is a slightly slanting stroke attached to the left of the lower portion of the vertical of the figure for 100. It seems that the writer has by oversight placed to the left the stroke that he should have attached to the right. Otherwise this stroke will have to be regarded as superfluous. We, therefore feel that the charter was actually given in G. 281 or 601 A.D. and that the reading originally proposed by Hira Lal is correct.

745. See no. II:II, Saṅgama, the village granted through these plates has been located in the Bilaspur District., See K. D. Bajpai and S. K. Pandey, *op.cit.*, 23; K.D. Bajpai,

expense of and substantially weakened the Śarabhapurīya power which was administered the final death blow at the hands of the Pāṇḍuvaṁśins of the line of Udayana who ruled over South Kosala and adjoining area in Vidarbha and Orissa for well over a century.

II. THE PĀṆḌAVAS OF MEKALĀ

The Pāṇḍava dynasty of Mekalā was first brought to light by the Bamhani plates of Śūrabala *alias* Udīrṇavaira.[746] The recently discovered Mallar plates of the same ruler[747] have added a little more to our knowledge of the history of the dynasty besides correcting some of the erroneous notions formed on the basis of the defective wording of the *praśasti* portion of the Bamhani plates.

Mekalā

In the opening stanza of both these grants the first member of the family is stated to have been born in Mekalā. Likewise the villages granted through both these charters are described as situated in Mekalā which is represented as divided into provinces each of which in its turn was subdivided into districts. It is, thus, obvious that Mekalā was the name of the area under the rule of the dynasty which is accordingly designated as the 'Pāṇḍava Dynasty of Mekalā'. The name Mekalā still survives in the range of hills called the Maikal range which serves as the connecting link between the Vindhyas and the Satpuras and stretches from the Khairagarh area to the Rewa region.[748] It is actually a spur of the Vindhya range, the eastern portion of which is called Amarakantak. In early Indian literature Mekala is referred to as the name of a mountain range, from which the river Narmadā takes its rise and is consequently called 'the daughter of Mekala' (*Mekala-kanyakā* or *Mekala-sutā*), as well as of a country and its inhabitants.[749] Applied in a territorial sense, it seems to have denoted the area round the Maikal range. When used for the country, the name is invariably spelt as terminating in long *ā* (Mekalā),[750] and this is supported by the records in question in both of which it is spelt likewise. The same

---

'New Light on the Early Pāṇḍava Dynasty of South Kosala', *ABORI, Diamond Jubilee Volume*, 435.

746. No. II:I.

747. No. II: II. Another stray plate of the dynasty has also been reported from Mallar. See *ABORI, Diamond Jubilee Volume*, 435-36.

748. H.C. Raychaudhuri, *Studies in Indian Antiquities*, 134: D.C. Sircar, *Studies in the Geography of Ancient and Mediaeval India*, 43, fn. 1.

749. For these references see *EI*, xxvii, 135; D.C. Sircar, *Studies in the Geography of Ancient and Mediaeval India*, 43, Ajay Mitra Shastri, *India as seen in the Bṛhatsaṁhitā of Varāhamihira*, 54.

750. In the historical texts of the Purāṇas also the name ends in long *ā*. See F.E. Pargiter, *The Purāṇa Text of the Dynasties of the Kali Age*, 51.

may be said regarding the Balaghat,[751] Mahurjhari[752] and Mandhal plates[753] of the Vākāṭaka king Pṛthivīṣeṇa II which also give Mekalā as the name of the country.[754] But from literature it is difficult to get an idea of the extent of the Mekalā country which must have differed from time to time with the fluctuations in political conditions. But we can reasonably infer from the present inscriptions that under the Pāṇḍavas, specially under Śūrabala, it had a wide extent covering a fairly large area of the Baghelkhand region of Madhya Pradesh and included the southern part of the Shahdol District, eastern part of the Mandla District and the northern part of the Bilaspur District.[755] The Mallar plates show that during the reign of Śūrabala a considerable part of the Bilaspur District including the Mallar region was also under the Pāṇḍuvaṁśins and it is said to have been included in Mekalā which, as we have seen above, served as the designation of the dominions of the dynasty in question and the application of the name was apparently extended even to fresh areas brought under the rule of the family from time to time.[756]

Lineage

In the very inaugural verse of our records the first member of the dynasty, Jayabala, is stated to have been born in the lineage of the Pāṇḍavas in the Mekalā country. Verse 11 of the Bamhani plates describes the lineage in which Śūrabala was born as *saumya* or 'of gentle nature'. But this seems to be a case of *śleṣa* or *double entendre* and the word is probably also intended to speak of the family as descended from the moon.[757] That this conjecture is correct is proved indisputably by verse 7 of the Mallar plates which, as if to leave no scope for doubt, clearly describes the family both as *saumya* (*i.e.*, 'of gentle nature') as well as *somasya vaṁśa* (*i.e.*, family of the moon).

751. *EI*, ix, 271, text-line 28. Also see *CII*, v, 81. F. Kielhorn, who originally edited these plates in *EI*, ix, thought that Mekalā was an error for Mekala. See *ibid.*, 271, fn. 9.
752. *Vidarbha Saṁśodhana Maṇḍala Vārṣika*, *1971*, 75, text-line 22.
753. *Ibid.*, *1977*, 171, text-line 17.
754. Some scholars are under the erroneous impression that while Mekala was the name of the country the word *Mekalā* denoted the capital of Mekala. A similar distinction is sought to be made between he names Kosala and Kosalā.
755. This finds support from the territorial divisions and localities referred to in the records of the family. B. Ch. Chhabra observes that 'the whole of Mekalā comprised the south-eastern part of the Rewa State, portions in the north of the Bilaspur District and some area in the east of the Mandla District'. See *EI* xxvii, 138.
756. The inclusion of a considerable part of the Bilaspur District including Mallar in Śūrabala's dominions is indicated not only by the findspot of this record but also by the identification of the village donated through it in the Bilaspur District.
757. The intended reading of the relevant portion of the verse in question in the Bamhani plates may actually be *saumyaḥ somasya vaṁśaḥ* (instead of *saumyaḥ so=yañ=ca vaṁśaḥ*) as in the Mallar plates.

It is not impossible that the claim to belong to the lunar lineage is also hinted at in the description of Śūrabala's father Bharatabala as possessıng fame resembling the rays of the moon.[758] Be that as it may, there is no doubt that the family was known both as Pāṇḍava as well as Soma-vaṁśa like the Pāṇḍuvaṁśins of South Kosala whose history will be discussed later.

Historical Outline

From the Bamhani and the Mallar plates of Śūrabala *alias* Udīrṇavaira we get the following genealogy of the dynasty :—

Jayabala
|
Vatsarāja
|
Nāgabala
|
Bharatabala
|
Śūrabala

Jayabala

Jayabala is the first member of the dynasty mentioned in our records which do not supply any information of historical interest about him. He is merely said to have been born in the lineage of the famous Pāṇḍavas in the Mekalā country. He is styled *rājan* and is described as the foremost amongst the ruling chiefs (*kṣitipati-tilaka*). He is described in conventional terms and is said to have acquired great renown and to have been endowed with the best of qualities and a handsome figure.[759]

Vatsarāja

Jayabala's son and successor, Vatsarāja, seems to have been more illustrious and powerful than his father. He is compared to the traditionally famous Vatsa king Udayana[760] and is said to have won victories in battles and assailed the enemies by the valour of his own arms and made the gardens attached to the houses of his enemies teem with wild beasts. He, too, is styled 'king' (*kṣitīśa* and *nṛpati*) and is represented as the foremost of the kings.[761] He married a lady named Droṇa-bhaṭṭārikā.

Nāgabala

Vatsarāja was succeeded by his son Nāgabala who was born of queen Droṇa-bhaṭṭārikā. He is described briefly in a single stanza[762] and that also

758. See nos. II:I verse 10; II:II, verse 6.
759. This description is found in the opening stanza of both the grants.
760. The comparison was obviously suggested by the name Vatsarāja.
761. This account is based on verses 2-3 of no. II:I and verse 2 of no. II: II.
762. See nos. II: I, verse 4; II: II, verse 3.

in a purely conventional manner. There is a vague allusion to his wars against his enemies in which his cavalry and elephantry are said to have played a leading role. But a prose passage, first introduced in connection with him and repeated with necessary alterations in regard to formal details with reference to his successors, styles him *mahārāja.* Whether he was the first member of the dynasty to assume the title *Mahārāja* cannot be ascertained as its absence like that of other epithets in connection with his two predecessors may be due to the fact that they are described only in verses which did not provide scope for the use of this title. But in case its absence with reference to the earlier rulers is deliberate, the assumption of this superior title by Nāgabala would indicate that he was more powerful than his predecessors and probably declared his independence and assumption of sovereign status, the earlier members of the family being feudatories of some other power. Nāgabala is further described as a devout worshipper of Maheśvara, a great honourer of the Brāhmaṇas and as highly devoted to the teachers and the supreme divinity.[763] His queen was Indra-bhaṭṭārikā.

Bharatabala

The son and successor of Nāgabala born of his queen Indra-bhaṭṭārikā was Bharatabala[764] who is described in greater detail than any of his predecessors,[765] which may be due to the fact that he was more powerful or that he was the immediate predecessor of the monarch responsible for issuing these charters. In the prose passage introducing him he, too, is given the title of *Mahārāja* and is represented as a devout worshipper of Maheśvara, a great respector of the Brāhmaṇas and as highly devoted to the teachers and the supreme divinity. He had Indra for his second name and is compared to Indra, the lord of gods, in the destruction of enemies and in valour and to god Agni in brilliance. Further, his birth from queen Indra-bhaṭṭārika is equated to that of god Kārttikeya from Pārvatī, the daughter of the lord of mountains, *i.e.*, Himavat. Verse 5 of the Mallar plates states that the ruling chiefs everywhere sang his praises in which they equated him to the epic hero Bharata, younger brother of Rāghava and born in the family of Daśaratha.[765a] He appears to have won some important successes against his enemies as indicated by the statements that he, like a gigantic quarter-elephant, covered all the quarters with a multitude of resounding trees in the form of overbearing enemies who were pulled down and torn asunder by

763. Our interpreatation of the relevant expression, *viz.*, *parama-guru-devat-ādhidaivata-viśeṣaḥ*, differs from that of others. For a detailed discussion, see abstract of and notes on the texts of these inscriptions.

764. This was the full form of the name. But he was also known simply as Bharata (see nos. II:I, text-line 15 and verse 8; II: II, text-line 21), indicating thereby that the name-ending *bala* found suffixed to the names of all but one members of the family has to be treated as something like a surname.

765. He claims as many as four stanzas (5-8) in the Bamhani plates and two verses (4-5) in the Mallar grant.

765a. The comparison is evidently based on the identity of names.

him and that he gave refuge to the Fortune of the host of his foes slain by him when she approached his arms. He married a lady, probably named Lokaprakāśā,[766] born in the Amaraja-kula in Kosalā. She is described in glowing terms, though the description is generally conventional in character. She is compared to the sacred river Jāhnavī, *i.e.*, Gaṅgā, descending on the earth from heaven on account of her crystal-like pure character and strict observance of self-restraint and self-discipline. She appears to have lived for a pretty long time as can be inferred from the statement that she attained a sublime status by dint of having grandsons and great-grandsons who were foremost among princes and champions of discipline and justice. The high praise bestowed on her probably indicates the great importance that the family attached to her marriage with Bharatabala, perhaps due to the accession of power and prestige it may have brought in its train. It is noteworthy in this connection that the spouses of the preceding two rulers, who are also mentioned, are not described in this manner.[767]

Śūrabala

Bharatabala was followed on the throne by his son *Mahāraja* Śūrabala who was also known as Udirṇavaira.[768] Besides the conventional description in the short prose passage which is also met with in connection with Nāgabala and Bharatabala,[769] only a single stanza is devoted to him in both

766. The manner in which the word *lokaprakāśā* is used makes one doubtful if it was really her name and not just a qualifying adjective describing her as 'well-known (literally, resplendent) in the world'. But if it is regarded as an adjective, we shall have to concede that the queen has been left unnamed though she is described in great detail otherwise It must be remembered, however, that in the prose passage introducing her son Śūrabala also her name is not mentioned though the names of the mothers of his two predecessors are clearly specified in the prose passage describing them. It has recently been suggested that the name of Bharatabala's wife and Śūrabala's mother was Mahādevī which is met with in the prose passage introducing Śūrabala in his Mallar plates. See B. Sitaraman and M.J. Sharma in *Studies in Indian Epigraphy*, iii, 187-88. But in that case we shall be facing the strange situation that whereas the title *devī* is used in the prose passages before the names of the mothers of Nāgabala and Bharatabala, it is omitted in the case of the issuing chief's mother. It may, of course, be argued that the word *mahādevī* has a *double entendre* and besides being the personal name of the queen also means 'chief queen'.
767. They are merely introduced as the mothers of Nāgabala and Bharatabala in the prose passages introducing them.
768. This name occurs independently in the prose passage at the beiginning of Śūrabala's Mallar plates. In fact, it is also mentioned in verse 11 of the Bamhani plates, but the wording of the stanza did not allow it to be recognised as a personal name and it was taken only as an adjective. This is the same as verse 7 of the Mallar plates.
769. But there is a significant difference. If Mahādevī was not the name of Bharatabala's queen, it will have to be conceded that Śūrabala's mother has been left unnamed. We feel that the name, which was possibly Lokaprakāśā, has been dropped by oversight.

the records.[770] He is said to have uprooted his enemies and overcome all the quarters by the pair of his lotus-like feet fervently rubbed by the heads of many a feudal chief subjugated by his perfect triple power.[771]

While it is not possible in the present state of our knowledge to determine the extent of the principality under the rule of the first four chiefs, it can be reasonably inferred from the localities mentioned in the two complete charters as well as their findspots that Śūrabala *alias* Udīrṇavaira ruled over a fairly extensive area including all the territories listed above as comprised in Mekalā.

Capital

In the absence of the mention of the place of issue of the grants of the family or any other information on the point, it is difficult to locate the capital of the Pāṇḍava kingdom of Mekalā. V.V. Mirashi seems to be inclined to identify it with Bandhogarh, about sixty miles north-west of Bamhani, the findspot of one of the grants of Śūrabala.[772] But he has not cited any evidence in support of his contention, the relationship of the Pāṇḍavas of Mekalā with Bhadrabāla,[773] the father of *Rājan* Vaiśravaṇa, known from an inscription found at Bandhogarh[773a] being unsubstantiable as will be shown in the sequel. K.D. Bajpai thinks that the capital of Jayabala's family was at Śarabhapura which he regards as the older name of Mallar.[774] While the possibility of the last known member of the family, Śūrabala, occupying the Mallar region cannot be gainsaid, there is absolutely no evidence to support the location of the dynasty's capital at Mallar. Moreover, as observed earlier,[775] the equation of Śarabhapura with Mallar is quite uncertain, if not untenable. It is, we feel, best to leave the question open till such time as some definite evidence comes to light.

Both the extant complete records of the dynasty are dated in the regnal years of the issuing chief and, therefore, the period of the Pāṇḍava rule over the Mekalā region has to be determined on other grounds. B.Ch. Chhabra has made an attempt to fix the chronology of the Pāṇḍavas on the basis of verse 11 of the Bamhani plates[776] which, according to him, contains

770. Stanza 11 of Bamhani plates and verse 7 of the Mallar grant.

771. The three powers are *prabhu-śakti*, *mantra-śakti* and *utsāha-śakti*. For the definition of these powers, see *Kauṭilīya Arthaśāstra*, VI.2.33. For other references, see P.V. Kane, *HDS*, iii, 171-72.

772. *Studies in Indology*, i, 235; *CII*, v, introduction, xxvi.

773. Mirashi spells the name as Bhadrabala with the object of connecting him with the Pāṇḍavas of Mekalā most of whom bore *bala*-ending names. See *ibid.*, introduction xxvi; *Studies in Indology*, i, 231-32.

773a. *EI*, xxxi 185-86, nos. xviii and xix and plate facing p. 186.

774. K.D. Bajpai, and S.K. Pandey. *op.cit.*, 23; K.D. Bajpai, 'New Light on the Early Pāṇḍava Dynasty of South Kosala' *ABORI*, *Diamond Jubilee Volume*, 436.

775. See *supra*, 90-5.

776. This stanza is repeated in the Mallar plates (verse 7) also.

a veiled allusion to the Vākāṭaka king Narendrasena who was Bharatabala's overlord. It has been suggested that there is a pun on the word *narendra* occurring at the end of this stanza which, while referring to Bharatabala, means 'king', whereas otherwise it stands for his Vākāṭaka overlord Narendrasena.[777] This suggestion, which is accepted by most scholars,[778] is apparently prompted by the assertion met with in some of the records of Vākāṭaka Pṛthivīṣeṇa II that the commands of his father Narendrasena were honoured by the lords of Kosalā, Mekalā and Mālava.[779] Regarding 435-470 A.D. as the regnal period of Narendrasena,[780] equating the second year of Bharatabala's reign[781] approximately to 460 A.D. and assigning a period of about twenty years for each reign, Chhabra arrived at 399-400 A.D. (roughly 400 A.D.) as the approximate date of Jayabala's rise to power.[781a] Mirashi also dates the accession of Jayabala to about 400 A.D. and places the reign of Bharatabala in *circa* 460-480 A.D.[782] D.C. Sircar favours a somewhat later date and places the reigns of Nāgabala and Bharatabala in the second half of the fifth century A.D.[783] However, a close examination brings to fore the difficulties in accepting these suggestions. First of all, as we have seen above, the Bamhani as well as Mallar plates belong not to Bharatabala but to his son Śūrabala *alias* Udīrṇavaira and the verse supposed to contain a reference to Narendrasena actually describes the latter. The misconception that the stanza in question describes Bharatabala was due to the omission by oversight of the conventional prose passage introducing Śūrabala in the Bamhani grant. The recent discovery of the Mallar charter containing this passage leaves no doubt about it. Thus, if the aforesaid verse actually refers to Narendrasena, though in a

777. *Bhārata Kaumudī* (Studies in Indology in honour of Dr. Radha Kumud Mukerjee), i, 219; *EI*, xxvii, 137 and 145, fn. 1.
778. V.V. Mirashi, *Inscriptions of the Vākāṭakas, CII*, v, xxv-xxvi and 83-84; *Studies in Indology*, i, 234-35; S.R. Goyal, *A History of the Imperial Guptas*, 276-77. But *contra* D.C. Sircar in *The Vākāṭaka-Gupta Age* (ed. R.C. Majumdar and A.S. Altekar), 92; *The Classical Age*, 223.
779. *CII*, v, 81, text-lines 27-28; *Vidarbha Saṁśodhana Maṇḍala Vārṣika* (Marathi), *1971*, 75, text-lines 22-23; *ibid 1977*, 171-72, text-lines 17-18.
780. This date was based on K.P. Jayaswal, *History of India* 150 *A.D.* 350 *A.D.*, 101. Mirashi (*Studies in Indology*, i, 231, fn. 2) is in favour of a slightly later date for the commencement of Narendrasena's reign which he places in the period 450 to 470 A.D.
781. This is the date of the Bamhani plates.
781a. *Bhārata-Kaumudī*, i, 219; *EI*, xxvii, 138.
782. *Studies in Indology*, i, 233. But if Jayabala was raised to power by Samudragupta, as Mirashi believes, his rise to power will have to be dated somewhere around 350 A.D. and the beginning of the reign of Bharatabala about 425 A.D., much earlier than the accession of Narendrasena.
783. *The Classical Age*, 223; *The Vākāṭaka-Gupta Age*, 92. He dates the Bamhani plates about the close of the fifth or probably the beginning of the sixth century A.D.

veiled manner, as the Pāṇḍava chief's overlord, the Pāṇḍava feudatory of Narendrasena would turn out to be Śūrabala and not his father Bharatabala. There is, however, actually no reference whatever to Vākāṭaka Narendrasena in this verse, and the word *narendra* has to be taken simply in the sense of 'king' and it is employed only as an adjective of Udīrṇavaira who is clearly named just before it. In fact, had there been no reference to the Mekalā king as obeying the orders of Narendrasena in the Vākāṭaka records, the idea of an indirect reference to the Vākāṭaka monarch in this stanza would not have suggested itself to any one. What is astonishing is that Chhabra and Mirashi proposed to correct incorrectly engraved word in verse 11 of the Bamhani plates to *sārvabhauma* which they rightly translated by 'sovereign' and 'paramount ruler' respectively.[784] Moreover, the same stanza also speaks of feudal chiefs falling at the feet of Udīrṇavaira which leaves no room for doubt that Śūrabala *alias* Udīrṇavaira, the issuer of these as also the Mallar plates, regarded himself as a paramount ruler with a number of feudatory chiefs acknowledging his sovereignty, there being absolutely no question of himself even nominally acknowledging anybody else's supremacy and making even a veiled reference to him. It has been observed by Chhabra with a view to explain away the so-called equivocal manner in which the allegiance to Narendrasena was supposed to have been expressed that Narendrasena's overlordship was more in name only, that Mekalā under the kingship of Bharatabala was an internally autonomous state, and that the prestige of its king was not much inferior to that of his suzerain or that both of them were perhaps more or less on friendly terms. It looks as if Bharatabala was not bound to acknowledge Narendrasena's overlordship in the charter issued by him, but that it was out of courtesy that he did so and that wilfully in an indirect manner.[785] However, if the Pāṇḍava king was so eager to refer to his Vākāṭaka overlord, however nominal, even by way of courtesy, he would have done so explicitly instead of resorting to such a veiled manner as would not allow it to be recognised without the help of some Vākāṭaka records referring to Narendrasena's overlordship over the Mekalā king. Moreover, the futility of all this exercise, which is inspired, as stated above, by some Vākāṭaka records, will become apparent the moment we realise that the Pāṇḍavas of Mekalā flourished after the Vākāṭakas had disappeared from the political map of India, as will be shown presently. The same is true of the suggestion to identify the Puṣyamitras, who, according to the famous Bhitari inscription,[786] 'had developed great power and wealth but were vanquished by the

784. *EI*, xxvii, 142 (fn. 3) and 145; *CII*, v, 86 (fn. 3) and 88. It must be pointed out, however, that the corresponding portion in the Mallar plates shows that this correction is unwarranted.
785. *EI*, xxvii, 137.
786. *CII*, iii, 53-54, text-lines 10-11, verse 4.

Gupta emperor Skandagupta, with Bharatabala who, it is argued, had transferred his allegiance from the Imperial Guptas to the Vākāṭakas and invaded the Gupta empire with the backing of Narendrasena.[787]

Fortunately, there are some stronger grounds which enable us to ascertain the period of the Pāṇḍavas of Mekalā. The family to which Bharatabala's queen Lokaprakāśā, who is said to have been born in Kosalā, belonged has been sought to be identified variously. B. Ch. Chhabra thought that possibly she belonged to the Pāṇḍava family of Kosalā.[788] V. V. Mirashi and D. C. Sircar pointed out the untenability of this suggestion, the former on the ground that two Pāṇḍava families (of Mekalā and Kosalā) must have been *sagotra*, if not *samānodaka*, and marriages between *samānodakas* or *sagotras* are not permissible according to Hindu law,[789] and the latter on the ground that the Pāṇḍava occupation of South Kosala took place at a later date.[790] The former thought that she belonged to the Śūra dynasty known from the Arang plate of its last known member Bhīmasena II[791] and was probably a daughter of Bhīmasena I, the fourth member of the family, while the latter held that she was probably a princess of the Śarabhapurīya family. But both the Bamhani and Mallar plates of Śūrabala inform us that Lokaprakāśā was born in the Amaraja-kula about which nothing was known at the time of the publication of the Bamhani plates. But after the discovery of the Mallar plates of Vyāghrarāja[792] there can be no doubt that the Amaraja-kula mentioned in the Bamhani and Mallar plates of Śūrabala is the same as the Amarārya-kula to which Vyāghrarāja and his brother Pravara-bhaṭṭāraka and father Jaya-bhaṭṭāraka belonged. The Amarārya-kula is generally regarded as the name of the Śarabhapurīya dynasty on account of the mention of Prasannapura which was evidently named after Prasannamātra and the names Jaya and Pravara which are known to have been born by the members of this dynasty. But as we have seen above,[793] this identification does not carry conviction and the Amarārya-kula kings Jaya-bhaṭṭāraka and Pravara-bhaṭṭāraka appear to have been ruling contemporaneously with the later members of the Śarabhapurīya dynasty in an area of Kosala not comprised in the latter's dominions and occupied the Mallar region about the close of the sixth or the beginning of the seventh century A.D. Therefore, Bharatabala, who married a princess of this family, cannot be assigned to a date earlier than the latter

787. S.R. Goyal, *op. cit.*, 276-77. It is generally believed that the early members of the Pāṇḍava dynasty of Mekalā were feudatories of the Imperial Guptas and that Bharatabala transferred his allegiance to the Vākāṭakas.

788. *Bhārata-Kaumudī*, i, 217; *EI*, xxvii, 138.

789. *Studies in Indology*, i, 234.

790. *The Classical Age*, 222.

791. *EI*, ix, 342-45.

792. See no. I: Appendix II. Also *EI*, xxxiv, 45-50.

793. See *supra*, 97-100. Also *vide infra*, no I: Appendix II.

half of the sixth century A.D. But even if the identification of the Amarārya-kula with the Śarabhapurīyas and consequently that of Jaya-bhaṭṭāraka with Jayarāja is conceded for the sake of argument, this date will not be affected materially. As we have shown above, the reign of Jayarāja has to be dated in *circa* 550-60 A.D. Even if Lokaprakāśā was sister or daughter of Jayarāja, *i.e.* Jaya-bhaṭṭāraka, the reign of her spouse Bharatabala cannot be dated earlier than the third quarter of the sixth century A.D. and it may have to be dated even later. And if she was a daughter of Pravararāja I, *i.e.* Pravara-bhaṭṭāraka, Bharatabala will have to be placed in the closing quarter of that century. The reigns of Bharatabala and Śūrabala may, therefore, be dated in the closing years of the sixth and the beginning of the seventh century A.D.

Another important evidence bearing on this question is afforded by the Malga plates of *Sāmanta* Indrarāja.[794] As we have seen above,[795] in regard to the formal features, general drafting, the list of addressees of the royal order about the grant, the privileges and exemptions conferred on the donee, the manner of recording date and other matters the Malga plates bear a close resemblance to the known grants of the Pāṇḍavas of Mekalā, and the scribes of the two sets of records appear to have been related to each other as brothers. The *Sāmanta* Indrarāja of the Malga plates, therefore, appears to have been related in some way or the other to the Pāṇḍavas though the exact nature of this relationship cannot be determind at present. It is also noteworthy in this connection that the only known charter of Indrarāja has been found in the Shahdol District of Madhya Pradesh wherein is also situated the provenance of one of the charters of the Mekalā Pāṇḍavas, *i.e.*, Bamhani plates. On palaeographical grounds the Malga plates are assignable to about the first half of the seventh century A.D.[796] and, as the similarity between this grant and those of the Mekalā Pāṇḍavas was not realised at the time of its appearance, it was conjectured by D.C. Sircar and S. Sankaranarayanan, who edited it for the first time, that Indrarāja ruled as a semi-independent chief either sometimes between the death of Maukhari Grahavarman about 605 A.D. and the establishment of Harṣavardhana's power over the erstwhile Maukhari kingdom shortly thereafter or sometime after Harṣavardhana's death in 647 A.D.[797] If the former was the case, Indrarāja, it has been suggested, might have owed allegiance to the Maukharis, while in the latter case the record will have to be placed roughly about the middle of the seventh century A.D. Be that as it may, the fact remains that in view of the very close similarities between the two sets of records it cannot be doubted that they could not have been separated by

794. *EI*, xxxiii, 209-14; *infra*, no. II: Appendix II.
795. *Supra*, 66-81. *Vide* also *infra*, no. II: Appendix II.
796. *EI*, xxxiii, 209.
797. *Ibid.*, 211.

any long interval of time and that the Mekalā Pāṇḍava charters cannot be placed much earlier than the end of the sixth or early years of the seventh century A.D.

In view of these facts the current notions about the history of the Mekalā Pāṇḍavas have to be thoroughly reconsidered and revised. In the light of the aforesaid evidence for the chronology we can reasonably conclude that the first known Pāṇḍava chief Jayabala rose to power about the beginning of the sixth century A.D. and his reign may be placed in *circa* 500-525 A.D. while those of the next three rulers may have covered the next seventy-five years. Śūrabala *alias* Udīrṇavaira, the last known member of the family who issued both the available complete charters, probably came to the throne around 600 A.D. The close of the fifth and the beginning of the sixth century A.D. witnessed a decline of the power of the Imperial Guptas which provided an opportunity for the rise of new political powers which at first acknowledged the suzerainty of the Guptas and later became independent after the fall of the Gupta empire. It was precisely during this period that the Maukharis, the Later Guptas and the Śarabhapurīyas found a place on the political map of India first as feudatories of the Guptas and then as sovereign powers about the middle of the sixth century A.D. The same appears to have been true of the Pāṇḍavas of Mekalā. The first two members of the dynasty, Jayabala and Vatsarāja, were probably feudatory chiefs owing allegiance to the Imperial Guptas, at least theoretically. The next ruler, Nāgabala, flourished at a time when the Gupta empire had collapsed and fully exploited this opportunity to assume sovereign status as indicated by his assumption not only of the title of *Mahārāja* but also of the superior epithet *Parama guru-devatādhidaivata-viśeṣa* which was normally borne by paramount rulers. His son Bharatabala and grandson Śūrabala *alias* Udīrṇavaira were also paramount rulers and further consolidated their position by annexing new territories.

Puranic References

The Pāṇḍavas of Mekalā are probably referred to in the dynastic accounts of the Purāṇas. According to the dynastic text as reconstructed by Pargiter, seven kings ruled in Mekalā for seventy years.[798] The preceding line refers to thirteen Puṣyamitras and Paṭumitras who are also supposed to have been connected with Mekalā. As pointed out earlier, scholars have generally identified the Puṣyamitras defeated by Skandagupta[799] with the Puṣyamitras

798. *Puṣyamitrā bhaviṣyanti Paṭumitrās=trayodaśa*
Mekalāyāṁ nṛpāh sapta bhaviṣyant-īha saptatiṁ.
—F.E. Pargiter, *The Purāṇa Text of the Dynasties of the Kali Age*. 51. According to B.C. Law, the *Viṣṇu Purāṇa* mentions ten kings who had Mekalā as their land of birth. See his *Ancient Indian Tribes*, ii, 28. But he has not cited any authority in support of this statement.

799. The reading of the portion of verse 4 of the Bhitari inscription supposed to refer to

mentioned in the Purāṇas who are further sought to be connected with the Mekalā Pāṇḍavas. While this identification is totally unwarranted in view of the chronological considerations outlined above, there is no room for doubt that the Purāṇa compilers were aware of the Mekalā Pāṇḍavas. This can be easily inferred from the fact that in a version of the *Viṣṇu Purāṇa* instead of the reconstructed reading *Puṣyamitrā bhaviṣyanti* we find *balavān Jayo bhaviṣyati* which is undoubtedly an allusion, though somewhat veiled, to the first Pāṇḍava king Jayabala.[800] It may perhaps be argued against this view that according to Pargiter the account in which the references in question occur relates to the third century A.D.[801] But it is now admitted that the dynastic accounts of the Purāṇas were not finalised in the early Gupta period as believed earlier and that they contain allusions even to some later members of the Gupta dynasty.[802] Even the portion under review which contains references to the Puṣyamitras and seven Mekalā kings and is believed to refer to conditions obtaining in the third century A.D. mentions the Nalas[803] who are known to have ruled in the fifth and subsequent centuries A.D. However, the Purāṇas give the number of Mekalā chiefs as seven, while we know only five Pāṇḍava rulers so far. We must, therefore, await future epigraphical discoveries which may bring to light some more members of the dynasty. It is equally likely that the predecessors of Jayabala were petty chieftains and their names have, therefore, been deliberately dropped in the official records of the dynasty.

Mekalā Pāṇḍavas and Bhadrabāla

V.V. Mirashi thinks that the Mekalā Pāṇḍavas were connected with some earlier chiefs known from a few early inscriptions found at Bandhogarh, some sixty miles to the north-west of Bamhani.[804] The *bala*-termination of the names of most of the Pāṇḍava chiefs has reminded him of *Mahāsenāpati* Bhadrabāla (-bala according to Mirashi), father of *Rājan* Vaiśravaṇa, mentioned in a couple of Bandhogarh inscriptions.[805] According to him, Bhadrabāla was an army-commander of the contemporary Magha king and that his son Vaiśravaṇa, who bore the title *Rājan*, probably ruled over a small

the Puṣyamitras is uncertain and some scholars are inclined to read it as *yudhy=amitāṁś=ca* instead of *Puṣyamitrāṁś=ca* so that there is no reference to any particular adversary but to enemies in general. See H.R. Divekar in *ABORI*, i, 99-103, and V.V. Mirashi in *JESI*, vi.

800. Cited by S.N. Roy in the *Historical and Cultural Studies in the Purāṇas*, 170.

801. F.E. Pargiter, *The Purāṇa Text of the Dynasties of the Kali Age*, 50 and 73.

802. See P.L. Gupta, *The Imperial Guptas*, i, 116-17, where attention is invited to some important Purānic references to Candragupta II, Kumāragupta I and Skandagupta.

803. F.E. Pargiter, *op. cit.*, 51:
Nala-vaṁśa-prasūtāś=ca vīryavanto mahābalāḥ.

804. *Studies in Indology*, i, 230 ff. Also see *Indica* (The Indian Historical Research Institute Silver Jubilee Commemoration Volume), 288 ff.

805. *EI*, xxxi, 185-86, nos. XVIII and XIX (text and translation of the inscriptions).

principality near Bandhogarh where two inscriptions of his reign have been found. He regards these two (Bhadrabāla and Vaiśravaṇa) as the ancestors of Jayabala, the first Pāṇḍava king of Mekalā known from the extant records of the dynasty.[806] For this purpose he rejects the theory identifying Bhadrabāla with the Magha king *Mahārāja* Bhadramagha as well as the identification of the former's son *Rājan* Vaiśravaṇa with the homonymous Magha chief who assumed the title *Mahārāja*, the latter on the ground of the difference in the titles.[807] It is futher suggested by him that *Mahārāja* Lakṣmaṇa, known from his Pali[808] and Singrauli[809] plates of the year 158 which is proposed to be referred to the Śaka era as against its commonly accepted attriubtion to the Gupta era,[810] and Balavarman, one of the Āryāvarta rulers exterminated by Samudragupta,[811] belonged to the Magha dynasty and that after overthrowing the Maghas, Samudragupta annexed the fertile region of Vatsa (Allahabad-Kosam region) and divided the hilly area of Baghelkhand among his feudatories including the Parivrājakas, the Uccakalpa Mahārājas and the Pāṇḍavas, the last being given the Mekalā region.[812]

There are insurmountable difficulties in accepting the above view. First of all, the name of the father of *Rājan* Vaiśravaṇa as recorded in the Bandhogarh inscriptions is Bhadrabāla, not Bhadrabala, and as such the identity of the name-endings which forms the basis of the above suggestion is non-existent. Secondly, while the grounds for the identification of *Mahāsenāpati* Bhadrabāla with the Magha king *Mahārāja* Bhadramagha are very weak as we have shown elsewhere,[813] the same cannot be said about the identification of *Rājan* Vaiśravaṇa with the Magha chief *Mahārāja* Vaiśravaṇa as the slight difference between the regal titles on which the differentiation between them is based is insignificant and is noticed in some other cases also.[814] What

806. *Studies in Indology*, i, 231-32.
807. *Ibid.* But *contra, ibid.*, 152ff., where these identifications are supported.
808. *EI*, ii, 363-365 and facsimile plate facing p. 364.
809. *ASI, AR*, for 1936-37, 88.
810. *Studies in Indology*, i, 233, fn. 2. The only ground given against the reference of this year to the Gupta era, which would make Lakṣmaṇa rule in 478 A.D., is the non-mention of the Gupta suzerain. We have several other instances of the Gupta feudatories not referring to their Gupta overlords in their records.
811. *CII*, iii, 7, text-line 21. Balavarman is generally identified with the homonymous predecessor of the Bhauma-Nāraka king Bhāskaravarman of Kāmarūpa. The ascription of Balavarman to the Magha dynasty is apparently inspired by the desire to bridge the gap between the last known Magha king Vijayamagha and the Gupta emperor Samudragupta. The same is true of the attribution of Lakṣmaṇa to the Magha dynasty.
812. *Studies in Indology*, i, 233. See also p. 165.
813. *Kauśāmbī Hoard of Magha Coins*, 25-26. See also *Itihās*,, iv, 39.
814. The Magha chief Bhīmasena is also styled *Mahārāja* in his Ginja and Bandhogarh inscriptions (Lüders' List, no. 906; *EI*, xxxi, 177, no. I) while the inscription on a terracotta sealing from Bhita calls him *Rājan* (*ASI, AR*, for 1911-12, 51, no, 27,

is most astonishing is that elsewhere Mirashi himself lends firm support to both these identifications.[815] Thirdly, the reference of the year 158 of the two grants of Lakṣmaṇa to the Śaka era is not supported by the palaeographic evidence which points to a late date.[816] Then again, there is nothing to substantiate the suggestion that Lakṣmaṇa and Balavarman were Magha chiefs. And lastly, as shown above, extant evidence does not warrant the enjecture that Jayabala was a contemporary of Samudragupta. On the other hand, he appears to have risen to power about the end of the fifth or the beginning of the seventh century A.D. It will, thus, follow that in the present state of our knowledge no relationship whatsoever can be postulated between *Mahāsenāpati* Bhadrabāla and the Pāṇḍavas of Mekalā.

Śūrabala *alias* Udīrṇavaira is the last known member of his dynasty and there is no knowledge as to what happened to the Pāṇḍava kingdom of Mekalā after him. We do not also know as to how long he continued to rule after the eighth year of his reign when he issued his Mallar charter. But while we are in dark about the subsequent history of the Mekalā Pāṇḍavas, we know of another line of rulers who also claimed to have originated from the celebrated Pāṇḍava lineage and commenced ruling in South Kosala about the same time as Śūrabala, the last known Mekalā Pāṇḍava monarch, was ruling over a large area including at least a part of the Chhattisgarh region. The termination of the Pāṇḍava rule in one area and its commencement in an adjacent area at approximately the same time cannot be regarded as totally accidental and the two Pāṇḍava families appear to have been related to each other although exact relation between them cannot be ascertained in the present state of insufficient information. It is noteworthy in this connection that besides tracing their origin from the Pāṇḍavas, both the families claim to belong to the lunar race. Then again, at least one of the members of the Kosala Pāṇḍava dynasty, like those of the Pāṇḍava dynasty of Mekalā, bore a name terminating in *bala*.[817] And lastly, if Udayana, the first known member of the Pāṇḍava ruling family of South Kosala, has been correctly identified with the homonymous chief whose inscription has been found at Kalanjar,[818] the earliest known Kosala

---

Pl. XVIII. 27). *Cf.* also the tiger-slayer type coins of Samudragupta on which we find the title *Rājan* and the Lyrist type coins of Samudragupta and Kumāragupta I, the legends on which give their names without any title. See Ajay Mitra Shastri, *Kauśāmbī Hoard of Magha Coins*, 23-24 and 27-28.

815. *EI*, xxvi, 298-99; *Studies in Indology*, i, 154-55.

816. The letters have a distinctly late appearance. The draft of the inscriptions, which is in almost correct Sanskrit, is also a pointer in the same direction. If the date of these records is referred to the Śaka era, these will be the earliest copper-plate grant found in India so far, while in fact it presents quite a developed appearance in all respects which is rather uncommon.

817. *Viz.*, Indrabala, the grandfather of Mahāśiva Tīvara.

818. For a verse quoted from this inscription, see *EI*, iv, 257, fn. 4. For an eye-copy, though not satisfactory, see A. Cunningham, *Archaeological Survey Reports*, xxi, 40, pl. ix. L. This inscription has not yet been edited.

Pāṇḍava chief would be ruling in an area not far away from the dominions of the Mekalā Pāṇḍavas. While these facts pointing to some sort of relationship between the two families cannot be gain said, there are a few important differences which may now be noticed. All but one known members of the Pāṇḍava dynasty of Mekalā bore *bala*-ending names, whereas, as pointed out earlier, only a single Pāṇḍava chief of Kosala had a name ending with *bala*. Secondly, the known records of the Mekalā Pāṇḍavas are composed in a mixture of prose and verse and incised in what are popularly known as nail-headed characters with certain southern peculiarities while all the copper-plate charters of the Kosala Pāṇḍavas are composed in prose alone and engraved in the box-headed variety of the Central India alphabet, the nail-headed characters and versified composition being reserved for stone inscriptions which are mostly private records.[819] All the Kosala Pāṇḍava chiefs whose copper-plate charters have come to light so far prefixed the word *mahat* to their names and it is possible that even those whose official records have not been reported to date did likewise.[820] No such practice appears to have obtained among the Mekalā Pāṇḍavas. Fourthly, the Kosala Pāṇḍavas after Nannarāja II adopted gupta-ending names without a single exception,[821] while not a single Pāṇḍava ruler of Mekalā bore such a name. Fifthly, all the Kosala Pāṇḍavas except only Indrabala bore names which were quite dissimilar to those borne by the Mekalā Pāṇḍavas. And lastly, all the Mekalā Pāṇḍavas appear to have been devout worshippers of Śiva though the sectarian title *Parama-Māheśvara* is formally applied only to three of them. As against this, all but the last know Pāṇḍava chiefs of Kosala were devotees of Viṣṇu. Some of these dissimilarities can be easily explained away in a satisfactory manner. It can, for instance, be argued that in Kosala the Pāṇḍavas gave up nail-headed characters and employed box-headed variety of the Central India alphabet in their copper-plate inscriptions because these characters had become popular for official records in South Kosala owing to their employment for nearly a century by the Śarabhapura chiefs who were their political predecessors in that area. The prefixing of the word *mahat* to the names of the Pāṇḍuvaṁśins of Kosala also may have been due to the same reason, as all the Śarabhapurīya monarchs except only Śarabha, Narendra and Prasannamātra had this word prefixed to their names. The difference in sectarian beliefs may well be attributed to personal predilections of the ruling chiefs instances

819. The only lithic record that may be treated as official is the Sirpur Lakṣmaṇa Temple inscription of the time of Śivagupta Bālārjuna.

820. We have yet to get official charters of the pre-Tīvaradeva chiefs and of Candragupta and Harṣagupta.

821. Śivanandin, the son of Śivagupta Bālārjuna, and the latter's brother Raṇakesarin are the only exceptions. But neither of these ascended the throne and Raṇakesarin was perhaps a secondary name.

of which are found in other dynasties also.[822] But the almost total dissimilarity of names and the abandonment of the *bala*-ending do not admit of an equally satisfactory explanation, for they mark an almost complete break and cannot be brushed aside on grounds of local conventions or similar other considerations. Then again, had the two lines of rulers belonged to the same family, it is strange that while a long account of the family beginning with Udayana is found in some of the inscriptions, not a single record refers to any of the Mekalā Pāṇḍava chiefs. In view of these facts we feel that the Pāṇḍuvaṁśins of Kosala probably represented a collateral branch of the same Pāṇḍava family which ruled over Mekalā for nearly a century,[823] though the final verdict on this question ought better to be preserved for future when fresh epigraphical discoveries may shed more light on this and other allied issues.

III. THE PĀṆḌUVAṀŚINS OF KOSALA

The next major ruling family of the Chhattisgarh region of Madhya Pradesh after the Śarabhapurīyas is represented by the Pāṇḍavas of South Kosala. Unlike the Pāṇḍavas of Mekala who found a place on the historical map of India just a little less than four decades ago, the Pāṇḍavas of the Chhattisgarh area have been known to historians for well over a century and a half[824] and our knowledge about them has grown fuller and fuller with the passage of time and we have now a fairly large number of records of their time, both official and private, which, besides bringing new facts to light, have contributed to remove some wrong notions which owed themselves to the inadequacy of the evidence available earlier or its faulty interpretation.

Lineage

One of the oldest extant records of the family, *viz.*, the Lakhneswar Temple (Kharod) inscription of Indrabala, calls the family *śaśi-kula* or lunar lineage.[825] A lunar origin for the dynasty is claimed in some other records also. Thus, the Aḍhabhāra plates of Nannarāja II refer to Tīvaradeva as

822. For example, the Vākāṭaka kings were Śaivas, but Rudrasena II changed over to Vaiṣṇavism. Among the Puṣpabhūtis of Sthāṇvīśvara we notice a change of religious leanings from generation to generation. There are several other instances.

823. Some scholars think that Bharatabala and Udayana were related as father and son. This problem will be considered later.

824. The Rajim plates of Tīvaradeva were discovered as early as 1785 and were first published in 1825, in the *Asiatic Researches*, xv, 499ff., with a version of the text supplied by Śrīvarmasūri and English translation by H.H. Wilson as well as a lithograph. See *CII*, iii, 291.

825. The inscription actually describes Indrabala as the very full moon in the sky that is the *śaśi-kula*. See V.V. Mirashi, *Studies in Indology*, i, 258, fn. 1.

born in the *śaśivaṁśa*,[826] whereas Śivagupta Bālārjuna is described as born in the *soma-vaṁśa*[827] or *śītāṁśu-vaṁśa*.[828] In the Sirpur Lakṣmaṇa Temple inscription of the time of Śivagupta Bālārjuna his granfather Candragupta is said to have been born in the *candr-ānvaya*,[829] while another Sirpur stone inscription of the reign of the same king refers to the family under the name *śaśadhar-ānvaya* in connection with Udayana.[830] Thus, we find that from the very beginning to the end the dynasty claimed to have belonged to the lunar race. And within the lunar race the dynasty traced its origin from the Pāṇḍavas. The Arang stone inscription of the time of Nannarāja I, for instance, states that Udayana was born of the Pāṇḍava-vaṁśa.[831] In all the three extant copper-plate charters of Tīvaradeva his father Nannarāja I is said to have adorned the Pāṇḍu-vaṁśa.[832] However, it is astonishing, though simply accidental, that while the claim to belong to the lunar race is met with in the records of the dynasty from the beginning to the end, that to an origin from the Pāṇḍu-vaṁśa or Pāṇḍava-vaṁśa is conspicuous by its absence in inscriptions after Mahāśiva Tīvara.[833] But the members of this dynasty are generally referred to in modern historical writings as Pāṇḍu-vaṁśins in order to distinguish them from the later Somavaṁśins who ruled over the Chhattisgarh region of Madhya Pradesh and the western part of Orissa.

Territories under the Dynasty

All the extant records of the family with the exception of the Kalanjar inscription of Udayana have been reported from the Chhattisgarh region. The family itself lays its claim to lordship over the Kosala country. In the inscription on the seals of the copper-plate charters of Mahāśiva Tīvara, for instance, we find the king assuming the title *Kosalādhipati*, 'Lord of Kosala', while in the charters themselves he is said to have obtained the lordship of the whole of Kosala.[834] It is only in the Aḍhabhāra grant of his son Nanna-rāja II that he is described as having earned the overlordship of the entire Kosala, Utkala and other *maṇḍalas* (provinces) by the valour of his own

826. No. III: V, text-line 5.
827. Nos. III: VI, text-line 4; VII, text-lines 4-5; VIII, text-line 4; IX, text-line 4; X, text-lines 4-5.
828. See verse 3 of the Senkapat inscription (no. III: XV).
829. No. III: XI, verse 4.
830. No. III: XII, text-line 3, verse 2.
831. No. III: I, text-line 7, verse 16.
832. Nos. III: II, text-line 16; III, text line 16; IV, text-lines 18-19.
833. Whether it indicates that the tradition of Pāṇḍava origin was forgotten cannot be ascertained. It is pertinent to note, however, that this tradition is not referred to in the records of the later Somavaṁśins also.
834. *Prāpta-sakala-Kosal-ādhipatyaḥ*. See nos. III: II, text-lines 16-17; III, text-line 16 (by oversight only the word *prāpta* is incised, the remainder being dropped); IV, text-line 19.

arms.[835] Strangely enough, however, Nannarāja himself is said to have acquired the lordship of the entire country (*maṇḍala*) of Kosalā.[836] It may, therefore, be reasonably inferred that the extension of the Pāṇḍuvaṁśin power in the east under Mahāśiva Tīvara was only a temporary phase and that the dominions of the Pāṇḍuvaṁśins primarily comprised Kosalā only. We do not find any specific mention of the territories under the rule of the later members of the dynasty, though the findspots of epigraphic records as well as the localities referred to in them point to the Chhattisgarh region as their principal dominion. The Senkapat inscription of the time of Śivagupta seems to indicate the incorporation of a part of the Vidarbha region of Maharashtra within the Pāṇḍuvaṁśin dominions;[837] but that, too, was only a passing phase. This question will be discussed at length at the appropriate place.

It is sometimes believed that the Chanda region of Vidarbha formed a part of the territorial possessions of the early members of the dynasty and it was from here that they invaded Kosala.[838] This view is based on the impression that the inscription of the time of Nannarāja[839] referring to the restoration by Bhavadeva, the fourth brother of Nannarāja, of a decayed Buddhist temple originally built by a king named Sūryaghoṣa was found at Bhandak in the Chanda District. There has been much uncertainty and debate about the actual provenance of this inscription. When the inscription was first published by Rev. Stevenson, Bhandak was given as its findspot.[840] Cunningham also attributed it to the same place.[841] Hira Lal,[842] D.R. Bhandarkar,[843] Moreshwar G. Dikshit and D. C. Sircar[844] did likewise. According to Kielhorn's information, however, the inscription was brought to the Central Museum, Nagpur, from Ratanpur (Bilaspur District, Madhya Pradesh).[845] V.V. Mirashi also initially accepted the view that it hailed from Bhandak and believed that Tīvaradeva's predecessors were ruling from that locality.[846] But shortly thereafter he felt convinced that the stone bear-

835. The expression in the original is *sva-bhuja-parākram-opārjita-sakala-Kosal-Otkal-ādi-maṇḍal-ādhipatya-prāpta-māhātmyasya*. See no. III: V, text-lines 5-7.
836. *Ibid.*, text-lines 8-9: *prāpta-sakala-Kosala-maṇḍal-ādhipatyaḥ*.
837. See no. III: XV, text-lines 6-7, verse 7.
838. R.C. Majumdar and A.B. Altekar (ed.), *The Vākāṭaka-Gupta Age*, 90-91; R. C. Majumdar (ed.), *The Classical Age*, 221.
839. See no. III: I. In the inscription the contemporary Pāṇḍuvaṁśin monarch is referred to as Nannarājādhirāja.
840. *JBBRAS*, i, 148ff.
841. *CASR*, ix, 127. For Cunningham's reasons for the attribution of this inscription to Bhandak, see *EI*, xxiii, 116-17.
842. *IA*, xxxvii, 208, fn. 20; lxii, 163; *ICPB*, 13, no. 14.
843. Bhandarkar's List, No. 1650.
844. *EI*, xxxi, 34; xxxiii, 256. Also see references in note 838 above which represent Sircar's view.
845. *JRAS*, 1905, 618.
846. *EI*, xxii, 17.

ing the inscription was found somewhere in Chhattisgarh and that the notion that it belonged to Bhandak was founded on erroneous information.[847] Later, on the testimony of Vinayakrao Aurangabadkar, he[848] and Y.K. Deshpande[849] pointed out that the inscription actually stood originally at Arang, about twenty miles south-west of Sirpur in the Raipur District of Madhya Pradesh. At the behest of Richard Jenkins, British Resident at Nagpur from 1807 to 1826, Aurangabadkar, who was in the former's service, undertook a tour of Chhattisgarh and submitted to him a report on the inscriptions in Chhattisgarh in the Moḍī characters which is presently deposited in the India Office Library, London.[850] According to this report, Aurangabadkar found the slab bearing the inscription of Bhavadeva Raṇakesarin affixed to a large temple at Aring, *i.e.*, Arang. He has given a transcript and a brief account of its contents in Marathi. The inscription, according to him, stated that "there was a king named Sūryaghoṣa...A relative of his fell from housetop and died. Becoming indifferent to mundane matters as a result of the sorrow occasioned by this incident, he erected a large temple of the sage. In his family was born a king named Udaye (ya)na. It is said that he belonged to the Pāṇḍava family.... His fourth son was Bhavadeva. He, too, was equally virtuous, brave and endowed with good conduct.... This king built a Jaina temple. He was a Jain by religion..."[851] This extract leaves no doubt that the inscription in question, which Vinayakrao Aurangabadkar had seen *in situ*, is none other than the one earlier believed to have come from Bhandak.[852] It appears, therefore, that the epigraph of Nannarāja I actually belonged to Arang, not

847. *Ibid.*, xxiii, 116-118. It has been suggested that the inscription was probably first removed from its original provenance to Ratanpur and later shifted to Nagpur where it was recorded as hailing from Ratanpur.

848. *EI*, xxvi, 227; xxxii, 252-54: *Studies in Indology*, i, 251-52.

849. As stated by Mirashi, the relevant information about this inscription from Vinayakrao Aurangabadkar's report was supplied by Y. K. Deshpande. Also see A. J. Rajurkar, *Candrapūracā Itihāsa* (Marathi), foreword by Y.K. Deshpande, 4-5.

850. MSS. No. Marathi D, 46.

851. या आरिंग्याचे महादेवालयाचे दगडावर संस्कृत अक्षर लिहिलेत्याची नक्कल...सूर्यधेय नामे राजा पृथ्वीपति... त्याचा कोन्ही एक आप्त माडीवरून पड्न मेला. त्याचे शोकास्तव वैराग्य आंगी आनून ऋषीच स्थान मोठ बांधल याचे वंशीचा राजा उदयेन नामक याजला पांडववंशीचा म्हणत होते... याचा चवथा पुत्र भवदेव नामक हाही त्यासारखा गुणवान, प्रतापवान, सदाचारसंपन्न... या राजान जैनाच मंदिर बांधते. हर जैन धर्मी होता Quoted by Mirashi in *EI*, xxxiii, 253, fn. 2.

852. I approached the authorities of the India Office Library with a request to supply a xeroxed or microfilmed copy of the relevant portion of Aurangabadkar's report. But the authorities expressed their difficulty in complying with the request as it is not possible for them to locate this portion of the manuscript in the absence of a person conversant with the Moḍī script in which Aurangabadkar's report is written.

Bhandak. However, D.C. Sircar still thinks that this inscription originally came from Bhandak, not Arang. In support of his contention he invites our attention to a fragmentary stone inscription from the Mahāmāyī temple at Arang noticed by Hira Lal in his *Inscriptions in the Central Provinces and Berar* which also, like the inscription under consideration, contained in line 13 the name or title Raṇakesarin.[853] Sircar, therefore, feels that the two inscriptions (one from Bhandak and the other from Arang) had similar, if not exactly the same, contents and that Vinayakrao Aurangabadkar must have noticed this (Mahāmāyī temple) inscription at Arang. He suggests that king Sūryaghoṣa had built two temples, one at Bhandak and the other at Arang, and that both of them were restored by Bhavadeva Raṇakesarin.[854] The Arang inscription referred to by Sircar has not been published in full, perhaps owing to its fragmentary condition; but if the brief account of its contents supplied by Hira Lal is to be relied upon, it cannot be the one noticed by Aurangabadkar. For, the Arang inscription described by Aurangabadkar was a Buddhist record and referred to the construction and restoration of a Buddha temple though it was wrongly taken as a Jain temple by him, evidently because of the use of the name Jina for Buddha. The Mahāmāyī temple inscription at Arang, on the other hand, is a Vaiṣṇava record as can be inferred from the fact that it opens with an invocation to Viṣṇu.[855] It will, thus, follow that the Arang inscription summarised by Aurangabadkar is undoubtedly identical with the so-called Bhandak (or Ratanpur) inscription and that in the present state of insufficient information, there is absolutely no evidence to substantiate the commonly accepted early Pāṇḍuvaṁśin occupation of Vidarbha.

Capital

All the known copper-plate charters of Mahāśiva Tīvara and his son and successor Nannarāja II were issued from Śrīpura which, as we have seen above, had already risen to the status of the capital of South Kosala during the reigns of the Śarabhapurīya chiefs Sudevarāja and Pravararāja. As no word like *vijaya-skandhāvāra, kaṭaka* or *vāsaka* is suffixed to the name, we may reasonably conclude that it continued to enjoy the status of the dynastic capital under these two Pāṇḍuvaṁśin chiefs also. We do not find any explicit reference to this town in the subsequent official charters of the family which are reticent about the place of their issue. But this silence is

853. *ICPB*, 110, no. 183.
854. *EI*, xxxii, 256.
855. The slab bearing this inscription was obviously affixed to a Viṣṇu temple which might be the same as that now called Mahāmāyin. Further, as the full contents of the inscription are still unknown, it is difficult to determine the exact position of the Raṇakesarin known from this inscription in the genealogy of the family, *viz.*, Bhavadeva Raṇakesarin grandson of Udayana, or Raṇakesarin, younger brother of Śivagupta Bālārjuna.

only casual and the discovery of a number of records of the time of Śiva-gupta Bālārjuna at Sirpur may be justifiably taken to indicate that the Pāṇḍuvaṁśin capital continued to be located at this town till the very end of the dynasty. As regards the pre-Tīvaradeva capital of the Pāṇḍuvaṁśins, we do not have any definite information as no copper-plate inscriptions of the earlier members of the family which might be expected to contain allusion to the place of their issue and thereby shed light on this question are now available. However, in all likelihood Śrīpura served as the capital of the family during this period also, though a final verdict on this issue must await discoveries of the official records of the earlier members of the dynasty referring to the issuing place.

Genealogy

The numerous stone and copper-plate inscriptions of the family discovered so far supply the following genealogy :—

- Udayana[856]
  - Indrabala
    - Nannadeva I[858]
    - Iśānadeva
  - Name lost[857]
    - 1
    - 2
    - 3 (Names are lost)
    - Bhavadeva Raṇakesarin[859]

(*Cont.*)

856. A. Ghosh (*EI*, xxvi, 267) mentions Sūryaghoṣa at the top of the genealogical table but states in note 1 that 'it is not definitely known whether he was an ancestor of Udayana'. However, the manner in which Sūryaghoṣa is mentioned in verse 5 of the Arang inscription of the time of Nannarāja I (no. III: I) shows that during the period in question he was treated as a very ancient ruler and had nothing to do with the Pāṇḍavas of South Kosala. He is mentioned simply because he had erected the Buddha temple the restoration of which forms the main theme of the inscription. The statement in verse 16 that Udayana sprang from the Pāṇḍava family also points in the same direction. Had Sūryaghoṣa been an ancestor of Udayana this statement would have been pertinently met with in connection with the former, and not with reference to the latter.

857. It is held by some that Udayana's son who is said in the Arang inscription of Nannarāja I to have had four sons was no other than Indrabala. See *A New History of the Indian People*, vi, *The Vākāṭaka-Gupta Age* (ed. R. C. Majumdar and A.S. Altekar), 90-91; *The Classical Age* (ed. R. C. Majumdar), 221 and 715 (genealogy of the Pāṇḍuvaṁśins). In that case we would have to take Nanna I, Īśānadeva and Bhavadeva Raṇakesarin as uterine brothers, while the name of the remaining son is lost.

858. He is called Nannadeva in the records of Tīvaradeva and Nannarājādhirāja in verse 40 of the Arang stone inscription of his time.

859. He is described as the fourth or youngest son of Udayana's son whose name is lost.

Tīvaradeva (or Mahāśiva-Tīvara)[860] — Candragupta

Nannarāja II[861] — Harṣagupta = Vāsaṭā, daughter of King Sūryavarman of Magadha

Śivagupta-Bālārjuna — Raṇakesarin

Śivanandin[862]

As has been pointed out earlier,[863] the Pāṇḍuvaṁśins of South Kosala were probably related to their counterparts in Mekalā. V.V. Mirashi postulated a lineal connection between these two lines and thinks that Udayana, the first known member of the Pāṇḍuvaṁśa of Kosala, was probably a son of Bharatabala, also known as Indra, who was till recently regarded as the last Pāṇḍava king of Mekalā.[864] If this view is accepted, Udayana's son Indrabala will have to be treated as a grandson of Bharatabala *alias* Indra. Mirashi actually refers to Udayana's son Indrabala as Indrabala II in order to distinguish him from the so-called Indrabala I, *i.e.*, Bharatabala who had Indra for his second name.[865] This suggestion is sought to be strengthened on the ground that in India a grandson is often christened after his grandfather.[866] This theory, however, needs to be modified substantially in view of the fact that Śūrabala *alias* Udīrṇavaira, and not Bharatabala *alias* Indra, was the last known member of the Pāṇḍava dynasty of Mekalā.[867] Therefore, if the lineal relationship between the two lines of the Pāṇḍava rulers is to be maintained, Udayana will have to be taken as the son of Śūrabala, and not of Bharatabala. If, however, the suggestion that Udayana was a son of Bharatabala is to be taken for granted, we will have to postulate that Bharatabala had two sons, *viz.*, Śūrabala

860. His name is dropped in the records of the time of Śivagupta Bālārjuna as he was not in the direct line of successsion.
861. Like his father, he is also dropped from the genealogical list in the later records of the family but is mentioned in the Senkapat inscription of the time of Śivagupta Bālārjuna (no. III: XV).
862. It is not known if he ever came to the throne.
863. See *supra*, 124-6.
864. *Studies in Indology*, i, 235-36.
865. *Ibid.*, 236, D.C. Sircar (*The Classical Age*, 222 and 716) also regards Indrabala as the full form of the secondary name Indra. But while it is almost certain that Bharatabala was also called Indra, there is nothing to indicate that he was known as Indrabala to justify his being designated as Indrabala I.
866. *Studies in Indology*, i, 236, fn. 1.
867. See *supra*, 121-2.

alias Udīrṇavaira and Udayana, and that the former, being elder, succeeded to his ancestral kingdom. But as we have shown above, while some relationship between the two lines cannot be denied, there are good many difficulties in regarding the Pāṇḍuvaṁśins of Kosala as the lineal descendants of the Pāṅḍavas of Mekalā.[868] We may, therefore, regard the two families as collaterally related to each other, the exact relationship being indeterminable in the present state of our knowledge.

Chronology

It is now universally accepted that the Pāṇḍuvaṁśins followed, and did not precede, the Śarabhapurīyas in the rule over South Kosala and Hira Lal's view to the contrary is no longer entertained by any historian.[869] However, as regards the flourishing period of the Pāṇḍuvaṁśins themselves, there is still a lot of controversy and uncertainty. The question has been generally debated by scholars with reference to the date of Tīvaradeva, one of the most prominent members of the dynasty.[869a] It will, therefore, be convenient to discuss the date of this ruler at some length and to determine the period of his predecessors and descendants in the light of his date.

General Alexander Cunningham suggested the period from 425 to 450 A.D. for the reign of Tīvaradeva.[870] But this date was too early to secure general acceptance. Moreover, it was based upon the supposed identification of Tīvaradeva's grand-nephew Śivagupta, Bālārjuna, the last known Pāṇḍuvaṁśin king, with the homonymous Somavaṁśin chief of Orissa[870] who, according to the traditional Orissan palm-leaf manuscripts known as *Mādalā-pañjīs*, ruled in the time of Yayāti or Yayātikesarin and on the acceptance of the date 474-526 (or 473-520) A.D. as proposed by Stirling.[870b] But it has been convincingly demonstrated that the evidence of the *Mādalā-pañjīs* is, generally speaking, not reliable for historical purposes and that the date of Yayātikesarin derived from them is totally unreliable and earlier by several centuries.[871]

Some earlier epigraphists were inclined to date Tīvaradeva's reign in the eighth century A.D. J.F. Fleet, while editing the Rajim plates (no. III:III)

868. See *supra*, 122-6.
869. See *supra*, 100-1.
869a. This is because of the notion that some definite evidences for determining the date of Tīvaradeva are available.
870. Cunningham, *ASR*, xvii, 17-18 and 28.
870a. *i.e.*, Śivagupta, the father of Mahābhavagupta I Janamejaya who was the first Somavaṁśin king of Orissa whose copper-plate charters have been found so far.
870b. *Asiatic Researches*, xv, 256ff., where it has been pointed out that while the traditions recorded in these palm-leaf manuscripts for the period prior to Yayātikesarin are totally inaccurate, the accounts from that point are reliable.
871. For a full-scale examination of the historical evidence of these texts, see J.F. Fleet in *EI*, iii, 325ff. *Vide* also D.C. Sircar, *Studies in the Yuga Purāṇa and other Texts*, 149-158.

and criticising the aforesaid suggestion of Cunningham, felt 'Tīvaradeva cannot be allotted to an earlier date than roughly about A.D. 800.'[872] F. Kielhorn placed a Sirpur stone inscription of the time of Śivagupta Bālārjuna in about the eighth or ninth century A.D. on palaeographical, linguistic and stylistic considerations.[873] Elsewhere, while editing the Kudopali plates of a feudatory of Mahābhavagupta II, he assigned this inscription to about the beginning of the ninth century and held that the Rajim plates 'undoubtedly belong to about the middle of the 8th century A.D.'[874] He further proposed to place the Nagpur (now Raipur) Museum inscription of Bhavadeva Raṇakesarin (actually of Nannarāja I) about the middle of the same century.[875] While editing the Sirpur Lakshmaṇa Temple inscription of the time of Śivagupta Bālārjuna, Hira Lal observed that its characters belong to the eighth or ninth century A.D.[876] D.R. Bhandarkar also took this general period for granted and proposed to identify Candragupta, who, according to the Sanjan plates of Amoghavarṣa I,[877] was defeated by the Rāṣṭrakūṭa king Govinda III, with the homonymous Pāṇḍuvaṁśin chief.[878] R. D. Banerji also subscribed to the same view about the date of Tīvaradeva.[879] It must be remembered in this connection that when this chronology was suggested for the Pāṇḍuvaṁśins, the chronology of the Vākāṭakas was also uncertain and on the basis of Fleet's identification of Devagupta, father of Rudrasena II's queen Prabhāvatīguptā, with the Later Gupta chief of that name[880] known from the Deo-Barnark inscription of Jīvitagupta,[881] they, too, were relegated to the eighth century A.D.[882] And since the copper-plate inscriptions of the Pāṇḍuvaṁśins, like those of the Vākāṭakas, are inscribed in

872. *CII*, iii, 294.
873. *IA*, xviii, 179. Kielhorn thought that the characters of this record bore close resemblance to those of the Ghosarwa inscription of the time of Devapāla.
874. *EI*, iv, 258. Elsewhere, he felt 'convinced that neither inscription can be older than A.D. 700'. See *IA*, xviii, 179.
875. *JRAS*, 1905. He observed that the characters of this inscription resemble in a general way those of the Kanaswa inscription of Śivagaṇa of the Mālava year 795. But elsewhere (*EI*, iv, 257-58) he states that the writing of the former is somewhat older than that of the latter and that the former may, therefore, be confidently assigned to the beginning of the eighth century A.D.
876. *EI*, xi, 184 and 185; *ICPB*, 100.
877. *EI*, xviii, 245, verse 22.
878. *Ibid.*, 240. 'There can be no doubt, observed Bhandarkar, 'that it (Pāṇḍava) was one of the paramount dynasties of the eighth and ninth centuries A.D.'
879. R.D. Banerji, *HO*, i, 134, 204 and 225. He accepted the identification of Rāṣṭrakūṭa Govinda III's adversary Candragupta with Tīvaradeva's homonymous brother and observed that the Pāṇḍuvaṁśins established their principality in the jungles of Eastern Gondwana in the seventh or eighth century A.D. He further states that it is impossible to place Tīvaradeva in the sixth century A.D.
880. *CII*, iii, 215.
881. *Ibid.*, 215, text-line 4.
882. *CII*, iii, 215.

box-headed characters, they were also assigned to about the same period. But the discovery of the Poona[883] and Riddhpur[884] plates, which give Candragupta (instead of Devagupta) as the name of Prabhāvatīguptā's father, demonstrated the erroneousness of Fleet's identification and established the contemporaniety of the Vākāṭakas and the Imperial Guptas, thus bringing the former a few centuries earlier than usually believed till that time. This naturally led to a re-thinking of the question of the date of the Pāṇḍuvaṁśins also and efforts were made to push them back to an earlier period. And no historian now believes in such a late date for the Pāṇḍuvaṁśins as the eighth or ninth century A.D.

D.C. Sircar and V.V. Mirashi were the first to suggest an earlier date for Tīvaradeva. The former observed that the Guptas, Vākāṭakas and Kadambas, who also employed box-headed characters in their records, are definitely known to have flourished earlier than 700 A.D. and that the same may be true about Tīvaradeva.[885] Mirashi first discussed this question at length while editing the Thakurdiya plates of Pravararāja and offered concrete suggestions.[886] He, too, took cue from the palaeographical evidence and rightly pointed out that Tīvaradeva cannot be referred to the eighth century A.D. simply because his records are incised in box-headed characters. He also invited attention to certain other points which also indicate, according to him, that Tīvaradeva flourished in the sixth century A.D., *i.e.*, a little over two centuries prior to the date to which he was assigned thereupto. Firstly, he proposed to identify king Sūryavarman, father of Vāsaṭā who, according to the Sirpur Lakshmaṇa temple inscription, of her son Śivagupta Bālārjuna, was married to Mahāśiva Tīvaradeva's nephew Harṣagupta, with the homonymous Maukhari prince known from the Haraha inscription engraved during the reign of his father Īśānavarman dated (Vikrama) and year 611 or 554 A.D.[887] as no other chief of that name is known from any other source.[888] Once this identification is conceded, Harṣagupta's father Candragupta would become a contemporary of Sūryavarman and his elder brother Tīvaradeva would have to be placed still earlier. Mirashi sought to strengthen this date for Tīvaradeva from the evidence furnished by some Viṣṇukuṇḍin records. The Ipur plates of Mādhavavarman Janāśraya issued in the thirty-seventh year of his reign describe him as *Trivaranagara-bhavana-gata-yuvati-hṛdaya-*

883. *EI*, xv, 41 and *CII*, v, 7, text-line 7.
884. *Ibid.*, 36, text-line 7.
885. D.C. Sircar, *The Successors of the Sātavāhanas in the Lower Deccan*, 129-30.
886. *EI*, xxii, 18-22. For his subsequent discussion on this question see *ibid.*, xxvi, 227-30; *Studies in Indology*, i, 237-47; *JESI*, iv, 1-5; vi.
887. *EI*, xiv, 115ff. This inscription records the renovation of a Śiva temple by Sūryavarman while he was on a hunting operation.
888. *EI*, xxii, 19; xxiii, 115-16 (where the genesis of the supposed Maukhari-Pāṇḍava alliance is outlined).

nandanaḥ, *i.e.*, the delighter of the hearts of the young ladies in the palace (or palaces) of Trivaranagara.[889] The same statement occurs in the Polamuru plates issued in the fortieth or forty-eighth year of his reign[890] in somewhat different words, *viz.*, *Trivaranagara-bhavana-gata-parama-yuvati-jana-viharana-ratiḥ*, *i.e.*, fond of sporting with the excellent young women in the palaces of Trivaranagara.[891] There is considerable difference of opinion regarding the real import of these expressions which have consequently remained obscure. According to E. Hultzsch the expression in the Ipur plates indicates that Mādhavavarman lived at Trivaranagara which, however, he was unable to identify.[892] K.V. Lakshman Rao, who first edited the Polamuru plates,[893] took this expression as an 'euphemistic way of telling us that Mādhavavarman had married a wife from the city of Trivara'.[894] Mirashi[895] and Sircar,[896] on the other hand, held that these expressions really appear to allude to Mādhavavarman's hostile relations with and victory over Trivaranagara rather than his marriage with a woman of that town.[897] That expression *trivaranagara* has been generally taken as a *ṣaṣṭhi tatpuruṣa* compound in the sense of 'the city of Trivara', Trivara being the name of the ruling chief whose capital it was and who was defeated by Mādhavavarman. Both Mirashi[898] and Sircar[899] are inclined to identify this Trivara with Mahāśiva Tīvaradeva, the Pāṇḍuvaṁśin ruler of Kosala, who was a powerful ruler and a victory over whom must have been a source of pride for Mādhavavarman who consequently thought it worth mentioning in his records. As regards the date of Mādhavavarman

889. *Ibid.*, xvii, 336, text-lines 4-5. Hultzsch translated the expression as 'who delights the hearts of the young women standing on (the top of) the palaces of Trivaranagara'. See *ibid.*, 337.
890. There is difference of opinion about the reading of the date.
891. *Journal of the Department of Letters*, University of Calcutta, xi, 59, text-lines 8-9; *JAHRS*, vi, 20. In D.C. Sircar's *The Successors of the Sātavāhanas in the Lower Deccan*, 335, the word *parama* is omitted, obviously due to oversight.
892. *EI*, xvii, 335. He observed that Trivaranagara can hardly be identified with the distant Tripurī.'
893. *Journal of the Department of Letters*, University of Calcutta, xi, 39.
894. *Ibid.*
895. *EI*, xvii, 19-20; *Studies in Indology*, i, 240-41.
896. *The Successors of the Sātavāhanas in the Lower Deccan*, 129, fn. 1; *The Classical Age* (ed. R.C. Majumdar), 208.
897. It must be noted that the expressions in question refers to not one but a number of ladies (*yuvati-jana*) whose hearts he pleased or with whom he sported. Moreover, the idea that a victorious king captivates the hearts of the damsels of the conquered city is sometimes met with in Sanskrit and Prakrit literature. In this connection Mirashi invites attention to the description in *Viddhaśālabhañjikā*, iv. 8 and *Gauḍavaho*, verse 1009. For extracts, see *Studies in Indology*, 241, fn. 2.
898. *EI*, xxii, 19-20; *Studies in Indology*, i, 240-41; *JESI*, iv, 2-3; vi, *NHIP*, vi.
899. *The Successors of the Sātavāhanas in the Lower Deccan*, 128-130; *The Vākāṭaka-Gupta Age*,(ed. R.C. Majumdar and A.S. Altekar), 89; *HCIP*, (ed. R.C. Majumdar), iii, *The Classical Age*, 208.

who must be a contemporary of Tīvaradeva to have successfully fought a battle with him, both invite our attention to the Polamuru plates of Mādhavavarman Janāśraya himself and those of the Eastern Cālukya king Jayasiṁha I,[900] which were found together. The former record the grant by Mādhavavarman of the village Pulombūru situated in the Guḍḍavāḍi *viṣaya* in favour of Śivaśarman, son and grandson respectively of Dāmaśarman and Rudraśarman and belonging to the Gautama *gotra* and the Taittirīya *śākhā*, on the occasion of a lunar eclipse on the fullmoon day of the month of Phālguna while the king was crossing the river Godāvarī in order to conquer the eastern region in the fortieth (or forty-eighth) year of his reign. The charter of Jayasiṁha I, issued in the fifth year of his reign, purports to grant the same village to Rudraśarman, son and grandson respectively of Śivaśarman and Dāmaśarman and belonging to the same *gotra* and *śākhā*. Rudraśarman, it is interesting to note, is called *pūrvāgrahārika*, 'the former owner of the *agrahāra*. There can be no doubt that Śivaśarman, the father of the donee of Jayasiṁha I's plates, was the same as the homonymous beneficiary of Mādhavavarman's grant. As the grant of Mādhavavarman was made in the fortieth or forty-eighth year of his reign, it may be reasonably supposed that his reign came to a close shortly thereafter. The recorded years of the reigns of the post-Mādhavavarman Viṣṇukuṇḍin chiefs Indrabhaṭṭārakavarman (27 years) and Vikramendravarman II (10 years[901]) and the Eastern Cālukya king Viṣṇuvardhana I (18 years) and the first five years of his successor Jayasiṁha I[902] total sixty. Assuming that Vikramendravarman I pre-deceased his father Mādhavavarman who had an extraordinarily long reign and the reigns of the Viṣṇukuṇḍin rulers may have extended a little beyond their recorded years and taking the lunar eclipsein to consideration, Mirashi arrives at 525-568 A.D. as the likely duration of Mādhavavarman's rule.[903] Sircar also dates approximately the reign of Mādhavavarman in the period *c.* 535-585 A.D.[904] According to this calculation, both Tīvaradeva and Mādhavavarman were ruling about the same time and consequently could have crossed arms.

As regards the exact regnal period of Tīvaradeva, Mirashi offered various suggestions at the different places where he discussed this problem. At first, primarily depending on the supposed contemporaniety of the Pāṇḍuvaṁśin chief Candragupta and the Maukhari prince Sūryavarman, he proposed to place Tīvaradeva in *c.* 530-550 A.D.[905] Somewhat later he brought

900. *EI*, xix, 254-58.
901. At that time the Chikkulla grant of the tenth year was the latest record of his reign (*ibid*., iv, 193-98). But recently copper-plate grants dated in the eleventh (*JIH*, xliii, 733-48) and fourteenth (*EI*, xxxvi, 7-12) years have come to light.
902. Jayasiṁha I's grant was made in the fifth year of his reign.
903. *EI*, xxii, 20-21; *Studies in Indology*, i, 241-44.
904. *The Successors of the Sātavāhanas in the Lower Deccan*, 107-112; *The Classical Age*. 208.
905. *EI*, xxii, 19.

down Tīvaradeva's accession by three decades and placed it in about 560 A.D. with a view to reconcile palaeographic and other evidences.[906] Elsewhere, he suggested some other dates, to wit, 550-565[907] and 535-555 A.D.[908] Of late, he has attempted to push back the date by a few decades and is now inclined to date Tīvaradeva's reign in *c.* 520-540 A.D.[909] Sircar favours a somewhat later date and thinks that Tīvaradeva 'flourished in the second half of the sixth century, probably about its last quarter.'[910] At one place he suggests for him the period *c.* 565-80 A.D.[911] Following Mirashi and Sircar, most other modern writers on the subject are favourably inclined in favour of placing Tīvaradeva about the middle of the sixth century A.D.[912]

However, a re-assessment of the evidence available earlier and some recent discoveries render it difficult to concede such an early date for Tīvaradeva. As will be obvious from the foregoing resumé, the two principal props of this theory are the identification of Sūryavarman, maternal grandfather of Śivagupta Bālārjuna, with the homonymous son of Maukhari Īśānavarman mentioned in the Haraha stone inscription of 554 A.D. and that of Trivaranagara referred to in the Ipur and Polamuru plates of Viṣṇukuṇḍin Mādhavavarman with the capital of Mahāśiva Tīvara, *viz.*, Śrīpura. To these must be added the currently universally accepted fact that the Pāṇḍuvaṁśins succeeded the Śarabhapurīyas. Let us first examine the identification of the two Sūryavarmans. A stanza met with in a Sirpur inscription of the time of Śivagupta Bālārjuna informs us that his mother Vāsaṭā was the daughter of king Sūryavarman who is stated to have been born in the family of the Varmans who were great on account of their overlordship over Magadha.[913] As stated above, this Sūryavarman is generally identified with the Maukhari prince of the same name. This identification is, however, not based on any

906. *Ibid.*, xxvi, 229. Assigning a reign of about fifteen years, he dated the end of Tīvaradeva's rule in about 575 A.D. See *Studies in Indology*, i, first ed. (1960), 234, fn. 2.

907. *Ganganatha Jha Commemoration Volume*, 223ff.; *Studies in Indology*, i, 239-40 and 244.

908. *Ibid.*, 247. This date is mentioned in the concluding part of the paper on the date of Tīvaradeva and is averred to have been proposed earlier in the article. But the date supported throughout the paper is 550-65 A.D., not 535-55 A.D.

909. *JESI*, iv, 3-4.

910. *The Classical Age*, 220.

911. *The Vākāṭaka-Gupta Age* (ed. R. C. Majumdar and A. S. Altekar), 90. It is added that he 'appears to have flourished about the middle of the sixth century.'

912. B.P. Sinha, *The Decline of the Kingdom of Magadha*, 443; *Readings in History and Culture*, 183-85. A strange case is, however, of Sudhakara Chattopadhyaya who clings, on the one hand to the antiquated dating of the Rajim and Baloda plates of Tīvaradeva in the about 800 A.D. (*Early History of North India*, 185 and 217) and insists, on the other hand, on the equation of Sūryavarman, father of Vāsaṭā, with the Maukhari prince of the name (*ibid.*, 268).

913. See no. III: XI, verse 16.

solid evidence. First of all, there is nothing to indicate that prince Sūryavarman known from the Haraha inscription succeeded his father on the Maukhari throne of Kannauj. When he got the Śiva temple repaired as stated in the Haraha inscription he was only a prince and his father Īśānavarman was on the throne. The inscription does not refer to him even as a crown prince even though it was evidently put up at his behest. His name does not figure in the genealogy of the Maukharis given on the numerous seals of the family nor is he known to have been mentioned in any literary work. There can consequently be no doubt that he did not come to the throne in the direct line of succession. It may, however, be argued that the seal-inscriptions mention only those in the direct line and not collaterals and Sūryavarman's name may have been dropped probably because he was a collateral.[914] But at the moment there is absolutely no evidence to allow us to come to any definite conclusion on this point. Consequently, the description of Sūryavarman as 'king' (*nṛpa*) cannot be justified in the present state of insufficient information.[914a] Secondly, as pointed out by A. Ghosh,[915] the Maukharis of the line of Harivarman were never regarded as a characteristically Magadhan dynasty. Even though a feudatory Maukhari family is known to have ruled over a small principality in the Gaya District of Bihar,[916] the family beginning with Harivarman to which Īśānavarman and his son Sūryavarman belonged had nothing to do with it. Then again, prior to the time of Īśānavarman's son and successor Śarvavarman the family of Harivarman had no pretensions to rule over Magadha and its territorial possessions were confined to Uttar Pradesh.[917] It is true that Īśānavarman claims to have fought battles in Orissa and Gauḍa[918] and he must have passed through Magadha in course of these expeditions; but these were in the nature of raids and do not represent any eastward expansion of the kingdom. They were primarily a power ruling in Uttar Pradesh and even

914. For this argument see Mirashi, *EI*, xxii, 19; B.P. Sinha, *Readings in History and Culture*, 181. Elsewhere (*EI*, xxiii, 115), Mirashi says that in the absence of sufficient evidence it is not possible to ascertain if Sūryavarman, being a younger son of Īśānavarman, never came to the throne.

914a. While for want of necessary evidence it is difficult to verify the suggestion that after the conquest of Magadha Śarvavarman appointed his brother Sūryavarman as the governor of the newly conquered province (B. P. Sinha, *Readings in History and Culture*, 181), the attempt to justify the use of the title 'king' for the Maukhari prince Sūryavarman does not appear to be judicious.

915. *EI*, xxiv, 283; xxv, 268.

916. For the records of this line see *CII*, iii, nos. 48-50, and for its history, R. C. Majumdar (ed.), *HCIP*, iii: *The Classical Age*, 67.

917. Sudhakara Chattopadhyaya, basing on the identification of the two Sūryavarmans, takes the statement of the Sirpur inscription of Vāsaṭā that her father was born in the family of the Varmans who ruled over Magadha as an evidence of the passing of Magadha under the Maukharis during the time of Īśānavarman. See his *Early History of North India*, 268-269.

918. *EI*, xiv, 117, verse 13.

after the later members of the dynasty came to control Magadha (or a part thereof),[919] they continued to have their headquarters at Kannauj. The Maukharis, therefore, could not justifiably be described as a Magadhan power. B.P. Sinha tries to meet this objection by arguing that 'the Sirpur inscription does not refer to Sūryavarman's dynasty as Magadhakula or a Magadhan dynasty' and that it only says that the Varman dynasty (*kula*) is famous for its supremacy over Magadha.[920] But it fails to carry conviction, for the inscription purports to say nothing more or short than that the Varmans were great because they were masters of Magadha.[921] Thirdly, even though all the known Maukhari chiefs without a single exception bore names ending in *varman*, the family to which they belonged could not be referred to simply as Varman. The Maukharis enjoyed a great reputation and played an important role in contemporary Indian politics for nearly a century (sixth-seventh century A.D.). Any relationship with, not to speak of birth in, such a family would have been a matter one could be justifiably proud of. Had Sūryavarman and his daughter Vāsatā belonged to the Maukhari lineage, the author of the inscription in question would not have missed this opportunity to glorify his patron and would not have contented himself by casually referring to it merely by the name ending. The Maukharis are nowhere spoken of as Varmans in inscriptions or literature even though there are numerous allusions to them in contemporary sources, and it is hardly believeable that a princess belonging to that family, who ought to have been justifiably proud of her celebrated lineage, would allow her widely respected family to be referred to in her own record[922] by such an enigmatic name as Varman merely because its members had *varman*-ending names. We know of several other ruling families with all their members bearing *varman*-terminating names; but on that account they are not styled Varman. Nor can it be argued that the composer of the *praśasti* was forced to use the name-ending *varman* instead of the family name Maukhari owing to metrical exigencies, for there was actually no such difficulty and he could have very well composed the relevant portion of the

919. A Maukhari seal has been reported from Nalanda. See EI, xxiv, 284ff. The seal belongs to a later member of the dynasty, to wit, *Mahārājādhirāja* Su.... son of Avantivarman. Also see the Deo-Barnark inscription of the Later Gupta chief Jivitagupta II (*CII*, iii, no. 46) which speaks of the confirmation of a land grant originally made by Bālāditya by *Parameśvara* Śarvavarman and *Parameśvara* Avantivarman who are undoubtedly the same as the homonymous Maukhari chiefs.

920. B.P. Sinha, *Readings in History and Culture*, 180.

921. It might be argued that Magadha being an important political centre for centuries, mastery over it might have been taken as a source of pride. But it lacks plausibility, for no such claim is made in the records of the Maukharis themselves or, for that matter, in the records of any other dynasty which came to obtain supremacy over Magadha.

922. The Sirpur Lakṣamaṇa Temple inscription in which the relevant verse occurs, was put up by the queen mother herself.

stanza in question as *Niṣpaṅke Magadh-ādhipatya-mahatāṁ jātaḥ kule Maukhare* the only alteration being the substitution of the expression *varmaṇām* by *Maukhare.*[923] It would thus be seen that the king Sūryavarman mentioned in his daughter's Sirpur inscription had no connection whatsoever with the Maukharis of Harivarman's line. And lastly, even if all these considerations were to be set aside, there are insurmountable chronological difficulties which render this identification totally untenable. As we learn from the Haraha inscription, the Maukhari prince Sūryavarman flourished in the third quarter of the sixth century A.D. As against it, the available evidence that the Pāṇḍava king Candragupta, who was a contemporary of Sūryavarman of the Varman family, could not have ruled much earlier than about the end of the seventh century A.D. As we have seen above,[924] the rule of the Śarabhapura chiefs who were the political predecessors of the Pāṇḍuvaṁśins in South Kosala, ended about the close of the sixth century A.D. and thereafter some other chiefs appear to have ruled before the Pāṇḍuvaṁśins could come to power. Mahāśiva Tīvara, the first Pāṇḍuvaṁśin chief whose copper-plate charters have come to light, was preceded by some other members of his family and between him and his brother Candragupta intervened the reign of the former's son Nannarāja II. It is, therefore, obvious that Maukhari Sūryavarman and the Pāṇḍava king Candragupta, who are sought to be made contemporaries, were separated from each other by an interval of more than a century. And consequently the two Sūryavarmans cannot be identified.

Let us now examine the other mainstay of this theory, *viz.*, the identification of the Trivaranagara mentioned in the Viṣṇukuṇḍin records with the capital of Tīvaradeva and the consequent contemporaniety of Tīvaradeva and the Viṣṇukuṇḍin chief Mādhavavarman Janāśraya. First of all, there is divergence of opinion regarding the import of the expression *trivaranagara*. K.V. Lakshman Rao was inclined to take it as the name of a locality and to identify it with Tewar, a village about 12 kms. west of Jabalpur in the Jabalpur District of Madhya Pradesh which was the capital of Cedi and thought that the Early Kalacuri king Śaṅkaragaṇa or most probably his father Kṛṣṇarāja was the father-in-law of Mādhavavarman.[925] It is well known that Tewar represents the ancient city of Tripurī or Tripura which was an important politico-cultural centre for about two millennia from the late

923. The Maukharis were also known as Mukhara and Maukhara, the two names occurring in the Haraha inscription of Īśānavarman (verse 3) and Bāṇa's *Harṣacarita* respectively.

S. Sankaranarayanan (*The Viṣṇukuṇḍins and their Times*, 228) also observes that had the author of the Sirpur *praśasti* thought of a Maukhari, 'he would have composed something like *utpanno Magadhādhipatya-mahatāṁ śrī-Maukharīṇāṁ kule*.

924. See *supra* pp. 95-109.

925. *Journal of the Department of Letters*, xi, 39-40.

Chalcolithic times to the end of the Kalacuri period.[926] The Sanskrit form of its name as found in literature and inscriptions was Tripura or Tripurī.[927] Its Prakrit form Tipuri is to be met with in a few copper coins datable to about second-first centuries B.C.,[928] while in the eleventh century A.D. it was commonly known as Tiori as stated by Al-Biruni.[929] It may be reasonably assumed that its modern name Tewar is a product of the process of Prakritisation of the ancient name Tripura (Tripura-Tiura-Tewar). One may even argue that the word *vara* in the expression *trivaranagara* is not really a part of the name of the city but an adjective qualifying the following word *nagara* and the actual name of the city would then be Trinagara which is the same as Tripura or Tripurī and the expression in question would mean 'three good cities'. It is interesting to note in this connection that Tripurī was probably so called as originally it consisted of three different settlements on the Narmada and its tributaries which were collectively known by the meaningful name Tripura or Tripurī.[930] This view is, however, quite untenable. Firstly, in epigraphs and literature this town is invariably mentioned as Tripura or Tripurī and never as Trinagara or Trivaranagara or even as Trivara.[931] Secondly, the Early Kalacuri chiefs Kṛṣṇarāja, Śaṅkaragaṇa and Budharāja and nothing to do with Tripurī which became the capital of the Kalacuris of Ḍāhala about the beginning of the eighth century A.D. And lastly, in the extensive archaeological excavations at Tripurī no trace whatsoever of the Viṣṇukuṇḍins has been found. We also know that during the time of Mādhavavarman Janāśraya the Tripurī region was under the rule of the Parivrājaka Mahārājas.[932]

S. Sankaranarayanan invites our attention to the age-old Indian poetic tradition of describing the womenfolks of the capital cities as having felt elated at the sight of their beloved princes and kings going round in the

926. For a summary of the results of excavations and the epigraphical references bearing on the subject, see my *Tripurī* (Hindi), 82-89 and 165-66.
927. For these references, see *ibid.*, 165-66 (inscriptions) and 167-68 (literature).
928. John Allan, *Catalogue of Indian Coins in the British Museum: Coins of Ancient India*, cxl-cxli, 239, pl. xxxv. 14-15.
929. E. Sachau, *Al-Beruni's India*, i, 202. K.V. Lakshman Rao (*Journal of the Department of Letters*, xi, 63) felt that Trivara is a partially Prakritised form of Tripurī which in due course gave rise to the form Tiwar of Tewar by which name Tripurī is currently known. A. Ghosh (*EI*, xxv, 269) thinks that 'there is much probability' in this view.
930. See H.D. Sankalia in the *Journal of the Madhya Pradesh Itihasa Parishad*, v, 59. *Cf.* the name Daśa-pura (modern Mandasaur, Madhya Pradesh) which has got to be explained in a similar manner.
931. Following the popular practice of naming the capital after the country or dynasty, Tripurī is sometimes referred to as Cedi-nagarī or Cedi-kula-*rājadhānī*. See Ajay Mitra Shastri, *Tripurī*, 3. Also *vide Abhidhānacintāmaṇi*, iv, 41; *CII*, iv, lxxxiii, fn. 4.
932. *EI*, viii, 284-88. Also vide my *Tripurī*, 32-33.

streets of the cities, particularly after their long absence due to some reason and finds the description of Mādhavavarman in his Ipur and Polamuru plates in tune with this tradition.[933] Therefore, according to him, there is no reference in this expression to any military expedition undertaken by the Viṣṇukuṇḍin monarch and he finds himself in agreement with E. Hultzsch in taking Trivaragara as a name of the place where the king resided. He further identifies it with the modern Tiruvuru (17° 10′ North and 30° 35′ East), the headquarters of the taluk of the same name in the Krishna District of Andhra Pradesh.[934]

Some other scholars are of the opinion that the expression *trivaranagara* cannot be taken as the name of any particular locality and is probably intended only as a general reference to the capture by Mādhavavarman of three excellent cities (*tri-vara-nagara*) and his dalliances with the damsels of the royal harems situated there.[935] It has also been suggested that the epithet, an ornamental one, 'means no more than that there were three flourishing cities in the Vishṇukuṇḍin kingdom where the king resided by turns.'[936]

The popular view at the moment is that Trivara is the name of a ruling chief defeated by Mādhavavarman and that the compound Trivara-nagara refers to his capital. And, as stated above, this Trivara is now generally identified with the Pāṇḍava king Tīvaradeva, and his capital (*nagara*) with Śrīpura. This suggestion also involves a number of unsubstantiable assumptions and as such does not admit of acceptance. The capital of the Pāṇḍuvaṁśins of South Kosala was known as Śrīpura and is invariably mentioned by this name in all the records of the dynasty. Had it ever been known as Trivaranagara after one of the most powerful members of the family, the name must have occurred at least in some of the inscriptions of his successors and it would not have been left to his avowed adversary alone to mention it. Moreover, howsoever renowned and powerful a monarch might have been, the capital was not generally known after his own name unless it was founded or re-settled and specifically so named by him.[937] Pāṭaliputra, for example, is nowhere spoken of as Candragupta-*nagara* or Aśoka *nagara* or Samudragupta-*nagara*. Then again, had Mādhavavarman really successfully raided the Pāṇḍava capital Śrīpura, he would not have referred to it in such a roundabout and obscure manner as he is supposed to have

933. For such descriptions see *Mahābhārata*, Śāntiparva, ch. 39; *Kādambarī*, 185; *Kathā-sarit-sāgara*, iii. vi. 223; *Bṛhat-kathā-mañjarī*, iii. 311-14, etc. These are cited by S. Sankaranarayanan in his *The Viṣṇukuṇḍins and their Times*, 230, fn. 45.
934. *The Viṣṇukuṇḍins and their Times*, Appendix iv. Also see *ibid.*, 46.
935. Ajay Mitra Shastri, 'A Note on the Ipur and Polamuru Plates of Mādhavavarman' *Sri Mallampalli Somasekhara Sarma Commemoration Volume*, *JAHRS*, xxxv, 168.
936. K.A. Nilakanta Sastri in *HCIP*, iii, *The Classical Age* (ed. R.C. Majumdar), 225.
937. For localities christened after the founders, *cf.* Pravarapura, Huṣkapura, Juṣkapura, Karṇāvatī, Śarabhapura, etc.

done. It would thus follow that the expression *trivaranagara* cannot be taken in the sense of 'the city of Trivara or Tīvaradeva' and has no bearing on the question of the date of Tīvaradeva. But even if we were to ignore all these facts for arguments' sake, chronologi calconsiderations present insurmountable hurdles against this identification. Till recently no Viṣṇukuṇḍin document dated in a well-known era was available and all the known records were dated with reference to the regnal years of the issuing chiefs. Consequently, the dates of individual members of the family were fixed tentatively on the twin grounds of the regnal years recorded in inscriptions and the data contained in the Polamuru plates of Mādhavavarman and Jayasiṁha I, to which reference has already been made. However, the discovery of the Tummalaguḍem (Ramanapeta Taluk, Nalgonda District, Andhra Pradesh) plates[938] issued by Vikramendravarman II in the expired Śaka year 488 corresponding to 566-67 A.D.[939] has put the Viṣṇukuṇḍin chronology on a more solid basis and we are no longer required to reconstruct it conjecturally on the basis of rather uncertain evidence as was the case hitherto. As Śaka 488 is stated to have corresponded to the eleventh year of Vikramendravarman's reign, his accession evidently took place sometime in 555-556 A.D. He was preceded on the throne by his father Indravarman (or Indrabhaṭṭārakavarman who ruled for at least twenty-seven years as indicated by the Ramatirtham plates dated in the twenty-seventh year of his reign.[940] Even if it is held that his reign did not extend beyond the twenty-seventh year, his accession cannot be dated later than 528-529 A.D. Some scholars are of the opinion that his father Vikramendravarman I did not come to the throne as he predeceased his father who had a rather extra-ordinarily long reign of over forty years.[941] But this surmise cannot be taken seriously in view of the fact that in the records of his successors Vikramendravarman I is given the regal titles *Rājan*[942] and *Mahārāja*[943] which should leave no room for doubt about his accession even though no record of his own reign has been reported so far.[944] Even assuming that he had a short reign covering just

938. Also known as Indrapālanagara plates.

939. *JIH*, xliii, 733ff.; S. Sankaranarayanan, *The Vishṇukuṇḍins and their Times*, 172-75.

940. *Ibid.*, 166-68; *EI*, xii, 133, text-line 16.

941. As pointed out earlier, D. C. Sircar favours the reading of the date of the Polamuru plates of Mādhavavarman as 40 which is followed by Mirashi. According to K.V. Lakshman Rao and R. Subba Rao, on the other hand, the plates were issued in the year 48. The latter view is favoured by S. Sankaranarayanan who is the latest writer on the subject. See his *The Vishṇukuṇḍins and their Times*, 180, text-line 41.

942. See Ramatirtham plates of his son Indrabhaṭṭārakavarman, text-line 5, *ibid.*, 166.

943. In the Tummalagudem plates of Vikramendravarm II, text-line 10, *Epigraphia Andhrica*, ii, 15.

944. Mirashi (*EI*, xxii, 20; *Studies in Indology*, i, 212-213) believes that Vikramendravarman I did not rule and holds that the regal titles may have been used for him

about a decade, his accession could not have taken place later than 518-519 A.D. His father Mādhavavarman Janāśraya ruled for at least forty or forty-eight years depending upon the reading of the date of his Polamuru plates. His accession, therefore, cannot be placed later than 478-479 or 470-471 A.D.[945] In any case, it is apparent and most important from our point of view that the close of his reign cannot be dated posterior to 518-519 A.D.[946] The allusion to his dalliances with the ladies of Trivaranagara is first met with in his Ipur plates issued in the thirty-seventh year of his reign. This episode, therefore, must have taken place in or prior to 515-516 A.D. in case the fortieth year was the last year of his reign. If, however, the Polamuru plates were granted in the forty-eighth year of his reign, this incident will have to be dated eight years earlier, *viz.*, in or anterior to 507-508 A.D. And the event may have to be placed still earlier in case some margin is allowed for the extension of the reigns of Mādhavavarman and Indravarman beyond their latest recorded years. If the expression *Trivaranagara* has to be taken as referring to Tīvaradeva, the latter will have to be shown to have assumed regal power before this date. But as we have seen above, the earliest date proposed for Tīvaradeva's accession so far is 520 A.D. which is five years posterior to the latest possible date for the event in question.[947] It is further noteworthy that even this early date for Tīvaradeva has been postulated with the sole object of establishing his contemporaniety with Mādhavavarman so that the interpretation of *Trivara-nagara* as Tīvara's capital may be retained. And when in spite of all this the contemporaniety of Tīvaradeva and Mādhavavarman could not be established, the accession of the latter was sought to be pulled down to 528 A.D. by ignoring the reign of Vikramendravarman, which is in total violation of the unimpeachable extant evidence in the form of the employment of regal titles for him in the inscriptions of his descendants.

It will follow from the foregoing discussion that the two principal grounds for placing Tīvaradeva in the sixth century A.D. are no more extant and the chronology of the Pāṇḍavas of South Kosala has got to be

---

by way of courtesy (*JESI*, iv, 5, fn. 24). But this insistence, which is inspired by the anxiety to establish the contemporaniety of Mādhavavarman and Tīvaradeva has no place in any scientific discussion.

945. In my paper entitled 'A Note on the Ipur and Polamuru plates of Vishṇukuṇḍin Mādhavavarman I' published in the *Śrī Mallampally Somasekhara Sarma Commemoration Volnme, JAHRS*, xxxv, these dates are wrongly printed as 489-490 or 482 A.D. (*ibid.*, 167). There are a few other misprints also.

946. Mirashi brings down this date by omitting the reign of Vikramendravarman I, which is totally unwarranted.

947. That the evidence of the Tummalagudem plates of Vikramendravarman II precludes the contemporaniety of his great grandfather Mādhavavarman with Tīvaradeva was first pointed out by the present writer in the *Śrī Mallampalli Somasekhara Sarma Commemoration Volume*, 165-168. Also see *JESI*, v, 20-25.

determined independently of the evidence of the Maukhari and Viṣṇukuṇḍin records.

Let us now proceed to discuss the evidences bearing on the question and try to ascertain the chronology of the Pāṇḍuvaṃśin rule. While discussing the chronology of the Śarabhapurīyas we have seen that the end of their rule cannot be placed much earlier than the close of the sixth century A.D. Even if one were to argue, as Mirashi did once,[948] that Pravararāja, the last known member of the dynasty, was overthrown by the Pāṇḍuvaṁśa and that the Pāṇḍava king who ousted him was none else than Tīvaradeva, the commencement of the latter's rule cannot be dated before the closing years of the sixth century A.D. It seems, however, that Tīvaradeva did not come to power immediately after Pravararāja and that the two were separated from each other by a sufficiently long interval of time.

There is enough evidence to show that the members of the Pāṇḍava dynasty ruled over South Kosala for quite some time before Tīvaradeva. Reference must be made in this connection to the Dhamatari and Kauvatal plates of the penultimate Śarabhapura chief Sudevarāja which refer to a certain Indrabalarāja as occupying the office of *Sarvādhikārādhikṛta* or Chief Minister. It is not possible in the present state of insufficient information to ascertain the identity of this Indrabalarāja. However, he is commonly identified with Indrabala, a son of the first known Pāṇḍuvaṁśa chief Udayana and grandfather of Tīvaradeva.[949] In case we were to accept this identification, Tīvaradeva's grandfather Indrabala will have to be regarded as occupying a subordinate, though important, position under Sudevarāja almost up to the latter's closing years. But there is sufficient evidence to prove that he also ruled as a sovereign ruler for some time. In a fragmentary inscription put up by Īśānadeva in the Lakṣmaṇeśvara temple at Kharod, about two miles to the north of Sheorinarayan in the Bilaspur District of Madhya Pradesh, his father Indrabala is described as one whose lotus-feet were adorned with the crest-jewels of all the monarchs.[950] He founded a town, christened Indrapura after his own name, which is referred to as the headquarters of a district (*viṣaya*) in the same record. His son Īśānadeva erected the temple of Lakṣmaṇeśvara (now known as Lakhneśvara at Kharod and granted a few villages for its maintenance. It will, thus follow that Indrabala began his career as a subordinate chief under Sudevarāja and ruled as a sovereign monarch after Pravararāja, and that he was succeeded by his son Īśānadeva. Nannarāja, another son of Indrabala, is

948. *EI*, xxii, 17.
949. *IHQ*, xx, 275; xxii, 63.
950. Text-line 22 of this still unpublished epigraph is deciphered by Mirashi (*Studies in Indology*, i, 258, fn. 1) as follows: *sarvve-āvan-īśvara-śiro-maṇi-rāji-rājat=pād-āmbujaḥ śaśi-kul-āmbara-pūrṇa-candraḥ Āsīd=bhuvaḥ patiḥ*. . .*pāsta-ripur=Indrabal-ābhidhānaḥ*. Also see Hira Lal, *ICPB*, 125, no. 208.

also known to have ruled in South Kosala.[951] His Arang (now Raipur Museum) stone inscription shows that another grandson of Udayana, Bhavadeva Raṇakesarin, also ruled in Kosala. We shall not be unjustified in assigning the period of a minimum of about four decades for the rule of Indrabala, Īśānadeva, Bhavadeva and Nannarāja, the reign of the last named king terminating about 630 A.D.[952]

Attention must be invited to a few other points which may lead one to date the accession of Tīvaradeva still later. As shown above,[953] we learn from the Mallar plates of Vyāghrarāja that two Amarārya-kula chiefs, *viz.*, Jaya-bhaṭṭāraka and Pravara-bhaṭṭāraka, ruled in South Kosala for some time after the Śarabhapurīyas. The date of the record has been variously read as year 4 or 41, which obviovsly refers to the reign of Pravara-bhaṭṭāraka. Provision will have to be made for the rule of these chiefs before the reigns of the members of Udayana's line. Similarly, provision will have to be made for the rule of Bhīmasena II, the last known member of the Rājarṣi-tulya-kula, known from his Arang plate dated in the Gupta year 282 or 601 A.D. and of the last known Mekalā Pāṇḍava chief Śūrabala Udīrṇavaira. If we provide for a period of about thirty years for the rule of these chiefs also, the commencement of the reign of Tīvaradeva would have to be dated in the second half of the seventh century A.D., to be more precise in *c.* 660 A,D.[954] It may perhaps be argued that if, as commonly held, Tīvaradeva's grandfather Indrabala was responsible for overthrowing the Śarabhapurīya dynasty, how could members of other families intervene between the Śarabhapura chiefs and the Pāṇḍuvaṁśins? It must be observed in this connection that the identification of Indrabalarāja mentioned in the copper-plate grants of Sudevarāja with the Pāṇḍuvaṁśin Indrabala is based simply on the identity of names which appears to be purely accidental. Then again, we cannot be quite sure about the duration of the rule of the Amarārya-kula, Rājarṣi-tulya-kula and the Mekalā Pāṇḍava chiefs in South Kosala. We have assigned them tentatively a period of just three decades on the assumption that the earlier members of these lines may have been ruling in a small part of Kosala or in a neighbouring area and that only the last known chiefs exercised their sway over the whole or a major portion of Kosala and that, too, only for a part of their reigns for which alone we have definite epigraphic evidence.

This date for Tīvaradeva finds support from some other evidences also. We learn from a stanza met with in a number of inscriptions of the Śailodbhava chief Dharmarāja II *alias* Mānabhīta that his younger brother

951. This is indicated by the Arang (so-called Bhandak) inscription which was put up during his reign.

952. Once Mirashi also admitted the necessity of allowing a few years (about thirty years) for the reigns of Tīvaradeva's predecessors. See *EI*, xxvi, 229. But of late, he appears to have preferred to ignore this fact vide *JESI*, iv, 1-2.

953. See *supra*. pp. 125-26

954. This chronology was first suggested by me *JESI*, v, 20-25.

Mādhava tried to oust him from his kingdom but was defeated in a battle fought at Phāsikā. Then out of desperation he joined king Trīvara, but both of them were again defeated at the foot of the Vindhyas.[955] Since Mādhavarāja II *alias* Sainyabhīta, grandfather of Dharmarāja II, is known to have been ruling in Gupta year 300 or 619-620 A.D.,[956] the reign of the latter must be referred to the second half of the seventh century A.D. This tallies well with the above date for Tīvaradeva who is evidently identical with king Trīvara of the Śailodbhava inscriptions. This identification, it may be mentioned, finds support from the Aḍhabhāra plates of Nannarāja II which describe his father Tīvaradeva as the lord of a number of provinces including Utkala.[957] Those who believe in an earlier date for Tīvaradeva regard king Trīvara as a later member of the Pāṇḍuvaṁśa who was named after his ancestor.[958] But this suggestion is unconvincing and uncalled for.

Palaeographic evidence also supports this date. It is admitted on all hands that the Arang stone inscription of the time of Nannarāja I is palaeographically later than the Arang plate of Bhīmasena II, dated Gupta 212 (=601 A.D.) by about half a century.[959] Mirashi also accepted this position, though in order to strengthen his date for Tīvaradeva he felt that the date of the Arang plate of Bhīmasena II should be read as Gupta 182,[960] and not as 282 as deciphered by Hira Lal.[961] But the first figure of the date is really 200, not 100,[962] so that Hira Lal's reading of the date appears to be correct.[963] It will thus follow that the Arang stone inscription of the time of Nannarāja I, father of Tīvaradeva, must be dated around the middle of the seventh century A.D.

A brief reference may now be made to some objections recently raised against placing Tīvaradeva in the second half of the seventh century A.D. It is

955. *Rājyaṁ labdhv-aiva darpād=aviganitatayā Mādhavo jyeṣṭha-bhāvān,*
Deśād=asmād=apāstuṁ kṛta-viṣama-matir=vigrahe Phāsikāyām |
Yuddhaṁ kṣobhena magno nṛpativaram=asau saṁśritas=Tīvar-ākhyaṁ,
Paścāt=ten-āpi sārdhaṁ punar=api vijito Vindhya-pādeṣu jīrṇaḥ ||
This verse is found in the Koddenda (*EI*, xix, 269, verse), Nivinna and Puri plates.

956. Mādhavarāja II's Ganjam plates were issued in this year. See *EI*, vi, 143. The identification of Mādhavavarman II Sainyabhīta of the Bugude plates and Mādhavarāja II of the Ganjam plates is taken for granted in the present discussion.

957. No. III: V, text-line 6. R.D. Banerji (*HO*, i, 134), N. P. Chakravarti and A. Ghosh (*EI*, xxv, 269-70) also favour this identification.

958. V.V. Mirashi, *Studies in Indology*, i, 247.

959. For a detailed discussion of this point, see A. Ghosh, 'Date of the Pāṇḍava Kings of Southern Kosala', *EI*, xxvi, 266-69.

960. *Ibid.*, xxvi, 227-29.

961. *Ibid.*, ix, 345, text-line 13.

962. The scribe by oversight attached the slightly slanting horizontal stroke to the lower portion of the symbol for 100 on its left instead of its upper portion on right.

963. Cf. D.C. Sircar, 'Durgarāja of the Śarabhapurīya Dynasty', *IHQ*, xxii, 62-63.

argued that a date for Tīvaradeva early in the sixth century A.D. will go well with Yuan Chwang's description of South Kosala while it will not agree with the chronology suggested in these pages. According to the Chinese traveller's account, the Kosalan 'king was a Kṣatriya by birth, a Buddhist in religion, and of noted benevolence.' He adds that there were 'above 100 Buddhist monasteries, and about 10,000 Brethern, all Mahāyānists'.[964] It is suggested that this description applies well to the time of Śivagupta Bālārjuna who extended his patronage to Buddhism,[965] but flourished much later than the period of Yuan Chwang's visit according to our chronology. A close examination of this account will, however, reveal that it is partially inaccurate and is of so general a nature as to be of no use in indicating the identity of the ruler in question. The statement that the king was a Buddhist is palpably erroneous as no Kosalan ruler from the Śarabhapurīyas to the Pāṇḍuvaṁśins was a Buddhist and the fact that all these chiefs were followers of Pauranic Hinduism is vouched for by their own inscriptions.[966] Not even Śivagupta Bālārjuna was a Buddhist. But, in keeping with the age-old Indian convention, all of them observed religious catholicity and so did Śivagupta. Such a catholic religious attitude could easily be mistaken as formal affiliation to one religion or the other, Buddhism in the present case, as has been done by Yuan Chwang in several cases. It is, therefore, clear that Yuan Chwang's account of South Kosala and its ruler has absolutely no bearing on the question of the date of Tīvaradeva.

According to our date for Tīvaradeva, Śivagupta Bālārjuna ruled in the eighth century A.D. The latter, as stated above, extended patronage to Buddhism. It has been doubted if Buddhism was flourishing in the Chhattisgarh region as late as the end of the eighth century A.D. There exists definite archaeological evidence to prove that Buddhism was in vogue in South Kosala not just up to the close of the eighth century A.D. but for a few centuries thereafter as well. The Ratanpur stone inscription of the time of Kalacuri Jājalladeva I, dated Kalacuri 866 (=1114 A.D.), for example, informs us that the king's spiritual teacher Rudraśiva was conversant with the writings of Diṅnāga and others.[967] The Koni stone inscription of the time of Pṛthvīdeva II, dated Kalacuri 900 (=1148-49 A.D.), states that its composer Kasela had mastered the Three Jewels and the *āgamas* of Śrīghana (*i.e.*, Buddha) and others.[968] These inscriptional references leave no doubt

964. T. Watters, *On Yuan Chwang's Travels in India*, ii, 200; Shaman Hwui Li, *The Life of Hiuen Tsiang*, 119.
965. One of his copper-plate charters and some of the stone inscriptions of his time record benefactions in favour of Buddhism.
966. Sūryaghoṣa, who flourished considerably earlier than Udayana and built a Buddha temple at Arang in memory of his son, is the only exception.
967. *Dig(ṅ)nāg-ādi-pramāṇa-vit.* V. V. Mirashi, *Inscriptions of the Kalachuri-Chedi Era*, *CII*, iv, pt. ii, 412, text-line 27.
968. *Jñātā ratna-trayasya prathitatara-matiḥ Śrīghana-ādy-āgam-aughe*. *Ibid.*, 470, text-line 27.

that Buddhism was prevalent in Kosala as late as the twelfth century A.D. This inference finds support from the excavated finds from Malhar, one of the most important towns of South Kosala. The finds of Period IV, dated 650-900 A.D., include baked clay sealings with the Buddhist creed.[969] Several Buddhist images like those of Buddha, Padmapāṇi Avalokiteśvara Hevajra and Tārā, datable up to the tenth century A.D., have also been reported.[970] The evidence is quite eloquent and leaves no doubt about the prevalence of Buddhism in this area during the early medieval period.[971]

To sum up, a date for Tīvaradeva in the latter half of the seventh century A.D. satisfactorily accounts for all the known historical facts and there is absolutely nothing against this view. It is, on the contrary, impossible to explain away the extant historical evidence in case Tīvaradeva is placed in the sixth century A.D.

With *c*. 660 A.D. as the date for the accession of Tīvaradeva, we may now proceed to outline the chronology of the rule of the Pāṇḍuvaṁśins in South Kosala. As stated above, we have to provide about three decades for the rule of the Rājarṣi-tulya-kula chief Bhīmasena II, the Amarārya-kula king Pravara-bhaṭṭāraka and Śūrabala *alias* Udīrṇavaira of the Pāṇḍava dynasty of Mekalā after the Śarabhapurīya rule which ended around 590 A.D. and before the establishment of the Pāṇḍuvaṁsins of Udayana's line in South Kosala. The latter event may, therefore, be dated about 620 A.D. Udayana had probably nothing to do with Kosala. But there is definite evidence to show that his son Indrabala and grandsons Īśānadeva, Nanna, and Bhavadeva ruled in Kosala before Tīvaradeva. Indrabala probably ruled from *c*. 620 to *c*. 640 A.D. It is difficult to ascertain in the present state of our knowledge if the two sons of Indrabala, *viz*., Nanna and Īśānadeva, ruled simultaneously or one after the other. In any case, we may roughly assign them a period of about twenty years, *c*. 640-*c*. 660 A.D. The brother of Indrabala, whose name is lost in the damaged portion of the Arang stone inscription of the time of Nanna, probably ruled simultaneously with Indrabala over a part of the Pāṇḍava kingdom in Kosala.[972] His son Bhavadeva may have succeeded him and ruled over the same

969. K.D. Bajpai and S.K. Pandey, *Malhar* 1975-77, 36.
970. *Ibid*., pls. xv-xvi, xviiA and xviiiB. In the description on pl. xvii the image of Hevajra is said to date from the eighth century A.D., while at p. 35 the Hevajra temple found in the excavations is described as of Period III which is dated from *c*. 300 to *c*. 650 A.D. There seems to be some confusion and the temple, if the image in question really belonged to it, actually appears to date from the eighth-ninth centuries A.D. The account of the temple complex seems to support this date.
971. For these objections and their examination, see V.V. Mirashi, 'The Date of Tīvaradeva', *JESI* vii, 1-4; Ajay Mitra Shastri, 'A Note on the Date of Tīvaradeva', *ibid*., 5-11.
972. He is styled *nṛpa* in verse 18. This reconstruction would imply a division of the Pāṇḍava kingdom of Kosala after Udayana.

area simultaneously with Nanna and Īśānadeva. It is also possible that Udayana was succeeded by Indrabala and the latter by his son Nanna on the throne while Īśānadeva and Bhavadeva governed parts of the Pāṇḍava kingdom of Kosala as Nanna's subordinates. The latest recorded date of Tīvaradeva is the ninth year of his reign when he gave his Baloda plates. How long thereafter he continued to rule cannot be determined in the absence of necessary evidence. But he may be assigned a reign of about twenty years, *c.* 660-*c.* 680 A.D. Only one record of his son and successor, Nanna II, has been found so far; but as it is not dated, the duration of his reign does not admit of ascertainment. But if he also ruled for about two decades, his reign may be placed in *c.* 680-*c.* 700 A.D. No record of the next two chiefs, Candragupta and Harṣagupta, has been reported to date. But if they, too, are supposed to have had a reign lasting twenty years each, their reigns may be dated from *c.* 700 to *c.* 720 and from *c.* 720 to *c.* 740 A.D. respectively. Harṣagupta's son and successor Śivagupta Bālārjuna is definitely known to have ruled for at least fifty-seven years as two of his copper-plate inscriptions were issued in that year.[973] Assuming that he continued to rule for a few years more thereafter, he may be taken to have closed his reign about the close of the eighth century A.D.

The above chronology, it must be pointed out, is provisional and may have to be modified in the light of future epigraphical discoveries, particularly dated records and records of those members of the dynasty who are at the moment known only from the inscriptions of their descendants. As and when such a modification becomes necessary, it is not likely to affect the general chronological framework to any considerable extent, the alterations being confined to matters of detail like the duration of individual reigns and the dates of their commencement and termination. As regards the general period of the commencement and the close of the Pāṇḍuvaṁśin rule in Kosala, no major change appears likely.

It will be seen that our chronology for the Pāṇḍuvaṁśins differs from the now commonly accepted scheme by about a century as regards the beginning of their rule and by nearly a century and a half as regards its end. It is comparatively close to the chronology adopted by earlier scholars like Kielhorn, Fleet and Hira Lal in regard to the close of the rule of the dynasty though there is considerable difference in matters of detail and the date of Tīvaradeva adopted in these pages falls over a century earlier than that proposed by these savants. These differences are forced upon us by a reappraisal of the entire evidence bearing on the problem in the light of recent epigraphical discoveries.

Historical Outline

Having thus settled the vexed problem of the chronology of the Pāṇḍuvaṁśins, their political history may now be outlined in brief.

973. This is the date of his Lodhia and incomplete Burhikhar (Mallar) plates.

Udayana

Udayana is the first member of the Pāṇḍuvaṁśa of Kosala to be mentioned in the records of the dynasty. No inscription of Udayana himself is known; but he is referred to in a couple of the inscriptions of his descendants, *viz.*, Arang stone inscription of Nanna I (no. III: I) and one of the Sirpur stone inscriptions of the time of Śivagupta Bālārjuna (no. III: XIII). He is generally identified with the homonymous Pāṇḍava ruler who is mentioned in a Kalanjar (Banda District, Uttar Pradesh) lithic record assigned to the ninth century A.D. as a king of the past and stated to have erected a brick temple of the god Bhadreśvara (Siva)[974] at Kalanjar.[975] It may be reasonably concluded that Udayana ruled over a principality including Kalanjar and adjoining area in Central India. In the present state of our knowledge it is not possible to ascertain if he advanced as far as South Kosala in course of his military expeditions. In all probability he himself had nothing to do with the Chhattisgarh region which was conquered by his successors. He had at least two sons: (i) Indrabala and (ii) his younger brother whose name has been lost.[976] It is not possible to determine his relationship, if any, with king Sūryaghoṣa who, according to the Arang stone inscription of Nanna I, built a temple of Buddha which, when in despair, was restored under the patronage of Udayana's grandson Bhavadeva Raṇakesarin.

Udayana's Successors

Udayana was succeeded by his eldest son Indrabala who is referred to in a number of dynastic records as he happened to be in the direct line of succession. He was the first member of the family who is definitely known to have ruled over at least a part of Kosala. A mutilated Kharod (Bilaspur District) Lakṣmaṇeśvara temple inscription states that Indrabala had

974. Some take it as a temple of Viṣṇu. See V.V. Mirashi, *Studies in Indology*, i, 236. However, it does not appear likely.

975. उदयन इति राजा यः कुले पाण्डवानां
सकलभुवननाथस्यास्य भद्रेश्वरस्य ।
पवनलुलितचिह्नं रम्यकान्तीष्टकाभि
गृह्विवरमतिभक्त्यां कारितं तेन पूर्व्वम् ॥

Quoted by Kielhorn in *EI*, iv, 257, fn. 4; *JRAS*, 1905, The inscription is yet to be published in its entirety. The record is sometimes erroneously referred as the Kalanjar inscription of Udayana himself. But the description of Udayana as a king of the past sets this notion at naught.

976. Indrabala is clearly spoken of as Udayana's son in a Sirpur lithic record of the time of Śivagupta Bālārjuna. See no. III: XIII, verse 2. In the Arang stone inscription of his son Nanna I he appears to have been referred to as Bala which by *double entendre*, mentions both him and Baladeva who were elder brothers of the unnamed son of Udayana and the epic hero Kṛṣṇa respectively. The comparison is evidently based on the identity of names or parts thereof.

destroyed his enemies and that his lotus-like feet were adorned by the rows of the crest-jewels of all the princes.[977] This should, notwithstanding the element of exaggeration involved in such eulogistic descriptions, leave no doubt that he ruled as a sovereign monarch for some time. He may be justifiably credited with the foundation of a town named Indrapura after his own name which is spoken of as the headquarters of a district (*viṣaya*) in the same inscription. What brought him to the Chhattisgarh region is not ascertainable at present. But the rise and expansionist policy of Harṣavardhana seem to have forced him to seek fortunes away from his ancestral kingdom, and he found a favourable climate in Kosala where the fall of the Śarabhapurīyas was followed by total political chaos which enabled him to carve out a small principality for himself. In this task he appears to have received valuable assistance from his younger brother whose name is lost but who is compared in the Arang lithic record of his nephew Nanna I to the epic hero Kṛṣṇa who followed his elder brother Bala and destroyed his numerous enemies.[978]

Indrabala is generally identified with the *Mahāsāmanta* Indrabalarāja who according to the Dhamatari and Kauvātāl plates,[979] occupied the office of *Sarvādhikārādhikṛta* under the Śarabhapurīya chief Sudevarāja.[980] Mirashi regards him as the grandson of the Mekalā Pāṇḍava chief Bharatabala *alias* Indra and conjectures that after the loss of Mekalā to the Uccakalpa *Mahārāja* Hastin he moved to Kosala where he ruled at first as a feudatory of the contemporary Śarabhapurīya chief Sudevarāja and later aggrandised himself at the cost of his suzerain and overthrew the next Śarabhapurīya king Pravararāja.[981] D.C. Sircar appears to be uncertain about this identification but states that in case this identification is to be accepted 'this son of Udayana did not inherit his father's kingdom, but went to the Śarabhapura court and accepted service under the Śarabhapurīyas whom he or more probably his immediate successors ultimately overthrew.'[982] But this identification, first proposed by Lochan Prasad Pandeya,[983] which is based only on the identity of names and the historical reconstruction based thereupon cannot be taken for granted in the present state of insufficient knowledge.[984]

977. For the original extract as transcribed by V.V. Mirashi, see note 950 above. *Vide* also Hira Lal, *ICPB*, 125, no. 208.
978. Comparison is made in several respects by the employment of words with two meanings (*śleṣa*). See verse 18 of the original and note 976 above.
979. See nos. I: IX, text-line 26; XII, text-lines 23-24..
980. This suggestion was first offered by Pandit Lochan Prasad Pandeya in a note on the Kauvatāl plates of Sudevarāja in *IHQ*, xxi, 294-95.
981. *Studies in Indology*, i, 236.
982. R.C. Majumdar (ed.), *The Classical Age*, 221. In *IHQ*, xxii, 63, he surmises that in case we were to accept this identification, Indrabala would have to be taken as a younger son of Udayana.
983. *IHQ*, xxi, 294-95.
984. This question has been discussed earlier. See pp. 114-15.

It is difficult to determine the order of succession after Indrabala. The employment of the title *nṛpa* for Indrabala's younger brother in the Arang inscription of Nanna I indicates that he wielded regal power. His fourth son Bhavadeva is also styled *nṛpa* and described as the 'lord of the earth' (*kṣiter=bharttā*). It would, thus, appear that Indrabala's younger brother ruled over a part of the Pāṇḍava kingdom in Kosala and was succeeded by his youngest son Bhavadeva. But since Bhavadeva's father is described as a loyal follower and helpmate of his elder brother Indrabala, we may reasonably conclude that he ruled as a subordinate chief acknowledging his elder brother's authority. The grant of some villages by Iśānadeva, a son of Indrabala, for the maintenance of the temple of Lakṣmaṇadeva at Kharod would indicate that he ruled after his father. But the description of another son of Indrabala, Nanna I, as *Rājādhirāja* seems to show that Nanna succeeded his father Indrabala on the ancestral throne of the dynasty. It is also pertinent to note in this connection that the next ruler of the dynasty who held sway over the entire Pāṇḍava realm of Kosalā, Tīvaradeva, was the son and successor of Nanna and that in the subsequent records of the family the line of succession is traced from Nannadeva I.[985] We may, therefore, conclude that either both Bhavadeva and Īśānadeva ruled over parts of the Pāṇḍava kingdom of Kosala as subordinates under Nanna I or all the three, *viz.* Nanna I, Bhavadeva and Īśānadeva, ruled independently and ultimately Nanna I succeeded in becoming the master of the whole of the Pāṇḍava kingdom either by forcibly exterminating his cousin and brother or in the course of succession when the last two chiefs died without leaving male issues to inherit their dominions. But before we leave this problem, another equally likely course of events must also be referred to. Bhavadeva's eulogistic description in the Arang inscription of his cousin Nanna I gives indication of his sovereign status and great power.[986] It is, therefore, not unlikely that Bhavadeva succeeded to the dominions not only of his father but also of his uncle Indrabala whose sons Nanna I and Īśānadeva may have been too young to wield power at the time of his death. And since the description of Bhavadeva is followed by the mention of his cousin Nannarāja I, it may be reasonably surmised that the latter inherited his territorial possessions from the former and that he may have permitted his younger brother Īśānadeva to govern a small area as his feudatory. The exact course of succession has to be left to be decided in the light of fresh evidence that may come to light in future.

Bhavadeva was also known as Raṇakesarin (literally, 'a lion in the battle') on account of his killing the maddened elephants of the enemies by his

985. Tīvaradeva, who claims to have acquired the overlordship of the whole of Kosala, is invariably referred to as the son of Nannadeva who is also named in a Sirpur inscription of the time of Śivagupta Bālārjuna. See no. III: XIII, verse 3. In this record he is also called Nanneśvara.

986. He is described in highly eulogistic terms in as many as fifteen stanzas.

sword in the battle-field.[987] He also assumed the *viruda* of Apriya-vaiśika, 'one disdainful of prostitutes' which is rather unusual.[988] Verse 32 of the Arang inscription of Nanna I informs us that he had earned another name, Cintādurga, by causing anxiety (*cintā*) to his enemies and by himself being difficult to assail at (*durga*) by warriors in combat. He extended active patronage to Buddhism and maintained the Buddha temple built by Sūryaghoṣa and it was under his patronage that the temple was repaired and the monastery attached to it was whitewashed and adorned with stepped well, gardens, etc.[989]

Īśānadeva was a follower of Paurāṇic Hinduism as can be reasonably inferred from the construction of and grant of some villages to the temple of Lakṣmaṇadeva at Kharod by him. Nannadeva I was probably an adherent of Śaivism. A Sirpur stone inscription of the time of Śivagupta Bālarjuna would have us believe that he covered the earth with Siva temples.[990]

The Arang stone inscription of Nanna I was earlier believed to have been found at Bhandak (now Bhadrāvatī) in the Chanda District of Vidarbha and it was accordingly held that Indrabala, Bhavadeva and Nannadeva I ruled over the Chanda region. But as shown above,[991] the inscription actually came from Arang and as such there is at the moment no evidence to support the Pāṇḍava rule over any part of the Vidarbha region during this period.

Mahāśiva Tīvara

Nanna I was succeeded by his son Mahāśiva Tīvara who is known from his three copper-plate charters that have come to light so far. The text-portion of these grants gives his name as Mahāśiva Tīvara, while in the legend on the seals attached to them he is referred to as Tīvaradeva. The legend on the seal being naturally brief, is expected to give the proper name of the king, while the text of the charters, which is much more detailed, gives an elaborate eulogy. It may, therefore, be reasonably assumed that Tīvara or Tīvaradeva was his personal name, Mahāśiva being his coronation name.[992] It is pertinent to note in this connection that it was a common practice among the Śarabhapurīyas and the Somavaṁśins who ruled over Kosala prior and posterior to the Pāṇḍuvaṁśins respectively to assume

987. See no. III: I, verse 20. Lion is smarter than elephant and the former is invariably represented as victorious over the former.
988. No. III: I, verse 28.
989. The description of the repair and restoration of the temple and the monastery is the main theme of the Arang inscription of Nanna I (no. III: I).
990. See no. III: XIII, verse 3.
991. See *supra*, pp. 152-55.
992. This name was repeated in the dynasty a little later by Bālārjuna who, however added the word *gupta* at the end to make it Mahāśivagupta. In this case also, Bālārjuna appears to have been the personal name and Mahāśivagupta the coronation name.

names beginning with *mahat*. This practice was evidently inherited by the Pāṇḍuvaṁśins from the Śarabhapurīyas. But while the Śarabhapurīyas generally assumed a single name to which they prefixed the word *mahat*[993] the Pāṇḍuvaṁśins appear to have assumed two names, one of which was personal and the other was assumed at the time of coronation, and it was to the latter name that the word *mahat* was added.[994] According to the evidence available at present, this practice was initiated by Tīvaradeva.[995]

The notion of Fleet that Tīvaradva was an adopted son of Nannadeva[996] was based on the reading *Nannadevasya tanaya-prāptaḥ*[996a] in text-line 16 of the Rajim plates. But the reading of the corresponding portion in the other two copper-plate charters (Bonda and Baloda) is *Nannadevasya tanayaḥ prāptasakala-Kosala-ādhipatyaḥ* which shows that the word *prāpta* is to be construed not with *tanaya* but with the following expression *sakala-Kosal-ādhipatyaḥ* which is omitted in the Rajim plates due to scribal error. As such, there exists no basis for this notion and Tīvaradeva was as much the real son of Nannadeva as Candragupta.[997]

Another scribal error in the Rajim plates led Fleet to believe that Tīvaradeva was a feudatory chief and that his paramount sovereign is mentioned in line 11 of this record.[998] He proposed to correct the expression *svāmī-bhavanapy-a-bahu-lapano* met with in the Rajim plates to *svāmī-bhavane=py-a-bahu-lapano* and found in it a mention of the palace of Tīvaradeva's overlord.[999] But this is again due to negligence on the part of the scribe, the correct expression found in other grants being *svāmī-bhavann=apy-a-bahu-lapano* which describes Tīvaradeva himself as *svāmin* or 'lord' and contains no allusion to his overlord. Moreover, there are clear indications in his records that he regarded himself as the paramount sovereign. His feet are said to have been rubbed by the edges of the crowns of many chiefs who had secured the five great sounds (*samadhigata-pañca-mahā-śabda*)

993. The only known exception is provided by Durgarāja who was also known as Mānamātra. The practice of prefixing the word *mahat* appears to have been initiated by Jayarāja.

994. In the case of the next three ruling chiefs of the dynasty the names known to us appear to have been coronation names. Confirmation of this conjecture has to be left to future epigraphic discoveries

995. If and when official records of the earlier members of the dynasty are found, the antiquity of this practice may have to be pushed back to an earlier date.

996, *CII*, iii, 293 and 298.

996a. Fleet rendered *tanaya-prāpta* by 'acquired as a son'. See *ibid.*, 293, fn. 3, and 298, fn. 2.

997. Fleet regarded Candragupta as Nannadeva's son by brith on the basis of a Sirpur stone inscription of the time of Śivagupta Bālārjuna (no. III: XIII, verse 4). See *ibid.*, 293, fn. 3.

998. *Ibid.*, 293.

999. *Ibid.*, 298 where this passage is translated.

bowing before him. The use of the title *Rājādhirāja* or *Adhirāja*[1000] for his father Nanna in the Arang stone inscription should leave no doubt that leave aside Tīvaradeva, his father had risen to paramount position.

The seal-inscription describes Tīvaradeva as *Kosalādhipati* or the lord of Kosala, while in the text of the charters themselves he is said to have acquired the overlordship of the whole of Kosala (*prāpta-sakala-Kosala-adhipatya*).[1001] This shows that the process of the subjugation of the Kosala region which was initiated by Indrabala was brought to a successful completion during the reign of Tīvaradeva who must have wiped out whatever small principalities might have been in existence in the area. But Tīvaradeva's military ambitions were not confined to Kosala and there is evidence that he carried his arms to and tried to annex adjoining areas of Orissa and possibly some other regions as well. The Aḍhabhāra plates of Nannarāja II inform us that his father Tīvaradeva and acquired mastery over the whole of Kosala, Utkala and other provinces by the prowess of his own arms (*sva-bhujaparākram-opārjita sakala-Kosal-Otkal-ādi-maṇḍal- ādhipatya-prāptal-māhātmyasya*).[1002] That the claim to have achieved possession of Utkala, etc., is not totally unfounded is indicated by the fact that Nannarāja, the issuer of the charter, himself is credited with the possessions of the province of Kosala alone.[1003] Some confirmation of this claim is found in a stanza met with in a record of the Śailodbhava chief Dharmarāja II *alias* Mānabhīta which states that shortly after obtaining the kingdom, his younger brother Mādhava made an attempt to drive him out of the kingdom but had to swallow discomfiture in a battle at Phāsikā; he then sought refuge under king Trīvara but was again defeated together with him in another battle fought at the foot of the Vindhyas and fled away.[1004] As shown above,[1005] king Trīvara of these records is none else than the Pāṇḍava monarch Tīvaradeva who was undoubtedly the most powerful member of his dynasty and engaged himself in a number of military expeditions.[1006] It appears that Tīvaradeva tried to take

1000. No. III:I, verse 40. Part of this word at the end is damaged, but the proposed restoration is fairly certain.

1001. Nos. III: II, text-lines 16-17; IV, text-line 19. In III: III, text-line 16, the words after *prāpta* and before the *visarga* are omitted due to oversight on the part of the scribe.

1002. No. III: V, text-lines 5-7.

1003. No· III: V, text-lines 8-9 (*prāpta-sakala-Kosalā-maṇḍal-ādhipatyaḥ*). This expression minus the word *maṇḍala* is literally identical with that employed for Tīvaradeva in his own charters.

1004. For the relevant stanza, see note 955 above.

1005. See *supra*, pp. 147-56

1006. Some scholars who placed Tivaradeva in the sixth century A.D. thought that king Trīvara of the Śailodbhava inscriptions was a later Pāṇḍava monarch of that name. But the discovery of the Aḍhabhāra plates of Nannarāja which credit his father Tīvaradeva with the possession of Utkala seems to have raised doubts about the correctness of this position in the minds of some of the scholars who

advantage of the struggle for succession in the Śailodbhava kingdom and apparently championed the cause of one of the claimants to regal power with the ultimate object of self-aggrandisement and success. It may perhaps be argued that the Śailodbhava inscriptions refer to Tīvara's discomfiture whereas the Aḍhabhāra plates lay claim to the acquisition of the Utkala-*maṇḍala*. However, it is not difficult to reconcile these two apparently conflicting claims. It appears that the Śailodbhava records actually refer to only one of the states in the protracted struggle which went on for quite some time with fluctuating vicissitudes sometimes favouring one party and sometimes the other party, but at the end Tīvaradeva was successful in annexing or controlling some adjoining area in Orissa at least for a short time. That this new acquisition did not last long is vouched for by the fact that Tīvara's son Nannarāja himself did not lay any claim to the Utkala-*maṇḍala*.[1007] It is sometimes argued that the Śailodbhava kingdom was known as Koṅgoḍa-*maṇḍala* whereas Tīvaradeva staked his claim to control the Utkala-*maṇḍala*.[1007a] But it presents no hurdles as the latter expression was probably intended as a general reference to Orissan territories without any specific implication. This event must have taken place after the ninth year of his reign as it is not mentioned in the Baloda plates issued in that year.

Some scholars believe that Tīvaradeva crossed swords with the Viṣṇu-kuṇḍin chief Mādhavavarma II Janāśraya also. But as pointed out earlier,[1008] this position can no longer be maintained in view of some recent epigraphical discoveries and chronological difficulties.

We learn from the Baloda plates that Tīvaradeva had a daughter who was married to a certain Nannarāja[1009] who is described as his 'dear son-in-law' (*priya-jāmātṛ*). He is said to have acquired the 'five great sounds' and may have ruled his fiei as a zamindar under him. It was at his behest that the grant recorded in the charter in question was made for feeding thirty persons daily. It is quite possible that the granted village was included in his *jāgīr*.

Tīvaradeva was a follower of Vaiṣṇavism and bore the sectarian title of *parama-Vaiṣṇava*, *i.e.*, a devout worshipper of Viṣṇu.[1010] It was in keeping

---

maintained it. *Contra* D.C. Sircar in *EI*, xxix, 39 and *ibid.*, xxxiv, 113. That no chronological difficulties are involved in this identification has been shown above.

1007. It is, however, interesting to note that some adjoining areas of Orissa continued to be under the Pāṇḍavas till the very end as indicated by the mention of certain localities in the records of Śivagupta Bālārjuna.

1007a. *EI*, xxxiv, 113.

1008. See *supra*, pp. 147-49

1009. No. III: IV, text-lines 25-26. It is somewhat interesting that Tīvaradeva's son and son-in-law had the same name. The name of his daughter has not been given.

1010. This perhaps marked a change in the family religion. As stated earlier, Tīvaradeva's father Nanna I was a Śaiva and is credited in a later record with the erection of a large number of Śiva temples.

with his faith that he depicted on his seal a seated figure of Garuḍa with outspread wings and grasping a snake with raised hood in each hand as the principal device and wheel and conch-shell as subsidiary devices.

Tīvaradeva was admittedly the greatest ruler of his family though his name is found omitted in all the subsequent records of the dynasty with the solitary exception of his son's Aḍhabhāra plates because he was not in the direct line of succession. He brought the entire Kosala country under his sway and it remained under the rule of his successors right up to the end of the dynasty. Not contented with this achievement, he meddled in the internal affairs of the Śailodbhava kingdom of Koṅgoda and this resulted in the extension, though only for a while, of his political control over the adjoining region of Orissa. Another line of the extension of his authority is possibly indicated by the village of Tīvarkheḍ near Multai on the Nagpur-Itarsi line of the Central Railway which may have been christened after the great Pāṇḍuvaṁśin ruler.

Nanna II

Before the discovery of the Aḍhabhāra plates it was believed that Tīvaradeva was succeeded by his brother Candragupta probably because the former passed away without leaving a male issue to inherit the kingdom. But the Aḍhabhāra charter showed for the first time that after Tīvaradeva the Pāṇḍava kingdom passed on to his son Nanna II (called Mahā-Nannarāja) who was evidently named after his illustrious grandfather.[1011] The Aḍhabhāra grant, still the only known record of Nannarāja II, was, however, left incomplete and the donation recorded therein was not made for some reason which is indeterminable at the moment. This is indicated not only by the absence of the seal but by the fact that an imprecatory stanza has been left incomplete even though much space was available at the bottom.[1012] The record having been left incomplete, the date has been left unrecorded.[1013]

Even though the grant mentioned in the Aḍhabhāra plates was intended to be made by Nannarāja, the preliminary portion of the inscription is devoted to the description of the attainments of his father Mahāśiva Tīvara whereas the donor himself is described very briefly. It is stated that he was the son of Mahāśiva Tīvara even as Pradyumna was of Kṛṣṇa, the enemy of Kaiṭabha, and was engaged in emulating the conduct of his father and meditated on the feet of his parents.

Nanna is said to have acquired the possession of the entire Kosalā-*maṇḍala*. The omission of reference to the Utkala-*maṇḍala*, which is men-

1011. See no. III: XIII. For a theory placing Nanna II's reign after Harṣagupta, see S. R. Nema, *Political History of the Soma-vāṁśī Kings of South Kosala and Orissa*, 114-116 and 124-128.

1012. For a detailed discussion of this question, see Ajay Mitra Shastri, 'A Note on the Aḍhabhāra Plates of Mahā-Nannarāja', *JOI*, xxiv, 67-69.

1013. The date is generally one of the concluding items of a copper-plate charter.

tioned in connection with his father's dominions, indicates the loss of Utkala either anterior to or during his reign. But if the wording of the record is to be relied upon, he maintained his control over Kosala intact.

Nanna II seems to find mention in the Senkapat stone-slab inscription of the time of Śivagupta Bālārjuna.[1014] This epigraph refers to three generations of a line of feudatory chiefs, *viz.*, Śivarakṣita, Devarakṣita and Durgarakṣita, the last two being related to the preceding chiefs as sons. Of these, Durgarakṣita was a contemporary of Śivagupta Bālārjuna and was ruling as a feudatory under him at the time the inscribed slab was put up. His father Devarakṣita was a contemporary and confidant of king Nannarāja and is stated to have received from him the Vindhyan territory extending up to the river Varadā which is evidently identical with the modern Wardha flowing through tne Vidarbha region of Maharashtra.[1015] There can be no doubt that king Nannarāja, benefactor of Devarakṣita, belonged to the Pāṇḍava dynasty and was a predecessor of Śivagupta. Of the two Nannarājas who preceded Śivagupta, *viz.*, (i) Nannarāja, son of Indrabala and father of Mahāśiva Tīvara, and (ii) Nannarāja, son and successor of Mahāśiva Tīvara, he has to be identified with ihe latter as the former would be too early to be regarded as a contemporary of the immediate predecessor of a feudatory of Śivagupta.[1016] If this identification is accepted, it will follow that sometime during the reign of Nanna II the Pāṇḍava kingdom witnessed an expansion on the west and came to incorporate a considerable part of Vidarbha. How long this portion of Vidarbha continued to be under the Paṇḍuvaṁśins cannot be determined for want of necessary evidence. A Rāṣtrakūṭa feudatory chief named Nannarāja is known to have been ruling in a part of Vidarbha about the close of the seventh and the beginning of the eighth century A.D.[1017] The relationship, hostile or otherwise, if any, between the two homonymous chiefs and the families represented by them is also unascertainable at present. Be that as it may, there is no doubt that the Pāṇḍava rule in Vidarbha represents an important episode in the annals of the dynasty. The date of the conquest of this area is not known. But it must have occurred after the date of his solitary known record which describes him as the lord of Kosala only.[1017a]

1014. No. III: XV, text-lines 5-6, verse 6.

1015. No. III: XV, verse 6. Also see *EI*, xxxi, 34, and *ibid.*, xxxiii, 255-256. Mirashi is not agreeable to this interpretation. See *ibid.*, xxxiii, 251-254.

1016. If this Nannarāja is to be identified with Tīvaradeva's father of that name, one would have to maintain the rather untenable position that four (or five if Nannarāja's reign is also included) Pāṇḍuvaṁśin reigns were co-eval with two generations of their subordinates. Moreshwar G. Dikshit and D.C. Sircar favour this identification without totally ruling the possibility of his equation with Nanna II. See *EI*, xxxi, 33-34.

1017. See his Akola and Multai plates dated Śaka 615 ond 631 respectively (*EI*, xxix, 109; *IA*, xviii, 230).

1017a. However, the possibility of the employment of the name Kosala in a wider sense

Like his father Tīvaradeva, Nanna II also was a follower of Vaiṣṇavism and enjoyed the sectarian epithet *Parama-Vaiṣṇava*. The grantee of his Aḍhabhāra plates was also a *Bhāgavata*, 'worshipper of Bhagavat', i.e., Viṣṇu. His own comparison with Pradyumna and that of his father Tīvaradeva with Pradyumna's father Kṛṣṇa is also of some interest in this context.

Candragupta

No record of the reign of Candragupta himself has been discovered so far and all our knwoledge about him is based on the records of his grandson's reign. But his description, though highly hiperbolic, in the Sirpur Lakṣmaṇa temple inscription leaves no doubt that he did assume regal power. It contains not only vague references to his military successes and other qualities but also employs for him the regal title *nṛpati* and describes him as the lord of the rulers of the earth (*avanibhṛtām adhīśvara*).[1018] Although there is no definite information on this point, there is little doubt that he succeeded Nanna II who might have died without a son to succeed him.

D.C. Sircar and Moreshwar G. Dikshit proposed to identify Nannarāja mentioned in the Senkapat inscription of the Śivagupta Bālārjuna with the homonymous father of Mahāśiva Tīvara and Candragupta. Now as Nannarāja is described as a contemporary of Devarakṣita whose son Durgarakṣita was a contemporary of Śivagupta, it will follow that the rule of the four generations, to wit, (i) Nannarāja I, (ii) Candragupta, (iii) Harṣagupta and (iv) Śivagupta Bālārjuna (and five reigns, *viz*., of these four chiefs and of Mahāśiva Tīvara), roughly corresponded to a couple of generations of their feudatories. And as Śivagupta is known to have had an extraordinarily long reign covering at least fifty-seven years, it is obvious that he must have come to the throne at an early age. In view of these facts, they assume that Tīvaradeva, Candraguptra and Harṣagupta had very short reigns. As no records of Candragupta and Harṣagupta have been discovered, it has been doubted if 'they actually ascended the Pāṇḍuvaṁśin throne and ruled for very short periods or ruled parts of South Kosala as viceroys of Tīvara', and it has been suggested that Śivagupta 'ascended the throne shortly, if not immediately, after Tīvara's death.'[1019] But as we have shown above, Nannarāja of this inscription should be

---

so as to cover some regions of Vidarbha under the rule of the dynasty cannot be gainsaid. In that case it is not impossible if this westward expansion took place prior to the issuance of the Aḍhabhāra plates or even during the reign of his father, Tīvaradeva, who is known to have aggrandised at the cost of other powers,

1018. See no. III: XI, verses 6-8. Moreshwar G. Dikshit and D.C. Sircar are not sure if Candragupta ascended the Pāṇḍava throne and toy with the idea that he and his son Harṣagupta governed parts of South Kosala as Tīvara's viceroys. See *EI*, xxxi, 33-34. But there seems to be no real basis for this assumption.

1019. *Ibid.*, xxxi, 34.

equated with the son, not father, of Tīvaradeva and the acceptance of this identification would render most of these assumptions unnecessary.[1020] Be that as it may, the fact remains that as Candragupta had to wait for two reigns, he must have come to the throne at a fairly advanced age.

The practicc of appending the word *gupta* to the royal names, which is known to have become popular hereafter,[1021] appears to have been initiated by him.

D.R. Bhandarkar identified Candragupta mentioned along with Nāgabhaṭa as defeated by the Rāṣṭrakūṭa emperor Govinda III in the Sañjan plates of his son Amoghavarṣa I with on Chandragupta. But this identification is rendered untenable not only by chronological difficulties but also by the facts that Candragupta, like Nāgabhaṭa was, in all probability, a ruler of Central India and that Kosala is mentioned in the inscription separately as one of the later conquests of Govinda III.[1022] Verse 6 of the Sirpur Lakṣmaṇa temple inscription apparently refers, though without naming, to the elder brother Candragupta who enjoyed regal power but followed him even as the plough-bearer (Baladeva) had followed the destroyer of Kaṁsa (Kṛṣṇa). According to H. Krishna Sastri, he had Adhikāradhavala for his name or surname.[1023] It would thus follow that Candrapupta had another elder brother in addition to Tīvaradeva who, however, preferred to be, or was, superseded by his younger brother.[1024]

Harṣagupta

Candragupta was succeeded by his son Harṣagupta who is known from references in numerous records, both official and private, of the reign of the next king Śivagupta Bālārjuna. In the introductory portion of the copper-plate charters of Śivagupta he is called Harṣadeva while the legend on the seals attached thereto gives Harṣagupta as his name. In most of these records he is credited with exercising regal power.

We learn from the Sirpur Lakṣmaṇa temple inscription that Harṣagupta married a lady named Vāsaṭā, daughter of king Sūryavarman who was born in the family of the Varmans great on account of their possession of

1020. Dikshit and Sircar do not rule out this possibility altogether but prefer the identification with Tīvara's father and feel that Nannarāja II may have had a short reign and may not have been as powerful a chief as his homonymous grandfather. See *EI*, xxxi, 32, fn. 4.

1021. Most of the later members of this dynasty as well as of the later Somakula bore *gupta*-ending names.

1022. *EI*, xviii, 245, Verse 22 mentions Nāgabhaṭa and Candragupta. For reference to the conquest of Kosala, see verse 24. For D.R. Bhandarkar's identification the two Candraguptas, see *ibid.*, 24.

1023, *Ibid.*, xi, 194, fn. 3.

1024. He was evidently different from Tīvaradeva who is known to have ruled as a sovereign monarch for quite some time.

Magadha. This Sūryavarman appears to have been an otherwise unknown local chief of Magadha and the dynasty to which he belonged was obviously known as Varman. The manner of mentioning this marriage is indicative of the importance that the Pāṇḍuvaṁśins attached to it, probably because it helped them materially in times of difficulty.[1025] However, Harṣagupta predeceased his spouse who build a Viṣṇu temple to prepetuate his memory.[1026]

Harṣagupta was a Vaiṣṇava and is said to have worshipped Acyuta all the time. The construction of a temple of Viṣṇu in his memory is also a pointer in the same direction.[1027]

Śivagupta Bālārjuna

Śivagupta Bālārjuna, son of Harṣagupta and Vāsaṭā, ascended the Pāṇḍuvaṁśin throne after his father's death. In his copper-plate charters he is called Mahā-Śivagupta and in the legend on seals, Śivagupta. In the private records on stone he is referred to either as Śivagupta or as Bālārjuna,[1028] there being only a solitary instance of the employment of the nama Mahā-Śivagupta.[1029]

Fortunately, we have a large number of inscriptions belonging to the reign of Śivagupta; but they do not contain much of interest to a historian. We learn from them that he enjoyed a long reign of not less than fifty-seven years.[1030] He had a younger brother named Raṇakesarin who is said to have helped him in his conquests.[1031] His son Śivanandin and maternal uncle Bhāskaravarman are also known. The latter was evidently a son of Sūryavarman of Magadha and a brother of Vāsaṭā and appears to have lived at the Pāṇḍuvaṁśin court at Śrīpura. It was at his instance that Śivagupta granted a village to a Buddhist monastery.[1032]

A line of feudatory Brāhmaṇa chiefs which gained the family's favour during the reign of Nanna II continued to govern in the same capacity during Śivagupta's reign. Śivagupta's contemporary of this line was Durgarakṣita who was responsible for the pious acts recorded in the Senkapat stone-slab inscription.

1025. No III: XI, verse 16. Alternatively the element of exaggeration may be due to Vāsaṭā who was responsible for pious deeds recorded in this inscription.

1026. *Ibid.*, verse 20.

1027. *Ibid.*

1028. Śivagupta: nos. III: XI, verse 41; XIII, verse 5; XIV, verse 2. Bālārjuna: nos. III: XI, verse 13; XII, verse 2; XIII, verse 5; XV, verses 4 and 10.

1029. No. III: XI, verse 12. As will be seen from the preceding note, this inscription mentions him as Śivagupta and Bālārjuna also.

1030. The Lodhia and the incomplete Burhikhar (Mallar) charters were given in the fifty-seventh year of his rule.

1031. No. III: XI, verse 12. Raṇakesarin is required to in line 13 of another fragmentary Sirpur inscription also. See Hira Lal, *ICPB*, 110, no. 183.

1032. Bhāskaravarman is mentioned in no. III: IX, text-line 13. For reference to Śivanandin, see *Archaeological Survey of India, Western Circle Progress Report* for 1904, 49, no. 2015.

Two villages mentioned in the Lodhia plates of the fifty-seventh year of Śivagupta's reign, Vaidyapālī and Khadirapadra, have been located in the Sambalpur or Kalahandi region of Orissa,[1032a] indicating thereby the inclusion of at least a part of the eastern part of Kosala in his kingdom. Whether it indicates a fresh conquest during his own reign or it continued to be under the Pāṇḍuvaṁśins from the time of Tīvaradeva, who is known to have extended his territorial possessions in Orissa, cannot be determined at present.

Śivagupta's reign marked a change in the family religion. He reverted back to Śaivism and is styled *Parama-Māheśvara* in his official records. Most of the records of his reign record activities connected with his newly adopted faith. This change finds reflection in the royal seal which now bears the figure of a humped bull and a *triśūla*, the mount and a characteristic emblem respectively of Śiva. But, though a devout Śaiva, he evinced tremendous religious catholicity extending his patronage to the followers of other faiths. He himself donated a village in favour of a Buddhist establishment and a private benefactor provided for a free feeding house for the Buddhist monks.[1033] As stated above, Śivagupta Bālārjuna's mother built a temple of Viṣṇu, the same as the so-called Lakṣmaṇa temple at Sirpur.

All the stone inscriptions of Śivagupta's reign are composed in Sanskrit stanzas couched in a highly flourishing *kāvya* style and show that classical Sanskrit literature flourished in Kosala under the Somavaṁśins.

The End

Śivagupta Bālārjuna is the last known Pāṇḍuvaṁśin monarch of South Kosala, and absolutely nothing is known of the fate of the dynasty after his rule which terminated around the close of the eighth century A.D. At present we have no evidence to ascertain if his younger brother Raṇakesarin and/or his son Śivanandin ruled after him.[1034] Even if they ruled, they could not maintain their control over the Chhattisgarh region intact for a

1032a. *EI*, xxvii, 322-23; *Journal of the Kalinga Historical Research Society*, i, 265-66.

1033. No. III: XII.

1034. Some scholars propose to identify king Raṇakesarin mentioned in a fragmentary inscription from Govindpur (old Nayagarh State, Orissa) with the homonymous Pāṇḍuvaṁśin chief who is believed to have succeeded his elder brother Śivagupta Bālārjuna (Binayak Misra in *JBORS*, xiii, 186-187). But this suggestion cannot be entertained as the inscription is decidedly much later than the time of the Pāṇḍuvaṁśins. See S.N. Rajaguru, *IO*, iv, 353. Attention is sometimes invited in this connection to a carnelian seal from Balpur (Raigarh District, Madhya Pradesh) belonging to the *Rāṇaka* Bālakesarin and bearing besides his name a rather strange animal which cannot be identified satisfactorily (*OHRJ*, iv, 58-59, pl. i; M. G. Dikshit, *Madhyapradeśa ke Purātattva kī Rūparekhā*,, 57, pl. xiii.50) and a couple of coins, one silver and the other gold, from the same site the fragmentary legend in which has been sought to be doubtfully restored as *Śrī-Kesarī* (Lochan

long time. For a stone inscription found built in a wall of the Rājīvalocana temple at Rajim, about twenty-eight miles south by east of Raipur, records the erection of a temple dedicated to Viṣṇu by the Nala king Vilāsatuṅga.[1035] The inscription mentions Vilāsatuṅga's father Virūparāja and grandfather Pṛthvīrāja also. It is evident that the region round Rajim in the Raipur District was under Vilāsatuṅga at the time of the construction of the temple in question which is undoubtedly the same as the modern temple of Rājīvalocana. The record has been assigned to about the eighth century A.D. on palaeographical grounds.[1036] Thus, it appears that the Nalas, who were the neighbours of the Pāṇḍuvaṁśins on the south, took advantage of the decline of the Pāṇḍuvaṁśin power after Śivagupta and Vilāsatuṅga succeeded in capturing the Raipur region from Śivagupta's weak successors.[1037] Whether Vilāsatuṅga's rule was confined to the Raipur region or he annexed some other parts of Chhattisgarh also cannot be

---

Prasad Pandeya in *JAHRS*, iii, 181). M. G. Dikshit seems to be in favour of identifying the issuer of these coins with Raṇakesarin, younger brother of Śivagupta Bālarjuna, and tries to connect the seal in question also with the Pāṇḍuvaṁśins, although no precise identification of Bālakesarin has been suggested (*Madhyapradeśa ke Purātattva kī Rūparekhā*, 57). Taking cue from Dikshit, it has been conjectured recently that the seal was issued by Raṇakesarin when he was serving under his elder brother who was on the throne while the coins were struck by him after he himself became king following the death of Śivagupta Bālārjuna (S. R. Nema, *The Soma-vaṁśī Kings of South Kosala and Orissa*, 144). However, Raṇakesarin and Bālakesarin are two quite different names and this alone, not to speak of other arguments, is enough to set aside their suggested identification. There is also nothing to support the proposed identification of Raṇakesarin of inscriptions with Kesarin of the above-mentioned coins. First of all, the reading of the legend on these coins is quite uncertain. And even if the restoration of the legend proposed by Lochan Prasad Pandeya is conceded, the omission of the word *raṇa* before Kesarī is inexplicable. It is, therefore, best to take the personages represented by the seal and the coins as the local chiefs of the area whose connection or otherwise with the Pāṇḍu-vaṁśa cannot be established for want of necessary evidence. For a full discussion on the seal, see C. S. Gupta, 'The Seal of Rāṇaka Bālakesarī', *JNSI*, xxxvi, 122-26.

1035. *EI*, xxvi, 49-58.

1036. V.V. Mirashi, *Studies in Indology*, i, 260. Elsewhere (*EI*, xxvi, 51), Mirashi proposed to date this inscription about 700 A.D. Cunningham, who noticed this record casually in *CASR*, xvii, 7, thought that the inscription is not datable later than the eighth or ninth century A.D. According to D.R. Bhandarkar (*PR, ASWI*, for 1903-04, 48), it belongs to about the middle of the eighth century A.D. Hira Lal thought that its characters 'appear to belong to the 8th or 9th century' (*ICPB*, 112, no. 188). We feel that the record has to be attributed to about the close of the eighth or the beginning of the ninth century when Śivagupta Bālārjuna had ceased to rule.

1037. Whether Vilāsatuṅga himself annexed this region or it was conquered by one of his predecessors cannot be ascertained at present. Likewise, we cannot determine in the present state of insufficient information as to how long the Nala rule lasted in the area.

determined in the present state of inadequate knowledge. Be that as it may, the fact remains that after Śivagupta we get no trace of the presence of Pāṇḍuvaṁśins in the Chhattisgarh region forming the western part of South Kosala which passed successively under the Nalas, Bāṇas and Kalacuris, and when the curtain rises again, they are found ruling in western Orissa which corresponded to the eastern part of Kosala.

IV. THE SOMAVAMŚINS

Lineage

Chiefs belonging to a dynasty referred to as Soma-kula in inscriptions ruled initially in western Orissa and gradually extended their sway over a large part of Orissa. There are definite indications that they were intimately connected with and probably belonged to the Pāṇḍu-vaṁśagwhich had earlier held sway over the entire Kosala country for nearly one and half centuries. To begin with, like the Pāṇḍuvaṁśins, the Somavāṁśins also traced their descent from the lunar line. All the members of the family are described in their official records as 'ornaments of the family of the moon' (*Soma-kula-tilaka*). One of the members of the dynasty, *viz.*, Mahāśiva-gupta II Yayāti, is figuratively styled 'the full moon on the clear horizon of the lineage of the cool-rayed (*i.e.*, moon)'.[1038] D.R. Bhandarkar argues that the earlier rulers of Kosala belonged to the Pāṇḍu-vaṁśa and if the Somavaṁśins belonged to the same line it will be difficult to explain as to why they did not mention this family name even once in their records.[1039] But this objection is untenable, for we have already shown that the name Pāṇḍu-vaṁśa or Pāṇḍava-vaṁśa is not met with even in a single record of the Pāṇḍuvaṁśins after the reign of Mahāśiva Tīvara, while all the records of the time of his grand-nephew trace the descent of the family from the moon.[1040] Secondly, the Somavaṁśins, like the Pāṇḍuvaṁśins (or, for that matter, the Śarabhapurīyas), adopted names beginning with the word *mahat*.[1041] Thirdly, following the practice obtaining among the later Pāṇḍu-vaṁśins,[1042] the Somavaṁśins also assumed *gupta*-ending names. Fourthly, it is noteworthy that these names, which were perhaps assumed at the time of coronation and are thus indicative of regal power, were different from the personal names which are often met with in the *praśasti* portion

1038. *Śīt-āṁśu-vaṁśa-vimal-āmbara-pūrṇṇa-candraḥ*, no. IV: XXI, text-line 15.
1039. *IA*, lxi, 241.
1040. See *supra*, pp. 132-37
1041. Śivagupta, father of Mahābhavagupta I Janamejaya, alone is mentioned in most of the records of his son without the prefix *mahat*.
1042. *Cf.* the names of the last three ruling chiefs of the family, *viz.*, Candragupta, Harṣagupta and Mahā-Śivagupta Bālārjuna. This practice is not known to have been prevalent in the earlier period.

or in connection with the specification of date in many inscriptions.[1043] This appears to be true of at least some of the Pāṇḍuvaṁśins chiefs also.[1044] Fifthly, repetition of names, specially in the third generation, is also common to the two families.[1045] Sixthly, the same is true of some of the names which are met with in both the dynasties. The name Śivagupta or Mahā-Śivagupta borne by the last known Pāṇḍuvaṁśin chief, for instance, is known to have been very popular among the Somavaṁśins.[1046] Similarly, the name Bhavadeva assumed by one of the early members of the Pāṇḍu-vaṁśa is found to have been very common among the Somakulins in the form of Mahābhavagupta. Likewise, the name Kesarin is found commonly associated with both the dynasties. Bhavadeva, one of the early members of the Pāṇḍu-vaṁśa, was also known as Raṇakesarin which, as we have seen above, also happened to be the name of the younger brother of the last known monarch of the same family, *viz.* Mahā-Śivagupta Bālārjuna. The Somavaṁśins are also referred to as as the Kesarī kings in the late medieval Orissan chronicles called *Mādalā-pañjī* indicating that in later times the dynasty was known popularly as Kesarin although this name is nowhere met with in the numerous records of the family itself which invariably refer to the dynasty as Soma-kula. That this tradition was not totally without foundation is vouched for by such kesarin-ending names as Uddyotakesarin and Karṇakesarin[1047] borne by two of the Somavaṁśin rulers. Some other local chiefs of the eastern part of South Kosalā flourishing during the Somavaṁśin period are also known to have borne similar names. To this category appear to belong Kesarin known from a couple of coins,[1048] Bālakesarin brought to light by a carnelian seal,[1049] both from Balpur in the Raigarh District, and Raṇakesarin mentioned in the Govindapur inscription.[1050] Seventhly, the Pāṇḍuvaṁśins are primarily

1043. *E.g.* Janamejaya, Yayāti, Bhīmaratha, Dharmaratha, Uddyotokesarin and Karṇakesarin, which are found mentioned in the non-formal portion of the epigraphic records and were apparently personal names.

1044. See, for example, Tīvaradeva and Bālārjuna which were obviously personal names of Mahāśiva and Mahā-Śivagupta respectively. The same appears to have been the case with some of the Śarabhapurīya chiefs, *viz.*, Prasannamātra and Mānamātra also.

1045. *Cf.* the names Raṇakesarin, Nanna and Mahāśiva which were repeated at least twice in the Pāṇḍu-vaṁśa, the last two in the third generation. In the Soma-kula this practice was too common to need illustration.

1046. This name is known to have been borne by not less than five Somavaṁśin rulers.

1047. While in the records of his own reign he is called simply as Karṇa or Mahāśivagupta, we learn from the commentary on verse 5 of the second Pariccheda of the *Rāmapāla-carita* of Sandhyākaranandin that the lord of Utkala defeated by a feudatory under the Pāla monarch Ramapāla was popularly known as Karṇakesarin. See *EI*, xxviii, 265.

1048. *JAHRS*, iii, 181.

1049. *OHRJ*, iv, 58-59, pl. i.

1050. S. N. Rajaguru, *IO*, iv, 353. For the plate, see Binayak Misra, *Orissa under the Bhauma-Kara Kings*, 74.

known to have been rulers of Kosala and this claim is explicitly met with in all the known inscriptions Mahāśiva Tīvara and his son Nannarāja II.[1051] Numerous copper-plate charters of the Somavaṁśins afford enough evidence to show their close connections with this area, specially during the earlier period. At the end of the three Chaudwar plates of Mahabhavagupta I Janamejaya, the king is styled *Kosalendra, i.e.*, 'lord of Kosala'.[1052] The Patna copper-plate grant of the eighth regnal year of Mahāśivagupta I Yayāti describes king Svabhāvatuṅga as the very moon causing moonlight that is the protection of Kosalas[1053] while in the Jatesinga-Dungri plates Mahāśivagupta III Yayāti is said to have been well-known for the *svayaṁvaras* in Kosalā.[1054] We have also instances of the appointment of officers specially to look after Kosalā. Thus, we find mention of the *Sandhivigrahin* of Kosalā in the Patna plates of the twenty-eighth regnal year of Mahāśivagupta I Yayāti,[1055] whereas the Balijhari plates of Uddyotakesarin speak of Rudradatta as the *Mahāsandhivigrahin* of Utkala and Kosalā.[1056] We learn from the Kelga plates of *Kumāra* Someśvara that his ancestor Abhimanyu had received the kingdom of Kosala as a favour from Uddyotakesarin of the Soma-kula.[1057] Then again, the villages granted through some of the copper-plate charters of the family were situated in Kosala and the donees of a few of the grants are reported to have been inhabitants of villages said to have been located in Kosala. To cite a few instances, the villages gifted away through the Sonepur[1058] and the second Kalibhana plates[1059] of Mahābhavagupta I Janamejaya, the Patna plates of the twenty-fourth year of the reign of Mahāśivagupta I Yayāti[1060] and the Jatesinga-Dungri plates of Mahāśivagupta III Yayāti[1061] are stated to have been situated in the Kosala-*deśa*, whereas in the case of the Chaudwar plates of Mahābhavagupta I Janamejaya,[1062] the Patna plates of the eighth year of the reign of Mahāśivagupta I Yayāti[1063] and his Nibinna plates[1064]

1051. The Aḍhabhāra plates of Nannarāja II credit his father Tīvaradeva with the overlordship of Kosala, Utkala and other *maṇḍalas*, while Nannarāja himself is described simply as the lord of the whole of the Kosala-*maṇḍala*.
1052. See nos. IV: VIII-X, verse 16.
1053. No. IV: XIV, verse 15.
1054. See no. IV: XXI, text-line 14.
1055. See no. IV: XVIII, text-line 69.
1056. No. IV: XXII, text-line 72.
1057. No. IV: XXVIII, text-lines 4-5.
1058. See no. IV: VI, text-line 13. The name is spelt as Kosalā.
1059. No. IV: XI, lines 4-5.
1060. No. IV: XVII, text-line 25.
1061. No. IV: XXI, text-line 18. We have here the name Kosala without the suffix *deśa*.
1062. Nos. IV: VIII-X, text-lines 4 and 11.
1063. No. IV: XIII, text-lines 5 and 10. In the latter line we have only Kosala, the suffix *deśa*, found in line 5, being omitted.
1064. No. IV: XV, text-lines 4-5 (Kosala-*deśa*) and 15 (Kosala).

and the Cuttack plates of Mahābhavagupta II Bhīmaratha[1065] not only were the donated villages situated in Kosala but the grantees were also residents of villages situated in Kosala or included in an administrative division forming part of Kosala. These affinities are too strong to be ignored in any discussion on the relationship between the Pāṇḍuvaṁśins and the Somavaṁśins and the Somavaṁśins who would, thus, appear to be very closely related to each other.

Let us now take note of some possible objections against this view. The big chronological gap that was supposed to separate the two dynasties is often cited as an argument against any lineal relationship between them. As stated above, Fleet, Kielhorn and other scholars were inclined to date the reign of Tīvaradeva in the eighth and that of his grand-nephew Mahāśivagupta Bālārjuna about the beginning of the ninth century. Later writers on the subject tried to push back the reign of Mahāśivagupta Bālārjuna to the first half of the seventh century. After a detailed palaeographical examination of a few of the copper-plate grants of the Somavaṁśins, J. F. Fleet arrived at the conclusion that these records 'cannot possibly be placed before A.D. 900' and that, on the whole, 'the characters are of the eleventh century, and that the kings mentioned in them are to be placed somewhere between A.D. 1000 and 1100.'[1066] But as we have shown above, consideration of the evidence that has come to light in the last few decades forces to date the termination of the Pāṇḍuvaṁśin rule in Kosala to about the close of the eighth century A.D. and, as will be seen in the sequel, scholars now generally favour dating the commencement of the Somavaṁśin rule at least a century earlier than the date suggested by Fleet. In view of these facts we now have only a small gap that separates the end of the Pāṇḍuvaṁśins and the beginning of the Somavaṁśins and this gap, too, may be filled up by future discoveries. Another possible argument against the connection between the two dynasties may relate to the characters used in their records. It is true that all the Pāṇḍuvaṁśin copper-plate grants are incised in box-headed characters while the records of the Somavaṁśins are written in the Nāgarī of the northern class. However, as we have seen above, the employment of box-headed characters was confined only to the copper-plate charters of the Pāṇḍuvaṁśins who appear to have continued their use by way of convention while all their lithic records dating from the reign of Mahāśivagupta Bālārjuna are incised in the Nāgarī characters. The reign of Mahā-Śivagupta, thus, seems to represent the transitional phase, and the Somavaṁśins gave up the use of box-headed characters as they were no longer popular. And lastly, attention may be invited to the differences in the legends and devices on the seals affixed to the copper-plate charters of the members of the two lines. This question was raised by

1065. No. IV: XVIII, text-lines 31 and 38 (Kosala in both the lines).
1066. *EI*, iii, 333.

H.C. Ray who pointed out that on the seals of the Somavaṁśins 'we miss the well-known *Garuḍa* of the Śrīpura kings' and have instead Gaja-Lakṣmī as on the seals of the Kalacuris of Tripurī and Tummāṇa. He showed awaraness of the use of different devices on seals by the different branches of the same tribe,[1067] but at the same time he took the difference in question to indicate that 'the founder of the new branch (Somavaṁśins)[1068] must have been separated from his relatives of the old branch (Pāṇḍuvaṁśins)[1069] by a comparatively long interval.'[1070] But the change of emblem on the royal seal need not be taken to be of much historical significance. For, sometimes we notice change in the royal emblem within the same family also, often coinciding with changed religious affiliations. When Ray wrote, seals of Tīvaradeva alone were known and, being a *Parama-Vaiṣṇava,* he naturally chose Vaiṣṇavite emblems for his seal. With the change over to Śaivism, Mahā-Śivagupta Bālārjuna, the last known monarch of the same dynasty, figured Nandin on his seal. Thus, the difference of seal-device is not necessarily indicative of any difference of branch of the same tribe or a long interval. As for the Gaja-Lakṣmī device, it could be adopted by any dynasty or ruling chief irrespective of sectarian leanings as she was supposed to symbolise royal fortune. This is exactly what we notice on the early Indian coins.

Trikaliṅga

The Somavaṁśins styled themselves *Tri-kaliṅg-ādhipati, i.e.,* 'Lord of Trikaliṅga'. The solitary exception to it was Śivagupta, father of Mahābhavagupta I Janamejaya and the earliest known member of the dynasty, for whom this title is not employed in any of the numerous records of his son and successor.[1071] This style is first found employed by the earliest known Eastern Gaṅga monarchs Indravarman and Sāmantavarman in their epigraphs dated (Gaṅga) years 39 and 64 respectively[1072] and subsequently by some later members of the same dynasty[1073] as well as some of the later

1067. By way of examples he pointed out that the Kalacuris of Tripurī and Tummāṇa adopted the device of Gaja-Lakṣmi for their seals, while the seals of the Kalacuris of Sarayūpāra (Gorakhpur region) and Kalyāṇa bear the figure of a bull. See *DHNI*, i, 395.

1068-1069. Names within parantheses are added by us.

1070. *DHNI*, i, 395-96.
The views expressed here differ radically from those in our paper in the Pupul Jayakar Felicitation Volume.

1071. No record of Śivagupta himself has been reported so far.

1072. *EI*, xxv, 281ff. (Indravarman); xxvii, 216ff. (Sāmantavarman).

1073. Vajrahasta V Anantavarman (*ibid*, iv, 191, text-line 46; ix, 98, text-line 41; xi, 151, text-line 50; xxiii, 72, text-line 44; xxxii, 314, text-line 38; xxxiii, 145, text-lines 39-40; xxxiv, 44, text-line 33), Rājarāja I Devendravarman (*ibid.*, xxxi, 196, text-line 45) and the latter's son Anantavarman Coḍagaṅga (*IA*, xviii, 164, text-lines 34-35 are the only later Eastern Gaṅga Kings to be designated *Tri-kaliṅg-ādhipati* in their own records. In the copper-plate charters of these three chiefs the expression

members of the Kalacuri dynasty of Tripurī..[1074] It is used erroneously for the Candella monarch Trailokyavarman in the Rewa plates of his vassal Kumārapāla of Kakareḍikā.[1075] While it is admitted on all hands that Trikaliṅga has a geographical connotation, there exists a wide divergence of opinion as regards the territory or territories actually denoted by it. This debate may be conveniently resolved into two main points, *viz.*, (i) it contains three areas known as Kaliṅga and (ii) it is the name of a single geographical unit. The former interpretation is based on the assumption that the name consists of two elements, *viz.*, (1) *tri* (three) and (2) Kaliṅga. A. Cunningham invited attention to the mention by Pliny (*circa* 23-79 A.D.) of the Macco-Calingae and the Gangarides-Calingae as separate peoples from the Calingae and concluded therefrom that the name Tri-Kaliṅga is probably old and that "the 'Three Kingdoms' were known as early as the time of Megasthenes, (4th century B.C.), from whom Pliny had chiefly copied his Indian Geography." He took the Three Kaliṅgas to denote the three kingdoms of Dhanakaṭaka or Amaravati on the Kṛishṇā, Andhra or Warangal and Kaliṅga or Rajamahendri. Thus, according to him, Tri-Kaliṅga corresponded with the province of Telingana which he took to be a slightly contracted form of Tri-Kaliṅga.[1076] Generally agreeing with Cunningham, A. C. Burnell points to Pliny's reference to Modogalingam which, in his opinion, stands for Muḍu-Kaliṅga or Three Kaliṅgas, *muḍu* being the

---

Trikaliṅga-mahībhuj is employed for the Eastern Gaṅga monarchs in general. We need not doubt the correctness of this description in view of the occurrence of the title *Tri-Kaliṅg-ādhipati* in the inscriptions of Indravarman and Sāmantavarman even though it is not met with in the intervening records.

1074. Rājaśekhara in his *Viddhaśālabhañjikā*, (acts i and iv) calls Yuvarājadeva I *Triliṅg-ādhipati* which according to some scholars (V.V. Mirashi, ***Inscriptions of the Kalachuri-Chedi Era, CII***, iv, Introduction, lxxviii), is probably an error for *Tri-Kaling-ādhipati*. However, as Triliṅga by itself is a well-known geographical term, this suggestion cannnot be regarded as conclusive. We have no definite evidence to indicate that this title was assumed by any member of the dynasty before Karṇa (or Lakṣmīkarṇa) for whom it is found applied in the Banaras grant issued in the very first year of his reign (*Ibid*., 244, text-line 34) as well as a few other inscriptions of subsequent years (*ibid*., 258, text-line 34; 277, text-line 4). The title is also employed for later members of the dynasty including Yaśaḥkarṇa (*ibid*., 294, text-line 23; 634), Narasiṁha (*ibid*., 322, text-line 3), Jayasiṁha (*ibid*., 328, text-line 21; 342, text-line 3) and Vijayasiṁha (*ibid*., 361, text-line 3; 366, text-line 4; 649).

1075. *IA*, xvii, 232, text-line 6. The writer of this charter of Kumārapāla, an erstwhile feudatory of the Kalacuris, used this title by oversight for his Candella overlord to whom Kumārapāla had transferred his allegiance. A few other epithets of the Kalacuris are also applied to Candella king, obviously by oversight.

1076. *The Ancient Geography of India*, 437-38. F. Kielhorn agreed with Cunningham in regarding Tri-Kaliṅga as the older name of Telingana. See *IA*, xvii, 225; *EI*, ii, 298.

Telugu word for 'three'.[1077] Taking a cue from these observations, most of the modern writers on the subject have tried to find out the three areas which could be called Kaliṅga. J. F. Fleet took Tri-Kaliṅga in the sense of three Kaliṅgas which, according to him, included Cuttack and probably the whole of Orissa.[1078] In the opinion of Ganga Mohan Laskar it included the whole of Kaliṅga with at least a few districts in its neighbourhood. He held that Kosala also formed a part of Tri-kaliṅga.[1079] B.C. Mazumdar[1080] and, following him, Binayak Misra[1081] and R. G. Basak[1082] identified the three Kaliṅgas with Kaliṅga proper, Koṅgoda and Utkala. R.D. Banerji also held that the 'country of Kaliṅga was divided from very early times into three parts and was called *Tri-Kaliṅga*'.[1083] While refraining from identifying the regions comprising the three Kaliṅgas he held that 'the vast country on the eastern shore of the Bay of Bengal, which extended from the Delta of the Ganges to that of the Godavari was called Kaliṅga in ancient times.'[1084] R. Subba Rao proposed to identify Tri-Kaliṅgas with Utkala or north Kaliṅga, Kaliṅga proper and Tel-Kaliṅga or south Kaliṅga and took the Tri-Kaliṅga country as extending from the Gaṅgā in the north to the Godāvarī in the south.[1085] H.C. Ray emphasises the intimate connection between the history of Orissa on the one hand and the Chhattisgarh division of the Central Provinces (now Madhya Pradesh) and the portion of the Madras Presidency (now Andhra Pradesh) lying to the north of the Godāvarī on the other and observes that Kaliṅga in its wider sense (*viz.*, Tri-Kaliṅga) included not only the area now known as Orissa but also considerable portions of the Central Provinces and northern Madras and this is the reason why the dynasties ruling in these areas assumed the title *Tri-Kāliṅg-ādhipati*[1086] D.C. Ganguli invites attention to the mention of Madhyama (middle) Kaliṅga in Eastern Gaṅga inscriptions and takes Tri-Kaliṅga as comprising the Godavari and Vishakhpatnam districts of the present state of Andhra Pradesh and the Ganjam district of Orissa which formed south, north and mid-Kalinga respectively.[1087] P. Acharya, who has discussed the question at length, does not seem to be clear regard-

1077. *Elements of South Indian Palaeography*, 23. For Pliny's references, vide R.C. Majumdar, *The Classical Accounts of India*, 342.
1078. *EI*, iii, 327 and 337. He also hinted at the likelihood of Trikaliṅg-*ādhipati* being a meaningless title.
1079. *JASB*, New Series, i, 3.
1080. *Orissa in the Making*, 172, 187, 194.
1081. *JBORS*, xiv, 145.
1082. *History of North-Eastern India*, 161.
1083. *HO*, i, 1.
1084. *Ibid.*, 2-3.
1085. *JAHRS*, vi, 201 and 203. This view is almost the same as that of R.D. Banerji.
1086. *DHNI*, i, 391 and 392.
1087. *IHQ*, viii, 29.

ing the extent of Tri-Kaliṅga,[1088] though at one place he appears to be in agreement with Ganguli.[1089] Although V.V. Mirashi renders Tri-Kaliṅga as 'three Kaliṅgas',[1090] he refrains from defining it and contents himself by averring that it was different from Kaliṅga, Koṅgoda, Utkala and Kosala.[1091] D.C. Sircar is also not sure as to 'whether the name Tri-Kaliṅga indicated three countries (*viz.*, Kosala, Kaliṅga and Utkala or Oḍra) collectively, or a particular tract of land lying probably between Kaliṅga and South Kosala',[1092] though he seems to be inclined in favour of the latter view.[1093]

However, if the extant evidence bearing on the subject is critically appraised, it would be found that the concept of Three Kaliṅgas (Tri-Kaliṅga) did not exist during the early period. We do come across allusions to Kaliṅga as a geographical unit in the records of the Mauryan emperor Aśoka[1094] and the Cedi ruler Khāravela,[1095] but nowhere it is mentioned as consisting of three divisions. Even otherwise up to about the beginning of the Christian era we have absolutely no evidence to indicate that Tri-Kaliṅga denoted three Kaliṅgas or three divisions of Kaliṅga. Let us, first of all, consider the references cited from the *Naturalis Historia* of Gaius Plinius Secundus, popularly known as Elder Pliny, which form the mainstay of the notion that even during the time of Megasthenes Tri-Kaliṅga was used as a collective name for three Kaliṅgas, *viz.*, Kaliṅga comprised three divisions. It is interesting to find that Pliny does not actually refer to three peoples called Kaliṅga and there is only apparent similarity between two or three of the names encountered in his work. He speaks of Maccocalingae as one of the many tribes of the Brachmanae who are described as inhabiting the hills while the tribes known as Calingae are said to be nearest the sea.[1096] The mention of the Mandei or the people of the Mahendra mountain range immediately following the Calingae should leave no room for doubt about the latter being the same as Kaliṅga while the Maccocalingae do not appear to have been connected with them in any way.

1088. 'Triliṅga, Trikaliṅga, Kaliṅga, Oḍra and Utkala', *OHRJ*, i, 73-92. The paper gives a dependable gist of practically all the earlier writings on the subject.

1089. *Ibid.*, 87.

1090. *Inscriptions of the Kalachuri-Chedi Era, CII*, Introduction, c. But at many a place he renders *Tri-kaliṅga-ādhipati* by 'the lord of Trikaliṅga', thereby leaving the impression that he treats Trikaliṅga as the name of a single province. See *ibid.*, 249, 262, etc.

1091. *Ibid.*, Introduction, c, fn. 6.

1092. *HCIP*, iv: *The Age of Imperial Kanauj*, 147. Elsewhere, Sircar observes that it is not impossible that Trikaliṅga was used to indicate parts of Kosala, Kaliṅga and Utkala. See *IHQ*, xx, 80, fn. 2.

1093. *Ibid.*, xx, 80.

1094. D.C. Sircar, *Select Inscriptions bearing on Indian History and Civilization*, i, second edition, 34, text-line 2.

1095. *Ibid.*, 214, text-line 1 (where Khāravela is styled *Kaliṅg-ādhipati*).

1096. R.C. Majumdar, *The Classical Accounts of India*, 341.

According to McCrindle's translation, the country of the Gangarides was quite different from the royal city of the Calingae which is mentioned after the former.[1097] It is only John Bostock and H.T. Riley who combine the two into a single people called Gangarides Calingae.[1098] It would, thus, follow that there is absolutely no reference to the three separate peoples known as Kaliṅga in Pliny's work. And as regards the expression *Modogalingae*, it cannot be taken as a Romanised version of the Telugu name Muḍu-Kaliṅga meaning 'Three Kaliṅgas', for, according to Pliny himself, it was the name of '*a single tribe*' inhabiting 'a very large island in the Gangas'.[1099] It would, we feel, be agreed that none of the countries proposed to be identified as three Kaliṅgas, not even the region commonly recognised as Kaliṅga, is an island in the Gaṅgā. We may, therefore, reasonably conclude that the view that the antiquity of the name Tri-Kaliṅga and of the concept of the 'Three Kaliṅgas' is as high as the early Maurya period is not supported by the available evidence. It must be noted in this connection that though the name Kaliṅga is frequently referred to in early Indian literature and inscriptions, we do not find a singe allusion to three Kaliṅgas. As regards the modern name Telangana or Telingana, it is apparently a derivative from Triliṅga found mentioned in somewhat later literature and inscriptions.[1100]

Moreover, in literature and inscriptions Kaliṅga is often distinguished from other regions of Orissa which are popularly taken to represent the three Kaliṅgas which, in turn, are supposed to have comprised the Tri-Kaliṅga country. The Jatesinga-Dungri plates of Mahāśivagupta III Yayāti, for instance, mention Kaliṅga, Koṅgoda and Utkala side by side in the same phrase,[1101] indicating thereby that these three countries were regarded as quite distinct from each other. The statement of the Brahmeśvara temple (Bhubaneswar) stone slab inscription of the time of Mahābhavagupta IV Uddyotakesarin that his predecessor Mahābhavagupta I Janamejaya, who is styled *Tri-Kaliṅg-ādhipati* in his numerous records, had captured the royal fortune of the Oḍra chief[1102] proves beyond doubt that Oḍra or Utkala had nothing to do with Tri-Kaliṅga. Likewise, the claim of the Talchar plate of the Kara king Śivakara III that his ancestor Śubhakara had reduced Kaliṅga to subjection[1103] points to the distinction between Oḍra, the home province of the Bhauma-Karas, and Kaliṅga. It is instructive

1097. *Ibid*.
1098. *Ibid.*, 350, note 8.
1099. *Ibid.*, 342.
1100. P. Acharya, "Triliṅga, Trikaliṅga, Kaliṅga, Oḍra and Utkala", *OHRJ*, i, 73-77. It is not impossible that Triliṅga itself may be a contracted form of Tri-Kaliṅga (obtained by dropping *ka*), perhaps due to contiguity with the latter.
1101. No. IV: XXI, text-line 14.
1102. No. IV: XXVI, verse 2.
1103. Binayak Misra, *Orissa under the Bhauma Kings*, 4.

to note in this connection that the Chinese traveller Yuan Chwang also refers to Oḍra (U-cha or Oda), Koṅgoda (Kong-yu-to) and Kaliṅga as distinct kingdoms. It is even more interesting to find him mentioning the first two as situated in Eastern India and the last one in Southern India.[1104] Rājaśekhara also makes a distinction between Kaliṅga and Utkala.[1105]

Let us now examine the opinion of those scholars according to whom Trikaliṅga was different from Kaliṅga and denoted a single geographical unit. To take only a few prominent attempts to locate it, G. Ramdas thought that the name meant 'high or elevated or hilly Kaliṅga' and signified the 'region of the Eastern Ghats from the upper source of the Mahānadī to about the source of the Languliya river in the south'[1106] or 'the tract of land comprising the Chhattisgarh districts of the Central Provinces (present Madhya Pradesh) and the hill states of Orissa.'[1107] R. C. Majumdar broadly agreed with this suggestion though he favoured the extension of its boundaries further south and held that most probably it was the designation of the hilly tract to the west of Kaliṅga.[1108] D. C. Sircar held doubtfully that Trikaliṅga was a tract of land between South Kosala and Kaliṅga and possibly included the Sambalpur region.[1109] Elsewhere, he seems to favour its identification with the eastern districts of South Kosala.[1110] According to Harekrishna Mahtab, who, too, is in general agreement with Ramdas, the Trikaliṅga kingdom comprised 'the entire region between the Rishikulya river and the Languliya river with the Zemindari of Jeypore in Koraput and the districts of Bastar, Bolangir-patan, Kalahandi and Sonepur and also the district of Sambalpur.'[1111]

Both the above views appear to be only partially correct, *viz.*, the first one as regards the constitution of the name as consisting of two parts and the second in regard to the partial location of the territory, and the correct position seems to lie somewhere between them. As we have seen above, even though Kaliṅga is frequently mentioned in literature and inscriptions from very early times, it is spoken of everywhere as a single territorial unit and there is absolutely no evidence of the existence of the concept of Three Kaliṅgas up to at least the middle of the first century A.D. There is, however, definite evidence to indicate that sometime between it and the sixth century A.D. the region of Kaliṅga came to be divided into three parts which came to be known collectively as Tri-Kaliṅga. The earliest references

1104. A. Cunningham, *The Ancient Geography of India*, 430-435. Cunningham's equation of Yuan Chwang's Kong-yu-to with Ganjam (*ibid.*, 432-434) is, however, erroneous
1105. *Kāvya-mīmāṁsā* (Gaekwad's Oriental Series, no. 1, Baroda, 1934), 93.
1106. *JBORS*, xiv, 547.
1107. *Ibid.*, 545-546. Also see *ibid.*, xv. 635ff.; *JAHRS*, i, 16-23.
1108. *EI*, xxiii, 70.
1109. *IHQ*, xx, 80.
1110. *Ibid.*, xx, 364.
1111. *History of Orissa*, i, 7.

to Tri-Kaliṅga, as we have seen above, are met with in the Eastern Gaṅga inscriptions. Thus, the Jirjingi grant of Indravarman I, dated (Gaṅga) year 39,[1112] and the Ponnuturu grant of Sāmantavarman, dated (Gaṅga) year 64,[1113] style the grantors 'Lords of Tri-Kaliṅga' (*Tri-Kaliṅg-ādhipati*). Their successors are also described as 'Kings of Tri-Kaliṅga' (*Tri-Kaliṅga-mahībhuj*) in the records of the later Eastern Gaṅga monarch Vajrahasta V and his descendants. We have evidence to show that Tri-Kaliṅga denoted three parts of Kaliṅga into which it had come to be divided during the early centuries of the Christian era. Thus, the Parbhani plates of Arikesarin a Cālukya Chief of the Telangana region, dated Śaka 888 (966 A.D.), avers that his ancestor Yuddhamalla ruled over Veṅgī together with the Three Kaliṅgas (*sa-Kaliṅga-trayīṁ Veṅgim*).[1114]

We have also some indications of the areas comprised in the Three Kaliṅgas in the inscriptions and literature at our disposal. Thus, we know that they included parts of Orissa, Madhya Pradesh and Andhra Pradesh. There are a few important evidences which must be kept in mind in this connection. As we have shown above, the Early Gaṅgas of Kaliṅga, who had their capital at Kaliṅganagara or Mukhalingam, styled themselves *Tri-Kaliṅg-ādhipati*. Even those rulers of the family who did not assume this title in their own records are called, in a general way, in subsequent inscriptions *Tri-Kaliṅga-mahībhuj*. That Mukhalingam in the Srikakulam District of Andhra Pradesh formed a part of Tri-Kaliṅga is clearly indicated by certain epigraphic references. An inscription from Mukhalingam, for example, informs us of the presence there of a temple dedicated to Trikaliṅgadeva to which were attached some singers and dancers whose headship was conferred on certain personages by the later Gaṅga ruler Anantavarman Coḍagaṅga.[1115] Kaliṅgapaṭṭana,[1115a] first referred to in the Siripuram grant of Anantavarman of *c.* fifth century A.D., has been identified with the modern port village of that name situated at the confluence of the river Vaṁśadhārā with the sea in the Srikakulam District.[1115b] An inscription dated Śaka 1036 from this place records the gift of a lamp to a divinity of Trikaliṅgapaṭṭana.[1115c] Another inscription dated Śaka 1074 mentions this place simply as Paṭṭana while referring to the nativity of the donor.[1115d] This was the only *paṭṭana* (port town) known for the entire Tri-Kaliṅga and the

1112. *EI*, xxv, 281ff.
1113. *Ibid.*, xxvii, 216ff.
1114. G.H. Khare, *Dakṣiṇacyā Madhyayugīna Itihāsācī Sādhane*, ii (Pune, 1934), 49, verse 2. It is possible to argue that the use of *sa-Kaliṅga-trayīm* instead of *sa-Trikaliṅgam* was due to metrical exigencies as we had actually argued elsewhere. But we now feel that this is simply impossible.
1115. *SII*, v, 1010.
1115a. As will be seen subsequently, it was also known as Trikaliṅgapaṭṭana.
1115b. *EI*, xxiv, 47ff.
1115c. *ARE*, 1934-35, No. 362.
1115d. *Ibid.*, 1934-35, No. 361.

same was called Trikaliṅgapaṭṭana in the eleventh century A.D. Subsequently (during the twelfth centry A.D.) it became the headquarters of the administrative division on the coast called Sāgarakhonna-viṣaya. A grant of the Eastern Cālukya king Guṇaga Vijayāditya III informs us that Tri-Kaliṅga was situated in Dakṣiṇāpatha.[1115e] Some other Eastern Cālukya records refer to the forest portion of Tri-Kaliṅga as forming part of the Cālukya dominions. According to the Masulipatam plates of Amma I (918-925 A.D.), for instance, his predecessor Vijayāditya IV (918 A.D.) ruled over the Veṅgīmaṇḍala together with the Tri-Kaliṅga forest (*Veṅgi-maṇḍalaṁ Tri-Kaliṅgāṭavi-yuktam*).[1115f] Likewise, we learn from the Kolavaram plates of Cālukya-Bhima II that Vikramāditya II (sometime after 925 A.D.) held sway over both Veṅgi-maṇḍala and Tri-Kaliṅga (*sa-Tri-Kaliṅgaṁ Veṅgi-maṇḍalam*).[1115g] The inclusion of Tri-Kaliṅga, obviously a part thereof, in the Veṅgi Cālukya kingdom finds support from some unexpected literary evidence also. The following stanza in the colophon of the medieval medical text entitled *Kalyāṇa-kāraka* by one Ugrādityācārya states that the work was composed at Rāmagiri which is described as adorned with structural as well as rock-cut temples and situated in the Tri-Kaliṅga country which was under the Veṅgi ruler :

> Veṅg-Iśa-Tri-Kaliṅga-deśa-janana-prastutya-sān-ūtkaṭa-
> Prodyad=vṛkṣa-latā-vitāna-nirataiḥ siddhaiś=ca vidyādharaiḥ /
> Sarve mandira-kandar-opama-guhā-caity-ālay-ālaṁkṛte
> Ramye Rāmagirāv-idaṁ viracitaṁ śāstraṁ hitaṁ prāṇinām//[1115h]

This Rāmagiri is apparently different from modern Ramtek near Nagpur which is generally believed to represent the Rāmagiri mentioned in the opening stanza of Kālidāsa's *Megha-dūta* (Pūrva-megha, verse 1). We propose to identify it with the homonymous locality situated in the Koraput District of Orissa bordering the Srikakulam District of Andhra Pradesh which alone would satisfy the description. The assumption of the title *Tri-Kaliṅgādhipati* by the Somavaṁśins, who also called themselves *Kosal-endra* or 'Lord of Kosala', would show that Tri-Kaliṅga must have abutted on or must have been very close to South Kosala. It must be remembered in this connection that the Pāṇḍuvaṁśins, who were lineal ancestors of the

1115e. *JAHRS*, v, 101f.

1115f. *EI*, v, 133, text-line 17.

1115g. *SII*, i, 43. The Arumbaka grant of Bāḍapa states that Ammarāja II (945-970 A.D.) at first ruled over the Veṅgi-deśa joined with Tri-Kaliṅga, but later left for Kaliṅga where he ruled for fourteen year (*EI*, xix, 137). This has been taken as an evidence of a distinction between Tri-Kaliṅga and Kaliṅga (*ibid.*, xxiii, 69); but here Tri-Kaliṅga may refer to the forest portion of the country while Kalinga may refer to the coastal region.

1115h. Cited by Nathuram Premi in his *Jaina Sāhitya aura Itihāsa*, second edition, 447, fn. 1.

Somavaṁśins, also ruled over South Kosala and when under pressure from other powers they were forced to shift eastward and southward, they naturally moved towards the Kalahandi-Koraput-Bastar region. For some time they could have continued to hold a part of Kosala together with the adjoining area. And lastly, the assumption of this title by some later members of the Kalacuri dynasty as well as the continuation of its use by the later Eastern Gaṅgas would show that it was a bone of contention among them as well as the Somavaṁśins and the Eastern Cālukyas. Therefore, the region of Tri-Kaliṅga or a part of it must have been situated not very far from their territories. Any identification of Tri-Kaliṅga must satisfy this condition.

While considering the question of the location of Tri-Kaliṅga, the fact that in ancient times natural barriers like mountains, rivers and seas played an important role seems to have been ignored.[1115i] Taking into consideration the above-mentioned political facts together with the geographical factors, we may conclude that the region comprising the Three Kaliṅgas had three distinct geographical features: (1) Eastern Ghats dividing Kaliṅga region into Western and Eastern parts; (2) the Mahānadī and the Godāvarī forming the northern and southern borders of Western Kaliṅga; and (3) the Indrāvatī dividing the Western Kaliṅga into North and South Kaliṅga, North Kaliṅga between the Indrāvatī and the Mahānadī and South Kaliṅga between the Godāvarī and the Indrāvatī. With this geographical overview we may attempt to locate the Three Kaliṅgas as follows: (1) South-Kaliṅga, bordered on the west and north-west by the Indrāvatī, on the south by the Godāvarī and on the east by the Eastern Ghats, comprised southern portion of Koraput together with a considerable part of Bastar and a small region of north-west Srikakulam; (2) North Kaliṅga, bordered on the north and west by the Mahānadī and on the south and east by the Eastern Ghats, consisted of northern Koraput and the adjoining south-eastern region of Kalahandi; and (3) East Kaliṅga-bordered the west by the Eastern Ghats, on the south by Godāvarī till it meets the Bay of Bengal, on the north by the Mahānadī where it empties into the Bay of Bengal and on the east by the Bay of Bengal—includes the whole of eastern Srikakulam and Vishakhapatnam together with the whole of Ganjam.

The above is only a very rough indication of the areas comprised in the Three Kaliṅgas, and it is impossible in the present state of disinformation to be more precise. Perhaps none of the kings who assumed the title *Tri-Kaliṅg-ādhipati* controlled at any time of their rule the whole of Tri-Kaliṅga; but even capture of a part of it, temporary or permanent, was thought enough to justify the assumption of this title. This was true of the Soma-

1115i. Even in these days of scientific and technological progress when many of the natural hurdles have been overcome their role in dividing the areas is not insignificant.

vaṁśins also as they could control only a part of Orissan region of Tri-Kaliṅga adjacent to South Kosala, *viz.*, Koraput-Kalahandi-Bastar.[1115j]

Genealogy

The inscriptions of the dynasty afford us fairly dependable information regarding the order of succession and genealogy though, as will be seen from the sequel, a few problems are still within the realm of guesswork and await future discoveries.

The first known member of the dynasty was undoubtedly Śivagupta[1116] on whose feet Mahābhavagupta Janamejaya, also styled Dharmakandarpa, is said to have meditated. No record of Śivagupta himself has come to light so far, but he is mentioned in all the records of Mahābhavagupta Janamejaya. Although the relationship between the two is nowhere clearly defined, their description may be reasonably taken to indicate that they were related as father and son respectively. Śivagupta's name is conspicuously omitted in the later records of the family which begin their historical narrative with Janamejaya.[1117]

Mahābhavagupta Janamejaya, son and successor of Śivagupta, is known from as many as thirteen records of his reign.[1118] As stated above, he is the first ruler of the dynasty mentioned in subsequent records. Being the first member of the family named Mahābhavagupta *alias* Janamejaya, he may be conveniently called Mahābhavagupta I Janamejaya I. *Rāṇaka* Malladatta, son of Dhāradatta, served as his *Mahāsandhivigrahin* or minister of peace and war from at least the sixth to at least the thirty-first year of his

1115j. The following stanza met with in a manuscript of the *Brahmāṇḍa Purāṇa* deposited in the Orissa State Museum defines Kaliṅga and Tri-kaliṅga respectively as (i) the land between the Ṛṣikulyā and Jhañjāvatī and (ii) that between the Jhañjāvatī and Vedavatī.

Ṛṣikulyāṁ samāsādya yāvad Jhañjāvatī nadī /,
Kaliṅgadeśa prakhyāto deśānā garhitas-tadā //
Jhañjāvatī samāsādya yāvad Vedavatī nadī /,
Trikaliṅgeti vikhyāto. . . . . //.

Cited by N.K. Sahu in the *Utkal University History of Orissa*, i (Bhubaneswar, 1964), 98, fn. 3.

The dependability of these stanzas is not beyond doubt; they contain grammatical errors and the last eight syllables of the second stanza are lost. They may represent the narrow definitions prevalent at the time the manuscript was copied, *viz.*, during the late medieval period. Anyway, not much significance can be attached to these stanzas, particularly, as they go against the unimpeachable epigraphic evidence.

For discussions on Tri-Kaliṅga, see Hiralal Shukla, *Prācina Bastar* 79-86; S. Tripathy, "Royal Titles of Trikaliṅgādhipati and Samasta-Gondramādhipati of the Early Medieval Orissan Epigraphs", *OHRJ*, xxxi, nos. 2-4, 143-151.

1116. In no. IV: V alone he is called Mahāśivagupta. It may be due to carelessness on the part of the writer, for in all the remaining records the name is given without the prefix *mahat*.

1117. Nos. IV: XII, XIV, XVI, XVII, XVIII, XXII, XXVI, XXVII, Supplementary Inscription III.

1118. Nos. IV: I-XI and Supplementary Inscriptions I-II.

reign.[1119] Sometime in or prior to the thirty-fourth year of Mahābhavagupta I's reign, he was succeeded in his office by *Rāṇaka* Dhāradatta[1120] who, though not stated anywhere, was evidently his son and grandson of his father Dhāradatta. The two Dhāradattas may, therefore, be called Dhāradatta I and Dhāradatta II. The line of the Dattas continued in service for quite a few generations and references to them are of great help in settling the order of succession.

Mahābhavagupta I Janamejaya I was followed by his son Mahāśivagupta Yayāti[1121] who, being the first monarch of this name, may be styled Mahāśivagupta I Yayāti I.[1122] Dhāradatta II, who had taken over as *mahāsāndhivigrahin* during the closing years of Mahābhavagupta I Janamejaya I, continued in office up to at least the twenty-fourth year of the reign of his son Mahāśivagupta I Yayāti I[1123] and was succeeded by Siṁhadatta, who also appears to have belonged to the same ministerial line, sometime in or before the twenty-eighth year of the king.[1124]

The son and successor of Mahāśivagupta I Yayāti I was Mahābhavagupta II Bhīmaratha who is known from two records of his own reign[1125] and a few later inscriptions.[1126] Siṁhadatta, who had joined ministerial service during the concluding part of Mahāśivagupta I, continued to hold the office up to at least the third year of Bhīmaratha.[1127]

That Mahābhavagupta II Bhīmaratha was succeeded by his son Mahāśivagupta II Dharmaratha is known not only from the records of the later members of the family but also from his own recently discovered Mahulpara plates.[1128]

The order of succession outlined above is based on solid epigraphic evidence and is consequently beyond doubt. However, the evidence is not

1119. He is mentioned in nos. IV: II-X. In the Vakratentali grant of the third year also there is reference to a *mahāsandhivigrahin*, but his name is not given. He may have been either Dhāradatta I or Malladatta himself.

1120. He figures for the first time in no. IV: XI issued in the thirty-fourth year.

1121. Six records of his reign are known. See nos. IV: XII-XVII. In addition to these records, he is also mentioned in nos. IV: XVIII-XX, XXII, XXVI, XXVII and Supplementary Inscription III. In IV: XX, the historical account commences with him.

1122. In the formal part of his own grants he is referred to as Mahāśivagupta and in the date portion as Yayāti. Later records mention him only by the latter name.

1123. He is last mentioned in a charter issued in this year. See no. IV: XVI

1124. See no. IV: XVII of this year where he figures for the first time.

1125. Nos. IV: XVIII and XIX. D.R. Bhandarkar (*List of Inscriptions of Northern India*, No. 1561) attributes no. IV: XIX to Mahābhavagupta I. But there is nothing to substantiate this view. D.C. Sircar tentatively attributes it to Mahābhavagupta Uddyotakesarin (*IHQ*, xx, 81) though he does not rule out its ascription to Mahābhavagupta II Bhīmaratha (*ibid.*, 80).

1126. Nos. IV: XX, XXII, XXVI, XXVII and Suppl. Inscr. III. In these records we find him mentioned as Bhīmaratha.

1127. He is mentioned in no. IV: XVIII issued in the third year.

1128. Nos. IV: XX, XXII, XXVI, XXVII and Suppl. Inscr. III. In the first grant issued by him he is spoken of both as Mahāśivagupta as well as Dharmaratha while in the remaining inscriptions he is referred to only as Dharmaratha.

that clear after Mahāśivagupta II Dharmaratha. We learn from the Balijhari[1129] and Sankhameri[1130] plates of Mahābhavagupta Uddyotakesarin and the Ratnagiri plates of his great-grandson Karṇa[1131] that Dharmaratha was followed by his *bhrātā* (uterine or step-brother) Naghuṣa (Nahuṣa) and the latter by his *anuja* (younger brother or cousin) Yayāti who was in turn succeeded by his son Uddyotakesarin. Unfortunately, no record of Nahuṣa himself has been reported so far and he is not mentioned in any other record with the result that it is difficult to determine his exact relationship with Dharmaratha. However, in the absence of any evidence to the contary we may tentatively regard him as a younger uterine brother of Dharmaratha. But as regards the next king, Yayāti, father of Uddyotakesarin, the latter's Mahada plate[1132] and the Brahmeśvara temple (Bhubaneswar) inscription of his mother Kolāvatī[1133] give his name as Caṇḍīhara. The latter record omits the name of Naghuṣa and supplies valuable information about Caṇḍīhara not available anywhere else. It states that Dharmaratha, probably also known as Rājamalla,[1134] died without leaving a son to succeed him. Thereafter various *bhaṭas* or soldiers overran the entire country and some time passed somehow with a great hero (*prabala-pravīra*) biding his time in another country. Then all the ministers installed Caṇḍīhara, son of Abhimanyu, grandson of Vicitravīra and great-grandson of Janamejaya, as the king.[1135] It would, thus, follow that Caṇḍīhara Yayāti[1136] belonged to a collateral line and was a cousin of Mahāśivagupta II Dharmaratha. The name of the great hero passing his time in another country is not mentioned, but in all probability he was none else than Caṇḍīhara himself. Notwithstanding the omission of Nahuṣa in the Brahmeśvara temple inscription, his accession on the Somavaṁśa throne cannot be doubted in view of the explicit evidence of the Balijhari, Sankhameri and Ratnagiri plates. In all likelihood he ruled during the troubled time which, according to the Brahmeśvara temple inscription, intervened between the passing away of Dharmaratha and the accession of Caṇḍīhara. Otherwise we shall be faced with the unlikely postula-

1129. No. IV: XXII, verses 6-10.
1130. The grant has not been published. See Suppl. Inscr. III.
1131. No. IV: XXVII, verses 6-10. These verses are almost bodily taken from no. IV: XXII and Suppl. Inscr. III.
1132. No. IV: Appendix II.
1133. No. IV: XXVI, Verse 7.
1134. No. IV: XXVI, verse 6 employs the word *rājamalla* while describing Dharmaratha. It may have been either a *viruda* or an adjective without much historical significance.
1135. No. IV: XXVI, verses 5-7.
1136. The identity of Caṇḍīhara and Yayāti is finally established by the fact that in the Balijhari, Sankhameri and Ratnagiri plates Yayāti is stated to have freed the two provinces of Kosala and Utkala, which were seized by the combatant troups, from the enemies while the same statement is made with reference to Caṇḍīhara only without explicitly naming the two provinces in the Brahmeśvara inscription.

tion that the Somavaṁśa throne was without a ruler for quite a few years. Mention must be made in this context of the Banpur plates[1137] which record a grant by Indraratha, son of Bhīmaratha by his queen Durgā. This Indraratha is undoubtedly the same as the homonymous ruler of the Somavaṁśa defeated by Rājendra Coḷa at Yayātinagara. We further learn from the Banpur grant that Indraratha had two younger brothers named Vaṅkaratha and Śaṅkararatha and had obtained the royal fortune of Kaliṅga through the favour of Dharmaratha and killed a certain Abhimanyu who had secured the kingdom by dubious means. There is no indication whatsoever that Vaṅkaratha and Śaṅkararatha ever assumed regal power. In the present state of our knowledge it is not possible to ascertain the exact place of Nahuṣa and Indraratha in the history of the dynasty. But that both of them came to power after Dharmaratha and anterior to Caṇḍīhara Yayāti admits of no doubt. As regards Nahuṣa, this fact is clearly stated in the official records of Uddyotakesarin and Karṇa. And for Indraratha, son of Bhīmaratha and brother (evidently step-brother)[1138] of Dharmaratha, too, there is no other plaee in the Somavaṁśin history. As will be shown below, Caṇḍīhara Yayāti was styled Mahāśivagupta. Therefore, in view of the alternate occurrence of the names Mahābhavagupta and Manāśivagupta in the Somavaṁśa, D. C. Sircar suggests that Nahuṣa, who is mentioned just prior to Yayāti in the Balijhari, plates, was known as Mahābhavagupta and that Indraratha was his another name.[1139] However, this conjecture fails to carry conviction as the Banpur plates, which give a fairly detailed description of Indraratha, do not record the name Nahuṣa. None of the above-mentioned three official charters of Uddyotakesarin and Karṇa refers to Nahuṣa by the other name Indraratha and the Coḷa and Paramāra inscriptions,[1140] which speak of the discomfiture of Indraratha at the hands of Rājendra Coḷa and Paramāra Bhoja respectively, do not mention the name Nahuṣa. Nahuṣa and Indraratha have, therefore, to be taken as two different personages. And the available evidence seems to indicate that Dharmaratha was followed by Nahuṣa and the latter by Indraratha. The latter's non-mention in the Balijhari, Sankhameri and Ratnagiri plates appears to have been due to strained relations between him and Caṇḍīhara Yayāti and his successors. Attention may, in this connection, be invited to the statement of the Banpur plates that Indraratha who was originally appointed a governor of Kaliṅga, which he had captured

1137. No. IV: Appendix 1. The inscription has been edited by K.B. Tripathy very carelessly and one cannot be quite definite about the correctness of the information given on its basis in the following lines.

1138. The Banpur grant is aware of Dharmaratha but does not mention him as brother of Indraratha while Vaṅkaratha and Śaṅkararatha, who as well as Indraratha were born of Bhīmaratha's queen Durgā, are described as such.

1139. *IHQ*, xxii, 303.

1140. *EI*, ix, 229 ff.; *SII*, i, 96 (Coḷa); *EI*, i, 222 ff. (Paramāra).

by his own valour, through Dharmaratha's favour, killed a certain Abhimanyu and enjoyed his fortune with the consent of the Brāhmaṇas. This Abhimanyu is perhaps identifiable with the homonymous father of Caṇḍīhara. This identification will explain satisfactorily as to why Abhimanyu's son Caṇḍīhara had to pass some time in wilderness when actually the Somavaṁśa kingdom was occupied by Indraratha after killing his father. The necessity for his anointment by all the ministers also can be easily accounted for by the civil war for succession. This Abhimanyu is said to have acquired the kingdom by highly unrighteous means, and it was after killing him that Indraratha became the king. We may, thus, conclude that after Dharmaratha the Somavaṁśa throne passed on successively to Nahuṣa, Indraratha and Caṇḍīhara Yayāti, Abhimanyu's occupation of the kingdom being only a *coup d'etat*.

The last named king, Caṇḍīhara, is also known from his own Jatesinga-Dungari plates in which he is referred to as Mahāśivagupta and Yayāti. In order to distinguish him from his earlier and later namesakes we may call him Mahāśivagupta III Yayāti II. This takes for granted that there was no other Mahāśivagupta between him and Dharmaratha and this assumption may have to be modified in the light of future discoveries. He is described as meditating upon the feet of Mahābhavagupta, who was in all probability Nahuṣa. As for Indraratha, he does not refer to himself by the *gupta*-ending name in his own Banpur grant. Moreover, it is clear from later records that there was a deliberate attempt to ignore Indraratha, probably because of hostility due to family feuds and humiliating defeats at the hands of outside powers. The Datta ministerial family continued in office during the period of Mahāśivagupta III Yayāti II *alias* Caṇḍīhara and his only known grant was executed by *Rāṇaka* Rudradatta, nephew of Siṁhadatta known from a record of Mahāśivagupta I Yayāti I and another of his son and successor Mahābhavagupta II Bhīmaratha, and grandson of Harṣadatta.[1141]

D. R. Bhandarkar is inclined to ascribe the Jatesinga-Dungari plates to Śivagupta, the first member of the Somavaṁśa known from the records of his son Mahābhavagupta I Janamejaya.[1142] But his view cannot be accepted in view of the mention in it of Rudradatta, nephew of Siṁhadatta, as holding the office of *Mahāsāndhivigrahin* which proves indisputably that the grant must be attributed to the post-Bhīmaratha period. Moreover, the description of the military successes of Yayāti in the present record tallies well with what is stated about him in the later records of the family. It may be pointed out in this connection that while Rudradatta figures in

1141. No. IV: XXI.

1142. *IA*, lxi, 241; *List of Inscriptions of Northern India*, *EI*, xix-xxiii, Appendix, 215-216, 403. This view seems to have been tacitly accepted by some scholars. See *EI*, xxiii, 249; *IHQ*, xx, 364.

subsequent records, there is no reference to him in any earlier inscription.[1143]

Mahāśivagupta III Yayāti II was succeeded by his son Mahābhavagupta IV Uddyotakesarin who is known from several of his own records[1144] as well as those of some later members of the dynasty.[1145] Rudradatta continued as the minister of peace and war under him at least till the eleventh year of his reign.[1146]

The Ratnagiri plates of Karṇa inform us that Mahābhavagupta IV Uddyotakesarin was followed by his son Janamejaya and the latter by his son Purañjaya.[1147] The recently published Nuapatna plates record a grant made by *Mahākumāra Yuvarāja* Dharmaratha during the reign of Janamejaya who is given the usual imperial titles.[1148] In view of the similarity of this record in certain features with the Kelga plates of Someśvara,[1149] a later member of the family, Janamejaya mentioned in it may be reasonably identified with the homonymous son of Uddyotakesarin and Dharmaratha was probably his son. Taking into consideration the facts that the names Mahābhavagupta and Mahāśivagupta were alternatively borne by the Somavaṁśin monarchs and that Uddyotakesarin and Purañjaya's younger brother Karṇa are known to have assumed these two names in this order, we may reasonably surmise that Janamejaya and Purañjaya were styled Mahāśivagupta and Mahābhavagupta respectively. If this is admitted, we may call them Mahāśivagupta IV Janamejaya II and Mahābhavagupta V Purañjaya respectively.

The successor of Mahābhavagupta V Purañjaya was his younger brother Mahāśivagupta V Karṇa who is known from two copper-plate grants[1150] and a stone image inscription[1151] of his reign. He is also mentioned under

1143. For a detailed discussion on this point, see *IHQ*, xx, 77-79. D.C. Sircar's assertion that Mahābhavagupta I Janamejaya's father is not mentioned as Mahāśivagupta in any record has to be modified a little as no. IV: V actually refers to him by this name. Sircar hints at the 'less probable' possibility of the Mahakosala Historical Society's plates (no. IV: XXIV) having been issued by Mahābhavagupta II Bhīmaratha (*IHQ*, xx, 79) and S.R. Nema accepts this suggestion (*Political History of the Somavaṁśī Kings of South Kosalā and Orissa*, 170-171). But we find it impossible to accept it as it would involve the rather improbable situation that Rudradatta became *Mahāsāndhivigrahin* during Bhīmaratha's reign and continued to occupy this office through the reigns of Dharmaratha, Nahuṣa, Abhimanyu, Indraratha and Caṇḍīhara Yāyati to the fourth year of Uddyotakesarin.

1144. Nos. IV: XXII-XXVI, Appendix II and Suppl. Inscr. III.

1145. Nos. IV: XXVII and XXVIII.

1146. No. IV: XXIV.

1147. No. IV: XXVII, verses 12-14.

1148. Suppl. Inscr. IV. Also see *Journal of the Orissa Research Society*, i, 29-33 and illustrations 3-8.

1149. No. IV: XXVIII.

1150. No. IV: XXVII and Suppl. Inscr. V.

1151. No. IV: Appendix III.

the name Karṇakesarin in a commentary on Sandhyākaranandin's *Rāma-carita.*[1152]

The Kelga grant of Someśvara[1153] informs us that Uddyotakesarin had anointed a certain Abhimanyu as the ruler of Kosala and that Someśvara ruled over it after the termination of Abhimanyu's rule. The relationship among these chiefs is not clear from the record. But it may be presumed with some justification that Abhimanyu was a younger brother of Uddyota-kesarin and was named after his grandfather. But there can be no certainty about it as well as about Someśvara who may have been another younger brother of Uddyotakesarin or more probably Abhimanyu's son.

In addition to the above, Raṇakesarin who is known from his Govinda-pur inscription may also have belonged to the Somavaṁśa. But his place in the dynasty cannot be ascertained in the absence of necessary information.[1154] The name of a chief called Viravarakesarin has been read in a short inscription in the Liṅgarāja temple at Bhubaneswar and it has been suggested, evidently on the basis of the termination *kesarin*, that he belonged to the Somakula.[1155] But the correct reading of the name, as pointed out by Suryanarayan Das,[1156] is Vīranarakesarī, and not Vīravarakesarī, and he is supposed to be none else than the Eastern Gaṅga king Narasiṁha. The *Mādalāpañjī*, a late chronicle of the Jagannātha temple at Purī, avers that the last Somavaṁśin ruler was Suvarṇakesarin who was vanquished by the Gaṅga king Anantavarman Coḍagaṅga. However, the historicity of the *Mādalāpañjī* has been rightly questioned and we cannot, therefore, be quite sure about the information furnished by it.[1157]

Chronology

The records of the Somavaṁśins, like those of the Pāṇḍuvaṁśins and the Śarabhapurīyas, are dated only in the regnal years of individual rulers without reference to any known reckoning with the result that there has been an unending controversy about their chronology which still continues to be in an unsettled state. Historians are, therefore, left with no option but to resort to other available sources in order to determine their general chronology.

On the basis of the traditions recorded in the *Mādalāpañjī*, a late local chronicle of the Jagannātha Temple at Purī, Andrew Stirling[1158] and, following him, other scholars including W. W. Hunter,[1159] Babu Rangalala

1152. *EI*, xxxiii, 264-265.
1153. No. IV: XXVIII.
1154. For some observations on this inscription, see note 1034 above.
1155. *IC*, iii, 122-125; *DHNI*, i, 478; *IHQ*, xxii, 306; *OHRJ*, i, 296-297.
1156. *Ibid.*, i, 302, text-line 2 and pl. 53.
1157. For a detailed examination of the historical value of the *Mādalāpañjī*, see *EI*, iii, 233ff.
1158. *Asiatic Researches*, xv, 254-305. At p. 265, he dates Yayāti's accession to 473 A.D.
1159. *Orissa*, ii, 183-191. He favoured 472 A.D. for the accession of Yayātikesarin.

Banerjee,[1160] Rajendra Lal Mitra[1161] and A. Cunningham[1162] regarded Yayāti as the founder of the Kesarin dynasty (Somavaṁśa) and dated his accession about the middle of the fifth century A.D. However, the unhistorical character of this chronicle soon became apparent[1163] and the necessity to find out other means for determining the period of the Somavaṁśa rule was realised.

J. F. Fleet subjected, for the first time, the palaeographic evidence of some of the copper-plate charters of Mahābhavagupta I Janamejaya, Mahāśivagupta I Yayāti and Mahābhavagupta II Bhīmaratha to a critical examination and observed that the 'general result of the palaeographic considerations, taken together' was 'that 'these records cannot possibly be placed before A.D. 900.' He was inclined to assign their characters to the eleventh century and to place the kings mentioned in these records somewhere between 1000 and 1100 A.D.[1164] F. Kielhorn thought that on palaeographical grounds the Kudopali grant of the time of Mahābhavagupta II Bhīmaratha could not be placed earlier than about the first half of the twelfth century A.D. and agreed with Fleet in dating the reigns of his three predecessors in about the eleventh century A.D.[1165] However, palaeographical considerations taken by themselves are not always dependable and there are eases where dates arrived at solely on this basis of palaeographic evidence had to be altered drastically. This has been the case with the Somavaṁśins themselves as nobody is now willing to place the early members of the dynasty in the eleventh century A.D. as advocated by Fleet and Kielhorn purely on palaeographic grounds.[1166] On the other hand, contacts with contemporary powers as gleaned from their own records as well as those of other ruling chiefs, particularly datable ones, would afford a more dependable chronological framework.

We learn from the two Baud copper-plate charters of Bhauma-Kara queen Pṛthvīmahādevī *alias* Tribhuvanamahādevī II, dated (Bhauma-Kara) year 158, that she was the daughter of Svabhāvatuṅga, king of Kosala (*Kosalādhipati*), who belonged to the lunar dynasty, and was born of Nṛttāmahādevī, daughter of a certain Yaśovṛddhi. The inscriptions further state that she had come to power as her husband Kusumahāra II *alias* Śubhākara IV and the latter's brother Lalitahāra II *alias* Śivakara III

1160. *IA*, v, 55; *JASB*, xlvi, 149 ff.
1161. *JPASB*, li, 9-14. Mitra proposed to place Yayāti's reign in 474-526 A.D.
1162. *CASR*, xviii, 17, 85 and 87. He placed Yayāti's accession in 475 A.D.
1163. For a detailed criticism of the *Mādalāpañjī* evidence, see Fleet in *EI*, iii, 334-340.
1164. *Ibid.*, 333. For a detailed discussion of palaeographical evidence, see *ibid.*, 328-332.
1165. *Ibid.*, iv, 256.
1166. Attention may in this connection be invited to the form of the initial *e* which, according to Kielhorn, proved most convincingly that the Kudopali charter could not have been written earlier than the first half of the twelfth century A.D. *Vide ibid.*, 255. D.C. Sircar points out that similar form of this initial vowel is met with in the Pāla inscriptions of the ninth and tenth centuries A.D. See *IHQ*, xx, 81.

had passed away without leaving any male issue, to succeed them.[1167] King Svabhāvatuṅga of the lunar dynasty is also mentioned in a short eulogistic supplement found at the end of the Patna plates of the eighth year of the reign of Mahāśivagupta I Yayāti.[1168] That he belonged to the Somavaṁśa is admitted on all hands. However, there is no unanimity as regards his identity. D.C. Sircar is in favour of identifying him with Mahāśivagupta I Yayāti himself.[1169] He invites our attention to another grant of the ninth year of Mahāśivagupta I Yayāti recording the grant of the village Candragrāma situated in the Maraḍa *viṣaya* in Dakṣiṇa Tosali, which is known to have formed part of the Bhauma-Kara dominions, in favour of a Brāhmaṇa resident of the village Śilābhañjapāṭī in the Oḍra country.[1170] The donated village Candragrāma and Maraḍa, the chief place of the district named after it, have been identified with modern Chandgaon, 32 miles south-east of Cuttack, and Barada or Marada Hariharapura in the Cuttack District respectively,[1171] whereas Śilābhañjapāṭī was obviously established by or christened after one of the Bhañja chiefs named Śilābhañja.[1172] By yet another charter given in the fifteenth year of his reign Mahāśivagupta I granted a village situated in the Gandhaṭapāṭī (or Gandhadapāṭī) *maṇḍala* in Kosala.[1173] Gandhaṭapāṭī, which has been identified with Gandharadi about 12 miles from Baud in the Phulbani District of Orissa,[1174] was evidently founded by or named after the Bhañja chief Śatrubhañja I *alias* Gandhaṭa and is mentioned in a few Bhañja grants.[1175] As suggested by Sircar, these records show that Mahāśivagupta I achieved some success against the Karas and drove their Bhañja feudatories away from Dhṛtipura in upper Orissa to Vañjulvaka in the Ganjam region. He further thinks that the Somavaṁśin monarch must have helped his daughter Tribhuvanamahādevī in securing the Kara throne against rival claimants and it was in that connection that he granted Candragrāma situated in the Kara territory and, therefore, the Bhauma-Kara year 158, the date of the above-mentioned Baud grants, and the ninth year of Mahāśivagupta I Yayāti, when the Patna charter registering the grant of Candragrāma was issued, could not have been far removed from one another.[1176]

1167. *EI*, xxix, 217, verses 12-13. As known from the later records of the family, this statement is not correct. Śivakara III had two sons who ascended the throne shortly afterwards.
1168. No. IV: XIII, verses 15-17.
1169. *JAS, Letters*, xix, 117ff.; *IHQ*, xxix, 155; *EI*, xxix, 224; *OHRJ*, i, 290-291; R.C. Majumdar (ed.), *HCIP*, iv: *The Age of Imperial Kanauj*, 148-149.
1170. No. IV: XIV, text-lines 25-26 and 33.
1171. Binayak Misra, *DMO*, 68, no. 9.
1172. There were more than one chiefs named Śilābhañja in the Bhañja dynasty.
1173. No. IV: XV, text-lines 4-5 and 16-17.
1174. Binayak Misra, *DMO*, 45; K.C. Panigrahi, *Chronology of the Bhauma-Karas and the Somavaṁśis of Orissa*, 32.
1175. Binayak Misra, *DMO*, 44-46, nos. 3, 4 and 14.
1176. *IHQ* xxix, 155; *OHRJ*, i, 291; *The Age of Imperial Kanauj*, 149.

And as regards the epoch of the Bhauma-Kara era, it has been suggested on the basis of some astronomical details found in the Daspalla grant of the Bhañja chief Śatrubhañja *alias* Tribhuvanakalaśa, dated year 198, probably of the Kara era,[1177] that it commenced in 831 A.D.[1178]

There are, however, some serious difficulties that militate against the above suggestions of Sircar. First of all, the recently discovered Orissa State Museum plates, which constitute the earliest known record of Mahāśivagupta I Yayāti, register a land-grant in the Gaṇḍitama *viṣaya* in the Oḍra country,[1179] thereby showing that coastal Orissa or Dakṣiṇa Tosali, which was earlier included in the Bhauma-Kara dominions, had passed under his control as early as the fourth year of his reign, if not earlier. And if, following Sircar's line of argument, we were to equate the fourth year of the reign of Mahāśivagupta I Yayāti with the Bhauma-Kara year 158, it would lead to serious anachronism. Basing on 831 A.D. as the epoch of this era fixed by Sircar, the equation would mean that Mahāśivagupta I Yayāti's fourth year was conterminous with about 989 A.D. and if he ruled for about thirty or thirty-five years,[1180] the termination of his reign would have to be dated around 1015 or 1020 A.D. But this is simply impossible, for we know definitely that his son and successor, Mahābhavagupta II Bhīmaratha, and his sons Mahāśivagupta II Dharmaratha and Indraratha ruled for at least thirteen, eleven and six years respectively,[1181] and even if we do not take the reigns of Nahuṣa and Abhimanyu intervening, according to our genealogical scheme outlined above, between those of Mahāśivagupta II Dharmaratha and Indraratha into consideration, we shall have to believe that Indraratha continued to rule at least up to 1045 or 1050 A.D. And this will militate against known historical facts. It is learnt from Coḷa records that a general of the Coḷa emperor Rājendra I had defeated Indraratha and captured his kingdom by 1022 A.D., whereas if the equation is conceded, Bhīmaratha, not Indraratha, must have been on the Somavaṁśin throne at the time of the Coḷa invasion.[1182] We have, therefore, to abandon this synchronism. Secondly, as pointed out by S.N. Rajaguru,[1183] the details of the date given in the Daspalla charter in question tally well with 23rd March, 934 A.D. also[1184] which would hint at 736 A.D. as the probable

1177. *EI*, xxix, 189-194. Also see *OHRJ*, i, 208-213.

1178. *IHQ* xxix, 155; *OHRJ*, i, 291, note 1; *The Age of Imperial Kanauj*, 150, note 51; *EI*, xxix, 191 (note 2), 224.

1179. No. IV: XII, text-line 17.

1180. His last known regnal year is 28. See no. IV: XVII.

1181. These are the only (in the case of Dharmaratha and Indraratha) or the latest (in the case of Bhīmaratha) known recorded years of their reigns.

1182. It must be pointed out that when Sircar wrote on the Somavaṁśins, the records of Dharmaratha and Indraratha were not known.

1183. *OHRJ*, i, 209-210.

1184. See L.D. Swamikannu Pillai, *Indian Ephemeries*, ii, 270. The details agree with 21st March, 812 A.D. also. But it is too early for our purpose.

epoch of the Bhauma-Kara era[1185] and the consequent equation of the Bhauma-Kara year 158 with 894 A.D. Therefore, the question of the epoch of the Bhauma-Kara era cannot yet be regarded as finally settled though in the light of known historical facts 736 A.D. appears preferable. And lastly, the identification of king Svabhāvatuṅga of the Baud and Patna plates with Mahāśivagupta I Yayāti is also not beyond doubt. The Baud grants unequivocally describe Svabhāvatuṅga as the lord of Kosala. The supplement at the end of the Patna plates also credits him with the protection of Kosalā.[1186] It appears, therefore, that Svabhāvatuṅga was regarded primarily as the ruler of Kosala. This description cannot be applied justifiably to Mahāśivagupta I Yayāti whose dominions, practically from the very beginning of his reign, appear to have comprised the twin provinces of Kosala and Oḍra.[1187] The reference to the minister of peace and war (*Sandhivigrahin*) attached to Kosala, Siṁhadatta, in the Patna plates of the twenty-eighth year of his reign[1188] seems to indicate that these two divisions had separate administrative organisations during his reign. Thus, the division of the Somavaṁśin kingdom into the two *rāṣṭras* (provinces) of Kosala and Utkala, which is explicitly alluded to in some later records of the family,[1189] had come into vogue as early as the time of Mahāśivagupta I Yayāti. He could not, therefore, have appropriately been called the lord of Kosala, for that would have amounted to his under-estimation by his daughter as well as his own court-poet. On the other hand, his father Mahābhavagupta I Janamejaya is explicitly styled *Kosalendra* (lord of Kosala) in some of his own records[1190] and none of his numerous inscriptions registers any grant in Oḍra or Dakṣiṇa Tosali. Further, the first stanza of the supplement tells us that Svabhāvatuṅga became king by his own valour which is an apt description only of a ruler who was the real founder of the family's greatness. It is appropriately applicable to Mahābhavagupta I Janamejaya with whom the historical account of the dynasty commences in the records of his successors. This description would obviously be inappropriate in the case of Mahāśivagupta I Yayāti. The tenor of description in the Patna plates also seems to support our contention. And lastly, the evidence of the Somavaṁśin and Bhauma-Kara inscriptions places the identification of Svabhāvatuṅga with Mahābhavagupta I Janamejaya on a firm foundation. The Brahmeśvara temple inscription of the

1185. S.N. Rajaguru thinks that this epoch of the Bhauma-Kara era finds support from the details of the occasion of the grant found in Śatrubhañja's Ganjam plates of year 198 also. See *OHRJ*, iv, 67ff.

1186. *Kosalā-pālana-kaumud-indu.*

1187. As pointed out earlier, the first record of his reign registers a grant in the Oḍra country.

1188. No. IV: XVII, text-line 69.

1189. No. IV: XXII, verse 9; no. IV:XXVI, verse 8.

1190. Nos. IV: VIII-X, verse 16.

time of Uddyotakesarin avers that Janamejaya killed the Oḍra king with a spear-head in a battle. No other member of the dynasty is credited with any involvement with or victory over Oḍra. Conversely, Svabhāvatuṅga as the only Somavaṁśin monarch mentioned in the Bhauma-Kara inscriptions, *viz.*, the Baud plates of Pṛthvīmahādevī. This combined evidence emanating from two different sources establishes the sameness of Janamejaya and Svabhāvatuṅga and points to Janamejaya-Svabhāvatuṅga's interference in the internal affairs of the Bhauma-Karas in order to help his daughter occupy the kingdom.[1191]

It will follow from the above discussion that the Bhauma-Kara era commenced in all probability in 736 A.D. and its year 158, when Pṛthvīmahādevī *alias* Tribhuvanamahādevī II was ruling, fell in the reign of Mahābhavagupta I Janamejaya.

The Kumuranga charter of Daṇḍimahādevī, dated (Bhauma-Kara) year 187 corresponding to 923 A.D.,[1192] is the last known Kara record registering a grant in Dakṣiṇa Tosali, whereas the first Somavaṁśin land-grant in Oḍra, which was earlier under the Karas, is recorded in the Orissa State Museum plates of Mahāśivagupta I Yayāti's fourth regnal year. If it is supposed that the fourth year of Yayāti fell one or two years after the date of the Kumuranga plates, *i.e.*, Bhauma-Kara year 188-89 or 924-25 A.D., we may tentatively date his accession in *c.* 920 A.D.

Another fixed point in the chronology of the Somavaṁśins is afforded by the records of Coḷa Rājendra I (1012-1044 A.D.) dated in the eleventh and subsequent years of his reign referring to his success against Indraratha in a battle at Yayātinagara. As the Gangetic expedition in course of which Rājendra's army is said to have captured Indraratha is first mentioned in a record of the eleventh year of Rājendra[1193] and a detailed account is found first in the Tīrumalai inscription of his twelfth year,[1194] we may safely date this episode and the end of Indraratha's reign around 1022 A.D. The victory of Paramāra Bhoja (known dates: 1020-1047 A.D.) over Indraratha referred to in the Udayapur *praśasti* of Udayāditya[1195] must be dated shortly before this event.

1191. S.N. Rajaguru (*OHRJ*, viii, 101ff.) and K.C. Panigrahi (*Chronology of the Bhauma-Karas and the Somavaṁśīs of Orissa*, 2-8) also uphold this identification, but most of their grounds are different from ours and unconvincing.

It must be stated that Sircar did not altogether rule out the possibility of Svabhāvatuṅga being another name of Mahābhavagupta I Janamejaya. See *JAS*, *Letters*, xix, 120.

1192. *JBORS*, v, 564-577.

1193. 476 of 1911. As pointed out by K.A. Nilakanta Sastri (*The Coḷas*, 238, note 51), this incident is not mentioned in the inscription of the tenth year.

1194. E. Hultzsch, *SII*, i, 95-99, no. 67.

1195. *EI*, i, 235, verse 19.

The above facts together with the regnal years of individual rulers referred to in their own records and an allowance for the extension of their reigns beyond the latest recorded years as well as for the reigns of chiefs whose records have not been reported so far enable us to fix the early chronology of the dynasty with some degree of certainty.

It may be added here that we come across a few allusions of a historical nature in some of the records of the early members of the dynasty. These include the success of Svabhāvatuṅga-Janamejaya and his son Mahāśivagupta I Yayāti over a Cedi king of Ḍahālā,[1196] the capture of thirty-two elephants after defeating a chief named Ajapāla in a battle by Mahāśivagupta I Yayāti,[1197] Mahābhavagupta II Bhīmaratha's victory over a chief named Rudra[1198] and Mahāśivagupta II Dharmaratha's success against Andhra and Gauḍa.[1199] However, the explicitly named chiefs are not known from any other source while the other chiefs cannot be identified with any degree of certainty in the absence of necessary details and as such are not of much use for our purpose.

The next fixed point in the history of the Somavaṁśa is the contemporaniety of its last known member Karṇa with the Pāla king Rāmapāla (*c.* 1077-1120 A.D.) and the Eastern Gaṅga monarch Anantavarman Coḍagaṅga (1078-1147 A.D.). The *Rāma-carita* (iii.45) of Sandhyākaranandin informs us that Rāmapāla did favour to the Utkala king, whom he had discomfited earlier and who hailed from the lineage of Bhava's adornment (*viz.*, lunar dynasty or Soma-vaṁśa), and protected the whole world from (the terror of) Kaliṅga after killing those robbers (of that place), an obvious reference to the soldiers of Anantavarman Coḍagaṅga.[1200] We learn from the commentary on another verse of the same work (ii.5) that the Utkala king in question was Karṇakesarin and that he was defeated by Jayasiṁha, Rāmapāla's feudatory of Daṇḍabhukti.[1201] Karṇakesarin of the commentary is evidently the same as the last known Somavaṁśin chief, who issued the Ratnagiri plates, whereas the Kaliṅga king from whose terror Rāmapāla claims to have rescued the entire world is no other than Anantavarman Coḍagaṅga who, too, in his Korni grant of Śaka 1034 or 1112 A.D., claims to have first defeated and then restored the Utkala king.[1202] These

1196. No. IV:XIII, verses 15-17.

1197. Nos. IV:XVI, verse 7; XVII, verse 8; XVIII, verse 8; XX, verse 7.

1198. No. IV:XX, verse 8.

1199. *Ibid.*, verse 9.

1200. भवभूषणसन्ततिभुवमनुजग्राह जितमुत्कलत्वंयः ।
जगदवति स्म समस्तं कलिङ्गतस्तान् निशाचरान् निघ्नन् ॥

1201. सिंह इति दण्डभुक्तिभूपतिरद्भुतप्रभावाकरकमलमुकुलतुलितोत्कलेशकर्णकेसरिसरिद्-
वल्लभकुम्भसम्भवो जयसिंहः ।

1202. *JAHRS*, i(iii), 106ff., text-lines 102-103.

allusions show that for some time during the weak rule of Karṇa, lower Orissa became a bone of contention between the Pālas and the Eastern Gaṅgas. However, finally it was annexed by Anantavarman Coḍagaṅga sometime between 1112 and 1114-15 A.D., the latter being the date of his Bhubaneswar (Liṅgarāja temple)[1203] and Puri (Mārkaṇḍeśvara temple)[1204] inscriptions. We may, therefore, date this event around 1113 A.D. The independent rule of Karṇa, which lasted for at least six years as indicated by his assumption of the imperial titles in the Ratnagiri plates issued in the sixth year of his reign, must have come to an end sometime in or before 1112 A.D., the date of the Korni plates, when he appears to have become a vassal of Anantavarman Coḍagaṅga, a position he appears to have held for sometime before he was finally extirpated. If the statement of the *Mādalāpañjī* that the last Somavaṁśin chief overthrown by Coḍagaṅga was Suvarṇakesarin has any historical worth, the close of Karṇa's rule will have to be dated a few years earlier. But in the present state of our knowledge we cannot be quite sure about it. The rule of the dynasty in South Kosala also came to an end about the same time.[1205]

In the light of the foregoing discussion the genealogy and the order of succession of the Somavaṁśins together with their approximate regnal periods may be reconstructed as given on p. 199.

Historical Outline

With the above background, an attempt may now be made to outline the political history of the dynasty.

Śivagupta

As we have seen above, Śivagupta is the first recorded member of the dynasty. He is known only from the official charters of his successor, Mahābhavagupta I Janamejaya, which refer to him with full paraphernalia of imperial titles borne by his descendants, viz., *Paramabhaṭṭāraka, Mahārājādhirāja* and *Parameśvara,*[1206] with the exception of only *Trikaliṅg-*

1203. *EI*, xxx, 31-32. Also see *OHRJ*, i(ii), 1 ff.

1204. *EI*, xxxiii, 184-185.

1205. K.C. Panigrahi (*Chronology of the Bhauma-Karas and the Somavaṁśis of Orissa,* 16) reads the date 549 in the Lalāṭendukesarī Cave inscription of Uddyotakesarin's reign and, referring it to the Gaṅga era commencing, in his opinion, in 496 A.D., takes it to correspond to 1015 A.D. But this is extremely doubtful. A likely veiled allusion to Janamejaya II's success against the Chindaka-Nāgas of Bastar in the Ratnagiri plates of Karṇa (*EI*, xxxiii, 265) may have some bearing on the vicissitudes the Somavaṁśins had to pass through in Dakṣiṇa Kosala. However, not much can be built upon such uncertain evidences.

1206. The title *Parameśvara* is left out by oversight in no. IV: XI, In no. IV : IV the title *Mahārāja* is used instead of the superior title *Mahārājādhirāja*, evidently due to negligence on the part of the writer.

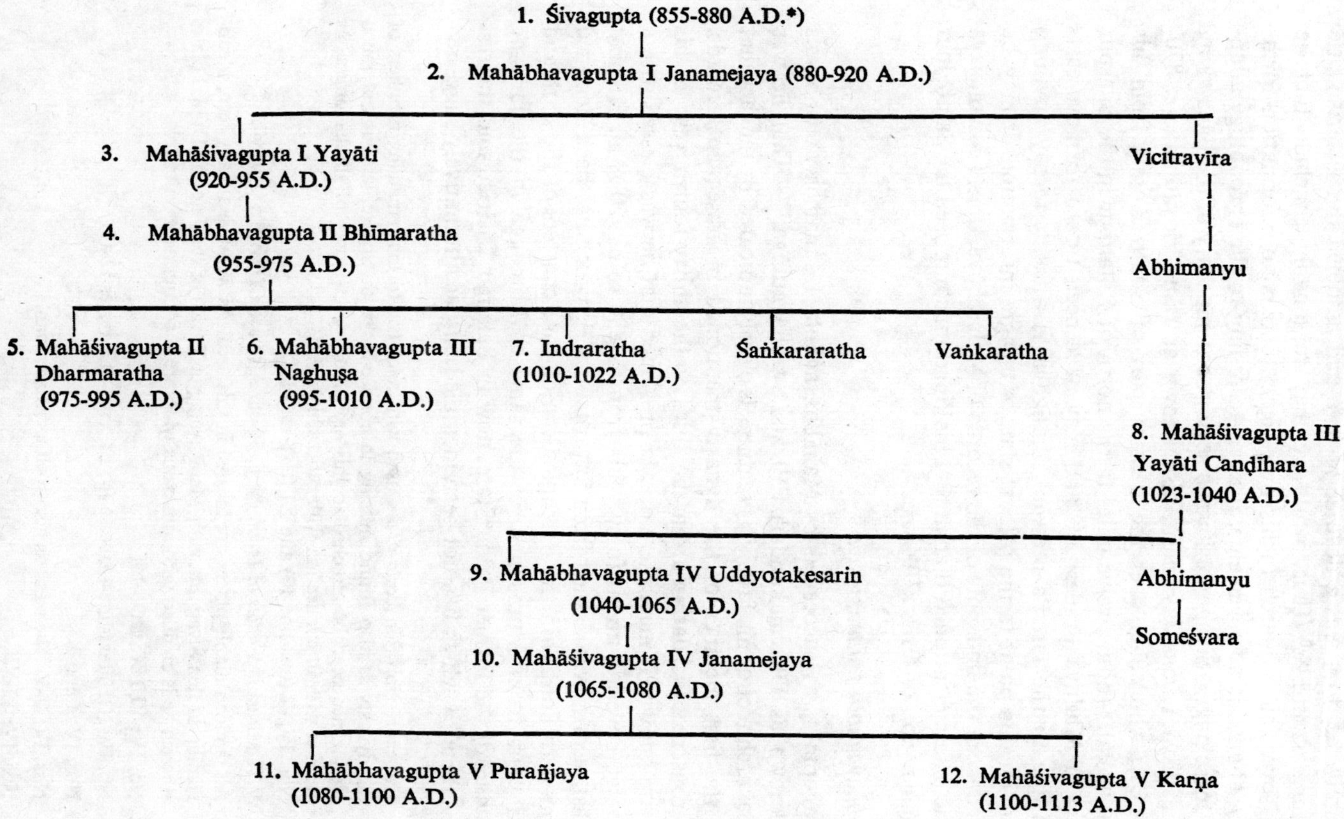

* The dates mentioned in brackets are only approximate.

āhipati which is found invariably attached to all the later members of the dynasty.[1207] From two of these records we learn that like the other chiefs of the family, he, too, was a devotee of Śiva and assumed the sectarian title *Paramamāheśvara.*[1208] Thus, while we may reasonably conclude that he was a sovereign monarch in his own right, there is no information forthcoming about his achievements, if any. According to the chronology adopted in these pages, Śivagupta I was a senior contemporary of the Bāṇa king Vikramāditya I *alias* Jayameru, also known as Bāṇa-Vidyādhara (*c.* 870-895 A.D.), who ruled over the western part of South Kosala from his capital at Pāli, about twelve miles to the north of Ratanpur in the Bilaspur District of Madhya Pradesh,[1209] and may have been forced to move eastwards due to the latter's pressure, though it is difficult to say anything definite on this point in the present state of meagre information. It may be inferred from the findspots of the records of Mahābhavagupta I Janamejaya and the places mentioned therein that his kingdom comprised the Sambalpur Balangir region of Orissa.[1210]

Mahābhavagupta I Janamejaya

Śivagupta was succeeded by Mahābhavagupta I Janamejaya who was also known as Dharmakandarpa[1211] and Svabhāvatuṅga.[1212] That he was the real architect of his family's greatness is clearly indicated by the fact that he is the first member of the dynasty mentioned in subsequent records. Numerous records dating from the third to the thirty-fourth year of his reign are known. It may, therefore, be presumed that he was blessed with a long reign covering about forty years from *c.* 880 to *c.* 920 A.D. His first and last records were issued from Suvarṇapura[1213] which has been identified with modern Sonpur in the Balangir District, four charters of the sixth and eighth years from Murasīman,[1214] the same as Mursinga in the Jarasing zamindari of the former Patna State, now in Balangir District, and the rest from Ārāma[1215] which has not been identified but, as alternatively suggested

1207. The expression *Somakula-tilaka* used with reference to the remaining members of the dynasty is also found missing in connection with Śivagupta. But not much significance need be attached to this omission, for instances of similar omissions are met with in connection with other chiefs also.

1208. Nos. IV:VI (text-line 10) and XI (text-lines 1-2).

1209. V.V. Mirashi, *Studies in Indology*, ii, 35-38. Also see *CII*, iv, lxxvi-lxxvii.

1210. All the identifiable places are located in this area. As we have already seen, identification of this Śivagupta with Mahāśivagupta Yayāti of the Jatesing-Dungri plates wherein he is credited with numerous widespread conquests is untenable.

1211. No. IV: VIII-X, verse 15.

1212. No. IV: XIII, text-line 44, verse 15; *EI*, xxix, 217, verses 12-13.

1213. Nos. IV: I and XI.

1214. Nos. IV: II-V. The name is also spelt as Mūrasīman.

1215. Nos. IV: VI-X.

by B. Ch. Chhabra,[1216] may have been situated close to Sonpur. In the absence of definite information it is difficult to determine as to which of these places served as his capital.[1217] These issuing places where the king was stationed in the different years of his reign at the time of making the grants in question, donated villages and the administrative divisions in which they were situated and the provenances of his records leave no doubt that he exercised firm control over the Sambalpur-Balangir region which formed the eastern part of Dakṣiṇa Kosala. This is in keeping with the style *Kosalendra* applied to him in some of his records.[1218] Whether he controlled any area in the Chhattisgarh region of Madhya Pradesh (western part of Kosala) cannot be ascertained at present, though such a possibility cannot be ruled out altogether.[1218a] The assumption, for the first time, by him of the title *Trikaliṅgādhipati,* 'Lord of Trikaliṅga', indicates that he laid his claim to and controlled at least a part of Trikaliṅga and that he pursued an expansionist policy.

Mahābhavagupta I Janamejaya appears to have been involved in a series of hostilities with the Kalacuris of Ḍāhala (Baghelkhand region of Madhya Pradesh) with Tripurī (modern Tewar in the Jabalpur District) as its capital. A short supplement at the end of the Patna plates of the eighth year of the reign of his son and successor, Mahāśivagupta I Yayāti,[1219] seems to refer to these incidents. It is stated that king Svabhāvatuṅga of the Somakula of Kosala, who, as we have shown above, is none else than Mahābhavagupta I Janamejaya himself, defeated the Caidyas, killed the soldiers of the Cedi king led by a certain Bhaṭṭapeḍi and recovered all the women earlier carried away by them. We are further told that from him (Svabhāvatuṅga) was

1216. *EI*, xxiii, 250. He was also willing to take it to mean 'pleasure garden' with a palace where the king occasionally resided. See *ibid.*, 250, note 6.

1217. In most cases we have references to the victorious camp stationed at these places (*samāvāsita-śrīmad-vijaya-kaṭakāt* or *samāvāsita-śrīmato vijaya-kaṭakāt*). In IV: IV we find mention of Mūrasīman, the best of towns (*pattana-vara*), while at anoother place (IV: V) the same place is mentioned without any such qualification. Ārāma is also referred to once (IV :VI) without any qualifying word. It is often assumed that if a place is mentioned by itself without any word like *vijaya-kaṭaka* or *vijaya-skandhāvāra* attached to it, it may be taken as capital. But it does not seem to be applicable in the present case, for two places, *viz.*, Mūrasīman and Ārāma, are mentioned in this manner. It may, of course, be argued that first Mūrasīman and then Ārāma became capital. However, the employment of the expression *samāvāsita-vijaya-kaṭaka* for them at other places renders this supposition untenable.

1218. Nos. IV: VIII-X, text-line 48.

1218a. L.P. Pandeya (*IHQ*, xx, 248, note 9) locates a village donated by Janamejaya and the headquarter of the district in which it was situated in the Chandrapur Taluk of the Bilaspur District.

1219. No. IV: XIII, verses 15-16.

born a son comparable to Viṣṇu who, caring two figs for the Caidya king Durgarāja,[1220] burnt and depopulated Ḍahālā.[1221] It is difficult to ascertain if we have here a reference to a single episode in which Svabhāvatuṅga was assisted by his son Mahāśivagupta I Yayāti or there is an allusion to two different stages of the conflict datable to two successive reigns, although the latter possibility seems preferable. Secondly, the Kalacuri-Cedi king Durgarāja is not known from any other source. It has, therefore, to be regarded as a *viruda* or secondary name of the contemporary Kalacuri chief. Let us now see if Kalacuri records throw some light on this question. We are told in the Bilhari stone inscription of Kalacuri Yuvarājadeva II that his ancestor Śaṅkaragaṇa *alias* Mugdhatuṅga, also known as Prasiddhadhavala, conquered the rows of the countries along the eastern coast and captured the Pāli country from the lord of Kosala.[1222] A Prakrit stanza in the Banaras plates of Karṇa also avers that Prasiddhadhavala took possession of Pāli thinking that in his family there will be many men eminent on account of their greatness.[1223] The Kosalendra from whom Mugdhatuṅga Prasiddhadhavala took away Pāli has been identified with the Bāṇa chief Vikramādityā I Jayameru (*c.* 870-*c.* 895 A.D.) whose inscription has been found in a temple at Pāli about 12 miles north of Ratanpur. As a result of this incident the Chhattisgarh region fell into the hands of Mugdhatuṅga Prasiddhadhavala (*c.* 890-*c.* 910 A.D.) who or one of his brothers placed in charge of this newly acquired territory by him[1224] came face to face with Mahābhavagupta I Janamejaya who controlled the eastern part of Kosala. It seems that the Kalacuri chief tried to penetrate into the Somavaṁśin dominions and this attack was repulsed successfully by Mahābhavagupta I Janamejaya, though in the initial stages of this conflict he had to suffer some reverses.

There is evidence of Janamejaya's deep involvement in Orissan affairs also. The Brahmeśvara temple (Bhubaneswar) inscription of the time of Uddyotakesarin avers that Janamejaya had captured the glory of the Oḍra king after killing him with a spear head. Oḍra or Orissa was at this time under the Bhauma-Karas and Pṛthvīmahādevī *alias* Tribhuvanamahādevī, daughter of Svabhāvatuṅga (*i.e.* Mahābhavagupta I), was on throne in the Bhauma-Kara year 158 (894 A.D.) as we learn from her two Baud charters issued in that year. These plates tell us that she came to throne as her

1220. K.C. Panigrahi (*Chronology of the Bhauma-Karas and the Somavaṁśīs of Orissa*, 2 and 50) proposes to read the name as Jyuvarāja (Yuvarāja) which is, however, not brone out by the facsimile.

1221. No. IV: XIII, verse 17.

1222. *CII*, iv, 211, verse 23.

1223. *Ibid.*, 242, verse 12.

1224. It is stated in several inscriptions of the Ratnapura branch of the Kalacuris that Kokalla (I) had eighteen sons, the eldest of whom ascended the throne at Tripuri and made his younger brothers chiefs of neighbouring provinces, See *ibid.*, 405, verse 6; 412, verse 5, etc.

husband Kusumahāra II *alias* Śubhākara IV and her husband's brother Lalitahāra II *alias* Śivakara III had died without leaving any heir to the royal throne.[1225] But this statement is belied by the later records of the family which inform us that Śivakara III had two sons who succeeded to the throne one after the other.[1226] It may, therefore, be reasonably conclud-ed that towards the close of Śivakara III's reign there was a civil war for succession in which Svabhāvatuṅga successfully intervened in favour of his daughter setting aside the claims of his son-in-law's brother's sons and it was in course of this episode that he may have killed Śivakara III who must have opposed his elder brother's widowed queen. In keeping with our chronology and the epoch of the Bhauma-Kara era this event must have taken place shortly prior to Bhauma-Kara year 158 or 894 A.D. While this military intervention did not result in the annexation of any new territory, it must have certainly contributed enormously to the extension of the political influence of the Somavaṁśins who must have come to be regarded as the supreme power in Orissa.[1227] This situation was, as we shall see below, fully exploited by the next chief, Mahāśivagupta I Yayāti.

Two recently discovered inscriptions inform us about a couple of Rāṣṭrakūṭa feudatories of Mahābhavagupta I Janamejaya. One of them, Mugdhagondaladeva, issued a copper-plate charter from a place, the name of which has been read as Prakaṭacittayotika. It appears from the details of the donated village that he governed, for sometime, the region along the river Tel. Though a feudatory and described as endowed with the five *mahā-śabdas*, he assumed the title *Mahārājādhirāja*, and a stanza in lines 16-18 seems to give a hyperbolic account of his conquests in Madhyadeśa, Kāñci, Kuntala and along the ocean. If at all there be any historical truth in this statement, he may be taken to have participated in these expedi-tions on behalf of his overlord. But it appears to be a mere play on words and no historical value need be attached to it.[1228] Another feudatory named Devapya, who also assumed the titles of *Mahārājādhirāja* and *Mahāmaṇḍaleśvara*, governed the Kolleḍā-*maṇḍala* situated along the Mahānadī in the twenty-third year of Janamejaya's reign.[1229]

Malladatta, son of Dhāradatta, and thereafter Dhāradatta, who was

1225. *EI.*, xxix, 217, verse 11.

1226. *Ibid.*, vi, 138, verses 7-8.

1227. According to S.N. Rajaguru (*IO*, iv, 364-365), however, Oḍra was only a district (*viṣaya*) of Uttara Tosali and did not denote Orissa proper as commonly believed. S.R. Nema (*Political History of the Somavaṁśī Kings of South Kosala and Orissa*, 202-203) accepts Rajaguru's opinion and identifies the Oḍra king killed by Janamajeya with a king of the Bhañja dynasty.

1228. Suppl. Inscr. No. II.

1229. Suppl. Inscr. No. I.

apparently the grandson of the earlier Dhāradatta and son of Malladatta,[1230] served as his minister of peace and war (*Mahāsāndhivigrahin*).[1231] As will be seen in the sequel, this Datta family continued to provide incumbents of this office for quite a few generations. Another minister (*mantrin*) named Sādhāraṇa, son of a certain Śobhana, is highly eulogised in a few records of Janamejaya. It is stated that his intellect was purified by the study of all the Arthaśāstras and Smṛtis, he was verily Bṛhaspati, preceptor of gods, in his knowledge of the Vedas, Vedāṅgas, Śikṣā, Kalpa and Itihāsa and that having entrusted him with all the responsibilities of the State, the king abandoned, himself to the enjoyment of mundane pleasures.[1232] He is mentioned as a minister in all the records dated from the seventeenth year.[1233] Hailing from a Brāhmaṇa family of Ṭakārī, he first figures in a record of the eighth year as *Mahāmahattaka* who served as the *dūtaka* of the grant in question.[1234] He rose to the position of a minister sometime in or before the seventeenth year,[1235] and in the three records of the thirty-first year, where he figures as the donee, he is mentioned both as *Mahattama* and a minister.[1236]

Mahābhavagupta I Janamejaya did not only consolidate his kingdom in the eastern part of Kosala and conquer some adjoining territories to justify his assumption of the title of *Trikaliṅgādhipati* but also participated in wider politics and thereby placed the Somavaṁśins on a firm footing and made them a power to be reckoned with in east Indian politics.

Mahāśivagupta I Yayāti

Mahābhavagupta I Janamejaya was succeeded by his son Mahāśivagupta I Yayāti whose known records are dated from the fourth[1237] to the twenty-eighth year[1238] of his reign and allowing a little margin for the extension of his reign beyond the latest recorded year he may be assumed to have ruled for about thirty-five years, *i.e.*, *c.* 920-*c.* 955 A.D.

1230. This relationship, which is not indicated in any record, is based on the assumption that a grandson is often named after his grand-father in India.

1231. The charters dated from sixth to thirty-first year mention Malladatta (Nos. IV: II-X) and the latest record issued in the thirty-fourth year (No. IV:XI) refers to Dhāradatta as *Mahāsāndhivigrahin.*

1232. Nos. IV: VI (verse 13), VII (verse 16), VIII-XI (verses 14-15).

1233. Nos. IV: VI-XI. The first of these records is of year 17 and the last one of year 34.

1234. No. IV: V.

1235. No. IV: VI.

1236. Nos. IV: VIII-X. In line 12 he is described as *Mahattama* while verses 14-15 eulogise him as a minister.

1237. No. IV: XII.

1238. No. IV: XVII.

Yayāti's charters dated between the fourth and fifteenth year of his reign were issued from Vinītapura[1239] which has been identified with the present Binkā on the Mahanadi in the Balangir District. However, the grants of the twenty-fourth and twenty-eighth years of his reign are stated to have been given from Yayātinagara[1240] which was obviously named after him. The fact that both the towns are stated to have been situated on the Mahānadī and are described in identical stanzas[1241] shows that they were identical and that Yayāti gave his name to the town earlier known as Vinītapura. The absence of the expression *samāvāsita-kaṭaka* or simply *kaṭaka* in a majority of cases[1242] and the highly hyperbolic description in many records[1243] seem to indicate that Vinītapura-Yayātinagara became the Somakula capital during Yayāti's reign and the extant evidence shows that it continued to occupy this position for quite sometime. It must, however, be distinguished from Abhinava-Yayātinagara or Yayātinagara (modern Jaipur in the Cuttack District),[1244] evidently named after the older Yayātinagara in Kosala,[1245] which appears to have become the capital of the later Somavaṁśins after Kosala had been placed under a viceregal line.[1246]

Mahāśivagupta I was engaged in a deadly battle with the Kalacuris of Tripurī. We learn from the concluding stanza of a short supplement appended at the end of the Patna grant of the eighth year of his reign that he vanquished the Cedi chief Durgarāja[1247] and put Ḍahālā aflame and depopulated it.[1248] It seems that the hostilities with the Kalacuris, which started during the previous reign, were continued by Yayāti who appears to have adopted an aggressive policy. Unfortunately, no Kalacuri ruler called Durgarāja is known to us at present. It was in all probability a *viruda* or secondary name of Yayāti's Kalacuri contemporary who was none else than Yuvarājadeva I (*c.* 915-*c.* 945 A.D.), or his son and

1239. Nos. IV: XII-XV.

1240. Nos. IV: XVI-XVII.

1241. Nos. IV: XIV, XVI-XVII, verses 1-4.

1242. In no. IV: XII we find the expression *samāvāsita-śrīmato vijayakaṭakāt* and in no. IV: XIII only *kaṭakāt*. No such expression is met with in any other record.

1243. Nos. IV: XII, verse 1; XIV, XVI-XVII, verses 1-4.

1244. Under the name Guhadeva-pāṭaka or Guheśvara-pāṭaka, it was earlier the capital of the Bhauma-Kara dynasty.

1245. Yayātinagara of Kosala seems to be mentioned in Dhoyin's *Pavanadūta*, verse 26. See *IHQ*, xx, 80-81, notes 2 and 3. Some scholars, however, take it to refer to the Orissan town of that name. See K.C. Panigrahi, *Chronology of the Bhauma-Karas and Somavaṁśis of Orissa*, pp. 14-15.

1246. For a detailed discussion of the evidence bearing on the distinction between the two Yayātinagaras, see *ibid.*, 12-15.

1247. Some read the name as Ju (Yu)varāja. See *ibid.*, 50.

1248. No. IV: XIII, verse 17.

successor Lakṣmaṇarāja II (*c.* 945-*c.* 970 A.D.), more probably the former. According to the *Viddhaśālabhañjikā* of the celebrated poet-dramatist Rājaśekhara, Yuvarājadeva I *alias* Keyūravarṣa assumed the title of *Triliṅgādhipati* which is generally taken to be an error for *Trikaliṅgādhipati.*[1249] One may perhaps argue that *Triliṅgādhipati* itself may be the intended title and the allusion may be to his victory over the Telugu country.[1250] It is pertinent to note in this connection that Andhra is included in the *Viddhaśālabhañjikā* in the list of the countries whose chiefs were defeated by Yuvarājadeva's armies. However, as the later Kalacuri kings are known to have borne the title *Trikaliṅgādhipati* while no member of the dynasty ever bore the other title *Triliṅgādhipati,* it may be reasonably assumed that the latter reading in the *Viddhaśālabhañjikā* is due to scribal error and that Yuvarājadeva I actually assumed the title *Trikaliṅgādhipati* in allusion to his raids in the Somakulin dominions. Secondly, and this is the clinching point, our evidence clearly shows that the event must have taken place in or prior to the ninth regnal year of Yayāti when Yuvarājadeva I, and not Lakṣmaṇarāja II, was on the Kalacuri throne. In view of these facts Yuvarājadeva I appears to have been the Kalacuri-Cedi antagonist of Yayāti, and the former may have had Durgarāja as his another name not known from any other source till now. Even making due allowance for the usual poetic exaggeration, one will have to concede that Yayāti did achieve palpable success against his Kalacuri adversary, and the raids of the latter's son and successor in Oḍra and Kosala during Bhīmaratha's reign appear to have been undertaken in retaliation against Yayāti's inroads in Ḍāhala.

It has been pointed out above that Mahābhavagupta I Janamejaya had placed his daughter Pṛthvīmahādevī *alias* Tribhuvanamahādevī on the Bhauma-Kara throne and had thereby secured a predominant position for his family in Orissa. It bore fruits during the reign of Yayāti who brought about an end of the Bhauma-Kara rule and annexed the territories so far held by the dynasty. The process started fairly early in his reign as indicated by his earliest charter issued in his fourth regnal year purporting to grant a piece of land in the Oḍra country.[1251] Another record dated in the ninth year of his reign registers a grant in Dakṣiṇa Tosali.[1252] It is interesting to note that land-grants in Dakṣiṇa Tosali are recorded in a number of

1249. *CII,* iv, lxxviii; Ajay Mitra Shastri, 'Kalachuri-Rāshṭtrakūṭa Relations in the Viddhaśālabhañjikā', *The Heritage of India* (L. N. Mishra Commemoration Volume, editors: U. Thakur and Y.K. Mishra), 267.

1250. For the Triliṅga country, see P. Acharya, 'Triliṅga, Trikaliṅga, Kaliṅga, Oḍra and Utkala', *OHRJ*, i, 73-78.

1251. No. IV: XII.

1252. No. IV: XIV.

Bhauma-Kara charters,[1253] the latest such charter being of the Bhauma-Kara year 187 falling in the reign of the Bhauma-Kara queen Daṇḍimahādevī.[1254] The cumulative evidence of these grants, as shown earlier, indicates that Oḍra or Dakṣiṇa Tosali had changed hands from the Bhauma-Karas to the Somakulins by about 924 A.D. Even if it is supposed that by the fourth regnal year of Yayāti only a portion of the Bhauma-Kara territory in Oḍra had passed over to the Somakulins, the transfer of the whole of Dakṣiṇa Tosali must have taken place only a few years later when we find Yayāti granting a village clearly stated to have been situated in Dakṣiṇa Tosali as such. Uttara Tosali or the Dhenkanal-Angul region, however, continued under the Bhauma-Karas till at least the Bhauma-Kara year 204 or 940 A.D. as indicated by a recently published grant of the penultimate Bhauma-Kara queen Vakulamahādevī.[1255] It may, therefore, be supposed that the remaining part of the Bhauma-Kara kingdom, *i.e.*, Uttara Tosali, passed on to Yayāti within a few years after 940 A.D., say in *c.* 945 A.D.[1256] Yayāti's grant of the ninth regnal year records a grant in favour of a resident of the village Śilābhañjapāṭī in Oḍra[1257] while the village donated through a record of the fifteenth year is described as situated in the *maṇḍala* named after Gandhaṭapāṭī.[1258] As pointed out earlier, Śilābhañjapāṭī and Gandhāṭapāṭi were named after the Bhañja chiefs and these records show the transfer of the Bhañja territory to Yayāti who drove away the Bhañjas to the Gañjam region. As a result of these successes Yayāti became the master of practically the whole of Orissa.

A few records of Yayāti himself as well as those of his descendants state that he defeated a certain Ajapāla in battle and captured thirty-two rutting elephants called Kāmadeva, etc. whose riders had been killed by his arrows.[1259] In the absence of details it is not possible to identify Ajapāla and locate the territory under him. But in view of its mention in so many records, it appears to have been an important achievement.

In consequence of the annexation of the Bhauma-Kara territory the Somavaṁśin kingdom was divided into two provinces of Kosala and Oḍra which were placed, for administrative reasons, under two different ministers

1253. Binayak Misra, *DMO*, 16-18, nos. 2, 8-10.

1254. *Ibid.*, 18, no. 10.

1255. *EI*, xxxvi, 307-312.

1256. Umakanta Subuddhi, *The Bhauma-Karas of Orissa*, 79.

1257. No. IV: XIV, text-line 23.

1258. No. IV: XV, text-lines 4-5.

1259. No. IV: XVI, verse 7; nos. IV: XVII-XVIII, verse 8; no, IV: XX, verse 7, K.C. Panigrahi sees in this stanza a reference to the rescue of 'the women brought to the elephant troop, evidently for the purpose of being carried away', which is not warranted by the text. Further, he takes Ajapāla as a common noun meaning 'the protector of elephant troop', See his *Chronology of the Bhauma-Karas and the Somavaṁśis of Orissa*, 2.

of peace and war, from the very beginning of Yayāti's reign. The Datta family was put in charge of Kosala. Dhāradatta II, who is mentioned as *Mahāsandhivigrahin* in the latest grant of Mahābhavagupta I Janamejaya, continued to hold the same office up to the twenty-fourth year of the reign of Yayāti and is mentioned in connection with all the grants in Kosala.[1260] Sometime in or before Yayāti's twenty-eighth regnal year Dhāradatta was succeeded by Siṁhadatta who is expressly referred to as the *Mahāsandhivigrahin* of Kosala.[1261] One Chicchaṭeśvara is mentioned as holding the same office in all the records registering grants in Oḍra or Dakṣiṇa Tosali.[1262] In some later records these two provinces are spoken of as the two *rāṣṭras* of the Somavaṁśin kingdom.[1263]

Mahāśivagupta I Yayāti was undoubtedly one of the most powerful members of the family to which he brought great glory and accretion of fresh territorries. His success against the Bhañjas and the Bhauma-Karas made him the undisputed lord of Orissa proper whereas he not only succeeded in keeping his Kosalan possessions intact against the mounting Kalacuri threat but also won a spectacular victory over his Kalacuri adversary. These successes put the Somavaṁśins firmly on all-India political map. It is perhaps due to this fact that under the name Yayātikesarī he is highly eulogised in the local traditions embodied in the *Mādalāpañjī*.

Mahābhavagupta II Bhīmaratha

Mahāśivagupta I Yayāti was succeeded by his son Mahābhavagupta II Bhīmaratha whose latest recorded regnal year is the thirteenth one.[1264] We may, therefore, assign him a reign of about two decades, *viz., c.* 955—*c.* 975 A.D.

The hostility with the Kalacuris of Ḍāhala, which marked the two earlier reigns, continued unabated during the reign of Bhīmaratha also. While the Somavaṁśin records maintain reticence in this matter, the Kalacuri inscriptions are eloquent regarding their success. The Bilhari stone inscription of Yuvarājadeva II refers to the raids of Lakṣmaṇarāja II (*c.* 945—*c.* 970 A.D.) in Kosala and Oḍra. We are told that he defeated the Kosala king and obtained an image of Kāliya from the Oḍra chief.[1265] Ignoring the distinction sought to be made here between the Kosala and Oḍra chiefs which is obviously due to poetic misconception or metrical exigencies or

1260. No. IV: XIII, XV and XVI.
1261. No. IV: XVII, text-line 69.
1262. Nos. IV: XII and XIV.
1263. No. IV: XXII, verse 9 speaks of Kosala and Utkala as two *rāṣṭras* while in no. IV: XXVI, verse 8, we find allusion to the two *rāṣṭras* without naming them.
1264. No. IV: XIX.
1265. CII IV, 213, verse 62.

born of the poet's desire to eulogise his patron's ancestor by attributing him two instead of a single conquest, it means in plain words that Lakṣmaṇarāja carried out raids in the Somavaṁśin territory, obviously with the object of retaliating Yayāti's inroads into Kalacuri dominions. Since Lakṣmaṇarāja's Kosala-Oḍra raids are not mentioned in the Karitalai inscription of his reign,[1266] they seem to have taken place in the later part of his reign. However, as the Somakula records maintain complete silence in this regard, it is difficult to ascertain the ultimate outcome of these adventures; but, on the whole, they seem to have been favourable to the Kalacuris although no territorial gain appears to have been involved.

The recently discovered Mahulpara plates of Dharmaratha mention a certain Rudra, probably described as an eastern chief (*purva-Rudra*), who is represented as pleased to hear the account of the movements of Bhīmaratha's sword and looking at the latter with his crown tremulous in a gesture of appreciation.[1267] This Rudra of the east cannot be definitely identified, but it is not impossible that king Rudra referred to in an inscription of his son *Yuvarāja* Bali-Akṣaya found at Boram (Manbhum District, W. Bengal)[1268] is intended. There are also some vague allusions to Bhīmaratha's military successes in his Cuttack plates[1269] as well as in the records of the later members of the family,[1270] but they are of no historical value.

Siṁhadatta, who figures as the minister of peace and war attached to Kosala in the latest charter of Mahāśivagupta I Yayāti, continued in the same office during Bhīmaratha's reign.[1271] From the Kudopali plates of his reign we learn about his feudatory *Rāṇaka* Puñja of the Māṭhara family who made a land-grant from his residence at Vāmaṇḍāpāṭī (probably the same as Bamra, Bangarh Tahsil, Sambalpur District) in the thirteenth regnal year of his patron. He, like his feudal lord, was a devout worshipper of Maheśvara but was also specially devoted to the goddess Kāleśvarī (perhaps a form of Kālī) by whose boon he believed to have got his fief comprising fifteen small villages (*pallikās*). He is said to have acquired the five great sounds (*samadhigata-pañca-mahāśabda*) and enjoyed the title of *Māṇḍalika* besides *Rāṇaka*. His seal is marked with the emblem of swan.[1272]

1266. *Ibid.*, iv, 188-191.
1267. No. IV: XX, verse 8.
1268. *JBORS*, ix, 416; Bhandarkar's List, No. 1755.
1269. No. IV:XVIII, verse 9.
1270. Nos. IV: XX (verse 8); XXII (verse 3); XXVI (verse 3).
1271. No. IV: XVIII, verse 22. This stanza eulogising Siṁhadatta is the same as verse 23 of no. IV: XVII which also describes him. But what is of special interest is that the same stanza is employed for describing Chicchaṭeśvara, the *Sandhivigrahin* associated with Oḍra, in no. IV: XIV (verse 20). The description cannot, therefore, be regarded as realistic.
1272. No. IV: XIX.

Bhīmaratha deserves credit for maintaining his territorial inheritance intact against the mounting Kalacuri aggressions. Whether there was any fresh territorial expansion during his reign cannot be ascertained. But there is no doubt that he paved the way for his successor's military aggrandisement.

Bhīmaratha had a number of sons out of whom at least three came to power one after the other after him.

Mahāśivagupta II Dharmaratha

Mahābhavagupta II Bhīmaratha was succeeded by his son, obviously the eldest one, Mahāśivagupta II Dharmaratha, who was probably also known as Rājamalla.[1273] His recently published Mahulpara grant, which supplies some valuable information of a historical nature about him not available from any other source, was issued in the eleventh year of his reign.[1274] He may, therefore, be supposed to have ruled for about twenty years, *viz.*, *c.* 975—*c.* 995 A.D.

A verse in the Mahulpara plates speaks of the chains of smoke rising from the cities (capitals) of Andhra and Gauḍa which were put aflame by Dharmaratha with ease as if in a sport.[1275] Besides this there are a few other allusions of a general nature to his military achievements as are also found in some other later records.[1276] However, the vagueness of the references to his success against Andhra and Gauḍa does not allow us to ascertain its exact nature. But there can be no doubt that his Andhra and Gauḍa adversaries must have belonged to the Eastern (Veṅgi) Cālukya and Pāla dynasties respectively. The Eastern Cālukya kingdom was torn asunder by internal family feuds over the question of succession to the throne, and, taking advantage of this situation, the Telugu Coḍa chief Jaṭā Coḍa Bhīma of Peḍakallu (Kurnool District) slew the Eastern Cālukya chief Dānārṇava and occupied the latter's kingdom and held it for twenty-seven years (973-1000 A.D.) after which it was re-occupied by Śaktivarman I with the help of Coḷa Rājarāja I.[1277] This period of twenty-seven years was regarded by Śaktivarman and his successors as an interregnum with-

1273. No. IV: XXVI, verse 6. But it may as well be only an adjective meaning 'wrestler among the kings' which is not an uncommon description of a king in early Indian literature.

1274. No. IV: XX.

1275. No. IV: XX, verse 9.

1276. No. IV: XX, verse 10 describes him as the cause of the destruction of the multitude of his foes. Nos. XXII and XXVII, verse 4 refers, in a general way, to his *digvijaya*. See also Suppl. Inscr. No. III, verse 4. No. IV: XXVI, verse 5 also contains a vague allusion to his conquests and compares him to the epic sage Paraśurāma.

1277. G. Yazdani (ed.), *Early History of the Deccan*, 486-487. See also R.C. Majumdar (ed.), *HCIP*, iv: *The Age of Imperial Kanauj*, 139-140.

out any king. It seems that Dharmaratha, like some other adventurers, also fished in these troubled waters and carried out a raid.

In Bengal, the Pālas were in critical straits immediately before and after the reign of Mahīpāla I (*c.* 988—*c.* 1038 A.D.). But as Dharmaratha closed his reign shortly after Mahīpāla's accession, his Gauḍa expedition must be dated during the period of Vigrahapāla II, father of Mahīpāla I, who had lost control of almost the whole of Bengal and ruled only in Bihar.[1278] Taking advantage of this precarious situation, Dharmaratha may have raided Bengal. However, these appear to have been merely military adventures without any territorial accretion.[1279]

Some records of the time of Mahābhavagupta IV Uddyotakesarin[1280] and Mahāśivagupta V Karṇa[1281] refer to Dharmaratha's military expeditions in the entire region from the Setu (Adam's Bridge) in the South to the Himalaya mountains in the north and from the eastern ocean (Bay of Bengal) to the western mountain, *i.e.* sun-set mountain.[1282] While there can be no doubt that all this hyperbolic description is a figment of imagination, pure and simple, we have dependable information in the Banpur plates of Indraratha about the expansion of the Somakula dominions in another direction during Dharmaratha's reign. Verse 12 of this inscription tells us that Indraratha, a step-brother of Dharmaratha, got, through the latter's favour the royal fortune of Kaliṅga, *i.e.*, he acted as Dharmaratha's viceroy in Kaliṅga.[1283] Thus, coastal Kaliṅga or a substantial part thereof was conquered by Dharmaratha. Perhaps this task was achieved by Indraratha who was, as usual, put in charge of this newly conquered province. But how long it remained under the Somakulins cannot be ascertained.

Under Dharmaratha, Sahadeva was the king's preceptor (*rāja-guru*), one Kumbhaṇḍipāla held the office of the minister of peace and war (*sandhi-vigraha-pada*) and the minister (*mantri-vara*) Netradeva acted as the chief of the records office (*Mahākṣapaṭalādhyakṣa*).[1284]

Dharmaratha kept the Somakula banner high and his military intervention in Andhra and Bengal and perhaps other parts of the country turned the Somakulins into an all-India power. He not only kept intact his

1278. *Ibid.*, 52-55.
1279. The identifications of Andhra and Gauḍa chiefs proposed here are different from those suggested earlier in *Studies in Indian Epigraphy*, i, 89. They are due toc hange in view regarding the Somavaṁśa chronology.
1280. No. IV: XXII and Suppl. Inscr. II, verse 5.
1281. No. IV: XXVII, verse 5.
1282 This amounts to a vague claim to the all-India sphere of influence of a *cakravartin* (*cakravarti-kṣetra*). Such claims are met with in connection with other chiefs as well and cannot be regarded as historical.
1283. No. IV: Appendix I, verse 12.
1284. No. IV: XX, verses 24-25.

inherited dominions but also added to it by conquering Kaliṅga. It is pertinent to note in this connection that his only known grant was situated in the Antaruda-*viṣaya* which, according to Bhauma-Kara records, was included in Dakṣiṇa Tosali.[1285]

Mahābhavagupta III Naghuṣa (Nahuṣa)

Our records contain conflicting statements regarding the history of the dynasty after Dharmaratha. According to the official charters of the time of Mahābhavagupta IV Uddyotakesarin and Mahāśivagupta V Karṇa,[1286] Dharmaratha was succeeded by his *bhrātā, i.e.* stept-brother or cousin, Naghuṣa (Nahuṣa) whereas the solitary Brahmeśvara (Bhubaneswar) temple inscription of Uddyotakesarin's mother Kolāvatī avers that the demise of Dharmaratha without leaving any son was followed by a political interregnum during which the country was subjected to foreign attacks.[1287] We may synthesise these statements by supposing that as Dharmaratha had no son,[1288] he was succeeded by Naghuṣa whose short reign was full of disturbances. He may have had a short reign of about fifteen years (*c.* 995—*c.* 1010 A.D.).

Unfortunately no record of Naghuṣa has been reported so far and no important event is clearly stated to have taken place during his reign in the records of the later members of the dynasty.[1289] But there are some indications that he had to face troubles from his own relatives. A verse in the Banpur plates avers that Indraratha had defeated the king of Uḍra in a battle and captured his fortune.[1290] As we have already seen, Uḍra formed part of the Somakula dominions right from the beginning of the reign of Mahāśivagupta I Yayāti. As such the vanquished Uḍra adversary of Indraratha was no other than Naghuṣa himself. This finds support from a perusal of the Banpur plates of Indraratha which show that Indraratha did not recognise Naghuṣa as Dharmaratha's successor. It may perhaps indicate that Dharmaratha's death was followed by some bitterness about succession and even though Naghuṣa ultimately succeeded to the throne, he was soon deprived of his possessions in Uḍra. The silence of the Brahmeśvara temple inscription also points in the same direction.

1285. Binayak Misra, DMO, 16, no. 2.
1286. Nos. IV: XXII, XXVII, verse 6; IV: Suppl. Inscr. III, verse 6.
1287. No. IV: XXVI, verse 6, states that for some time after Dharmaratha's passing away both the provinces (*rāṣṭra-dvaya*) were occupied by various soldiers. There is no mention of any king between Dharmaratha and Caṇḍihara Yayāti even though Naghuṣa and Indraratha are known to have intervened between them.
1288. If he had any, he may have predeceased him.
1289. Nos. IV: XXII, XXVII and IV: Suppl. Inscr. III, verses 6-7 contain only vague praise and allusions to his military exercises.
1290. No. IV: App. I, verse 12.

Indraratha

Naghuṣa's death appears to have been followed by a scramble for power between Indraratha and a collateral line of the family claiming descent from Mahābhavagupta I Janamejaya, with success ultimately going to the former. Indraratha, born of another queen (Durgā) of Bhīmaratha and thus a step-brother of Dharmaratha was a natural claimant to the throne. Even after defeating Naghuṣa, lord of Uḍra, he continued to govern the province of Kaliṅga which was allotted to him by Dharmaratha till the end of Naghuṣa's reign. But after the death of Naghuṣa he naturally staked his claim to the Somakula throne which was, however, challenged by a certain Abhimanyu who is said to have appropriated to himself the lordship of the earth (*i.e.*, kingdom) by foul means. There is no doubt that this Abhimanyu was no other than the homonymous father of Caṇḍīhara and son and grandson respectively of Vicitravīra and Janamejaya.[1291] Abhimanyu was probably backed by a certain Vatsarāja whose whereabouts are not known. Indraratha rushed from his viceregal province of Kaliṅga and killed Abhimanyu and many officials supporting his claim in the battlefield. Thereafter with the approval of the Brāhmaṇas he assumed kingship and firmly entrenched himself at the ancestral capital Yayātinagara from which he issued his Banpur plates.[1292] He assumed all the sectarian and regal titles found employed for other Somakula monarchs but did not adopt the *gupta*-ending coronation name for reasons that cannot be ascertained at present.[1293] He is represented to have controlled 'three kingdoms' (*trairājya*)[1294] which probably included Kosala, Uḍra and Kaliṅga. His Banpur plates record grant of a village situated in the Koṅgoda-*maṇḍala* or Ganjam region.[1295]

Till the sixth year of his reign when his only extant grant was issued, Indraratha appears to have been ruling in full glory. But he continued to rule for a few more years till at least 1022 A.D. when he was defeated by Coḷa Rājendra I at Yayātinagara in course of his Gangetic expedition. According to the Coḷa records, Rājendra carried away a 'large heap of family-treasures together with many (other) treasures after having captured Indraratha of the ancient race of the moon' and seized Oḍḍa-*viṣaya* and Kosalai-nāḍu.[1296] This expedition appears to have been undertaken primarily with a view to thwart the activities of Indraratha who had aligned

1291. See No. IV: XXVI, verse 7.
1292. No. IV: App. I. Much of the information outlined above is derived from verses 13-14.
1293. This name is not found in his Banpur plates which forms his only known record.
1294. No. IV: App. I, verse 14.
1295. All this information is based on the text of the Banpur plates as published by K.B. Tripathy (No. IV: App. I). The plates stand in need of a better edition which may afford some more dependable information.
1296. K.A.N. Sastri, *The Coḷas*, 207.

himself with the Later Cālukya king Jayasiṁha II Jagadekamalla (*c.* 1015-1042 A.D.) who, setting aside the claims of Rājendra I's nephew Rājarāja, had placed the latter's step-brother Vijayāditya VII Viṣṇuvardhana on the throne of Veṅgi.[1297]

Indraratha had to face invasions of other contemporary powers also. The Udepur *praśasti* informs us that he was defeated by the mercenaries of the Paramāra king Bhoja (*c.* 1000-*c.* 1047 A.D.).[1298] Gāṅgeyadeva (*c.* 1015-1041 A.D.), the Kalacuri king of Tripurī, is also credited with success against the Utkala king who was none else than Indraratha.[1299] A branch of the Kalacuris was already established in the western part of South Kosala with Tummāṇa (modern Tumāṇ, Bilaspur District) in *c.* 1000 A.D. by Kaliṅgarāja and it must have thwarted the Somavaṁśin expansion in that direction. Kaliṅgarāja's son and successor, Kamalarāja (*c.* 1020-*c.* 1045 A.D.), aided his overlord Gāṅgeyadeva in his Utkala campaign.[1300] The Paramāras and the Kalacuris appear to have allied themselves with the Coḷas and the raids of these three powers against Indraratha were not totally unconnected with each other.[1301] Whether the Kalacuri and Paramāra invasions preceded the Coḷa expedition or all the three invasions were undertaken at the same time cannot be determined, though the former postulation appears more likely. Be that as it may, after his defeat in the battle at Yayātinagara, Indraratha was probably taken captive and perhaps killed and the entire Somakula kingdom lay waste and wrapped in total anarchy for some time.[1302]

Mahāśivagupta III Caṇḍīhara Yayāti

According to the Coḷa records, Indraratha was taken captive by Rājendra I together with his family[1303] and as such even if Indraratha had a son, he was not left to succeed him. As we have seen above, in the civil war for

1297. *Ibid.*, 205-206 and 237, note 48; G. Yazdani, (ed.) *Early History of the Deccan*, 327 ff., 489.
1298. *EI*, i, 235, verse 19.
1299. *CII*, iv, xc, cxx-cxxi. Mirashi's identification of Gāṅgeya's Utkala adversary with the Kara king Śubhākara II (*ibid.*, xc) is erroneous. Whichever of the two above-mentioned proposed epochs of the Bhauma-Kara era is accepted, Śubhākara II would be much too early to be a contemporary of Gāṅgeyadeva. Equally untenable is his conjecture that during this campaign the Somakula king Mahāśivagupta I Yayāti was defeated by Gāṅgeyadeva (*ibid.*, xc, cxxi). For, no scholar now dates the end of Mahāśivagupta I Yayāti's reign later than 1000 A.D.
1300. *Ibid.*, cxx-cxxi.
1301. This inference is justified in the light of the Kulenur inscription (*EI*, xv, 330) which records the victory of Caṭṭadeva *alias* Kundarāja, a cousin of Jayasiṁha II Jagadekamalla, over the elephant troops of the allied enemies.
1302. Nos. IV: XXII and XXVII, verse 9; XXVI, verse 6. See also IV: Suppl. Inscr. III, verse 9.
1303. K.A. Nilakanta Sastri, *The Coḷas*, 207.

succession that followed the death of Nahuṣa Indraratha had killed Abhimanyu, son of Vicitravīra and grandson of Janamejaya, who had staked his claim to the Somakula throne. Thereafter, during Indraratha's reign Abhimanyu's son Yayāti *alias* Caṇḍīhara[1304] was left with no option but to spend a few years in self-imposed exile.[1305] But after the catastrophe at Yayātinagara which threatened the very existence of the kingdom, Yayāti was brought back and installed on the Somavaṁśin throne by all the *amātyas* (ministers). While in the records of his successors he is referred to as Yayāti and Caṇḍīhara, in his own Jatesinga-Dungari charter he mentions himself as Mahāśivagupta (III) Yayāti.[1306] The immediate task Mahāśivagupta III faced after accession was to drive the enemies out and restore normal conditions in the kingdom which was badly mauled and devastated by the aforesaid invasions.[1307] He proved himself equal to this task and, as stated in the records of his son and successor, Mahābhavagupta IV Uddyotakesarin, he freed both the *rāṣṭras* (provinces) of Kosala and Utkala, which were occupied by enemy forces, from all the troubles.[1308] He was, therefore, perfectly justified in claiming that he had acquired the title of *Trikaliṅgādhipati* by the prowess of his arms.[1309] His Jatesinga-Dungari (also called Mārañja-Mura) charter gives a somewhat detailed account of his conquests which, though a bit exaggerated, is not totally baseless. He is described as the self-chosen husband (*i.e.*, lord) of Kaliṅga, Koṅgoda, Utkala and Kosalā, the burning fever to the Karṇṇāṭa, Lāṭa and Gurjara kings and as the very wind in carrying away the garments of Gauḍa and Rāḍhā. While we may easily concede that Koṅgoda, Utkala and Kosala were included in his dominions and that he may have claimed a vague suzerainty over the whole of Kaliṅga, there is absolutely nothing to substantiate other claims, though the possibility of his undertaking raids against some of these countries cannot be denied altogether. He is further represented as addicted to the *kāñcī* (girdle) of the ladies and as a *bhū-viṭa* (paramour of the earth).[1310] There seems to be pun on the word *kāñcī* and some success against the Coḷas is intended to be claimed. This claim need not be regarded as purely hyperbolic as Caṇḍīhara did free his kingdom from the Coḷa occupation and may have chased and pursued the Coḷa invaders in course of his operation emancipation.[1311]

1304. In IV: XXII, XXVII and Suppl. Inscr. III, verse 8 as well as in XXI, text-lines 18 and 44 he is called Yayāti, while in IV: XXVI, verse 7 and in IV: App. II, text-line 1 he is mentioned as Caṇḍīhara.

1305. No. IV: XXVI, verse 6.

1306. No. IV: XXI, text-lines 17-18 and 43-44.

1307-1308. For references, see note 1302.

1309. No. IV: XXI, text-lines 15-16.

1310. D.C. Sircar thinks that *bhūviṭa* may be an error of Draviḍa meaning the Coḷas (*JBORS*, i, 295; *HCIP*, v: *The Struggle for Empire*, 211). But even if *bhūviṭa* is taken to be correct, the allusion to Kāñcī would serve the same purpose.

1311. This account is based on no. IV: XXI, text-lines 13-15.

It will be seen from the above that Caṇḍīhara's achievements were in no way insignificant. He had restored the sunken fortunes of the family which now got a new lease of life for another little less than a century and an important position in contemporary Indian politics. The grateful posterity remembered him reverentially and it is no wonder that high praise is showered on him in the records of his descendants. In his own charter he is compared to the Pauranic heroes Nala, Nahuṣa, Māndhātṛ, Dilīpa, Bhagīratha and Bharata while in records of Uddyotakesarin and Karṇa he is described as a representative of Madhusūdana (Kṛṣṇa) and a conqueror of the world (*viśva-vijayin*).[1312] One of these inscriptions says that he was saluted by the whole earth.[1313]

Rāṇaka Rudradatta, nephew of the above-mentioned Siṁhadatta and grandson of Harṣagupta, held the office of the minister of peace and war (*Sandhivigrahin*) under Caṇḍīhara.[1314] As the charter in question records the grant of a village in Kosala, Rudradatta was evidently attached to Kosala. [1315] From a later record we learn his father's name which was Devadatta as well as the fact that he hailed from Ayodhyāpura.[1316]

The only known record of Caṇḍīhara is dated in the third year of his reign and it is difficult to decide for how many more years he continued to rule. But we would not be far wrong if we place his reign in *c.* 1022-*c.* 1040 A.D.

Mahābhavagupta IV Uddyotakesarin

Mahāśivagupta III Yayāti *alias* Caṇḍīhara was succeeded by his son Mahābhavagupta IV Uddyotakesarin for whom we have a number of records dated between the fourth and the eighteenth years of his reign.[1317] We may, therefore, tentatively assign him a reign of about twenty-five years (*c.* 1040-*c.* 1065 A.D.). That Uddyotakesarin maintained his hold over the twin provinces of Kosala and Uḍra or Utkala intact is indicated by his Mahakosala Historical Society's plates recording grant of a village in the Sambalpur tract [1318] and the Balijhari charter registering a grant in Oḍra[1319] as well as by the construction of a temple at Bhuvaneswar by his mother

1312. Nos. IV: XXII, XXVII and Suppl. Inscr. III, verse 8.
1313. No. IV: XXVI, verse 8.
1314. No. IV: XXI, text-lines 45-46.
1315. We have already seen that the practice of having separate ministers of peace and war for Kosala and Utkala started during the reign of Mahāśivagupta I Yayāti. But it is difficult to ascertain if this practice was continued during Caṇḍīhara's reign. It is known to have been discontinued by his son.
1316. No. IV: XXIV, text-line 35.
1317. Nos. IV: XXII-XXVI, App. II, and Suppl. Inscr. III.
1318. No. IV: XXIV.
1319. No. IV: XXII.

Kolāvatī[1320] and the presence of some records of his reign on the Khaṇḍagiri hill in the Puri District.[1321]

Mahāsandhivigrahin Rudradatta, son of Devadatta, nephew of Siṁhadatta and grandson of Harṣadatta, who is already known to us from Caṇḍīhara's only known record, continued in office during his son's reign also at least up to his eleventh regnal year.[1322] As we have pointed out earlier, after the annexation of the Bhauma-Kara territory during the reign of Mahāśivagupta I Yayāti the practice of having separate *Sandhivigrahins* for Uḍra and Kosala was initiated and the members of the Datta ministerial family were associated with Kosala. But in the two grants of Uddyotakesarin's fourth regnal year, Rudradatta is mentioned as the *Mahāsandhivigrahin* of both Utkala and Kosala.[1323] Whether the practice of appointing separate ministers of peace and war for the two main provinces of the kingdom was discontinued by Uddyotakesarin himself or by his father and for what reasons cannot be determined at present. But it was obviously inspired by administrative reasons and not much historical significance attaches to it. The inference drawn from this fact that the Utkala country came to form a part of the Somavaṁśin kingdom sometime about the second quarter of the eleventh century[1324] is, therefore, unwarranted.

Uddyotakesarin is credited with some military successes in the Bhuvaneswar inscription of his mother. It is stated that he vanquished all the hostile forces of Ḍāhala, Uḍra and Gauḍa with ease in a childish sport as it were. He is further described as the unique protector of the earth extending up to the four oceans and is compared to the traditional celebrities like Pṛthu, Māndhātṛ and Bharata.[1325] Since Uḍra is known to have formed part of Uddyotakesarin's dominions, the word *coḍra* (generally split as *ca Uḍra*) appears to be an error for Coḍa.[1326] The Ḍāhala contemporary of Uddyotakesarin was the Kalacuri king Karṇa or Lakṣmīkarṇa (*c.* 1040—*c.* 1073 A.D.) who also assumed the title of *Trikaliṅgādhipati*, which may allude to his claim to success against the Somavaṁśins, though his records are reticent about any such victory. In Gauḍa, Pāla king Nayapāla and then his son Vigrahapāla III were in power during this period. Both these chiefs were involved in hostilities with Karṇa; but ultimately a peace treaty was signed and the latter's daughter Yauvanaśrī was married to Vigrahapāla III.

1320. No. IV: XXVI.
1321. Nos. IV: XXIII and XXV. The placement of Abhimanyu in charge of Kosala is also indicative of his hold over Kosala.
1322. No. IV: XXIV.
1323. Nos. IV: XXII and Suppl. Inscr. III.
1324. *OHRJ*, i, 295; *HCIP*, v: *The Struggle for Empire*, 211.
1325. No. IV: XXVI, Verses 9-10.
1326. According to D.C. Sircar (*JBORS*, i, 296), the Uḍra king defeated by Uddyotakesarin was one of his own subordinates or one of his father's adversaries (*HCIP*, v: *The Struggle for Empire*, 212).

The condition of the Pālas during this period was so precarious that there is nothing surprising if Uddyotakesarin carried out a raid in Gauḍa without much difficulty. Whether Uddyotakesarin's raids against Karṇa were undertaken independently or Karṇa joined his son-in-law Vigrahapāla III during Uddyotakesarin's Bengal raid cannot be ascertained in the present state of insufficient information. Rājādhirāja I (1018-1052 A.D.), Rājendra II (1052-1064 A.D.) and Vīrarājendra I (1063-1070 A.D.) were the Coḷa contemporaries of Uddyotakesarin. But his claim to a victory over the Coḷas appears to be only a figment of poetic imagination unless we assume that he assisted his father in driving away the Coḷa occupants from the Somakula kingdom.[1327]

It is learnt from the Kelga plates of *Kumārādhirāja* Someśvara that Uddyotakesarin appointed a certain Abhimanyu as his sub-king in Kosala.[1328] This Abhimanyu, in view of the common practice of naming the grandson after the grandfather, may have been a brother of Uddyotakesarin. This arrangement, which was made sometime after the eleventh year of his reign,[1329] was apparently intended to check the encroachments of the Kalacuris of the western part of South Kosala and the Chindaka-Nāgas while the king himself remained in Utkala to contain the Gaṅga onslaughts. Abhimanyu was followed by *Kumārādhirāja-parameśvara* Someśvara. This arrangement seems to have worked well and achieved its objective till the termination of Uddyotakesarin's rule.

Like his predecessors, Uddyotakesarin was also a devout Śaiva and, unlike the seals attached to other Somavaṁśin charters, the seal of his Mahakosala Historical Society's plates bears the figure of a horned Nandin topped by a crescent. His mother Kolāvatī, who hailed from the solar race, was also a staunch Śaiva and built the temple of Brahmeśvara Śiva at Ekāmra (Bhubaneswar) and endowed it with some beautiful maids, evidently for entertaining the god and the audience with dance and dramatic performance.[1330] But Uddyotakesarin observed religious catholicity and appears to have extended patronage to Jainism as well, as may be reasonably inferred from a couple of short inscriptions of his reign at the Khaṇḍagiri hill.

Mahāśivagupta IV Janamejaya

Uddyotakesarin was followed by his son Janamejaya who may be reasonably assumed to have adopted the coronation name Mahāśivagupta.

1327. This is quite likely. *EI*, iv, 191, text-line 41.
1328. No. IV: XXVIII, text-lines 4-5.
1329. No. IV: XXIV, which records a grant in Kosala, was issued in the eleventh year.
1330. No. XXVI, verses 11-15.

His only recorded date is the fifth year of his reign[1331] and he may be tentatively given a rule of about fifteen years from *c.* 1065 to *c.* 1080 A.D. The Ratnagiri plates of his nephew Karṇa, which devote a couple of verses to him, do not supply any information of historical interest about him except perhaps a veiled allusion to his victory over a Nāga chief,[1332] who may possibly be identified with the Chindaka-Nāga chief Someśvara I (1069-1097 A.D.) of Bastar. The latter also claims to have won a victory over the Uḍra chief and captured six lakhs and ninety-six villages of Kosala.[1333] The recently discovered Nuapatna plates of his reign inform us that a certain *Yuvarāja* Dharmaratha, who enjoyed the titles *Paramabhaṭṭāraka* and *Mahākumārādhirāja-Parameśvara,* acted as his sub-king in Paścima-Kaliṅga[1334] which does not admit of a proper identification but may have denoted some area on the west of Kaliṅga.[1335] His exact relationship with Janamejaya cannot be ascertained, though not improbably he may have been his son.

During this period the Somakula kingdom was threatened by the Gaṅgas on the south and the Kalacuris of Kosala and the Chindaka-Nāgas on the north. The Gaṅga king Rājarāja I Devendravarman (1070-1078 A.D.), son and successor of Vajrahasta V Anantavarman, claims that his general Vanapati defeated the kings of Utkala and Kosala. The Kalacuri chief Pṛthvīdeva I (*c.* 1065-*c.* 1090 A.D.) also probably achieved some success against the Somavaṁśins as may be inferred from his assumption of the title *Sakala-Kosalādhipati* (lord of the whole of Kosala) in his Amoda plates dated 1069 and 1079 A.D.[1336]

Rāṇaka Malladatta, who evidently belonged to the oft-mentioned Datta ministerial line and may have been a son of and succeeded Rudradatta, was Janamejaya's *Sandhivigrahin.*[1337]

Mahābhavagupta V Purañjaya

Mahāśivagupta IV Janamejaya's son and successor Mahābhavagupta V Purañjaya (*c.* 1080-c- 1100 A.D.) has left no record of his own and is known only from a couple of verses in the Ratnagiri plates of his brother and successor Karṇa.[1338] One of these stanzas refers to his victory over the Gauḍa. Ḍāhala, Kaliṅga and Vaṅga kings.[1339] Of these successes there

1331. No. IV: Suppl. Inscr. IV, text-line 5.
1332. No. IV: XXVII, verses 12-13.
1333. Hira Lal, *ICPB*, 161-162, no. 273.
1334. No. IV: Suppl. Inscr. IV, text-lines 9-10.
1335. According to some (K.S. Behera, "Administrative System under the Somavaṁśīs", *Early Indian Political and Administrative Systems* (ed. D.C. Sircar), 89-90), the Kosala portion of the Somavaṁśin kingdom was known as Paścima-Kaliṅga.
1336. *CII*, iv, 400, text-line 5; 406, text-line 24. Mirashi (*ibid.*, cxxi) takes the claim to be an empty boast in view of the absence of any record of his reign in the eastern part of Kosala.
1337. No. IV: Suppl. Inscr. IV, text-line 41.
1338. No. IV: XXVII, verses 14-15.
1339. No. IV: XXVII, verse 15.

is no confirmation from any other source and it is unlikely that he would have thought of embarking on such military adventures at a time when the very existence of the Somavaṁśa kingdom was in jeopardy due to the growing menace of the Eastern Gaṅgas, Chindaka-Nāgas and the Kalacuris of Kosala. Anantavarman Coḍagaṅga (1078-1142 A.D.) and Chindaka-Nāga Someśvara I were supreme in Kaliṅga and the Bastar region respectively and were constantly encroaching upon the Somakula dominions. In Bengal, Rāmapāla (*c.* 1077-*c.* 1120 A.D.), who resurrected the fallen fortunes of the Pāla dynasty and claims to have defeated the last known Somakula chief in the later part of his reign, was on the throne. Jājalladeva (*c.* 1090-*c.* 1120 A.D.), son and successor of Kalacuri Pṛthvīdeva I, also claims to have seized in battle but later released at his mother's behest Someśvara (evidently the homonymous Somavaṁśin chief who came to power in Kosala after Abhimanyu and issued his charter from Suvarṇapura) and exacted tribute from the king of Dakṣiṇa Kosala.[1340] In view of these facts the claim to victory over these powers is either a mere figment of poetic imagination or may refer to some minor skirmishes in which he might have attained some success.

Mahāśivagupta V Karṇa

Mahābhavagupta V Purañjaya was succeeded by his younger brother Mahāśivagupta V Karṇa, the same as Kārṇakesarin of the literary tradition,[1341] the last Somakula monarch whose records dated in the sixth and seventh years of his reign have come to light.[1342] As we have seen above, he had to face defeat at the hands of the Pāla king Rāmapāla and was finally deprived of his territorial possessions in Utkala by the Gaṅga king Anantavarman Coḍagaṅga who became undisputed lord of lower Orissa sometime between 1108 and 1114-15 A.D. The first date is provided by the Mukhalingam plates which tell us that the Gaṅga king had first defeated and then reinstated the Utkala king[1343] and the second by his Bhubaneswar (Liṅgarāja

1340. *CII*, iv, 413, verses 22-23. In the Sheorinarayan plates of Ratnadeva II (*ibid.*, 421, verse 8) and the Kharod stone inscription of Ratnadeva III (*ibid.*, 537, verse 6) there is mention of Jājalladeva's victory over Bala and Bhujabala of Suvarṇapura respectively. Scholars are generally inclined to identify both Bala and Bhujabala with the Somavaṁśin prince Someśvara. See *ibid.*, cxxiv-cxxv, 420, 534; *IHQ*, xxii, 304; *HCIP*, v: *The Struggle for Empire*, 213.

1341. This name is mentioned in a commentary on Sandhyākaranandin's *Rāma-carita*. In the Tumburu plates of Anantavarman Coḍagaṅga, dated Śaka 1051, he is called Karṇarāya. See *Bhāratī* (Telugu), 1968, pp. 2ff.

1342. Nos. IV: XXVII and Suppl. Inscr. V.

1343. *EA*, iv, pp. 33ff. This statement is also met with in his Korni plates of Śaka 1034 (1112 A.D.) which was so far taken to be the earliest reference to this episode and accordingly this event was dated sometime between 1112 and 1114-15 A.D. This episode is referred to in several subsequent records.

temple)[1344] and Purī (Mārkaṇḍeśvara temple)[1345] inscriptions which clearly indicate his final occupation of this region, evidently after the extirpation of Karṇa. We may, therefore, tentatively date his reign in *c.* 1100-1113 A.D. If, however, we were to place reliance on the *Mādalā-pañji* tradition according to which Suvarṇakesarin was the last Somavaṁśin monarch extirpated by Coḍagaṅga, the termination of Karṇa's reign may have to be dated a little earlier. But the historicity of this tradition may be kept pending till the discovery of more dependable evidence.

Karṇa ruled as a sovereign monarch in lower Orissa till at least the seventh year of his reign as may be justifiably inferred from his Ratnagiri and the recently discovered Kamalpur plates of the sixth and seventh years respectively,[1345a] both referring to him with full imperial titles and as ruling from Yayātinagara which is, in all probability, identical with Jajpur in the Cuttack District and Jajnagar of the Muslim historians. Sometime thereafter he became a target of the rival expansionist designs of Rāmapāla and Anantavarman Coḍagaṅga both of whom tried to set him up as their respective protégé for the time being. However, ultimately, the latter got the upper hand and overthrew Karṇa who appears to have held a subordinate position under his victorious Gaṅga adversary before being finally overthrown sometime about 1113 A.D.

A certain Kṛṣṇadeva held the office of *Sandhivigrahin* and Chittaladeva that of *Mahākṣapaṭalin* (Chief of Records Office) during the reign of Karṇa. They are described hyperbolically in one of his records.[1345b]

The Kosalan possessions also slipped away from the Somavaṁśins about the same time or a little later. As we have seen above, Uddyotakesarin had invested Abhimanyu with the rulership of Kosala and after the close of Abhimanyu's rule *Kumārādhirāja* Someśvara had assumed power and appears to have flourished towards the close of the eleventh and in the early years of the twelfth century A.D. That he was not in possession of the whole of the Kosalan region under the Somakula is indicated by the Kamalpur plates of the seventh year of Karṇa's reign which show that his Māhārāṣṭrakūṭa feudatory named Jayārṇama (correctly, Jayārṇava) was ruling over the Birmaharajpur area in the Balangir District in that year[1346] and may have continued to rule for a few years thereafter. What happened to his fief after him is not known. But the Somavaṁśin rule in the eastern part of Dakṣiṇa Kosala was wiped out in the early years of the twelfth century as a result of the Kalacuri, Chindaka-Nāga and Telugu-Coḍa encroachments. We have already referred to Kalacuri Jājalladeva I's victory over Someśvara as well as the Chindaga-Nāga chief Someśvara's encroachments

1344. *EI*, xxx, 31-32.
1345. *Ibid.*, xxxiii, 184-85.
1345a. Nos. IV: XXVII and Suppl. Inscr. V.
1345b. No. IV: XXVII.
1346. Suppl. Inscr. V.

in Kosala. The Chindaka-Nāga occupation of Kosala was carried out through their Telugu-Coḍa feudatories. The Telugu-Coḍa feudatory Yaśorāja (about the middle of the eleventh century) is credited with the occupation of Kosala while his great-grandson Someśvara II, who flourished in the early years of the twelfth century, is described as the 'lord of the entire Kosala' and issued his Patna Museum[1347] and Kumarīsiṁhā[1348] plates from Suvarṇapura (Sonepur in the Balangir District) wherefrom the only extant charter of the Somavaṁśin Someśvara was also issued.[1349] Thus, the Somakula rule was wiped out both in coastal Orissa and the eastern part of South Kosala in the first quarter of the twelfth century, in the former region by the Eastern Gaṅga monarch Anantavarman Coḍagaṅga and the latter region by the Kalacuris of the western portion of Kosala and the Chindaka-Nāgas aided by their Telugu-Coḍa feudatories.[1350]

1347. *EI*, xix, 97 ff.

1348. *Journal of the Kalinga Historical Research Society*, i (iii), 29ff.

1349. No. IV: XXVIII.

1350. For a fuller discussion of the termination of the Somakula rule in Kosala, see *EI*, xxviii, 324; *IHQ*, xxii, 304-305; *HCIP*, v: *The Struggle for Empire*, 213-214. For a detailed discussion on the genealogy and chronology of the Telugu-Coḍas, see *EI*, xxviii, 286-289.

It has been suggested on the basis of certain similarities in the Kelga plates of Somavaṁśin Someśvara (No. IV: XXVIII) and some Telugu-Coḍa records that the Somakulin Someśvara may have been named after and may have acknowledged for a time the sovereignty of his Chindaka-Nāga namesake, Someśvara I. See *HCIP*, v: *The Struggle for Empire*, 214, 217-218.

INDEX

The following abbreviations have been used: *a*-author, *b*—book or ancient text, *c*—chief, *d*—deity, *dyn*—dynasty, *k*—king, *m*—mountain, *p*—place, *q*—queen, *r*—river, *t*—title. Where a word occurs in the text and the footnotes, only the former has been listed. Words occurring only in the footnotes have been indicated by n after the page number.

ERRATA

Page	*Line*	*Read*	*For*
6 n.22	2	chiefs are attached must	chiefs must
15	11	Vatsa which was	Vatsa was
16 n.112	5	*u & samvatsara*	*ū & sambatsara*
16 n.112	8	epithet	eipthet
17	6	the earliest record	the record
17	21	pronounced	pronounced
19	25	*-oddharaṇa-*	*-oddhararaṇa-*
24	1 & 16	of *v* & receiving	*v* & receving
35 n.230		*nṛśansā & °hanso°*	*nṛśaṅsa &° haṅso°*
37 n.267	2	paurṇamāsī	paurṇāmāsī
39	4	words	word
39 n.272b	4	but do not	but not
41 n.278	2	a couple	couple
42	9	inscription	inscriptions
42 n.280	3	times, is	times, in
49	16	matter	mater
51	13	there	here
56 n.373	4	for *u*	for *ū*
59	14	correct letter	correct letters
60 n.416	1-2	pronunciation	pronounciation
61 n.436	2	*tṛjagatī*	*tṛjagataī*
65 n.517	1	*jagat = traya*	*jaga-traya*
66	24	charters[526a]	charters
73	13	charters	characters
76	4	later members	members
82	26	Banerji	Benerji
83	36	plate	plates
84	32	antity	unity
86 n.610	8	°मीदृक्स्या°	°मीहक्स्या°
86 n.611	1 & 2	कालिकम् & °मनाहार्यं°	°कालिकंम् & °मनाहयं°
86 n.613	5	अनाच्छेद्य°	अनाछेद्य°
87 n.614	5	अमुकस्य	अमुकल्य
87 n.614	8 & 13	°नुपूर्व्यं & दत्तं	°नुपूर्व्वं & तत्तं
87 n.614	16 & 17	°नृं पाणां & पार्थिवेन्द्रान्	°नृपाणां & पार्थिवेन्द्रान
104	22	on the seals attached	attached
106 n. 698	1	*Bhānugupto*	*Bhānugupta*
106 n. 698	2	*= ānugatyena*	*= ānugatyen*
108	15	years	year
110	29	seal-	real-
111	7	and, taking advantage	advantage
111	24	on proper left	left
118 n. 754	3	the	he

Page	*line*	*Read*	*For*
124	10	correct an	correct
125	10	the two	two
126	22	determined	determind
126	31	sometime	sometimes
130	7 & 9	conjecture & sixth	enjecture & seventh
132	12	reserved	preserved
135 n. 851	1 & 3	सूयंघोष & आणून	सूयंघेय & आनून
135 n. 851	6	हा	हर
140	1	felt that	felt
141	28	year	and year
142	16	the	that
142 n. 895		xxii	xvii
142 n. 897	1	refer	refers
144 n. 912	4 & 6	in about & of that	in the about & of the
146 n. 922	1	Lakshmaṇa	Lakṣamaṇa
148 & 148 n. 929	19 & 3	Buddharāja had & or	Budharaja and & of
149	6	Trivaranagara	Trivaragara
150	17	of the	of
150 n. 943	1	Vikramendravarman	Vikramendravarm
152 n. 950	2	*sarvv-*	*sarvve-*
154	16	282	212
158 n. 915	4	°गृंह्वरमतिभक्त्या	गृह्विरमतिभक्त्यां
162 & 163	12 & 6	*Kosal-*	*Kosala-*
163	14 & 16	had & *-prāpta-*	and & *-prāptal*
163	19	possession	possessions
164	8 & 27	stages & fief	states & fiet
166	14 & 19	the	tne & ihe
167 & 168	17 & 11	of the time of & our	of the & on
168	17	brother of	brother
168 n. 1022	2 & 3	identification of & 241	identification & 24
169 & n.1031	16 & 1	name & referred	nama & required
170 n. 1034	12	on	in
172	12	Pāṇḍu-vaṁśa	Pāṇḍu-vaṁśag
172	17-18	Mahāśivagupta III Yayāti	Mahāśivagupta II Yayāti
173	2	Pāṇḍuvaṁśin	Pāṇḍuvaṁśins
174	2 & 9	of Mahāśiva & Kosala	Mahāśiva & Kosalas
176	4	awareness	awaraness
176	21	*Trikaliṅga*	*Trikaliṅga*
176 below n.1070		*The	The
180	9	Ganges	Gangas
183 & 184	2 & 30	century & bordered on	centry & bordered
186 n.1120 & 187	9-10	issued & contrary	itsued & contary
188	17	place	plaee
192	20	cases & the	eases & this
205	15	Jajpur	Jaipur